CREATIVITY
AND
TRADITION
IN
FOLKLORE

CREATIVITY AND TRADITION IN FOLKLORE

New Directions

EDITED BY

Simon J. Bronner

UTAH STATE UNIVERSITY PRESS
Logan, Utah
1992

Copyright © 1992 Utah State University Press
All rights reserved

Utah State University Press
Logan, UT 84322-7800

Library of Congress Cataloging-in-Publication Data

Creativity and tradition in folklore: new directions / edited by
  Simon J. Bronner.
    p. cm. —(Publications of the American Folklore Society. New
  Series)
    "In honour of W.F.H. 'Bill' Nicolaisen"—P. [1].
    Includes bibliographical and index.
    ISBN 0-87421-158-1
    1. Folklore. 2. Oral tradition. 3. Communication in folklore.
4. Creativity (Linguistics) 5. Nicolaisen, W.F.H. I. Bronner, Simon J.
II. Nicolaisen, W.F.H. III. Series.
GR71.C74   1992
398—dc20   92-6652
                                                              CIP

Book and jacket design by Joanne Poon.

A Publication of the American Folklore Society
Patrick B. Mullen, General Editor

In Honor of W. F. H. "Bill" Nicolaisen

CONTENTS

Acknowledgments ix

1 Introduction 1
   SIMON J. BRONNER

   Ballad and Song

2 Some Songs of Place and Ballads of Name 41
   IAN A. OLSON

3 The *Aisling* and the Cowboy... and Factory Girl 57
   D. K. WILGUS AND ELEANOR R. LONG-WILGUS

4 "The Dollar and the Devil": From Poem to Traditional Song? 71
   W. K. MCNEIL

   Narrative

5 Pearl Bryan in Legend 93
   RONALD L. BAKER

6 The Legend Conduit 105
   LINDA DÉGH

7 Narrating in Socialist Everyday Life: Observations on Strategies of Life Management in Southeast Europe 127
   KLAUS ROTH

8 "I Saw the Trees Had Souls": Personal Experience Narratives of Contemporary Witches 141
   ELIZABETH TUCKER

9 The Fruit of the Womb: Creative Uses of a Naturalizing Tradition in Folktales 153
   CRISTINA BACCHILEGA

Language and Cultural Knowledge

10   On the Naming of Places and Kindred Things   169
WILBUR ZELINSKY

11   Paremiological Minimum and Cultural Literacy   185
WOLFGANG MIEDER

12   What, If Anything, Is a Scotticism?   205
J. DERRICK MCCLURE

13   Words and Things in Gaelic Scotland   223
ALEXANDER FENTON

Community and Identity

14   The Forgotten Makars: The Scottish Local Poet Tradition   239
MARY ELLEN BROWN

15.   Celebration of the *Slava* by a Serbian Family in England   255
VENETIA NEWALL

16.   Tradition, Change, and Hmong Refugees   263
ROGER E. MITCHELL

17   Elaborating Tradition: A Pennsylvania-German Folk Artist Ministers to His Community   277
SIMON J. BRONNER

W. F. H. Nicolaisen: A Selected Bibliography   327

Contributors   339

Index   345

ACKNOWLEDGMENTS

I appreciated the advice of May Nicolaisen, David Buchan, Ron Baker, Bill McNeil, Phillips Stevens, Jr., Peter Voorheis, Dan Ward, and Elizabeth Tucker when this project was just an idea. When the time came for action, contributors responded quickly to the call to honor Bill Nicolaisen on the theme of creativity and tradition and answered my requests graciously. Offices for university relations and the vice-president for academic affairs at SUNY Binghamton generously lent their support. Additionally, Patrick B. Mullen, editor of the Publications of the American Folklore Society, deserves credit for his encouragement throughout the project.

The project would never have seen the light of print had it not been for the assistance of the Center for Research and Graduate Studies directed by Howard Sachs at Penn State Harrisburg. Renee Horley processed the original manuscript, and Douglas Manger, an able editorial assistant, worked on the revisions. Donna Horley of the Humanities Division meanwhile handled much of the correspondence. My thanks go out to them, and *a gross Dank*, as one says here in the Dutch Country, to Bill Nicolaisen for all he has given us.

—Simon J. Bronner
Harrisburg, Pennsylvania
U.S.A.

INTRODUCTION

SIMON J. BRONNER

Tradition . . . guides and safeguards continuity in a world of change without restraining or jeopardizing individual ingenuity. There is a toughness and a persistence about folk culture from which even the most independently minded escape only with difficulty. Yet—and this is the fascinating miracle of all folk cultures—the filter of individuality, of creative identity, of recognizable personality, prevents the products of tradition from becoming faceless and interchangeable.

—W. F. H. Nicolaisen from his presidential
address to the American Folklore Society, 1983

Bill Nicolaisen inspires the understanding that individuals creatively, strategically, control their cultural traditions. Working in folklore and related fields, he has seen lore, literature, and life as connected processes of creativity and tradition. Although we still encounter reductive interpretations of folklore as repetition, of literature as originality, the spirit of this volume—and indeed of Bill Nicolaisen—is to seek connections across categories and to find meanings in the creativity and tradition that express our humanity.

"Tradition" connotes a type of awareness, a natural order coming from the social and historical character of communicative encounters of people acting in communities (see Popper 1965:120–35; Acton

1953; Zaretzke 1982). Tradition may thus be treated as a given in a society, but in more modern terms people invoke it to organize belief and action by selectively employing and adjusting social precedent. As Dan Ben-Amos has pointed out, the use of "tradition" in folkloristic analyses applying modern approaches varies. Literally, "tradition" comes from the Latin for handing down or handing over and therefore contains the idea of transmission so crucial to the modern concept of folklore. In general usage, it carries the idea of repetition based on cultural precedent. Ben-Amos summarizes the folkloristic uses of tradition as generally implying "the knowledge of customs, rituals, beliefs, and oral literature as defined and practiced by a particular group, and as transmitted within its confines from generation to generation" (Ben-Amos 1984:105; see also Bronner 1986b; Gailey 1989).

The concept of individual creativity and cultural tradition working interdependently provides guideposts for documenting and interpreting folklore that take into account the collective precedent as well as the particular special performance. It presents folklore as an active force in people's lives and interprets it by explaining the choices made and the creativity applied. Folklore changes as people adapt it to different situations and needs. Folklore becomes manipulated knowledge; it is expressed as a blend of personal and social influence. Retaining a connection to the idea of folklore as characterized by repetition and variation ("variation in repetition," Nicolaisen insists), this conceptual matrix offers human terms of tradition and creativity to revise the mechanical associations of an earlier day. Thus it suggests the operation of folklore in complex human, or, more exactly, social and cultural contexts, rather than in mere linguistic terms.

The linking of creativity and tradition suggests the modern philosophy that "the ability to create is not limited to artists or writers but extends to many more, and perhaps to all, areas of human activity and endeavor" (Kristeller 1983:106). This ideal succeeds the Romantic notion of art as the sole domain of exceptional cultivated minds as existing free of tradition, as an expression of originality or genius that can create something where nothing existed previously.[1] As philosopher Paul Oskar Kristeller points out, "Perhaps the concept of genius has been less widely used in recent decades since it is definitely an 'elitist' notion, whereas in an egalitarian age such as ours it is claimed and believed that everybody, not only some gifted and talented artists, is original and creative" (Kristeller 1983:108). Relatively modern in conception, creativity in many ways opens up the process of art for review. Indeed, "creativity" did not become an accepted part of English vocabulary until the period between 1934 and 1961 (Kristeller 1983: 105).[2]

Creativity calls attention to individual artistry in varied forms, made subject to relative social standards of appropriateness or excellence. There is not, then, one capitalized Tradition in art, but a multiplicity of traditions to explore, for tradition in its multiple, abstract existence does not form a simple contrast with creativity (Kristeller 1983:111). Tradition thus revised does, however, recognize value in tradition as well as in elite notions of artistic creativity. We may recognize situations in which the pressure to repeat precedent is strong when tradition may be reintroduced or reestablished as a creative contribution. In any case, innovation is based on an understanding of traditional precedents. Creativity and tradition are intertwined, and represent the complex processes of humans expressing themselves to others in ways that carry value and meaning.

The concept of the interdependence of creativity and tradition in folklore studies has been in formation at least since the 1910s, when Franz Boas, for one, questioned a West European tendency in folklore studies of viewing folktales as intact, uniform units and tellers as passive repeaters of texts (Boas 1940:403). In fieldwork among Native Americans, Boas found varying levels of originality in the performance of folklore and he explained differences with reference to personality and social context. He underscored his view by referring to tale tellers as "individual artists" (Boas 1940:451–90). A pivotal study bringing out the artistry of the tale teller was Mark K. Azadovskij's *Eine sibirische Märchenerzählerin* (A Siberian Tale Teller) for the Finnish monograph series *Folklore Fellows Communications* (1926). Instead of following the convention of analyzing the texts for conformity to ancient tale types, Azadovskij considered the teller's personality and present surroundings and how those shaped her creative choice of individualized imagery and style within the Siberian narrative tradition (see Azadovskij 1974, 1975; Nicolaisen 1976a:326–27; Thompson 1977:451–53; Cocchiara 1981:539–40; Kirshenblatt-Gimblett 1989: 132–33; see also Litwin 1917). Cultural anthropologists and European ethnologists studying small homogeneous groups took further notice of the critical roles of context and creativity in narrative formation, and offered that even societies thought to be "primitive" undergo change and interpersonal dynamics. Thus folklore reveals culture in continuous development (see Boas 1925, 1938; Malinowski 1954, 1961; Dégh 1969, 1978; see also Lord 1960, Rosenberg 1970).

Within American folklore studies, Daniel Crowley labeled the problem of reconciling anthropological attention to dynamics and literary concern for stability in folklore in "Tradition and Creativity," the introduction to *I Could Talk Old-Story Good* (1966). In this study of Bahamian folk narratives, he observed that "no tale, no matter how sacred or traditional, can be told twice in exactly the same way without improbable feats of memory," and therefore, "variation both intentional and accidental confuses the problem of studying diffusion patterns, and threatens the validity of anticipated results" (Crowley 1966:1). Narrators are not merely receptacles for tradition, he concluded, but rather are choosers, arrangers, and performers. He added that "the pattern of creative activity within the forms of one's own society is valid not only in such folk arts as pottery or storytelling, but equally in the most extreme forms of personal self-expression in modern European painting" (Crowley 1966:136). This approach, advanced by Crowley and many others, revealed the communicative use of folklore in social settings as a process basic to human expression (see Dégh 1969, 1978; Abrahams 1970b; Paredes and Bauman 1972; Ben-Amos 1972; Ben-Amos and Goldstein 1975; Bauman 1977; see also Bascom 1955; Jansen 1957; Dorson 1972, 1978; Toelken 1979).

This concept took on particular force after the 1970s when, influenced by dramatic changes in human mobility and mass communications, new models appeared emphasizing the small frames of symbolic social interactions within a mass society (see Bauman 1989; Bronner 1986b:94–130). Such frames included family gatherings and factory and office settings, with folklorists putting forth studies of emergent types of tradition such as personal-experience stories, gestures, photocopied humor, and conversational lore. Looked at as process, folkloric performance could be found in the interactions of suburban teens in cars or college students or doctors and lawyers or even folklorists. "Folk" as a social unit, Alan Dundes stated in an oft-cited declaration, "can refer to *any group of people whatsoever* who share at least one common factor. It does not matter what the linking factor is—it could be a common occupation, language, or religion—but what is important is that a group formed for whatever reason will have some traditions which it calls its own" (Dundes 1980:6–7). As an emergent force, folklore did not have to dwell on the stability of a society or the timelessness of its products but could be examined for its role in implementing change. As Barbara Kirshenblatt-Gimblett noted, folklorists could study the "stimulus that sociocultural change provides not only for persistence and revitalization, but also for the creation of folklore." She offered the example of immigrant groups in North America being generally studied in terms of the folklore they lost in the process of settling down rather than in terms of the creative adjustment, change, and gain in folklore made, not to mention the varieties of contexts they experienced (Kirshenblatt-Gimblett 1978:109–10).

The prevalence in folkloristic inquiry of tradition and creativity is demonstrated by eighteen entries between 1977 and 1989 (the period when these terms appeared with significant frequency) in the Modern Language Association's bibliographic database. Of these eighteen titles, ten belong to authors engaged in folklore research (Tucker 1977; McCarthy 1978; Conroy 1979; Dow et al. 1980; Evans 1982; Santino 1985; Peacock 1986; Joyner 1988; Briggs 1988; Jones 1989; see also Bronner 1986c; Mieder 1987; Tu 1987). Further underscoring the contribution of this folkloristically based inquiry to scholarly discourse generally was an essay entitled " 'Creativity' and 'Tradition' " by philosopher Paul Oskar Kristeller (at a surprisingly late date in philosophy, he admits) in a journal devoted to the history of ideas because of the great "recent literary and popular discussion" of the linked terms (Kristeller 1983:105). Another philosopher explained that "tradition has been widely disregarded or disparaged by philosophers and intellectuals generally, mostly in the interest of a rationalism which has persevered throughout the period of modern philosophy and has only in the last couple of decades come under serious attack" (Zaretzke 1982:85). In questioning an elitist construction of "Western Civilization," "tradition" appears philosophically essential to accounting for a multicultural world. Indeed, the ideas expressed during the 1980s about tradition and creativity speak to the modern redefinition of the arts and to the emphasis on change and variation in contemporary societies (see Kristeller 1979). Observing the "mystical syncretism" of Indonesian folk religion, for example, James Peacock noted that tradition can encourage, rather than hinder (as Westerners tend to think), change. He argued that "traditional symbols, ideas, and practices subtly slip into the present national and ethnic consciousness, through the innovative efforts of Sukarno and others, resulting in a kind of social change... Heirs, many of us, of a culture that glorifies rationalizing reformism, we can usefully reflect on the dynamic power, in Indonesia and elsewhere, of creative traditionalism" (Peacock 1986:351).

The idea of "creation," or "bringing something into being," what philosopher John Hope Mason refers to as the Judaeo-Christian and neo-Platonic view or the "character of the creator," has occupied a dominant position in Western history (Mason 1988). In this view, creation implies unity, stability, order, harmony, and spirituality. "Creativity" in tradition implies less of a superhuman model. It exists more at the level of an artisan's work; in myths, it is the tool of tricksters and smiths rather than deities, Mason points out. Thus creativity, particularly cultural creativity, implies multiplicity, change, conflict, and physicality. Creativity emerges from everyday struggle and the action of people considering the tensions between old and new, individual and society (see Mason 1988; Bronner 1986a, 1986c; Martin 1990).

Why should this concern for creativity in everyday interaction and tradition attract scholarly attention? Michael Owen Jones answers by stating that "solutions to problems about the nature, generation, and functions of specific traditions provide understanding of the pervasiveness and role of tradition generally in people's lives. They contribute to an appreciation of what people are capable of and what they accomplish. They direct attention to a sphere of interaction often taken for granted or relegated to secondary importance but significant in its own right—that of how we do things and express ourselves on a day-to-day basis" (Jones 1989:262). The study of creativity in tradition identifies structures, acts, processes, and individuals involved in cultural expression, and as such it explores the essence of our humanity—our ideas, our capacities, and our ability to express them. The study of creativity in tradition moves internally toward studying consciousness, outwardly toward culture—and both are mediated by art.

Verbal and nonverbal behavior as a whole are typically governed by similar cultural processes. In social situations, such behaviors are not easily separable, and as Bill Nicolaisen points out, "crafts are indeed the tangible, material counterparts of the stories, songs, sayings, beliefs, customs, and so on, which we usually summarize as lore; and the role of the craftsman or craftswoman does not differ to any marked extent from that of the tradition bearers in the area of verbal art" (Nicolaisen 1990:44). Moreover, craftsmanship or artisanship is a model of creativity within tradition appropriate to cultural expression generally, for it recognizes individuals making use of materials at hand in response to audience and environment, and injecting variety into a process of repetition (see Nicolaisen 1984a:268–70; Nicolaisen 1990: 41–42; see also Gailey 1989; Martin 1990).[3] Following the lead of Bill Nicolaisen, this volume places creativity before tradition to suggest that individuals create, that is, express themselves, within a psychological and cultural context (see Nicolaisen 1990:45).

☙ ☙ ☙

W. F. H. (as he goes by formally, or "Bill," as he prefers to be called socially) Nicolaisen has been deeply involved in linking creativity and tradition, and it is his particular approach set against the background of his personal experience that will be explored here. It's an appropriate time to do so because his retirement from teaching alerts scholars to assess his influence over more than forty years, spanning two continents and several major paradigm shifts.

Bill was born Wilhelm Fritz Hermann Nicolaisen on June 13, 1927, in Halle/Saale, in east-central Germany, near Leipzig. His father was a professor of agriculture. As a child, Bill devoured folktales. The Second World War disrupted his education, indeed his life, and from 1945 to 1946 he worked on a farm before attending the University of Kiel from 1948 to 1950 to extend his boyhood passion for folktales to the study of language and literature. In 1950 he attended the King's College, Newcastle-upon-Tyne, now the University of Newcastle in England. He returned to Germany to study at the University of Tübingen, where he received his Dr. Phil. *magna cum laude* in comparative linguistics, English, and German in 1955. Having been awarded a "Scholarship for Advanced Studies in Arts" from the University of Glasgow, he later received Bachelor and Master of Letters degrees (1956, 1970) in Celtic Studies. His dissertation had been on the river names of the British Isles ("Die morphologische und semasiologische Struktur der Gewässernamen der britischen Inseln") and in Glasgow, he focused on Scottish river names ("Studies in Scottish Hydronymy").

By the 1950s, then, he had fastened on language and literature for his career. At universities in Glasgow and Dublin he taught German language and literature and from 1956 to 1969 he worked in the School of Scottish Studies at the University of Edinburgh as head of the Scottish Place-Name Survey. He had research interests in language (particularly place names), in folklore (narrative and balladry), in literature (medieval classics and Scottish poets and novelists), and in cultural history (Scotland, the British Isles, and Scandinavia). During this period, he had a long tenure—from 1957 to 1965—as assistant, later associate, editor of *Scottish Studies*. Wedding him to Scotland even more was his marriage to May Marshall in 1958. (They had first met at an evening class in Gaelic when Bill forgot his book and May let him share hers.) Bill and May eventually had four children with good Scottish or Scandinavian names—Fiona, Kirsten, Moira, and Birgit.

In the fall of 1966, Bill came to Ohio State University in the United States as visiting professor of English and folklore at the invitation of prominent folklorist Francis Lee Utley.[4] In 1967, he returned to the University of Edinburgh, becoming the acting head of its School of Scottish Studies in 1968. The following year, he left for the United States to take a position of associate professor in the English Department at the State University of New York at Binghamton. He quickly reached full professor status, and in 1985 the school honored him with the coveted title of distinguished professor of English and folklore. He gradually expanded his research interests to the United States, but has continued research in Europe, and particularly Scotland, returning there often on sabbaticals, on summer grants, and for special positions.

Nicolaisen's background takes in the roots of folklore scholarship. In Germany, known for the influence of the Brothers Grimm and folktale research, Nicolaisen came under the tutelage of internationally renowned folklorists Kurt Ranke, first president of the International Society for Folk Narrative Research and editor-in-chief of the *Enzyklopädie des Märchens,* and Walter Anderson, author of the classic monograph *Kaiser und Abt: Die Geschichte eines Schwanks* (The Emperor and the Abbot: The History of a Jest, 1923) that used the Finnish historic-geographic method of folktale analysis.[5]

Ranke explored the nature and function of narratives and the ongoing power of narration in everyday life. Ranke, Nicolaisen points out, went beyond the limits of the historical-geographical method to ask: "What are the creative impulses that operate behind the phenomenological manifestations of the diverse kinds of folk-narrative and that have given them such different contents, such various forms and such variable functions?" (Nicolaisen 1989:115). Nicolaisen continues,

"What really matters to Ranke in this context is the discovery of the imaginative shaping individual in the creative process or, put differently, the actualization of the communal spirit and soul in the poetic individual" (Nicolaisen 1989:115–16).

Walter Anderson also introduced Nicolaisen to comparative folktale research and opened its methods for scrutiny.

> Walter Anderson introduced me, as one of two students, into the mysteries of archetype and oicotype and the diffusion of folktales, as part of his seminar on "Vergleichende Märchenforschung" [Comparative Folktale Research]. After having at first displayed appropriate and genuine astonishment at the clearly demonstrable existence of geographically far-flung and historically evolved, or maybe devolved, internationally known genres and types of folknarrative, even the undergraduate mind began to ask for more, and certainly for more substantiating information with regard to the local manifestations of each type, on an oicotypal level, so to speak. [Nicolaisen 1976a:324]

From his work with Ranke and Anderson, as Nicolaisen recalls, other questions emerged: "How is it possible, I ask, for a viable and vital folk tradition to continue over a span of centuries without apparent diminution? Where do its invigorating impulses come from? Who are those responsible for its continuing existence and vitality, and what gives them satisfaction in this dynamic process in which they are so essentially and existentially involved?" (Nicolaisen 1990:42). Considering the prevailing paradigm then, Nicolaisen remembered that the answer to such questions "would have been a simple one, given with all the uncompromising force of well-established, scientific certitude: Das Volk singt und erzählt [The folk sing and narrate]. The people themselves as a community in anonymous acts of creation and re-creation keep traditions alive and add to and subtract from them" (Nicolaisen 1990:42).[6]

Folklorists addressing these difficult questions are likely to consider the role of the environment and of the individual. Nicolaisen has suggested regarding "folkness not in terms of societal status but as an appropriate behavioral response to the stimulus of certain circumstances—a cultural *register* rather than a cultural *level*" (Nicolaisen

1990:41). As a student of linguistics, Nicolaisen recognized register as a reference to a form of language appropriate to a limited situation (see also Bauman 1977:17). As Nicolaisen explains,

> the concept it represents is an inclusive one embracing that desirable triad of text, texture, and context, and because, on the other— and this perhaps more importantly—it emphasizes use rather than trait, object, mode of communication, level and size of social aggregation, or a demand for artistry, though potentially leaving space for all of them. The concept of *register* also acknowledges rightly the absence of that scholarly fiction—at least in contemporary terms although probably also in historical perspective—of the homogeneous folk society and ultimately of isolatable "folk persons" who in their individual lives act and communicate always in the folk manner... we all share various peculiar folk cultural characteristics and items which we use in selective situations whenever the folk cultural register makes it appropriate to do so. We are not folk all the time, nor are we never folk, although the importance of the folk cultural register in our lives varies considerably, ranging from near-complete domination to minor significance on rare occasions. [Nicolaisen 1980a:139]

Together with the linguistically derived idea that textual structures and variable situations guide the nature of expression, the act—or art—of storytelling largely informs Nicolaisen's viewpoint. Nicolaisen recognizes that narratives breed variation because they are reconstituted in performance, although their integrity as stories is maintained. They always leave something out; they are the "inevitable and necessary result of social interaction, of the need to narrate oneself and each other in never-ending fictions" (Nicolaisen 1991:10). When Nicolaisen says that "without stories we could not survive; without stories we would be disoriented; without stories we would be lost; without stories we lack assurance as to who we are or who we could be," he reveals tradition as shaping, sustaining, and always varying (Nicolaisen 1991:5–10).

Rather than tradition restricting culture to stable uniformity, tradition embraces variation and creativity. Nicolaisen's argument is not for the abandonment of texts, but for "their integration into a fuller and more rounded interrogation," for "it is necessary to know whether a tale is a variant of an identifiable type, both for matters of comparison and for the sake of placing the teller in a tradition." Further, "it is necessary to describe and analyze fully the personal versions of the variant of that type, or rather such versions in their ever repetitive and yet ever innovative realizations. Of course it is necessary to explore in great detail the biographical environment of the tellers (singers, artisans, etc.) in question, as well as their world views and predilections. Of course it is necessary to establish the place of a tale in a storyteller's repertoire." In sum, Nicolaisen concludes that

> faced with all these necessities, I am arguing that, beyond these legitimate scholarly activities the teller's tale be studied in a conscious and deliberate effort to rid us once and for all of any misunderstandings regarding the creative forces in tradition and the central role of region and the individual within it. Only then can we sweep aside all those mistaken notions which bedevilled folklore scholarship for far too long depriving it of its full and proper impact, and only then can we begin to become sensitive to the real source of vitality, as well as variability, in the folk-cultural register. Creativity is as personal as the human imagination and human craftfulness. [Nicolaisen 1990:45]

Variation in folklore is creative, in other words, because it is the result of "deliberate, intentional, and therefore far from accidental, changes and choices introduced by the individual folk artist whose creative genius is not content with mere imitative repetition in the process of appropriating a variant of a tale (or song) as his or her own personal version. Far from being at odds with each other, creativity and tradition, individual and community, together produce vital variability thus keeping alive the very items that their integrated forces help to shape" (Nicolaisen 1990:45).

Nicolaisen eloquently described the dynamic, rather than opposition, of creativity and tradition in his presidential address to the American Folklore Society in 1983.

> The folk-cultural response offers the expected but—and this is important—while shunning startling and disconcerting innovation, leaves room for judicious improvement and personal creativity. It favors the status quo, prefers circumscribed individuality to total

conformity or anarchic chaos, shuns eccentricity but has room for foolishness and wisdom; it lays great store by the accumulated common sense of generations though refracted through individual prisms and takes a few measured risks within an overall atmosphere of security. In folk culture audacity never outstrips sagacity. Tradition prevails but not without change, continuity creates balance and yet there is disruption, sometimes disconcerting, sometimes refreshing, sometimes both; repetition never becomes boring, community and individual are at ease with each other. [Nicolaisen 1984a:269]

In his phrasing, there is reference to the adaptive nature of folklore. Folklore, Nicolaisen suggests, gains its vitality from its use, from human responses to a complex environment. Folklore allows people to adapt to, or comment on, other people; it carries power because it draws on a social grounding with room for individual expression.

For Nicolaisen, folklore is therefore basic to our humanity because it acts on the very dimensions surrounding us as humans: space and time. Storytelling, for example, allows people to tell the past in the way they wish it had occurred, to create themselves, to cope with the present, and to manage an uncertain future. "Through stories we create innumerable pasts," Nicolaisen observes, "while rehearsing possible futures through advice, injunctions, prophecy, divination, detailed directions in order to make the actual future less overwhelming when it happens" (Nicolaisen 1990:41; see also Nicolaisen 1985a). Broadly speaking, Nicolaisen asserts that "as long as we, as folk, are tethered to time, our stories will tell of it, will transform it, will use it as a major organisational and structural principle. True timelessness is beyond our imagination. Maybe these stories whether legends or folktales, will teach us to live fuller and more effective lives in the present... " (Nicolaisen 1980b:318; see also Nicolaisen 1983a, 1984d).

Of space, and its extension into concepts of habitat and community, Nicolaisen is even more definite. He cautions that our sense of space is less developed than that of time: "The human dilemma is not so much that we are where we are and that we are bounded and determined by what we call the passage of time, in all its manifestations and punctuations, but that we have to be what we are when we are, and cannot be earlier or later" (Nicolaisen 1980c:14). Besides the question of "when?" is the question of "where?" followed by the philosophical question of "why there?" Thus folk activity in a situation, set against a landscape, or more generally a habitat, contains spatial concepts of *location, region,* and the *interaction* of place and people (see Nicolaisen 1973a:5). "All folk-cultural creativity," Nicolaisen declares,

> is in essence regional (or somehow home specific). Consequently, at least one important element in the forging of diversity in folk-culture is the sense of, and response to, region, (to "home"). Naturally, this is a spatial concept and a synchronic one which, while eminently mappable in its many co-existing traits, does not account for diachronic change. It is also a concept which comfortably locates the group as structured community. Community thus inhabits the region, is living region, and folk-culture has a large share of that regional community life. [Nicolaisen 1990:40]

Tradition thus offers a commentary on the human perception of space and on human adaptation to the environment.

This premise led Nicolaisen to suggest a mission for folklore study embedded in a geography, broadly defined, of tradition. This seemed appropriate since some of folklore study's basic questions involve queries of movement across space and time and of the character of creative expression in selected spaces and times as they are interpreted by individuals. Tapping into linguistics again, Nicolaisen asserts that the idea behind *dialect* involves basic folkloristic concerns. He sees

> no reason why a vernacular architecture should not have its *dialects,* why the folk idiom could not be expressed in terms of *dialect,* why an area delimited by material culture isoglosses should not be a folk cultural *dialect* area, or why von Sydow's "oicotypical districts" could not be viewed as regions of folk-narrative *dialect. Dialect* appears to be the very metaphor that pays attention to both sameness and difference, to variation and repetition, to variant and type.... It certainly would make a welcome parallel to *register.*[7] [Nicolaisen 1980a:145]

This outlook had the advantage, he thought, of unifying traditional expressions, verbal and nonverbal (*Wörter und Sachen,* he called it, or "words *and* things"). Nicolaisen had hopes eventually of mapping folk culture in America as an applied form of folklore study (see

Nicolaisen 1971, 1973, 1975a; see also Rooney et al. 1982). In keeping with his concern for human intention and creativity, he especially wanted to visualize the ways that people "*make* regions" (Nicolaisen 1976b:147). Although the hope for an American folk atlas has yet to be realized, Nicolaisen offered that the "geographic" approach, a result of which could yet be the mapping of folk culture in all its variation, has had a profound implication for folklore studies. It implies greater interchange and cooperation among folklorists, and a goal toward which the particularistic collection and interpretation of folklore will lead. He reflects that

> at the very best, such an approach will nail the slogan "variation in repetition" to its masthead and will view vernacular folk culture as a whole with its registers, isoglosses, and dialects. The task is not really as difficult as it sounds. It just means farewell to myopia and welcome to a grander vision. It means enthusiasm and the willingness to think afresh. Above all it means a king-sized dose of good will. Under such favorable conditions variant, dialect and region will easily be seen as different facets of the same diamond, and the exploration of the geography of tradition will truly become an exploration of the geography of culture and of the geography of the human mind. [Nicolaisen 1980a:146–47]

We might view the materials of folklore that have dominated Nicolaisen's research—names and narratives—as very personal and yet simultaneously collective expressions given to a "geography of the human mind." Bill once admitted in an interview that when he started out in academe he thought that naming and narrating were distinctly separate subjects, and it is true that students of names—although naming is very much part of tradition—have not been abundant in folklore studies.[8] His work led him to find them inextricably linked. He said that "both are basic activities of human beings to master, to structure their world." In his presidential address to the American Folklore Society, he suggested that names and narratives both reveal themselves as "reconcilable twin approaches to human individuality in its enmeshings with" the past. They "are products of two of the most essential speech acts in the human repertoire, those of naming and narration. One, through the device of identifying reference, gives structure to a chaotic world; the other, through story, creates pasts which inform the present and take the sting out of the future. *Homo nominans* and *homo narrans* seem to be at odds with each other and yet strive toward the same goal, respond to the same need: the humanism of satisfying, strategic survival" (Nicolaisen 1984a:271, 260).

His first publications, beginning in 1957, were on place names; to show their relations in time and space and their cultural connections to the views of ethnic communities through history, he collected narratives attached to them. His work culminated almost twenty years later in *Scottish Place Names,* a monumental volume that won the Chicago Folklore Prize for outstanding contribution to folklore studies. Appreciate the immensity of his task by considering that to complete the volume he needed to translate seven languages and mine sources in archaeology, folklore, sociology, local history, geography, literature, linguistics, and law.

In relation to the concept of creativity and tradition, Nicolaisen's name studies follow a path from product to process to individual. As he put it in 1976,

> Onomastics has been my academic bread and butter and my own intellectual entertainment for a quarter of a century. During these twenty-five years I have moved from an initial preoccupation with the product—the name, via fascination with the process-naming, to an infatuation with the producer—Man. I have no doubt that this quest for *homo nominans* has largely been a journey towards a discovery of self, and—incorrigible optimist that I am—I am convinced that, if one embarks on that journey, one will somewhere along the road get (be vouchsafed, one would have said last century) the teeniest-weeniest glimpse of the divine—in us. [Nicolaisen 1976d:158–59]

With relation to folklore, Nicolaisen explored through onomastics the functions that naming provides for individuals and the ways that names establish identities for family, occupational, social, ethnic, religious, and moral groups (see Nicolaisen 1984c). More than reiterating that names reflect folklore, he showed that people acculturate space (or objects and other people) by using folklore to *create* names, as in the "application of facets of popular belief and the localization of migratory legends" (Nicolaisen 1976d:146). Summarizing his view, Nicolaisen stated in "Folklore and Names" that the communicating word thrives as instruction, as celebration, as entertainment, as ornamentation, as grooming, as preening, etc. and in its textual, verbal embedding the name thrives with it. This environment of context, or usage acts, provides both situational stimulus and conditioned outlet for what one might loosely term folk naming or, with a little more precision, the onomastic response appropriate to the folk cultural register: the nickname, the by-name, the private name, the unofficial name, the register-bound boy's or girl's name, the house name, the incident name, the retrieval or secondary reinterpretation, the creation of meaning for the meaningless name, the folk acculturation of names from sources outside the register or their modification according to folk principles. [Nicolaisen 1984c:17]

While this perspective stresses the control that individuals have over their naming choices, tradition offers varieties of cultural knowledge as a basis for naming and other symbolically expressive choices. Nicolaisen has proposed that such knowledge resembles the use of dialects: "We all acquire an onomasticon as well as a lexicon," he wrote, "and use it appropriately in recognition, in thinking, and in talking. The result is a large number of onomastic idiolects, individual name repertoires, with the range and degree of competence varying from person to person. Naturally, each such onomastic idiolect is strongly influenced by its community of name users and name givers, who make up an onomastic dialect area that is also culturally and socially stratified" (Nicolaisen 1980d:41–42).[9]

This combination of behavioral, social, linguistic (and literary), and dialectal considerations is further evident in Nicolaisen's studies of narrative. Nicolaisen considers narrative, and the process of narrating, broadly as based in four categories usually named in English as ballad and song, literature (poetry and novel), legend, and tale.[10] Pointing out that "narration" has etymological roots in Latin and Greek words (*gnarus* and *gnosis,* respectively) for knowledge and skill, Nicolaisen states that "the idea of narrative can therefore be claimed to refer to 'a mode of knowledge emerging from action'—one knows by doing— or, equally plausibly, as knowledge activated through the word in time—one translated knowing into telling. The storyteller, in this sense, finds his place close to the gnome, the teacher, the wise man, the one who narrates because he has gnosis and is gnarus—'the skilful sage'" (Nicolaisen 1984b:177). Speaking on legends, for example, Nicolaisen hypothesizes that they "are necessary narrative transactions shared by teller and listener in the folk-cultural register, in response to certain behavioural stimuli and to certain negotiated motivations and interests. Legends, through entertaining narration, through translating knowing into telling, craftsmanlike give structure to mere sequence of events and create . . . a textured, believable past" (Nicolaisen 1984b:177).

Nicolaisen's stress on the relation of narrative to individual tellers and their creation of a believable past is especially evident in "AT 1535 in Beech Mountain, North Carolina," published in the Scandinavian journal *Arv* (1980). Working back from presently told tales of "The Heifer Hide," as they are known in Beech Mountain (they are indexed as "The Rich and the Poor Peasant" in the Aarne-Thompson tale-type index), he traces the sources of the tales through a family genealogy, attitudes toward the tales and their performance through the family tree. "Ray [Hicks], when he had finished his story," Nicolaisen wrote, "asked me if I had noted certain details. When I told him that I had, he informed me with great pleasure that these were small additions that he himself had added to the story as he had heard it from his grandfather, in order to make it his own. Hattie, on the other hand, insisted on telling me several times that her version was exactly as she had heard it from her father—it was her father's story, not her own" (Nicolaisen 1984a).

Nicolaisen's research led to another question: How is it that we recognize these stories as versions? In his narrative studies, particularly of legends and ballads, Nicolaisen has examined the linguistic structures that guide formation into narrative. Insisting that legends as narratives do have form, despite the pronouncements of some scholars who view their content as predominant, he compares them to the structuring of personal experience stories (Nicolaisen 1985b, 1987). In the study of ballads he reveals what he calls the "episode-forming," or structuring potential of place names in ballads, as well as the ballad singer's distinctive, varied uses of incremental repetition (Nicolaisen 1973b, 1978). He also compares folk ballad form to literary poetic form to point out similarities in "the art of narration" and the "vast difference between the immediately shared, simultaneous experience of story-teller and audience in oral tradition and the almost unpredictable relationship between the lonely writer and the elusive reader in the realm of written, visual stories" (Nicolaisen 1983b:138–39; see also Nicolaisen 1983c).

Form. Structure. Style. Performance. Function. Context. Habitat. Register. Response. Identity. Dialect. Region. Community. Variant. Variation. Repetition. Vitality. The lexicon used by Nicolaisen brings out the wholeness of expression at the hands of artisans in its varied environments. He uses these terms within the larger concept of creativity and tradition to uncover our basic ideas "within a certain context and against the background of a certain reality that really matters, for it is here that the tension—not the contradiction but the tension—between creativity and tradition keeps folk culture alive and well" (Nicolaisen 1986a:127). International in its scope, regional, local, and individual in its affecting presence, folklore "is interwoven into the whole texture of culture" (Nicolaisen 1970–71:23).

Nicolaisen's passion for studying creativity and tradition in folklore carries over into his remarkable publishing and presentational record, and his organizing and teaching activities. He has published over 300 articles in over 60 different scholarly journals (see the selected bibliography of his works in this volume); he has published over 120 reviews; and he has presented papers at ten to twelve professional meetings a year worldwide. He has held leadership posts in fourteen learned societies; among his special achievements have been the presidencies of the New York Folklore Society, the Middle Atlantic Folklife Association, the American Folklore Society, the American Name Society, and the International Congress of Onomastic Sciences. He is a vice-president of the International Society for Folk Narrative Research, the secretary-general of the International Committee of Onomastic Sciences, cofounder of the Society for North American Cultural Survey, founder of the Council for Name Studies in Great Britain and Ireland, and founder of the Folk Narrative Section of the American Folklore Society. He is a fellow of the Finnish Academy of Science and Letters, of the American Folklore Society, and of the Center for Medieval and Early Renaissance Studies. His research has been supported by the American Council of Learned Societies, the National Endowment for the Humanities, the Carnegie Trust for the Universities of Scotland, and the SUNY Research Foundation. He has been the editor of five special issues of scholarly journals. His work is hardly done, despite his retirement from teaching.

Bill will continue his research and professional activities, now from a new home base in the northeast of Scotland. Since 1973, he has been working on what he regards as the major project of his scholarly life, a dictionary of Scottish place names. In all these endeavors, he is the consummate colleague. He offers good cheer, humor (with a special fondness for a good pun), encouragement, and assistance. Despite his extraordinarily busy schedule, he insists on making time for writing letters and visiting, for keeping up with friends and colleagues, and for putting in a good word wherever he goes.

As Professor Nicolaisen, Bill has had a tremendous impact as a teacher and mentor. I should know. It was his course on folklore which I took as a wide-eyed freshman that changed my life path. And I wasn't the only one.[11] He had both large introductory classes and smaller seminars. He would reach out to freshman and graduate student alike. I vividly see him standing in front of a lecture hall packed with students waiting to be convinced of the relation of this subject to their lives. He showed how folklore raises the texture of culture we all can feel:

> If you have ever heard a joke—let us say, about Spiro Agnew—liked it and told it again, you are one of the folk. If you have ever avoided flying on Friday the 13th, you are one of the folk. If you have ever demanded "Trick or Treat" at Halloween, you are one of the folk. If you say "Bless you" or "Gesundheit" when somebody sneezes, if you have ever told the story of "Cinderella" or "The Sleeping Beauty" to your children at nighttime or to your Kindergarten class, if you have ever played "Musical Chairs," if you have ever counted "Eenie, meenie, mine, mo...," if you have ever written something on a bathroom wall—you are one of the folk... Folklore is right among us because "we are the folk." [Nicolaisen 1970–71:22]

He had us interview and collect material from our families; he had us go into the Binghamton community and discover its ethnic, regional, and religious dimensions. He understood our Old-World roots and our individual searches for independence; he reflected on rural, regional, and ethnic subcultures, and contemplated the transformations of the electronic present. He riveted our attention on small items like names with brilliant observations (sometimes calling the roll took a very long time!), and made us well aware of the social meanings in broad items like landscape. He forced us to know the region and even more importantly its people. He forced us to think for ourselves about our cultural existence, our past and our future. Folklore in this New York maelstrom was a study of compassion and relevance.

"I don't 'teach' in a strict, chalk-and-blackboard sense," Bill told a newspaper interviewer, "I always say I'm trying to make people aware of things...(to) open their eyes—so that when they go out there in the community, they see things (and) know how to interpret them" (Mittelstadt 1981:19). Concerned with effective and innovative teaching, he participated in forums at the school and received teaching honors. He offered his experience teaching folklore as the heart of a humanistic mission, that of studying and interpreting human expressiveness. "In my undergraduate folklore class at Binghamton," he insisted,

> I . . . [expose] students to actual folk material and its analysis, in addition to making participants go out and collect such material. I use recordings a great deal but also bring live folk artists into class, and at present we are also preparing a folk concert to be given by singers and musicians in our midst, at the very end of the course. It has been my experience that the student generation of today responds easily and gladly to the impulses received in such an exposure, and there is hope that their responsiveness will lead to a new responsibility. [Nicolaisen 1970–71:23]

He went beyond the campus to offer courses in the heart of the ethnically rich Triple Cities area; within the campus, his office filled with the sounds of guidance and wisdom from professor to student. He taught his subject, to be sure, but he also preached sensitivity, curiosity, insight.

As professor, Bill offered a variety of folklore courses. He taught a basic introductory course in folklore followed by specialized offerings in American Folklore, Studies in Folklore, Ballads, American Folk Myths, Ethnic Folk Culture, Volksmärchen und Kunstmärchen (for the German Department), and Folklore and Literature, in addition to classes on linguistics and onomastics. He brought his warm presence right into the midst of students in his service as a fellow of Hinman College, a student residential complex in the university, and into the community in his support for the regional Scottish society. As a student, I was pleasantly surprised to discover that contrary to the arrogant professorial stereotype, Bill talked to students outside class and was interested in our lives as well as our grades. He could be seen at the pool with his children, at the cafeteria trading stories with staff, and in the theater performing with students in a campus play. His office was a joy to enter. It had the hallmarks of an inspired scholar—books were everywhere, papers were piled high, and the floor was barely visible. A Scottish stone rubbing vied with a painting of a covered bridge for space on the wall, and over his desk hung a reminder in German that life was manageable and joyful. His head buried in his work, he would sense a student approaching, swing his chair around, and beam a welcoming smile. His caring extended to all of God's creatures. He protected "Misty" in his office and sometimes even talked to her. Misty, I should say, was a poor plant left an orphan by departing students; Bill took her in and had her growing again in no time. His students were sure it had something to do with Bill's generous bestowal of a name and narrative as well as water and sunlight.

Bill led students in semesters abroad, helped international students adjust to the Binghamton campus, advised students of English, counseled students specializing in folklore, and assisted the student newspaper and yearbook. Administrators at the universities adored his service as director of graduate studies of English and director of the linguistics program, in addition to his chairmanship of long-range planning and many search committees for the university. But for students, it was his love of his subject, his enthusiasm for learning, his graceful delivery of knowledge, his caring for the campus community and all those within it that made him outstanding. It is these qualities that also distinguish his scholarship.

***

The essays in this volume explore creativity and tradition with special reference to research topics and cultural areas explored by Bill Nicolaisen. The essayists are eminent colleagues on both sides of the Atlantic. They honor him with this volume, using this opportunity to move the study of creativity and tradition forward onto the international scene. The volume is therefore a tribute to Bill's long scholarly reach and to folklore as a field of inquiry into the creative mind in culture.

The progression of the volume is generally from essays working on the genres of tradition (represented clearly in ballad and song) to questions of transmission and process (especially in the "blurred genres" of narrative) to matters of language, composition, adaptation, and innovation (in more abstract headings of "language and cultural knowledge" and ultimately in "community and identity").

The first section on ballad and song raises questions about the structure, function, variation, transmission, and creation of narrative songs in tradition. Ian Olson opens by examining the connections of places and names in the performance of Scottish folk ballads. Considering the creative updating of tradition, D. K. Wilgus and Eleanor Long-Wilgus reveal the influence of ancient Irish vision-poems into songs as varied as cowboy and factory girl laments in America. From these previous essays slanted toward the structure and content of tradition, we move to the role of the individual and media. In his essay on one song often considered part of oral tradition in twentieth-century America, W. K. McNeil looks at the song's source in one man's poetry.

Continuing the emphasis on the fundamental impulse to create pasts through stories, the next section offers perspectives on the use of narrative in various historical and cultural situations. Ronald L. Baker offers a transition from the previous section by examining a historical event in America that inspired narrative response in both ballad and legend—the murder of Pearl Bryan in 1896 near Fort Thomas, Kentucky. In her study of a "legend conduit," Linda Dégh concentrates on a narrative event—a recently held conversation among Hungarian neighbors—and she addresses questions of creative transmission of traditional material within this immediate context. Klaus Roth in his essay offers a perspective on the character and function of narrating as a folk-cultural response to social and political conditions in Bulgaria. Moving back to the American scene in Nicolaisen's backyard of Binghamton, New York, Elizabeth Tucker contributes her work on everyday narrating—personal experience stories "from our own lives that illustrate or illuminate who we are and what we have accomplished." Cristina Bacchilega closes the section with an essay questioning the creative manipulation of folktales by collectors and editors who made semiotic connections of gender and nature.

Basic to the construction of creative expression such as narrative in tradition is the use of language and its association with cultural knowledge. The section after narrative on language and cultural knowledge thus explores this topic with reference to names, proverbs, and speech as they are used and perceived variously. In his philosophical essay, Wilbur Zelinsky raises the fundamental relationship between humans culturally constructing their environment by analyzing place names as a most basic creative tradition, "the creation of reality." Wolfgang Mieder follows by also inquiring into the ways that humans identify their cultural wisdom as well as their surroundings. He brings out studies of "paremiological minimum," the basic repertoire of proverbs known by someone as a member of a society. In so doing he raises issues of the changing definitions of cultural literacy subject to creative additions within various modern cultural traditions. J. Derrick McClure further explores how cultural traditions are perceived both from within and outside a society. Digging into history, he examines classifications of words considered distinctively Scottish by English and Scottish speakers. Alexander Fenton has a similar sensitivity to the relative nature of his subject, and he makes a creative cultural connection in historical tradition between words and the things they represent in his study of terms used for material culture among Gaelic Scottish speakers.

Scotland is also the setting of Mary Ellen Brown's study of local poets in the next section on community and identity. Her study and the ones that follow particularly look at individuals creatively using tradition to affect their social connections to one another. Brown examines traditional sources for localized poetry and the communicative process which, as she says, "converts the everyday to art." Venetia Newall moves the reader to England where she describes a Serbian family's creative adjustment of a traditional festival, and food feast, based on their needs as members of an ethnic minority and other features of their identity. Roger Mitchell offers a study of refugees from Laos that suggests the need for ongoing attention—for scholarly and applied purposes—to folkloric processes in the many population shifts currently occurring in the world. Mitchell observes an area in the upper Midwest of the United States that took in Hmong refugees after the Vietnam War. Mitchell finds that in their new setting the Hmong use proverbs as an active force in the process of adaptation. I close the volume with a study of a folk artist who creatively expressed the values, and fears, of his Pennsylvania-German valley community in stone and on paper.

The essays are bound by a unifying interest in the control and complexity of cultural expression. Some essays concentrate on the structure and content of tradition (e.g., Wilgus and Long-Wilgus, Mieder, Bacchilega, Baker); others focus on function and context (e.g., Olson, Roth, Newall, Bronner, Tucker). Process, event, and transmission receive their due, especially as they have a role in the repetition and variation, or tradition and creativity, of cultural knowledge (e.g., Dégh, Mitchell, Baker, Bronner, Zelinsky). Involved in studies of process beyond the nature of social interaction are the factors of media in popular culture, literature and literacy, environment, and politics. Many essays touch on these factors, particularly the ones by Brown, Bacchilega, Baker, McNeil, and Roth. Some studies dwell on the present (e.g., Tucker, Mitchell, Dégh, Newall), others probe history for insights (e.g., McClure, Fenton, Brown), and others work to bring both into view (e.g., Mieder, Zelinsky, Bacchilega, Baker, Bronner, Roth). On the creative side, we have studies that consider individual artists, poets, singers, storytellers, and organizers (e.g., Bronner, McNeil, Brown, Olson, Tucker, Dégh, Newall).

Some readers may find the genres represented under the umbrella of "folklore" rather wide; the term covers vocabulary, names, proverbs, sayings, songs, poems, legends, jokes, stories, beliefs, and crafts. All, however, have a connection to traditionally learned knowledge and expresson as part of culture. And within these pages you should recognize expressions decidedly non-folkloric but with a relation to the folk-cultural register (see especially McNeil, Brown). Zelinsky perhaps covers the most cultural ground, asking about the very nature of naming, although he relies primarily on European-American examples, official and otherwise. Mieder's essay is comparative with considerations of German, Russian, and American studies of popular proverb tradition. As might be expected, Scottish language and literature receive considerable attention (Olson, McClure, Fenton, Brown), and space is given to custom and song in England and Ireland (Newall, Wilgus and Long-Wilgus). Hungarian, Serbian, Italian, and Bulgarian narrative communities are examined (Dégh, Newall, Bacchilega, Roth), and within America, one can read of Hmong and German language and arts (Mitchell, Bronner). Other American studies examine Anglo-American song and emergent American narrative traditions (Wilgus and Long-Wilgus, Tucker, McNeil, Baker). The contributors themselves are diverse, representing Nicolaisen's scholarly journey from central Europe to Great Britain to America.

We devote this volume, then, to varieties of a concept, and we dedicate it to Bill Nicolaisen for his inspiration to all of us who carry forward the challenges of documenting and interpreting our folklore so revealing of our ever-changing surroundings, our ever-complex selves, our ever-profound humanity. As humans we come together on the common ground of culture, despite severing tides. From thought to action, from names to narrative, from words to things, ingenuity stirs about, while tradition, as Bill writes, "guides and safeguards" us.

In closing, I think of one of Bill Nicolaisen's favorite examples of folklore from the Scottish ballad "Annan Water."

> And wae betide ye, Annan Water
> This night that ye are a drumlie river!
> For over thee I'll build a bridge
> That ye never more true love may sever.[12]

Creatively adjusted constantly for different places and situations, the song has been performed and used variously by its singers and listeners. It suggests the power of folklore to relate the human condition and the urge for salvation through togetherness. Its underlying message still endures in our time. It speaks in names and narrative of everything that severs. It applies creativity to express its themes poignantly and persuasively. It invokes tradition to heal so much that is broken and fractured (Nicolaisen 1984a:265–66). The water metaphor in culture drew Bill Nicolaisen's attention in his first publications and underlined the close of his dramatic presidential address to the American Folklore Society more than twenty-five years later. He affirms, as we do in this book, that "there are still cascades of texts out there and klondikes of folklore" (Nicolaisen 1984a:271). Let's get to them so we might comprehend the flow of creativity and tradition through our lives.

NOTES

1. Commenting on artistic biases in the modern era, T. S. Eliot in 1919 asserted that "in English writing we seldom speak of tradition, though we occasionally apply its name in deploring its absence. We cannot refer to 'the tradition' or to 'a tradition'; at most we employ the adjective in say-

ing that the poetry of So-and-so is 'traditional' or even 'too traditional.' Seldom, perhaps, does the word appear except in a phrase of censure" (Eliot 1960:3). Eliot's protest is that the fine arts have overemphasized the individual to the detriment of his or her art. "No poet, no artist of any art," he says, "has his complete meaning alone. His significance, his appreciation is the appreciation of his relation to the dead poets and artists. You cannot value him alone, you must set him, for contrast and comparison, among the dead" (Eliot 1960:4).

As representation of "tradition" was considered suspect in Western social constructions of "art," so too was the representation of "creativity" in definitions of cultural tradition until relatively recently. In the sciences during the late nineteenth century, Sigmund Freud was influential in presenting creativity as a psychologically adaptive device common to all individuals. Sander Gilman in *The Jew's Body* (1991) argues that Freud's advocacy for this view was driven by the social and cultural context of Europe which at the time considered creativity a mark of intellectual superiority among a dominant group and simultaneously a sign of physical disorder among discriminated groups such as Jews (see pp. 128–49). Freud, who had a Jewish background in Austria, thus removed creativity from a discourse on race and disease to one on a force present in all human beings. In Freud's theories sexuality was this force since he believed that creativity sublimated fundamentally human anxieties; others such as Franz Boas have characterized creativity as a force that drives a psychological feeling for form—a need to express and an urge to create (Boas 1955:9–10; see also Jones 1980; Bronner 1985).

Franz Boas's influential advocacy in anthropology for the universal and culturally relative nature of creativity was also probably motivated by a reaction to the racial science of the nineteenth century. Boas was a German Jew who emigrated to the United States and like Freud, Boas used folklore and folk art extensively to make his case for links between individual creativity and cultural tradition (see Herskovits 1953:73–101).

2. The word "creativity" is absent from the first edition of the Oxford English Dictionary (1893). There is reference to "creativeness," the general state of creating, but it lacks the later artistic association of "creativity" (see Mason 1988). The second edition (1933) lists creativity with mostly twentieth-century references (the earliest usage listed is 1875), and suggests the influence of philosopher Alfred North Whitehead during the 1920s in spreading use of the term.

3. Nicolaisen affirms Walter Benjamin's argument that "the storytelling that thrives for a long time in the milieu of work—the rural, the maritime, the urban—is itself an artisan form of communication, as it were. It does not aim to convey the pure essence of the thing, like information or a report. It sinks the thing into the life of the storyteller, in order to bring it out of him again." To Nicolaisen, narration therefore "significantly happens in an 'atmosphere of craftsmanship,' serving those who are craft-ful while being itself a craft" (Nicolaisen 1984b:175; see also Benjamin 1968:91).

4. Francis Lee Utley (1907–74) is a significant figure in folklore studies gen-

erally, and in Nicolaisen's career particularly. Utley shared many research interests with Bill. He was active in onomastics (president of the American Name Society and editorial board member of *Names* from 1957 to 1963), linguistics (executive councils of the American Dialect Society and Modern Language Association), folk narrative (president of the American Folklore Society), medieval studies (executive council of the Medieval Academy of America), and English literature (president of the College English Association). For his bibliography, see Amsler 1975, and for testimonies to his impact on medieval studies see Mandel and Rosenberg 1970. For accounts of his life and career, see Wilgus 1974; Finnie 1975. Nicolaisen dedicated his essay "Some Humorous Folk-Etymological Narratives" (1977) to Utley and contributed "Place-Names in Bilingual Communities" (1975c) to a memorial issue of *Names* for Utley; he also discussed some of Utley's research on naming in "Onomastic Activities in the United States" (1975b).

5. Kurt Ranke (1908–85) as editor, organizer, writer, and teacher helped to shape the international study of folk narrative. Nicolaisen states that "it would be difficult to imagine the study of folklore in Germany after World War II and the burgeoning of international folk-narrative research in the last three decades without the profound influence of his scholarship, his remarkable ability and his sage counsel and guidance" (Nicolaisen 1986b:110). Ranke was chair of folklore at the University of Kiel during the 1950s and moved to Göttingen in 1960. Among his notable accomplishments were the founding of the journal *Fabula* and the International Society for Folk Narrative Research. He was editor-in-chief of the *Enzyklopädie des Märchens, Folktales of Germany* (University of Chicago Press, 1966), and *European Anecdotes and Jests* (Copenhagen, 1972). For more discussion of Ranke and his ideas, see Köhler-Zülch 1986; Nicolaisen 1986b, Nicolaisen 1989; Harkort, Peeters, and Wildhaber 1968. Nicolaisen in "Kurt Ranke and Einfache Formen" (1989) compares Ranke's ideas to another important influence, through his writings, on Nicolaisen—Max Lüthi (1909–   ). See Lüthi 1970, 1984, 1989.

Besides being a world authority on folk narrative, Walter Anderson (1885–1962) also had research interests in language, folk song, and Estonian and Finnish folklore. He published other monographs in the Folklore Fellows Communication Series in 1939 (*Johannes Bolte: Ein Nachruf*, No. 124), in 1951 (*Ein volkskundliches Experiment*, No. 141), and in 1956 (*Eine neue Arbeit zur experimentellen Volkskunde*, No. 168). Stith Thompson described Anderson as a "cosmopolitan scholar." Thompson goes on to say:

> He has issued several of the most thorough monographic studies of a folktale and has striven constantly to improve the technique developed by Krohn and Aarne. He has been convinced of the fundamental soundness of the historic-geographic method and has not hesitated to defend it when it has been attacked. Anderson's knowledge of the tale is probably unsurpassed, certainly in respect to the Baltic and Slavic fields, and he has been generous in helping other scholars, particularly

young students, in discovering elusive material. His own standards of scholarship are very exacting, so that slipshod work by others is not likely to escape his caustic censure. [Thompson 1977:401]

For an overview of Anderson's illustrious career, see Ranke 1962; Levin 1963. Nicolaisen studied with Anderson at Kiel before moving on to Tübingen and further education in Scotland. Regarding the concept of creativity and tradition, it is also worth footnoting here the later scholarly context of German folklore scholarship, especially with the influence of the "Tübingen School" under the leadership of Hermann Bausinger, who moved folklore toward an empirical cultural science concerned with changing folk traditions in the modern world (see Bausinger 1968; Dow and Lixfeld 1986).

6. Nicolaisen explains Anderson's theory of self-correction as the idea that "the people themselves as a community in anonymous acts of creation and re-creation keep traditions alive and add to and subtract from them. The mere mention of individual composers was then seen as a fictionalizing characteristic of the genre" (Nicolaisen 1986a:126). The theory (sometimes called the "law of self-correction") therefore emphasizes stability in line with an original tradition. Stith Thompson, for example, summarizes Anderson's idea: "Intelligent hearers often correct careless tellers and in that way bring the tale back nearer to the regular tradition. The hearer of many versions of a tale naturally constructs a kind of standard form as a composite of what he has heard, and thus keeps the tale from going off at purely fortuitous tangents." Anderson assumed, therefore, that the "gifted raconteur" follows older tradition, keeping it stable, rather than introducing creativity, and this explains the "remarkable stability of the essential story in the midst of continually shifting details" (Thompson 1977:437).

7. In this quotation, and in many other writings, Nicolaisen uses the term "oicotype" suggested by Swedish folklorist Carl Wilhelm von Sydow (1878–1952). Von Sydow took the term from botany in which it denotes a genetic variety of plant that adapts to a certain environment through natural selection and thus differs somewhat from other members of the same species. In folklore, according to a common definition, "the term refers to local forms of a tale type, folksong, or proverb with 'local' defined in either geographic or cultural terms. Oicotypes could be on the village, state, regional, or national level. The concept oicotype differs from the notion of subtype in that the oicotype is tied by definition to a very specific locale" (von Sydow 1965:220). Nicolaisen and other folklorists emphasizing variable transmission also have adapted von Sydow's related term "active bearer of tradition." Countering the idea that tales move by themselves in some superorganic stream, von Sydow argued that the vitality of folklore depends on transmission by active bearers of tradition. Summarizing von Sydow's views, Alan Dundes stated that folklore is transmitted

only if and when one active bearer communicates such a tale to another active bearer. If an active bearer migrates from a place before imparting his materials, the folklore may die out in that place. If in the new place, either because of language or culture, the active bearer fails to continue his active role, the folklore may not survive. Von Sydow admits that it is possible for passive bearers to become active bearers in the event of the death or departure of an active bearer in a community. But in any event, von Sydow believes that the number of active bearers is relatively small and that the transmission of folklore is carried out in irregular leaps and bounds, rather than by means of a smooth regular wave in the form of a concentric circle diffusing outward from a center point of origin. [von Sydow 1965:219; see also von Sydow 1977]

8. As Nicolaisen has pointed out, scholars more often associate name studies with linguistic rather than folkloristic scholarship (see Nicolaisen 1968). Nonetheless, prominent folklorists taking up name studies have included Archer Taylor, Francis Lee Utley, Herbert Halpert, Warren Roberts, W. Edson Richmond, Bruce Jackson, Alan Dundes, Ronald L. Baker, Robert M. Rennick, and Jan Harold Brunvand. Drawing further folkloristic attention to onomastics, Jan Harold Brunvand devoted a chapter of his introductory textbook *The Study of American Folklore* (1986) to "Folk Speech and Naming," and he also edited and introduced a special issue of the journal *Names* on "Names in Folklore" (September 1968). In addition, a special issue of *Names Northeast* appeared on "Folklore and Names" (vol. 3, 1984), and Kelsie Harder regularly prepares a "Namelore" column for the *Tennessee Folklore Society Bulletin*.

9. "Idiolect" uses the Greek root of *idio* meaning "own, personal." The dictionary definition offers idiolect as the speech of an individual, considered as a linguistic pattern unique among speakers of his or her language or dialect. It also has a linguistic connection to the association of "idiom" with vernacular traits (Nicolaisen 1980a:143–45), and, as Gary Alan Fine argues, an adaptation to "idioculture," or individualized culture creation within small groups (Fine 1979).

10. Nicolaisen considers the cultural biases in German and English terminology for narrative genres in "German *Sage* and English *Legend*: Terminology and Conceptual Problems" (1988). See also Ben-Amos 1976; Abrahams 1976; Honko 1989.

11. Among Bill Nicolaisen's students who have gone on to advanced degrees in folklore and who have published folklore research have been Judith Levin, Cristina Bacchilega, Kathy Kimiecik, David Gay, and William Healy. He also exerted influence on students and university policy as a member of the English Department's dissertation and examination committee (1970–71, 1972–73), committee on study in Britain (1970–74), joint faculty and student graduate committee (fall 1973), chair of the graduate review committee (1986), supervisor of workshops in expository writing (1970–72), supervisor of teaching of English to foreign students (1970–74), director of the graduate program in English (1972–73), adviser for the specialization in English literature and language (1977–89) and English literature and folklore (1979–81, 1984–89), chair of the criti-

cal languages instruction committee, and chair of the linguistics program (1985–89). For other comments on his approach to students, see Mittelstadt 1981.

12. These are lines from a version of the Scottish ballad "Annan Water" quoted by Bill Nicolaisen in "Names and Narratives" (1984a). "Annan Water" refers to a dangerous river that used to present in narrative song the drowning death of a lover trying to reach his beloved from whom he is separated. Beyond the name's reference to rivers on the actual Scottish map, Nicolaisen asserts, "it is a symbol for everything that divides, separates and disrupts, a poignant reminder that all is not well in this world and that so much that is broken and fractured still has to be healed" (1984a:265–66).

REFERENCES

Abrahams, Roger D.
- 1970a   A Singer and Her Songs: Almeda Riddle's Book of Ballads. Baton Rouge: Louisiana State University Press.
- 1970b   Creativity, Individuality, and the Traditional Singer. Studies in the Literary Imagination 3:5–34.
- 1976   Genre Theory and Folkloristics. Studia Fennica 20:13–19.
- 1983   Interpreting Folklore Ethnographically and Sociologically. *In* Richard M. Dorson, ed., Handbook of American Folklore. Bloomington: Indiana University Press, pp. 345–50.

Acton, H. B.
- 1953   Tradition and Some Other Forms of Order. Proceedings of the Aristotelian Society, New Series, Vol. 53, 1952–53. London: Harrison and Sons, pp. 1–28.

Alvey, Gerald
- 1984   Dulcimer Maker: The Craft of Homer Ledford. Lexington: University Press of Kentucky.

Amsler, Mark E.
- 1975   A Bibliography of the Writings of Francis Lee Utley. Names 23: 130–46.

Anderson, Walter
- 1923   Kaiser und Abt: Die Geschichte eines Schwanks. Helsinki: Folklore Fellows Communication No. 42.

Azadovskij, Mark
- 1926   Eine sibirische Märchenerzählerin. Helsinki: Folklore Fellows Communications No. 68.
- 1974   A Siberian Tale Teller. Translated by James R. Dow. Austin: Center for Intercultural Studies in Folklore and Ethnomusicology, Monograph Series No. 2, University of Texas at Austin.
- 1975   A Siberian Narrator (1960). *In* Felix J. Oinas and Stephen Soudakoff, eds., The Study of Russian Folklore. The Hague: Mouton, pp. 79–89.

Bascom, William
   1955   Verbal Art. Journal of American Folklore 68:245–52.
Bauman, Richard
   1977   Verbal Art as Performance. Rowley, Massachusetts: Newbury House.
   1989   American Folklore Studies and Social Transformation: A Performance-Centered Perspective. Text and Performance Quarterly 9:175–84.
Bausinger, Hermann
   1968   Folklore Research at the University of Tübingen: On the Activities of the Ludwig-Uhland Institut. Journal of the Folklore Institute 5:124–33.
Ben-Amos, Dan
   1972   Toward a Definition of Folklore in Context. *In* Américo Paredes and Richard Bauman, eds., Toward New Perspectives in Folklore. Austin: University of Texas Press, pp. 3–15.
   1976   (ed.) Folklore Genres. Austin: University of Texas Press.
   1984   The Seven Strands of *Tradition:* Varieties in Its Meaning in American Folklore Studies. Journal of Folklore Research 21:97–131.
Ben-Amos, Dan; Goldstein, Kenneth S.
   1975   (eds.) Folklore: Performance and Communication. The Hague: Mouton.
Benjamin, Walter
   1968   Illuminations, ed. Hannah Arendt, trans. Harry Zohn. New York: Harcourt, Brace & World.
Biebuyck, Daniel P.
   1969   (ed.) Tradition and Creativity in Tribal Art. Berkeley: University of California Press.
Boas, Franz
   1925   Stylistic Aspects of Primitive Literature. Journal of American Folklore 38:329–39.
   1938   Mythology and Folklore. *In* Franz Boas, ed., General Anthropology. Boston: D. C. Heath, pp. 609–26.
   1940   Race, Language and Culture. New York: Free Press.
   1955   Primitive Art. 1927 repr. New York: Dover.
Briggs, Charles L.
   1988   Competence in Performance: The Creativity of Tradition in Mexicano Verbal Art. Philadelphia: University of Pennsylvania Press.
Bronner, Simon J.
   1986a   Grasping Things: Folk Material Culture and Mass Society in America. Lexington: University Press of Kentucky.
   1986b   American Folklore Studies: An Intellectual History. Lawrence: University Press of Kansas.
   1986c   The House on Penn Street: Creativity and Conflict in Folk Art. *In* John Michael Vlach and Simon J. Bronner, eds., *Folk Art and*

    Worlds. Ann Arbor, Michigan: UMI Research Press, pp. 123–49. Repr., Logan: Utah State University Press, 1992.
1988 Art, Performance, and Praxis: The Rhetoric of Contemporary Folklore Studies. Western Folklore 47:75–102.
Brunvand, Jan Harold
 1968 (ed.) Special Issue on Names in Folklore. *Names* 16:197–298.
 1986 The Study of American Folklore: An Introduction. 3d ed., New York: W. W. Norton.
Cocchiara, Giuseppe
 1981 The History of Folklore in Europe. Trans. John N. McDaniel. Philadelphia: Institute for the Study of Human Issues.
Conroy, Patricia L.
 1979 Creativity in Oral Transmission: An Example from Faroese Ballad Tradition. Arv: Scandinavian Yearbook of Folklore 35:25–48.
Crowley, Daniel J.
 1966 I Could Talk Old-Story Good: Creativity in Bahamian Folklore. Berkeley: University of California Press.
Dégh, Linda
 1969 Folktales and Society: Story-Telling in a Hungarian Peasant Community. Trans. Emily M. Schossberger. Bloomington: Indiana University Press.
 1978 (ed.) Studies in East European Folk Narrative. Bloomington: Indiana University Folklore Monographs Series, No. 25.
Dorson, Richard M.
 1971 American Folklore and the Historian. Chicago: University of Chicago Press.
 1972 Oral Styles of American Folk Narrators (1960). *In* Folklore: Selected Essays. Bloomington: Indiana University Press, pp. 99–146.
 1978 Folklore in the Modern World. *In* Richard M. Dorson, ed., Folklore in the Modern World. The Hague: Mouton, pp. 11–51.
Dow, James; Lixfeld, Hannjost
 1986 (eds.) German *Volkskunde:* A Decade of Theoretical Confrontation, Debate, and Reorientation (1967–77). Bloomington: Indiana University Press.
Dow, James R.; Rippley, La Vern J.; Benjamin, Steven M.
 1980 Amana Folk Art: Tradition and Creativity among the True Inspirationists of Iowa. *In* Papers from the St. Olaf Symposium on German-Americana. Occasional Papers of Society for German-American Studies No. 10. Morgantown: Department of Foreign Languages, West Virginia University, pp. 19–30.
Dundes, Alan
 1962 From Etic to Emic Units in the Structural Study of Folktales. Journal of American Folklore 75:95–105.
 1980 Interpreting Folklore. Bloomington: Indiana University Press.

1986 The Anthropologist and the Comparative Method in Folklore. Journal of Folklore Research 23:125–46.
Eliot, T. S.
1960 Tradition and the Individual Talent (1919). In Selected Essays. New York: Harcourt, Brace & World, pp. 3–11.
Evans, David
1982 Big Road Blues: Tradition and Creativity in the Folk Blues. Berkeley: University of California Press.
Fine, Gary Alan
1979 Small Groups and Culture Creation: The Idioculture of Little League Baseball Teams. American Sociological Review 44:733–45.
Finnie, W. Bruce
1975 In Memoriam: Francis Lee Utley, 1907–1974. Names 23:127–29.
Gailey, Alan
1989 The Nature of Tradition. Folklore 100:143–61.
Gilman, Sander
1991 The Jew's Body. New York: Routledge.
Glassie, Henry; Ives, Edward D.; Szwed, John F.
1971 Folksongs and Their Makers. Bowling Green, Ohio: Bowling Green University Popular Press.
Handler, Richard; Linnekin, Jocelyn
1984 Tradition, Genuine or Spurious. Journal of American Folklore 97:273–90.
Harkort, Fritz; Peeters, Karel C.; Wildhaber, Robert
1968 (eds.) Volksüberlieferung: Festschrift für Kurt Ranke. Göttingen: Otto Schwartz.
Herskovits, Melville
1953 Franz Boas: The Science of Man in the Making. New York: Charles Scribner's Sons.
Hobsbawm, Eric; Ranger, Terrence
1983 The Invention of Tradition. Cambridge: Cambridge University Press.
Honko, Lauri
1989 Folkloristic Theories of Genre. Studia Fennica 33:13–28.
Jansen, William Hugh
1957 Classifying Performance in the Study of Verbal Folklore. In W. Edson Richmond, ed., Studies in Folklore. Bloomington: Indiana University Press, pp. 110–18.
Jones, Michael Owen
1980 A Feeling for Form, As Illustrated by People at Work. In Nikolai Burlakoff and Carl Lindahl, eds., Folklore on Two Continents: Essays in Honor of Linda Dégh. Bloomington: Trickster Press, pp. 260–69.

1989   Craftsman of the Cumberlands: Tradition and Creativity. Lexington: University Press of Kentucky.

Joyner, Charles
  1984   Down by the Riverside: A South Carolina Slave Community. Urbana: University of Illinois Press.
  1988   Tradition, Creativity and the Appalachian Dulcimer. International Folklore Review 6:74–77.

Kirshenblatt-Gimblett, Barbara
  1978   Culture Shock and Narrative Creativity. *In* Richard M. Dorson, ed., Folklore in the Modern World. The Hague: Mouton, pp. 109–22.
  1989   Authoring Lives. Journal of Folklore Research 26:123–50.

Köhler-Zülch, Ines
  1986   In Memoriam Kurt Ranke. Zeitschrift für Volkskunde 82:105–7.

Kristeller, Paul Oskar
  1979   The Modern System of the Arts (1951, 1952). *In* W. E. Kennick, ed., Art and Philosophy: Readings in Aesthetics. New York: St. Martin's Press, pp. 7–33.
  1983   "Creativity" and "Tradition." Journal of the History of Ideas 44: 105–14.

Levin, Isidor
  1963   Walter Anderson: 10.10.1885 in Minsk-d. 23.8.1962 in Kiel. Deutsches Jahrbuch für Volkskunde 9:293–311.

Litwin, A.
  1917   "Sonye di Khakhome." In *Yidishe neshomes*, vol. 3. New York: Folksbildung, pp. 1–20.

Lord, Albert
  1960   The Singer of Tales. Cambridge: Harvard University Press.

Lüthi, Max
  1970   Once Upon a Time: On the Nature of Fairy Tales. Trans. Lee Chadeayne and Paul Gottwald. Bloomington: Indiana University Press.
  1984   The Fairytale as Art Form and Portrait of Man. Trans. Jon Erickson. Bloomington: Indiana University Press.
  1989   The European Folktale: Form and Nature. Trans. John D. Niles. Philadelphia: Institute for the Study of Human Issues.

Malinowski, Bronislaw
  1954   Magic, Science and Religion, and Other Essays. Garden City, New York: Doubleday/Anchor.
  1961   Argonauts of the Western Pacific (1922). New York: E. P. Dutton.

Mandel, Jerome; Rosenberg, Bruce
  1970   (eds.) Medieval Literature and Folklore Studies: Essays in Honor of Francis Lee Utley. New Brunswick, New Jersey: Rutgers University Press.

Martin, Charles E.
   1990   "Creative Constraints in the Folk Arts of Appalachia." *In* Barbara Allen and Thomas J. Schlereth, eds., Sense of Place: American Regional Cultures. Lexington: University Press of Kentucky, pp. 138–51.

Mason, John Hope
   1988   The Character of Creativity: Two Traditions. History of European Ideas 9:697–715.

McCarthy, William Bernard
   1978   Creativity, Tradition, and History: The Ballad Repertoire of Agnes Lyle of Kilbarchan. Ph.D. diss., Indiana University.

McDowell, John H.
   1988   (ed.) Performance in Contemporary African Arts. Journal of Folklore Research (Special Issue) 25, nos. 1–2 (January–September).

Mieder, Wolfgang
   1987   Tradition and Innovation in Folk Literature. Hanover, New Hampshire: University Press of New England.

Mittelstadt, Mike
   1981   SUNY Prof. Helps Others Explore "Roots." Vestal News, May 14:19.

Nicolaisen, W. F. H.
   1968   The Prodigious Jump: A Contribution to the Study of the Relationship Between Folklore and Place-Names. *In* Fritz Harkort, Karel C. Peeters, and Robert Wildhaber, eds., Volksüberlieferung: Festschrift für Kurt Ranke. Göttingen: Otto Schwartz, pp. 531–42.
   1970–71   National and International Folklore. Bulletin of the Pennsylvania State Modern Language Association 49 (Fall/Spring):17–24.
   1971   The Mapping of Folk Culture as Applied Folklore. *In* Dick Sweterlitsch, ed., Papers on Applied Folklore. Bloomington, Indiana: Folklore Forum Bibliographic and Special Studies, No. 8, pp. 26–30.
   1973a   Folklore and Geography: Toward an Atlas of American Folk Culture. New York Folklore 29:3–20.
   1973b   Place Names in Traditional Ballads. Folklore 84:299–312.
   1975a   Surveying and Mapping North American Culture. Mid-South Folklore 3:35–40.
   1975b   Onomastic Activities in the United States. Onoma 9:555–73.
   1975c   Place-Names in Bilingual Communities. Names 23:167–74.
   1976a   Folk and Habitat. Studia Fennica 20:324–30.
   1976b   The Folk and the Region. New York Folklore 2:143–49.
   1976c   Scottish Place-Names. London: B. T. Batsford.
   1976d   Place-Name Legends: An Onomastic Mythology. Folklore 87:146–59.

1977   Some Humorous Folk-Etymological Narratives. New York Folklore 3:13.
1978   How Incremental is Incremental Repetition? *In* Patricia Conroy, ed., Ballads and Ballad Research. Seattle: University of Washington, pp. 122–35.
1980a   Variant, Dialect, and Region: An Exploration in the Geography of Tradition. New York Folklore 6:137–49.
1980b   Time in Folk-Narrative. *In* Venetia Newall, ed., Folklore Studies in the Twentieth Century. Woodbridge, Suffolk: D. S. Brewer, pp. 314–19.
1980c   Space in Folk Narrative. *In* Nikolai Burlakoff and Carl Lindahl, eds., Folklore on Two Continents: Essays in Honor of Linda Dégh. Bloomington, Indiana: Trickster Press, pp. 14–18.
1980d   Onomastic Dialects. American Speech 55:36–45.
1983a   Concepts of Time and Space in Irish Folktales. *In* Patrick K. Ford, ed., Celtic Folklore and Christianity: Studies in Memory of William W. Heist. Santa Barbara: McNally and Loftin, pp. 150–59.
1983b   Scott and the Folk Tradition. *In* Alan Bold, ed., Sir Walter Scott: The Long Forgotten Melody. London: Vision and Barnes and Noble, pp. 127–42.
1983c   Theodor Fontane's "Sir Patrick Spens." *In* James Porter, ed., The Ballad Image: Essays Presented to Bertrand Harris Bronson. Los Angeles: Center for the Study of Comparative Folklore and Mythology, University of California, pp. 3–19.
1984a   Names and Narratives. Journal of American Folklore 97:259–72.
1984b   Legends as Narrative Response. *In* Paul Smith, ed., Perspectives on Contemporary Legend. Sheffield, England: Center for English Cultural Tradition and Language Papers Series No. 4, University of Sheffield, pp. 167–78.
1984c   Folklore and Names. Names Northeast 3:14–21.
1984d   The Structure of Narrated Time in the Folktale. *In* Le conte pourquoi? Comment? Paris: Editions du Centre National de la Recherche Scientifique, pp. 417–36.
1985a   Rehearsing the Future in the Folktale. New York Folklore 11:231–38.
1985b   Perspectives on Contemporary Legend. Fabula 26:213–18.
1986a   Response to Porter. Western Folklore 45:125–27.
1986b   Obituary: Kurt Ranke (1908–1985). Folklore 97:110–11.
1987   The Linguistic Structure of Legends. *In* Gillian Bennett, Paul Smith, and J. D. A. Widdowson, eds., Perspectives on Contemporary Legend, Vol. II. CECTAL Conference Paper Series No. 5. Sheffield: Sheffield Academic Press, pp. 61–76.
1988   German *Sage* and English *Legend:* Terminology and Conceptual Problems. *In* Gillian Bennett and Paul Smith, eds., Monsters

with Iron Teeth: Perspectives on Contemporary Legend III. Sheffield, England: Sheffield Academic Press, pp. 79–87.
1989   Kurt Ranke and Einfache Formen. Folklore 100:113–19.
1990   Variability and Creativity in Folk-Narrative. *In* Veronika Görög-Karady, ed., D'un conte...a l'autre: la variabilité dans la littérature orale. Paris: Editions du Centre National de la Recherche Scientifique, pp. 39–46.
1991   Why Tell Stories? Fabula 31:5–10.

Paredes, Américo; Bauman, Richard
1972   (eds.) Toward New Perspectives in Folklore. Austin: University of Texas Press.

Peacock, James L.
1986   The Creativity of Tradition in Indonesian Religion. Journal of the History of Ideas 44:105–13.

Popper, Karl R.
1965   Conjectures and Refutations: The Growth of Scientific Knowledge. New York: Basic Books.

Ranke, Kurt
1962   Walter Anderson (1885–1962). Fabula 5:n.p.

Rooney, John F.; Zelinsky, Wilbur; Louder, Dean R.
1982   (eds.) This Remarkable Continent: An Atlas of United States and Canadian Society and Cultures. College Station, Texas: Texas A&M University Press for the Society for the North American Cultural Survey.

Rosenberg, Bruce
1970   The Art of the American Folk Preacher. New York: Oxford University Press.

Santino, Jack
1986   The Folk *Assemblage* of Autumn: Tradition and Creativity in Halloween Folk Art. *In* John Michael Vlach and Simon J. Bronner, eds., Folk Art and Art Worlds. Ann Arbor: UMI Research Press, pp. 150–70. Repr., Logan: Utah State University Press, 1992.

Stekert, Ellen Jane
1965   Two Voices of Tradition: The Influence of Personality and Collecting Environment upon the Songs of Two Traditional Folksingers. Ph.D. diss., University of Pennsylvania.

Thompson, Stith
1977   The Folktale. Berkeley: University of California Press.

Toelken, Barre
1979   The Dynamics of Folklore. Boston: Houghton Mifflin.

Tu, Ching-I
1987   (ed.) Tradition and Creativity: Essays on East Asian Civilization. New Brunswick, New Jersey: Transaction Books.

Tucker, Elizabeth Godfrey
1977   Tradition and Creativity in the Storytelling of Pre-Adolescent Girls. Ph.D. diss., Indiana University.

Von Sydow, C. W.
   1965   Folktale Studies and Philology: Some Points of View (1948). *In* Alan Dundes, ed., The Study of Folklore. Englewood Cliffs, New Jersey: Prentice-Hall, pp. 219–42.
   1977   Selected Papers on Folklore. 1948 repr., New York: Arno Press.

Wilgus, D. K.
   1974   Francis Lee Utley. Western Folklore 33:202–4.

Zaretzke, Kenneth
   1982   The Idea of Tradition. Intercollegiate Review 17:85–98.

BALLAD
AND
SONG

2

SOME SONGS OF PLACE AND BALLADS OF NAME*

IAN A. OLSON

Bill Nicolaisen offers the fundamental insight that ballads are structured mainly through names; *homo nominans* and *homo narrans* strive toward the same goal (Nicolaisen 1973, 1984, 1988):

> As I came in by Dunnideer
> And doon the Netherha
> There were fifty thousand hielanmen
> All marchin to Harlaw.

He also gives us a humanistic secret drawn from his compassion for people and their lives. To paraphrase, time may render a place name lexically meaningless, but *people* will retain it nevertheless if it means something to them, if it encompasses or enriches their existence. For if people do not utter, write, and use names, especially of places, those names follow their "meanings" into oblivion.

---

*I am most grateful to the following for their help and advice: David Buchan, Willie Donaldson, Sandy Fenton, Flora Garry, Peter Hall, Hamish Henderson, Lizzie Higgins, Jack Philip, and the kind and helpful staff of the Reference and Local Studies Departments of Aberdeen City District Library.

GEORDIE (CHILD 209) OR GIGHTIE'S LADY (GREIG-DUNCAN 249)

The quiet road on the outskirts of Aberdeen where I spent my childhood had long been stranded by the passage of time and the forging of new routes into the city. Cut off from its origin on the Great Northern Road (which now sweeps in along the banks of the River Don—the northern boundary of the city) it still, however, ascended the ring of hills surrounding Aberdeen to pass by the ancient settlement of Hilltown (or Hilton as it has become) before descending to the junction of the towns of Old and New Aberdeen. Over the centuries Back Hilton Road had changed little since the days when it was the principal route into the city—the Via Regis or King's Highway—and in the 1940s was still a magnificent tree-lined avenue surrounded by fields and with an open stream running down its length. If you followed it up and over the hill, you passed by a boundary stone marking the edge of the Freedom Lands of Aberdeen and remnants of the great forest of Stocket (both given to the citizens by King Robert the Bruce in 1319). The remains of a stone circle encountered further down the hill marked over four thousand years of settlement in the area. If you then descended further down the ridge past the farm of Ash-hill and through the old clachan of Kittybrewster (where a great cattle market was held every Friday), you came to a choice of roads at a V-shaped junction known locally (although not marked on any map) as "Split the Winds."

The right-hand road led directly into the New Town of Aberdeen around the mouth of the River Dee, its southern boundary. This option was a comparatively recent luxury as until the eighteenth century a great unpleasant marsh had barred the way. (At least it was finally drained completely; in persistently rainy weather unfortunate footballers on the fields of Powis School in the north still find themselves sinking into the ancient marsh of Old Aberdeen). Originally, therefore, the Highway at this point veered to the left, becoming Causeyend (causeway end) as it met the made road which connected Old and New Aberdeen.

"Split the Winds"? Nicolaisen emphasizes the importance of constantly used names which appear on no maps in his classic *Scottish Place-Names* (1976), and "Split the Winds" was only one of many used by the citizens to navigate Aberdeen. The official route guide, therefore, was of little use to me when working my way through college as a tram conductor. Aberdonians boarding my tram further back along the Great Northern Road at "The Fountain" (long since moved further into town to confuse matters) would proffer me fares to such places as "The Queen." (Victoria's statue imperiously obstructed the pavement at the end of the direct road through the old marshlands at its junction with the comparatively recent Union Street which by 1822 ingeniously bridged over a warren of medieval streets in New Aberdeen).

If passengers were continuing left (north) up Union Street to where it became the Castlegate with the Market Cross, they asked for "Jimmy Hay's" (although that gentleman had not owned the Athenaeum eating house on the square since 1906); if turning right (south) they would ask for "The Monkey House" (the pillared entrance to the Northern Assurance Company where generations of Aberdonians trysted their future spouses). Old folk wanting the south end of Union Street asked for "Babbie Law's"—although the good lady had not dispensed refreshment to travellers there since the early nineteenth century.

Best of all were requests for places such as "Fitty" (or even "Futty"), for this was how the little fishing community at the end of the quays off the Dee (note the Auld Alliance terminology) had been named since the earliest records. The city fathers officially named it "Footdee" in the nineteenth century (a delightful attempt to add *meaning* as well as gentility), but no one ever used it from that day to this.

If we leave "Split the Winds" and travel in towards the city along Causeyend, we come to a hollow between two hills. Go up the hill to the right and you follow the Gallowgate, which then gradually descends to the focal point of the new town, the Castlegate, overlooked by the Tolbooth, the original prison tower. The "gate" is of course a road, but to confuse matters the first section from Causeyend was once known as Porthill, as one of the city gates bestrode it halfway up until 1768. On the other hand the road from Causeyend leading up the hill to the left is known as Mounthooly[1] and leads north to the old town along the Spital road (although the leper hospital it passed has been gone for almost four hundred years).

On the crossroads itself, until a massive roundabout was added, stood the house of a settled traveller family "discovered" by the great Hamish Henderson of the School of Scottish Studies in the early 1950s. The amazing repertoire of the mother, Jeannie Robertson, rapidly revealed to the world the prodigious folk culture of the despised travelling people; all that had been written previously about the "lost" balladry and folktale of Scotland had to be totally revised.

Jeannie Robertson became internationally known, and her repertoire and performances were studied with great care. She often claimed that she was "true" to the ballads she sang and varied nothing that had been handed down to her.[2] As far as she was concerned she had her versions—if you wanted others you were welcome to go to other singers—and she certainly did not create or re-create as she performed. This would make what follows, to my mind, rather interesting.

The great ballad (*muckle sang*) entitled "Geordie" (209) by Francis James Child exists throughout Britain and North America. Basically it tells of the (usually) successful attempt of a high-born wife to plead for the life of her noble husband. He has been condemned to death for an often unspecified crime, although a frequent charge is of killing and selling the King's deer. It has been suggested that the husband was one of the great Gordon lords who had come north to hold and pacify the rich farmlands of Aberdeenshire with the Normans (and spent seven centuries thereafter in almost continuous warfare with their neighbors until they channelled their courageous recklessness into a regiment of the British Army).

Although several versions of the ballad refer to this spirited family as the protagonists, only one that I am aware of actually sets the scene in the Tolbooth of Aberdeen (Bronson 1966: III, 281 [Child Ballad 209, Variant 34] and Greig-Duncan 249D). Moreover, when Gavin Greig, the schoolmaster at New Deer, and the Reverend James Bruce Duncan of Lynturk collected some three thousand folksongs from the North-East in the decade before the First World War they found eleven versions of "Geordie."[3] None of these, however, gives anywhere in North-East as being the scene of the *crime*. Most have the vagueness of the commonest version sung today in folk clubs:

> Ah, my Geordie never stole nor calf nor cow
> He never hurted any
> Stole sixteen of the king's royal deer
> And he sold them in Bohenny.

Twenty years ago I passed a signpost to Bohenny when travelling up the Great Glen to Inverness after a long and nauseating six-hour sea voyage from the Outer Hebrides. Too tired to stop that day, I have never found it since and the Gazetteer categorically denies its existence. On the other hand, over thirty years ago in Aberdeen I heard Jeannie Robertson sing:

> Slew sixteen of the King's royal deer
> And selt them on Mounthooly [sold]

JOHNIE COCK (CHILD 114) OR JOHNNIE O' BRAIDISLEYS (GREIG-DUNCAN 250)

If we halt at Mounthooly and retrace our steps along Causeyend, past "Split the Winds," we can nowadays ignore the climb up to Hilton and instead continue out the Great Northern Road along the banks of the Don, the northern boundary of Aberdeen. We pick up the old highway at the end of the city at Persley Den and Mugiemoss. The old road, now a four-lane highway, swings inland up the flank of Brimmond Hill as the Tyrebagger Road. At its summit the broad lands of the North-East open out before us, with the great mountain barrier of the Mounth to the south, the wide plains of Deeside above, the beautiful hill range of Bennachie ahead with the village of Monymusk nestling in the woods of Paradise at its foot, and above to the north, the valley of the Don and the farmlands of Buchan beyond.

This is one of the richest song and ballad countries in the world as Peter Buchan, Walter Scott, Francis Child, Gavin Greig and James Duncan, James Carpenter, Alan Lomax, Bertrand Bronson, Hamish Henderson, and many others have testified. Perhaps the finest of these ballads is "Johnnie o' Braidisleys"; Francis Child called it "this precious specimen of the unspoiled traditional ballad" (1882–98:III, 1).

> John awoke one May morning
> Called for water to wash his hands
> Go lowse to me my twa grey hounds [unleash]
> That lie bound in iron bands, bands,
>   *That lie bound in iron bands.*

Ignoring his mother's pleas, this high-born poacher sets off deerhunting, is betrayed in the act to the King's foresters whom he kills (all but one) in pitched battle while mortally wounded himself. The ballad unfolds and reaches its inevitable climax in a series of vivid, almost cinematic scenes. If there ever was an original hero he has been subsumed into a universal folk drama concerning the inexorability of fate, life, and death with no winners and no triumph. Carried by a variety of powerful tunes, the ballad is sung to this day in the midst of gripped audiences swept into the unfolding action by the chorus of the repeated last line, moved by its chilling power.

Unusually, the ballad has been largely confined to Scotland, and according to Bronson is mostly sung nowadays in the North-East, where "living traditional singers continue to provide us with fresh variants." I have recorded this ballad over five years from Jeannie Robertson's daughter, Lizzie Higgins, on a number of different occasions and in a variety of settings, and have noticed two main points. Firstly, she also appears to have a fixed version in her mind, and if she by chance departs from it, she interrupts her singing or adds a postscript to ensure that the audience has the full and "proper" version as it was given to her. Like her mother, she sings of "Johnnie the Brine" and differs from her in virtually only one word—the single place name in their version. Secondly, she sings the story as *true*; her mother, from whom she learned the song, showed her the very spot where the hero died.

I do not want to enter the controversy between those who maintain that the ballad singer creates or re-creates the ballad in a formulaic manner (or did so in earlier periods of history) and those who do not accept this view, except to contrast the rigidity with which traditional performers often seem to stick to their ballad versions compared to the formulaic mode they clearly adopt when storytelling. When storytelling, performers elaborate a basic skeletal structure as the teller interacts with the audience.

Over and above this is the often striking contrast in the mode of delivery. The storyteller interacts as strongly as possible with the audience, with often much movement, gesture, and eye-contact. The voice changes in speed, pitch, and volume for contrast and effect. But what happens when the same person stops to perform a great ballad? Flora Garry, one of the North-East's finest poets and now aged ninety, describes the phenomenon as so many have before. In her case she recalls being a little girl in her mother's farm kitchen during a regular visit of a traveller woman, Mrs. [Kirsty?] McGuire:

> The pack was undone. This was a dark tartan rug spread out on the stone floor, containing her wares. These were mostly drapery

goods like women's overalls, pillowcases, tape, bits of lace, cheap brooches and bottles of scent... My mother and the "deem" [maid] always bought something. They didn't linger long over the transactions. The afternoon's work lay ahead. It was at this point that Mrs. McGuire sang if she felt like it.

She just looked down at the floor, her bundle ready to lift, and suddenly became another person as she sang. I can only describe the sound as a loud, prolonged, menacing kind—very frightening, but exciting. I was both sorry and relieved when she took her leave.[4]

When singing "Johnnie the Brine," Lizzie Higgins enters a setting different from that of her mother[5]; it is a little village that has been visualized by many another North-East singer when "possessed" by this remarkable song. We usually end with

> Now Johnny's guid bend-bow is broke   [good]
> An his two grey hounds are slain
> His body lies in Monymusk
> An his hunting days are deen, deen   [done]
> *His hunting days are deen*

You will remember my pointing out Monymusk, under the Hill of Bennachie, by the woods called Paradise.

SLEEPY TOON (GREIG-DUNCAN 356)

If we continue out the old highway, it swings north again to cross the river Don at Inverurie. The main road now runs inland again along the northern flanks of the Bennachie range before coming hard up against the grim moorlands and mountains of the Highland line where it must either turn north or south. The mountain passes are guarded by the fortified towerhouses of the great lords—similar to those which watch over the Mounth passes to the south along Deeside. Bennachie is a lovely mountain with an almost unscathed Iron-Age fort on its principal peak. It is a favorite Nicolaisen climb, and from its slopes a ballad country within a ballad country unfolds below.

By around 1840 an agricultural revolution had done away with the little communities which had farmed in common, using the run rig system, and which had supported a variety of small tradesmen.[6] Larger amalgamated units now dominated the scene, working to a scientific crop rotation. They were still called "touns"—or "ferm-touns" rather—but they now comprised a farmer and his family, employing "farm servants." Semi-independent crofters scraped a living from reclaimed marginal land and they and their children formed much of the farm servant labor pool. In many ways it was a cyclical economy; you worked until you had enough capital to rent or buy a place of your own, and employ others in turn. Those who worked the biggest amalgamations—the "muckle fermers"—soon drew away from this democratic situation to live like lower gentry. Farm servants were usually housed in barrack-like outhouses called "chaumers" (*chambres?*) and were fed in the kitchen. Less commonly they lived in self-catering units called "bothies."

Between 1840 and 1890 a series of "bothy ballads" were composed—very often by known authors—that described the cycle of life on the farms from the point of view of the employees. They often have a standard formula: the singer describes his employment agreement ("feeing") with the farmer at the hiring fair and the promises made regarding equipment and conditions. He then recounts the actual conditions met when taking up employment, and his leaving after a term of six months in the hope of finding better conditions elsewhere. The farmer and his family (and fellow workers) are "given their character" in no uncertain manner. It was also the heyday of the skilled Horseman, and their pride in their prowess and their horses shines through many of these songs. Unusually for folksongs, these "bothy ballads" are unique to the North-East of Scotland.[7]

From the top of Bennachie you can look down on the ferm-toun of Christ's Kirk on the Green in the parish of Kennethmont; around a century ago it gained the more ironic name of Sleepytoon. Beyond it is the market town of Insch, and in the great moor towards the west, the village of Rhynie. Adam Mitchell struggled to farm Sleepytoon from the 1840s to 1858, employing five servants. Around 1854 one of these was a William (Boyd) Clark, who composed the following:

> I happened at last Whitsunday
> I tired o' my place
> And I gaed up to Insch to fee   [went]
> My fortune for to chase.
> > *And sing errie errity adie a'*
> > *Sing errie errity an'.*

I met in wi' Adam Mitchell
To fee we did presume
He's a fairmer in Kennethmont
Lives ower at Sleepytoon   [over]

"If you and I agree" he says
"You'll have the fairest play
For I never bid my servants work
Above ten hours a day."
. . . .
A pair o' blues they led the van   [blue-gray horses]
So nimbly as they go
And a pair o' broons that follows them   [browns]
That never yet said no.
. . . .
And ilka day he hurried [us] on   [each]
The hills and valleys rang
We never got a moment's rest
For his damnd eternal tongue
. . . .
Gin we were doon at Rhynie's Muir   [if only; down; moor]
And garin' the gless gang roon   [making the glass go round]
We will tell them o' the usage
We got at Sleepytoon.

We'll maybe see Old Adam yet
Jist at his dish of brose   [just]
And we'll gie 'im our pocket napkin   [give]
To dicht his snuffy nose.[8]   [wipe]

It has a fine catchy tune and is still going strong after 130 years. By 1910 it had at least five minor variants, with four variants of the name of the starting scene and two of the finishing. How it will look in another 130 years is impossible to say. The proud horsemen, the bothies and chaumers, the hiring fairs have all long since gone—but they live on in song as do the names of their touns and villages. Poor Adam Mitchell seems bound for immortality, snuffy nose and all.

THE BATTLE OF HARLAW (CHILD 163 AND GREIG-DUNCAN 112)

North of Sleepytoon there stands on a small hill the remains of the castle of Dunnideer. It is one of the oldest castles in Scotland (built around 1260) but the vitrified fort and earthworks beside it show that the hill has been a strongpoint for well over two thousand years. All that remains of the great tower is the west wall, with a window overlooking the Highland passes. Watchers in July 1411 saw an army of some ten thousand Highlandmen pour through the northernmost gap with intent to break out into open country and through to Aberdeen. Donald Macdonald, Lord of the Isles, inheritor of the ancient Norse kingdom of Somerled, had arrived from the island of Skye to support his claims to the recently vacant Earldom of Ross, whose vast enclaves spread as far south as the valley of the Dee.[9]

The invaders passed by the Hill of Netherhall, avoided the castle of Balquhain, and occupied the high ground across the King's Highway as it ascended the Hill of Harlaw from Inverurie. Here, on the morning of July 24, they were suddenly attacked by a well-armed force of some one thousand men in forward defense from Aberdeen. It was led by the Earl of Mar and included his mighty vassals, the castellans of North-East Scotland, together with the Lord Provost of Aberdeen and the burgesses of the city. The ferocious battle that ensued was brought to a bloody standstill only by nightfall and there were fearful losses on either side. Over half the North-East men died, including the Provost and his burgesses, and few of the noble lords returned to their castles. Macdonald withdrew his army home that night, leaving his exhausted opponents to bury the dead. "Red Harlaw" remains etched on our memory to this day.

When Sir Walter Scott, busy as ever inventing Scotland's history, turned his attention to this battle, he portrayed it as a pivotal event in Scottish history, when Lowland Saxon civilization triumphed over Celtic barbarism, and until very recently most (Lowland) historians have held the same view.

Macdonald had inherited one of the oldest titles in Scotland, had attended Oxford and the English court, and had an excellent claim. Mar, on the other hand, had recently gained his Earldom by murdering the previous Earl and by besieging and marrying the widowed Countess. Such actions had come as no surprise to those familiar with this violent, illegitimate son of the Wolf of Badenoch, brought up by his Gaelic-speaking mother in the Highlands.[10]

The concept of a "national deliverance," therefore, begins to blur into a feudal conflict between two cousins which engulfed both their great vassals and the "small folk" of either side. As it turned out, Donald's son Alasdair eventually inherited the Earldom of Ross, but the Lordship of the Isles was assimilated to the Crown in 1494 and the Earldom of Mar petered out soon after. Perhaps the only winners in the long run were the descendants of the noble vassals, the great families such as the Forbeses, Irvines, and Leslies who remained secure in their towers throughout the North-East, many to this day.

Had Scott and subsequent historians listened carefully to the great ballad of "The Battle of Harlaw" (sung in the North-East to this day) and studied the names it celebrates, they might have come to a better understanding of the battle's part in Scottish history:[11]

> As I cam in by Denniedeer
> And doon by Netherha   [down]
> There was fifty thousand Hielandmen
> A' marchin to Harlaw.
> > *Wi my dirrum doo dirrum doo*
> > *Daddie dirrum dey.*
>
> ....
>
> The Hielandmen wi' their lang swords   [long]
> They laid on us fu' sair   [full sore]
> And they drove back oor merry men
> Three acres breadth and mair.   [more]
>
> ....
>
> The first ae stroke that Forbes struck   [single]
> He gart McDonald reel   [made]
> And the neist ae stroke that Forbes struck   [next]
> The brave McDonald fell.
>
> ....
>
> On Mononday at mornin'
> The battle it began
> On Saturday at gloamin'   [dusk]
> Ye'd kentna wha had won   [not known who]

The ballad singers do not celebrate the ruthless opportunist Earl of Mar, but his vassal, "brave" Lord Forbes (who is not recorded as having been present, but whose family and castles thrive to this day). They symbolically kill off the "brave" Macdonald, to explain the withdrawal of his forces.[12] They leave the dreadful and inconclusive battlefield to the dead of either side, great and small:

And sic a weary burying	[such]
The like you never saw	
As was the Sunday after that	
On the muirs down by Harlaw	[moors]
Gin onybody spier at you	[if anyone asks]
For them that is awa	[away]
Ye'll tell them plain and very plain	
They're sleepin' at Harlaw.	

CONCLUSION

As we look around Harlaw we see that Picts, Celts, Saxons, Normans, Scots, all have left their names on the landscape of the North-East: Pitgair, Balquhain, Inveramsey, Glenlogie, Dubston, Tullos, Bograxie, Whiteford, Netherton. These are no quaint remnants of bygone ages and peoples, for although their original "meanings" may have faded they are fully incorporated into the way of life of the North-East people, are blended into daily usage, are as vital as the day they were first formed. They are a living nexus of ferm-touns and settlements, hills and woods, rivers and roads. Sentiment may delay the slide of an unused word into oblivion but can seldom prevent it. If a name has persisted for hundreds or even thousands of years in such a landscape it is because it has proved both satisfactory and satisfying to the peoples that have accumulated there over time.

In addition to this, the North-East people retain an idiosyncracy which emphasizes Nicolaisen's view that names are keys to the understanding of human existence. When, for example, the battlefield of Harlaw was described to me by a local farmer, he said: "It's the same farmer has the land."

The Maitlands have farmed the lands of Balhaggardy on which Harlaw was fought since before that day in 1411 until the present time. The farmer's curious description of them refers not only to this remarkable continuity—for that could have been expressed better as "the same family"—but also to the fact that in this part of the world the farmer *is* his land; their identities merge.[13] When he takes on the land he commonly is given its name (in full or corrupted) and the man, the fields, the forests and the streams become a single entity with a single identity, and a single name. It may seem a rather mystical attitude for such a down-to-earth people; Flora Garry's poem conveys its spirit well:[14]

> They carried him feet first out into the sunlight
> (Waste of time, the best hay day of all Summer).
> The polished cars and the coach's glasswork glittered.
> Into the country town they drove decorously,
> Past the garages, villas and railed-in gardens,
> To the bright geometric, well-groomed cemetery...
>
> It should have been far otherwise for him.
> Evening and the clover wet with dew,
> The time he used to wander by the whin-dykes,
> Eyeing fences, cattle-beasts and water troughs,
> Scythe in hand to snick the seeding thistles.
> Then would have been the hour of his own choosing,
> He in a plain strong box of his own making,
> And the farm lads, their spades well-greased and keen-edged,
> In a sheltered corner of the sixteen acre.
> Just a natural, necessary field job,
> Done with competence and expedition,
> Prelude to sleep and tomorrow's work and weather.

NOTES

1. For a discussion of these Aberdeen place names (including "Split the Winds"), see G. M. Fraser's *Aberdeen Street Names* (1911) together with Nicolaisen's review of the 1986 reprint with foreword by Moira Henderson in *Aberdeen University Review* 52 (1988):235–36.
2. Hamish Henderson would not necessarily agree. See his 1980 essay "The Ballad, the Folk, and the Oral Tradition" in *The People's Past*, ed. E. J. Cowan (Edinburgh: Edinburgh University Student Publications Board), pp. 69–107.
3. The background to the Greig-Duncan Collection is treated in Ian Olson's "The Greig-Duncan Folk Song Collection: Last Leaves of a Local Culture?" in *Review of Scottish Culture* 5 (1989):79–85.

4. I am grateful to Flora Garry for permission to quote from this letter of 24 February 1989.
5. Bronson 1966: III, 9–10 (Child Ballad 114, Variant 13); Jeannie Robertson, Archive, School of Scottish Studies.
6. The best account of this transition is given by Ian Carter in his *Farmlife in Northeast Scotland 1840–1914* (Edinburgh: John Donald Publishers Limited, 1984).
7. Much of the background to this section has come from Peter Hall, either verbally, or from his essay, "Farm Life and the Farm Songs," which introduces Volume 3 of the *Greig-Duncan Folk Song Collection* (1987), or from his M. Litt Thesis, "Folk Songs of the North-East Farm Servants in the Nineteenth Century" (University of Aberdeen, 1985).
8. This is a conflation of several versions, largely from Greig-Duncan 356 (Volume 3).
9. William Mackay's account of "The Battle of Harlaw" in *Trans. Gaelic Society of Inverness* 30 (1919–22):267–85, is counterbalanced by that of the Aberdonian W. D. Simpson in his *The Earldom of Mar* (Aberdeen: The University Press [Aberdeen University Studies No. 124], 1948). David Buchan discusses the historical accuracy of the ballad in "History and Harlaw" in *Ballad Studies*, ed. E. B. Lyle (London: Folklore Society, 1976).
10. *Nomen ipse loquitur* (the name speaks for itself). The Wolf, Alexander, Earl of Buchan and younger son of King Robert II, was eventually excommunicated for burning Elgin Cathedral to the ground in 1390. This was the culmination of many years of terror and destruction in the Highlands and Lowlands. Not a nice man.
11. Once more I have made a conflation of several versions, especially from Bronson 163 and Greig-Duncan 112 (Volume 1).
12. The ballad singer's chivalric view of Macdonald and his army is born out by the annual exchange of swords for many years after by the families of Alexander Irvine of Drum (Deeside) and Eachainn Ruadh Maclean (Macdonald's second in command), who slew each other in mortal combat. If the pibroch commemorating Maclean ("Lament for Red Hector of the Battles") was composed at this time this makes it our oldest known pibroch (and the same applies to the Harlaw ballad). Forbes family members insist they were present at the battle in their "Memoirs of the House of Forbes" (MS at Castle Forbes), p. 139.
13. The custom of calling the farmer by the name of his farm is not confined to the North-East of Scotland (it occurs, for example, in the Faroes and parts of Europe); we just make the most of it.
14. From the poem "Decently and in Order" by Flora Garry and reprinted by her kind permission from *Bennygoak and other Poems* (Aberdeen: Rainbow Press, 1975). The subject is modeled on her uncle, Joseph Campbell, who farmed the lands of Upperboat on the River Don, three miles south of Harlaw. She notes, however: "Jo *was* a nicer man. But, he *was* his land" (letter of 23 December 1989).

REFERENCES

Bronson, Bertrand H.
  1966   The Traditional Tunes of the Child Ballads, 4 vols. Princeton: Princeton University Press.
Child, Francis James
  1882–98 The English and Scottish Popular Ballads, 5 vols. Boston and New York: Houghton Mifflin.
Nicolaisen, W. F. H.
  1973   Place Names in Traditional Ballads. Folklore 84:299–312.
  1976   Scottish Place-Names. London: B. T. Batsford.
  1984   Names and Narratives. Journal of American Folklore 97:259–72.
  1988   The Toponomy of Remembered Childhood. Names 36:133–42.
Shuldham-Shaw, Patrick; Lyle, Emily B.
  1981–87 (eds.) The Greig-Duncan Folk Song Collection. Vol. 1 (Nautical, military and historical songs), Vol. 2 (Narrative songs), Vol. 3 (Songs of the countryside). Aberdeen: Aberdeen University Press (Vols. 4–8 [in preparation]: Songs of courtship, love, and parting; general notes and indexes).

3

THE *AISLING* AND THE COWBOY... AND FACTORY GIRL*

D. K. WILGUS AND ELEANOR R. LONG-WILGUS

Bill Nicolaisen's work underscores the importance of comparative studies, both in the comparative analysis of traditional texts (Nicolaisen 1978; see also Wilgus 1958) and in considering the relationships between folk poetry and literature (Nicolaisen 1983; see also Long 1980). The present study serves as an affectionate tribute to those concerns, as well as constituting an extension of our continuing interest in one of their more intriguing objects: the influence of Irish poetic tradition upon popular song in Ireland and in the United States.

That influence was traced by D. K. Wilgus in "The *Aisling* and the Cowboy" (1985), which showed how the ancient Irish vision-poem (*aisling*) has manifested itself in various types of Irish songs of political resistance, courtship, and lamentation and in American songs about miners and loggers culminating in "The Cowboy's Lament" (Laws 1964:B1). A subsequent report (Wilgus 1988) documented the persistence of the *aisling* tradition in Australian folk poetry as well as at home. The group of songs to be discussed here bears further witness to the pervasive imprint of a medieval Irish literary convention upon

---

* D. K. Wilgus had begun work on this article when he was stricken with the medical problems that culminated in his death on Christmas Day 1989. Despite lengthy periods of hospitalization, he continued with its preparation and had completed a rough draft at the time of his demise. The present article was prepared from that rough draft by his widow, Eleanor R. Long-Wilgus.

creativity in modern balladry and song on both sides of the Atlantic Ocean.

The *aisling* of historical tradition is a first-person narrative in which a *Natureingang* ("As I walked out...") leads to an encounter, either in a dream or in a waking vision, with a lady who may be either young and beautiful or old and ugly. The ensuing dialogue in either case sometimes takes the form of a political prophecy (as in the Granuaile and *Sean Bhean Bocht* cycles, respectively), sometimes the form of a courtship (as in the "Dawning of the Day" cycle and in the tradition represented by Chaucer's Wife of Bath's Tale). Many Irish versions of the *aisling* model, however, consist of a political prophecy lacking the *Natureingang* "frame"; conversely, the "frame" may serve to introduce a courtship or a lament lacking both the vision and the prophecy aspects of the prototype.[1]

Our first example is an *aisling*-type which introduces courtship dialogues with differing outcomes. In renditions delivered fifteen years apart, Sarah Makem illustrates the ways in which a resourceful singer responds to the demands of her immediate social context and her aesthetic values by drawing upon the variant traditions available to her, in this case the two major types known as "The Country Girl" and "The Factory Girl."

In both types, there is a class difference between the wealthy suitor and the poor girl. The "Country Girl" version describes an encounter in which the girl first protests on the ground of the difference in their stations, but in the course of the dialogue allows herself to be persuaded to marry her interlocutor. The "Factory Girl" version is traceable to the medieval French *pastourelle* and the English "Collier Laddie" tradition, in which the poor girl rejects the attentions of a wealthy suitor for the love of a man of her own class.

Sarah Makem's first text, composed for inclusion in a commercially distributed anthology, follows the "Country Girl" pattern, but suppresses any reference to the wealth of the suitor; this permits the inference that the interlocutor is, after all, someone with a background similar to her own.

THE FACTORY GIRL

1. As I went a-walking one fine summer's morning,
   The birds on the branches they sweetly did sing.
   The lads and the lasses together were sportin',
   Going down to yon factory, their work to begin.

2. I spied a wee damsel, more fairer than Venus,
   Her skin like the lily that grows in the dell,
   Her cheek like the red rose that grew in yon valley,
   She's my own only goddess, she's a sweet factory girl.

3. I step-ped up to her, it was for to view her,
   When on me she cast a proud look of disdain.
   "Stand off me, stand off me, and do not insult me,
   For although I'm a poor girl, I think it no shame."

4. "I don't mean to harm you, or yet, love, to scorn you,
   But grant me one favor: pray where do you dwell?"
   "I am a poor orphan, without home or relations,
   And besides I'm a hard workin' factory girl."

5. Well, now to conclude and to finish these verses,
   This couple got married and both are doin' well.
   So, lads, fill your glasses and drink to the lasses
   Till we hear the dumb sound of the sweet factory bell.
               —Mrs. Sarah Makem, Co. Armagh, Northern
               Ireland, 1967 [Topic 12T128]

Sarah Makem's second text, collected for archival purposes fifteen years earlier, follows the "Factory Girl" pattern but departs from it in that the girl eventually marries above her station after all, presumably in consequence of new opportunities made available to her through her employment in the factory.

THE FACTORY GIRL

1. As I went a-walking, one fine summer's morning
   The birds on the branches they sweetly did sing
   The lads and the lasses together were sportin'
   Going down to yon factory, their work to begin.

2. I spied a wee damsel, more fairer than Venus
   Her skin like the lily, not one could excel
   Her cheeks like the red rose that grew in yon valley
   She's my own only goddess, she's a sweet factory girl.

3. I step-ped up to her, it was for to view her
   When on me she cast a proud look of disdain
   Stand off me, stand off me and do not insult me
   For although I'm a poor girl, I think it's no shame

4. I don't mean to harm you, I'm sure I would scorn it
   But grant me one favour: Pray where do you dwell?
   Kind sir, you'll excuse me, for now I must leave you
   For yonder's the sound of the factory bell

5. I have lands, I have houses adorned with ivy
   I've gold in my pocket and silver as well
   And if you go with me, a lady I'll make you
   So try and say yes, my dear factory girl

6. O love and sensation rules many a nation
   To many a young girl perhaps you'd look well
   I am a poor girl, without home or relations
   And besides I'm a hard-working factory girl

7. It's true I did love her but now she won't have me
   And all for her sake I'll go wander awhile
   Over high hills and valleys where no one shall know me
   I'll mourn for the sake of my factory girl.

8. Now this maid's [sic] she got married and become a great lady
   Become a great lady of fame and renown

> She may bless the day and the bright summer's morning
> She met with the squire and upon him did frown
>
> 9. Well now to conclude, and to finish these verses
> This couple got married, and both are doing well
> So, lads, fill your glasses, and drink to the lasses
> Till we hear the sweet sound of the factory bell.
> —Mrs. Sarah Makem, Co. Armagh, Northern Ireland, 1952 [Kennedy, 1975:501; BBC18536]

Both texts exhibit the singer's lively sense of what is appropriate in a given context. In the "Country Girl" version, abbreviated in response to the constraints imposed by time limitations on commercial segments, she elected to delete material referring to the wealth of the suitor, converting the courtship into one between equals that rescues her from "the dumb sound of the factory bell." In the "Factory Girl" version collected fifteen years earlier under more relaxed conditions, she preserved the rejection of the *landed* suitor (the "squire"), but amplified her text to suggest that factory labor acts as a more reliable vehicle for upward mobility through marriage than the old agricultural nexus of relationships. By manipulating the traditional options available to her in each case, she demonstrated her own clear preference for matrimony as the outcome of courtship encounters and her tacit endorsement of the industrial revolution as a widener of opportunities for sexual choice. Manipulation of this kind is typical of the kind of creativity we have elsewhere called "rationalizing"—conscious or unconscious editing of traditional materials to bring them into conformity with the singer's personal value system (Long 1973).

We believe it is safe to argue that what the "Country Girl/Factory Girl" syndrome represents is no more and no less than the "successful courtship" variation of the broader *aisling* theme. The tune certainly belongs to the "Lord Randall" family which carries so many *aisling*-type texts, including "The Cowboy's Lament." As we have repeatedly argued elsewhere, it is unwise—to say the least—to judge by the supposed antiquity of either sentiment or earliest printed variant, yet Irish song tradition is rich in courtship dialogues between Catholic and Protestant, peasant and aristocrat, poor and wealthy, all of which are happily resolved as in the "Country Girl" version. And the earliest text we have discovered is a "Country Girl" printed in a songbook in Waterford in 1836.[2]

[stanza omitted]
So lads, fill your glasses and drink to the lasses
Till we hear the dumb sound of the sweet factory bell.
—Mrs. Sarah Makem, 1967

Another development of the *aisling* tradition describes an encounter with one who is lamenting over a tragedy or disaster, as in "The High Blantyre Explosion" and "The Lost Jimmy Whalen" (Wilgus 1985: 288–94). It too has had an interesting progress through Irish and American folksong, beginning with the lamentation of a cuckolded husband.

THE OLD MAN ROCKING THE CRADLE

1. It was the other night that I chanced to go rovin'
   Down by the wee river, I joggin' along,
   I heard an old man makin' sad lamentations
   About rockin' the cradle and the child not his own.
   Chorus
   "Hi hi, hi ho, Hi dilly [laddie] lie easy.
   Perhaps your own daddy will never be known.
   I'm seein' [sitting here] and sighin' and rockin' the cradle,
   And nursing the [a] babby [sic] and I all alone [that's none of my own].

2. "She goes out every night to a ball or a party
   And leaves me here rockin' the cradle alone.
   And it's by the Lor' Harry, if ever you marry,
   You're sure to be rockin' the cradle alone.

Chorus
3. "So come all you young men that's inclined to get married,
   Take my advice, leave the women alone.
   For it's by the Lor' Harry, if ever you marry,
   You're sure to be rockin' the cradle alone."
   Chorus

—Paddy Tunney, Co. Donegal, Ireland
[Topic 12TS289]

In Ireland, "The Old Man Rockin' the Cradle" has frequently been assimilated to the Christian folk legend represented by "The Cherry Tree Carol" (Child 54); originally, it is said, the cuckold was Joseph and the song a lullaby sung to the infant Jesus (Lomax 1960:357–58; Kennedy 1975:484). The tune, like that of "The Country Girl," is a member of the "Lord Randall" family, and the song has also been collected from Canadian tradition (Lomax 1960:357; Peacock 1965:2, 478–79). The form best known in the United States, however, was explained to John Lomax by an American Gypsy as a lullaby sung by a cowboy to a "dogie" (orphan calf) too feeble to run with the rest of the herd, and therefore "cradled" on the saddle pommel of the cowboy's horse (Lomax 1960:357).

GET ALONG LITTLE DOGIES

1. As I was walkin' one mornin' for pleasure
   I met a cowpuncher a-ridin' along.
   His hat was throwed back and his spurs was a-jinglin'
   As he approached us a singin' this song.
   Chorus

"Hoopie-ti-yi-o, get along little dogies
It's your misfortune and none of my own.
Hoopie-ti-yi-o, get along little dogies
For you know Wyomin' will be your new home.

2. "Early in the mornin' we round up the dogies
To mark 'em and brand 'em and bob off their tails,
Drive up the horses, load up the chuck wagon,
And throw the dogies upon the trail.
Chorus

3. "It's hoopin' and yellin' and drivin' the dogies,
Oh how I do wish that you'd go on.
It's hoopin' and yellin', go on little dogies,
For you know Wyomin' will be your new home.
Chorus

4. "If ever I marry 'twill be to a widow
With six little orphans that's not my own,
If ever I marry 'twill be to a widow
With a great big ranch and a ten-story home."
Chorus

—Cartwright Brothers, 1928
[Columbia 15410-D; Mx 147579]

Alan Lomax has pointed out the relationship between this cowboy song and the Irish lament (which is known in Ireland as *Hushabu Cliabhán* or "Cradle Hushaby") without reference to the underlying *aisling* tradition; he provides a variant whose chorus closely resembles that of the Irish text.

Hushie-ci-ola [cf. *Hushabu cliabhán*], little baby, lie easy,
Who's your real father may never be known,
O it's weeping, wailing, rocking the cradle,
And tending a baby that's none of your own.
[Lomax 1960:373]

Another Irish version of the cuckold's lullaby lacks the *aisling*-type frame; the background is updated and the narrative more detailed.

ROCKING THE BABY TO SLEEP

1. She is just forty-five and a tidy wee wife.
   She's five years younger than me.
   She's full of enjoyment, loves plenty of fun,
   And she sometimes goes out on a spree.

   When I stop at home, the baby to mind,
   The house in good order to keep,
   With a fire burning bright, you can sit there all night,
   Just rockin' the baby to sleep.
   Chorus
   Singin' too-la-lay-o, go to sleep, baby,
   Sleep, little baby, don't let you cry.
   Too-la-lay-o, go to sleep, baby,
   Mama'll be home to bye-and-bye.

2. Just as I rocked the baby to sleep,
   I took a short walk down the street,
   And to my surprise, I saw with my eyes
   Me wife with a soldier six feet.

   She said she loved fun, she'd be home when she was done,
   She was only takin' a peep.
   They were kissin' and courtin' each other all night,
   And me rockin' the baby to sleep.

Chorus

3. Some love to roam from their own native home,
   But I by the fireside keep,
   With a fire burning bright, you can sit there all night,
   Just rocking the baby to sleep.
   Chorus

>—Mary Ann Cunningham, Co. Down, Northern Ireland, 24 July 1970. [UCLA T7-73-30]. Recorded and copyrighted by Hugh Shields. [Ulster Folk Museum, Shields T-1970-30][3]

This version must have circulated in Ireland at least by the early decades of the twentieth century, for it appears in a 1924 recording by the American country singer Riley Puckett.

ROCK ALL OUR BABIES TO SLEEP

1. Show me the lady that never would roam
   Away from her fireside at night,
   And never go roaming after the boys
   But would sit by her fireside at night.

   My wife she's one of a different kind
   Oft-times cause me for to weep,
   She's off from her home, she leaves me alone
   To rock all our babies to sleep.
   Chorus
   (Yodel)

> To rock all our babies to sleep.
> (Yodel)
> To rock all our babies to sleep.
>
> 2. Just the other night while out for a walk
>   I happened to stroll down the street,
>   And to my surprise I saw with my eyes
>   My wife with a man of six feet.
>
>   She said, "It's no harm. Don't raise no alarm.
>   Don't make any fuss on the street."
>   She tickled my chin. She told me, "Go in,
>   To rock all our babies to sleep."
>   *Chorus*
>
>   Riley Puckett, 1924
>   [Columbia 107-D; Mx81633]

Jimmie Rodgers recorded the same song a few years later with lyrics that seem to further update the material.

> ROCK ALL OUR BABIES TO SLEEP
>
> 1. Show me the lady that never would roam
>   Away from her fireside at night,
>   And never go roaming out after the boys,
>   But would sit by her fireside so bright.
>
> 2. My wife she is one of the different kind,
>   Often caused me a lotta grief.
>   She's off from her home, she leaves me alone
>   To rock all our babies to sleep.
>
> 3. I remember one night when I came home,
>   I came in as quiet as a lamb.
>   They must have had company, for when I walked in,
>   I heard the back door when it slammed.
>
> 4. I walked right in and looked all around.
>   I never thought she would cheat.
>   Without a doubt, she had just gone out
>   And left all our babies to sleep.

5. Just the other night while out for a walk,
   I happened to stroll down the street,
   And to my surprise I saw with my eyes
   My wife with a man of sixteen.

6. She says it's no harm, don't raise no alarm,
   Don't make any fuss on the street.
   She tickled my chin, told me to go in,
   And rock all our babies to sleep.
   —Jimmie Rodgers, 21 October 1932
   [Mx BS58963–1; Victor 23721 et al.]

From courtship to cowboys, from political protest to marital complaint, the influence of the classic Irish *aisling* is ubiquitous, and can be readily traced through melodic traditions, the modulation of its narrative themes, and evidence of textual conservatism embedded even in what appear to be massive innovations in traditional song materials. A creative folksinger like Sarah Makem is thus provided with both a solid verbal, thematic, and musical foundation and a rich variety of traditional alternatives out of which to shape idiosyncratic, but not at all independent, texts in accordance with her own values and the demands of the immediate context.

NOTES

1. In this connection, we should like to suggest that perhaps the "Four Black Sheep" of Tristram Potter Coffin's recent analysis (Coffin 1983) owes at least as much to the *aisling* tradition emanating from Ireland as to the circumstances hypothesized in that analysis.
2. National Library of Ireland, IR 6551: Song Books, Waterford. Numerous examples of Catholic/Protestant and other "successful courtship dialogue" songs (including additional "Country Girl" variants) are to be found in our as-yet-unpublished catalogue of Irish narrative songs in the English language. A small but useful discography/bibliography of "Country Girl" variants is available in Kennedy (1975:529).
3. We are deeply grateful to Hugh Shields for his permission to reproduce Mrs. Cunningham's version.

REFERENCES

Child, Francis James
    1965   The English and Scottish Popular Ballads. 1882–88 repr. New York: Dover Publications.

Coffin, Tristram Potter
    1983   Four Black Sheep Among the 305. *In* James Porter, ed., The Ballad Image: Essays Presented to Bertrand Harris Bronson. Los Angeles: Center for the Study of Comparative Folklore and Mythology, University of California, pp. 30–38.

Kennedy, Peter
    1975   Folksongs of Britain and Ireland. London: Cassell & Co., Ltd.

Laws, G. Malcolm, Jr.
    1964   Native American Balladry. Rev. ed. Philadelphia: The American Folklore Society.

Lomax, Alan
    1960   The Folk Songs of North America in the English Language. Garden City, N.Y.: Doubleday and Company.

Long, Eleanor R.
    1973   Ballad Singers, Ballad Makers, and Ballad Etiology. Western Folklore 32:225–36.
    1980   Young Man, I Think You're Dyin': The Twining Branches Theme in the Tristan Legend and in English Tradition. Fabula 21:183–99.

Nicolaisen, W. F. H.
    1978   English Jack and American Jack. Midwestern Journal of Language and Folklore 4:27–36.
    1983   Theodore Fontane's "Sir Patrick Spens." *In* James Porter, ed., The Ballad Image: Essays Presented to Bertrand Harris Bronson. Los Angeles: Center for the Study of Comparative Folklore and Mythology, University of California, pp. 3–19.

Peacock, Kenneth
    1965   Songs of the Newfoundland Outports. 3 vols. Ottawa: National Museum of Canada, Anthropological Series No. 65, Bulletin No. 197.

Wilgus, D. K.
    1958   Shooting Fish in a Barrel: The Child Ballad in America. Journal of American Folklore 71:161–64.
    1985   The *Aisling* and the Cowboy: Some Unnoticed Influences of Irish Vision Poetry on Anglo-American Balladry. Western Folklore 44:255–300.
    1988   The Poet in Hell: Australia and Ireland. Mississippi Folklore Register 22:3–16.

"THE DOLLAR AND THE DEVIL":
From Poem to Traditional Song?

W. K. MCNEIL

In the following account of a poem that ended up as a song and possibly entered folk tradition I have, of necessity, concentrated on the contributions specific individuals made to the song and attempted to point out whether or not their various additions and deletions fitted with folk tradition, in particular that of the southern Appalachian mountains. The argument here is for greater consideration to be given to the history of individual items before assigning them to the status of folklore. Bill Nicolaisen has always held to that standard in his numerous publications, and this essay honors his inspiration.

In the 1970 *Yearbook of the International Folk Music Council*, Archie Green comments on a November 1924 Okeh label recording of "The Dollar and the Devil" by Henry Whitter. Green describes the song as "a highly important example of folk attitudes toward the established, formalistic church in fundamentalist-oriented communities." In a footnote Green suggests that Whitter derived his text from an eight-stanza Holy Roller song, "The Two Rulers," collected in 1936 by Lillian Crabtree in Overton County, Tennessee (Green 1970:47–48). The song may indeed express folk attitudes but does not have the fundamentalist roots Green asserts. From evidence now available it seems that the text of the song originated in a poem by long-time North Carolina poet-laureate James Larkin Pearson.

Born September 13, 1879, on Berry's Mountain in Wilkes County,

North Carolina, Pearson became the poet laureate of his native state on August 4, 1953, and retained the position until his death on August 27, 1981, seventeen days shy of his 102nd birthday. A product of inadequate rural schools, by his own estimate Pearson achieved no more than fifteen months of formal schooling (Pearson 1971:xxiv).[1] His real education came from reading practically every book he could find. At age seven he started his own library with three or four schoolbooks and eventually amassed over four thousand volumes, which now compose the nucleus of the James Larkin Pearson Library at Wilkes Community College in North Wilkesboro, North Carolina.

Even earlier Pearson had shown an inclination for rhyming. In an autobiographical sketch for his last poetry collection he recalled how this tendency first became evident:

> One cold winter day when I was four-and-a-half years old, my father had me out with him somewhere on the farm. All at once he asked me, "Jimmy, are you cold?" Without taking any time to study out my answer, it came like a flash, and I said:
> "My fingers and toes,
> My feet and my hands,
> Are jist as cold
> As you ever see'd a man's."
> Back at the house a few minutes later, my father told my mother what I had said, and they were both scared. They were afraid their boy was going to be a poet. No such disease had ever been known in the family on either side, and they didn't know what to do for it. So they just had to wait and watch for further developments. They began to notice that my baby words were often falling into a rhymed and measured pattern. They hoped I would outgrow the disease, but it seems that I never did. [Pearson 1971:xxi]

The poetry "disease" continued throughout his life, his last efforts coming when he was in his late nineties.

Pearson's work first appeared in print in 1895 when he was sixteen. One of his later poems, "Fifty Acres," was widely printed, appearing in among other publications *Bartlett's Familiar Quotations*. It also resulted in his being included in *Who's Who in America* although, as Pearson said, "when I was not publishing anything for awhile the Who's Who people dropped me—thinking, I suppose, that I had passed over

Jordan" (Pearson 1971:xxv). Although he received acclaim for "Fifty Acres" and several other poems, some poems got away from him. One piece of verse penned in 1916 was later printed as an anonymous poem in the December 2, 1944, edition of his hometown newspaper. Titled "When the War Is Going to End," Pearson later called it his "worst poem" (Pearson 1971:268).[2] Nevertheless, on December 22, he wrote a letter to the editor of the paper and cleared up the question of authorship (Pearson 1971:270–71).[3]

He was less fortunate, however, with a poem written in 1911 under the title "When the Dollar Rules the Pulpit." So completely did this work get away from Pearson that it was copyrighted by at least two commercial recording artists and, as mentioned above, collected and identified as a Holy Roller gospel text. Pearson's efforts to receive credit and payment for his poem were unsuccessful and his lyrics from 1911 are still generally attributed to others. About the only persons now aware of Pearson's authorship are those who personally knew the man.

"When the Dollar Rules the Pulpit" apparently first appeared in *The Fool-Killer*, the monthly magazine of humor Pearson published between 1910 and 1929. At its peak *The Fool-Killer* achieved a circulation of 50,000 but, in 1911, it must have been considerably smaller (Pearson 1971:270).[4] Pearson published the poem twice more, in *Pearson's Poems* (1924) and in *Plowed Ground: Humorous and Dialect Poems* (1949). His text follows:

WHEN THE DOLLAR RULES THE PULPIT

In this world of frills and fashions,
    Where the churches are so fine,
And the trade-mark of religion
    Is the classic dollar sign,
There's a rule that never faileth,
    And you'll always find it true—
When the Dollar rules the pulpit,
    Then the Devil rules the pew.

There may be a heap of singing,
    And an awful sight of prayer,
And the sermon may be answered
    With an "Amen!" here and there;

But as sure as Joe's a Dutchman,
  Or old Shylock was a Jew,
When the Dollar rules the pulpit,
  Then the Devil rules the pew.

When the money gets to talking,
  And the Master's voice is still,
And the preacher swaps a sermon
  For a twenty-dollar bill;
That's the time old Mister Satan
  Gets the churches in a stew—
When the Dollar rules the pulpit
  And the Devil rules the pew.

When religion goes a-begging,
  And the Bible is forgot,
And the preacher preaches nothing
  Only scientific rot,
Then the faithful old believers,
  They are getting mighty few—
When the Dollar rules the pulpit
  And the Devil rules the pew.
[Pearson 1911:226 LT]

After the 1911 publication, the poem apparently languished until the early 1920s. Reportedly a musical setting for the lyrics appeared in gospel songbooks in the 1920s, but I have been unable to find these sources.[5] In 1924, thirteen years after Pearson's initial publication and, coincidentally, the same year the verse appeared in *Pearson's Poems*, the lyrics made the first of their several appearances on commercial recordings. This was the Henry Whitter recording with a new title, "The Dollar and the Devil," which has been called the first disc that "poked fun at commercialized religion" (Green 1970:48). How did the poem go from Pearson's monthly humor sheet to country song? Possibly early country recording artist Dock Walsh played a part in the transition.

According to Pearson's daughter, Dock Walsh read the poem and made a melody for it, one which was played by Walsh several times around Wilkes County.[6] Walsh, too, was a native of the county and, in fact, he and Pearson were from adjoining communities; undoubtedly the two were aware of each other. Born Doctor Coble Walsh on July

23, 1901, at Lewis Fork, he became Wilkes County's first country recording artist on October 3, 1925, when he cut four sides in Atlanta for the Columbia label. He continued to record, both on his own and with the band "The Carolina Tar Heels," until 1932. Walsh made one final record, an album for the Folk-Legacy label, five years before his death in 1967.

Prior to his recording career Walsh spent four years, 1921 to 1925, as a public schoolteacher and it was possibly during this time that he set Pearson's poem to music, although the poet's daughter is uncertain about the specific year of the Walsh tune. Walsh, who had what was for that time and place a good education, could have been aware of the poem, which originally appeared when he was ten. More likely, though, he knew of it through its publication in *Pearson's Poems*. That volume was issued on March 1, 1924, so it is possible that Walsh set the poem to music shortly thereafter, in time for Whitter's recording session in October. All of these considerations are, of course, based on the assumption that it was Walsh's tune that was used by Whitter.

That Walsh could have influenced Whitter is not as farfetched as it might seem initially. Whitter, a native of Grayson County, Virginia, lived about forty miles from the Ferguson community where Walsh was reared. By October 1924, Whitter had completed four recording sessions for the General Phonograph Corporation, Okeh Record Division; one record issued from his second session on December 12, 1923, was a big hit in western North Carolina. This was "Lonesome Road Blues" and "Wreck on the Southern Old '97," two sides released in January 1924. Whitter's record inspired Walsh to try to make his own recordings. Walsh wrote Okeh but received no encouragement. Columbia responded, however, and he made his first recordings for that company. Since Walsh contacted Whitter's company and the two men lived relatively close to each other, they may have had personal contact, at which time Walsh could have performed his setting of the Pearson poem for Whitter.

At this late date it will probably never be known if such interaction took place or, for that matter, if Walsh's tune is the one used by Whitter. On the recording, Whitter seems to be unsure of the melody, his vocal sounding almost like a different tune from that of his instrumental break; this situation suggests the possibility that it had been recently learned orally. To my knowledge Walsh's melody was never copyrighted; so, unless it is the one used by Whitter, it has passed into oblivion. Pearson apparently did not appreciate Walsh's setting his poem to music, but his reaction was not strong.[7] The same cannot be said for his attitude about Whitter's recording, which was probably released in June 1925 but evidently did not come to Pearson's attention for several months (Cohen 1975:65).[8] The first indication that Pearson knew of Whitter's record is a letter of January 6, 1926, to the Register of Copyrights at the Library of Congress. He asks, "Will you please tell me what constitutes an infringement of copyright, and what steps should be taken in case of such infringement?" He proceeds to recount the publication on March 1, 1924, of *Pearson's Poems* containing "When the Dollar Rules the Pulpit" and then offers the following comments:

> I have just learned that a large phonograph corporation has taken one of my poems from the above mentioned copyrighted book and had it set to music and reproduced (with instruments and singing) on a phonograph record, and this record is being sold all over the country. This was done without my knowledge or consent and without giving me credit as author of the poem. I am on the track of another one which I think they have used in the same way. Have ordered the record and am waiting for it to arrive before I can be sure about the second one. But I know about the first one. The words are sung and accompanied by instrumental music. Four words have been changed, but it is my original copyrighted poem.

The letter concluded with several questions:

> Now shouldn't my copyright protect me in such a case? And can't I demand and get a royalty on the sales of the records? If so, how much royalty should I expect to get, and what steps should I take to get it? Also, can't I demand that my name be placed on the records as author of the poem?
> If I find that the company has used more than one poem in that way, does each one constitute a separate infringement?[9]

The Library's reply cannot be found.

Even before contacting the Library of Congress Pearson sought legal counsel, for on January 21, 1926, he received a letter from his attorneys containing a copy of a letter from Ralph Peer of the General

Phonograph Corporation, Okeh Record Division. Peer referred to a letter of January 2 from the lawyers concerning infringement of copyright in the recording of "The Dollar and the Devil." Basically, Peer denied any infringement of copyright because, according to his interpretation, in mechanical reproduction the Copyright Act of 1909 provided for protection of musical compositions only. Peer further noted, "It is our understanding that the song which we have recorded is traditional in character, but regardless of this point it seems to us that the copyright act very clearly limits our liability to owners of copyrights on musical compositions."[10]

There can be little doubt that Whitter's lyrics came from Pearson's poem, although Whitter may have acquired them indirectly from Walsh or from some other party. The only changes between Okeh 40352 and the 1911 poem are minimal and of the sort that might occur when one is recalling verses orally rather than reading them from a printed page. The first verse is exactly the same except that the line "There's a rule that never faileth" which may have sounded a bit too poetic, was changed to "There's a rule that never fails" and "where" and "there" are substituted for "when" and "then," a change that is consistent throughout the Whitter text.

Pearson's second verse is shifted to the fourth stanza; his third verse becomes Whitter's second. Several minor changes occur here, including alteration of the line "the preacher swaps a sermon" to "swaps his sermon" and the phrase "gets the churches in a stew" becomes "gets his church's business too." The fourth verse of the original is Whitter's third verse and, again, the changes are minor. The phrase "only scientific rot" is changed to "a scientific rot" and "then the faithful old believers" becomes "there's a people—old believers." Whitter's fourth verse (Pearson's second) also has some slight alterations. "A heap of singing and an awful sight of prayer" becomes "a lot of singing and an awful lot of prayer" and the phrase "as sure as Joe's a Dutchman, or old Shylock was a Jew" becomes "as sure as Job's a Dutchman and old Shylock was a Jew."

Understandably, Pearson felt that he had a strong case against Peer and his company. Exactly what happened next is uncertain, but at some point between January 21 and August 3, 1926, Pearson acquired an additional lawyer who practiced in Washington, D.C., his first cousin, Robert H. McNeill.

Correspondence between lawyer and client reveals that McNeill applied himself diligently to the task. His letter of August 3, 1926, must have greatly pleased Pearson: "I feel confident that we are going to get something out of your phonograph case. I have paid the costs and the defendant has written me showing a disposition to arrive at an understanding on some basis. I may go to New York and discuss the details soon."[11] Twenty-four days later, on August 27, 1926, McNeill was still confident, writing Pearson, "I have proposed to the General Phonograph Company that we will settle their infringement of your poem for $750 cash, plus a royalty on all records hereafter sold." He added, "The Phonograph Company is considering it and I am confident that they will pay us $500 at least."[12]

Apparently, McNeill's confidence was premature, for by the end of the next month he still had not received an answer. On September 29 he wrote Pearson: "We expect a definite answer to our compromise proposition from the General Phonograph Company on the 15th instant or sooner. We are confident it will be satisfactory."[13] Yet, over two months later, on December 8, 1926, McNeill reported that all offers had been rejected and suggested that more forceful measures were necessary: "The last time I was in New York, I had hoped to get settlement of this case. I offered to settle for $600 and a royalty, but it was turned down at that time, and I have had nothing since. I think now we had better proceed with the case by taking your deposition. That would probably bring them to terms."[14]

Pearson evidently accepted McNeill's recommendation but did not get around to acting on it immediately. Possibly he was hoping that he would not have to take the matter to court. Whatever the reason, it was not until March of 1928 before his deposition was taken. Apparently, during the previous fifteen months, the General Phonograph Company had not changed its official attitude. McNeill wrote Pearson on March 3, 1928, "I am in receipt of a letter today from Mr. Darby, the attorney handling your case in New York, that the case will probably be on for trial in April."[15] Two weeks later, Pearson received a letter from Walter C. Darby, the New York attorney, stating "I have been endeavoring to get an answer from the attorneys for the defendant in this case as to whether they would stipulate the taking of the depositions or whether it would be necessary for us to take a motion. I have also approached them regarding settlement. I have not had a reply to my letter to date. However, I am writing again to-day asking that they give the matter their immediate attention."[16]

If there were any other letters concerning the proposed suit they are no longer extant, but the outcome of the matter is not in doubt. Sometime after the correspondence with the General Phonograph Company Pearson wrote an undated manuscript "When to Get a Copyright" that was apparently intended for publication in *The Writer's Monthly* and which provides a history of the entire affair (Pearson Library Papers). This paper indicates that even before Whitter's recording Pearson was having "difficulties" with his poem. The manuscript also explains why Pearson did not copyright "When the Dollar Rules the Pulpit" upon its initial publication and also suggests that the piece may have come in an indirect manner from Pearson to Whitter and other singers.

> About February, 1911, I wrote a poem to which I didn't attach much importance. In fact, it was not a poem—it was a mere rhyme or jingle containing some homely philosophy and a catchy refrain. I had written hundreds of better things, and had printed most of them in a small obscure paper of which I was editor. I had never thought of getting a copyright on the paper or any of its contents. So the poem in question went into the paper just as the others had done, and I didn't consider it worth a second thought. But a few days after the paper went out I began to notice that my "poem" was being copied in other papers here, yonder, and everywhere. I saw it in a number of papers and clippings of it were sent to me from different parts of the country. Usually my name was attached, but in a few cases no credit was given. But the point is that my poem which I thought to be of no value had made a hit, and it was out going about in the world without any copyright on it.
>
> A few years later when I collected my poems from the four winds to make a book, I of course included the "popular hit" with the others and copyrighted the book in my own name. That was all I could do, and I thought that was enough. I thought the copyright covered every poem in the book, even though most of them had been previously printed without copyright.
>
> Now for the next act. One day last winter I made the discovery that a big phonograph corporation in New York had taken my poem and had it set to music and reproduced (both records and music) on a phonograph record which they were selling by the thousands all over the country. I consulted a local lawyer who thought I

had a case and that I could certainly get damages, or at least a royalty on the sales of the record. Then I secured the service of a regular copyright lawyer in Washington who agreed to look into the merits of the case. But when it became known that the poem had been first printed and widely copied without copyright, all my hopes were dashed to the ground. I couldn't do a thing. It seems that the poem had become public property by reason of having been published without copyright, and my later copyright on the book wasn't worth a cent in that case. The phonograph company goes right [on] making and selling the record of my poem, and I can't get a cent. Can't even get my name on the record as author of the words.

Hereafter, I am going to copyright everything I write before it ever gets into print or at the time of its first publication.[17]

Pearson's claim that Whitter's record was "selling by the thousands all over the country" should not be taken too seriously. Although sales figures apparently no longer exist, Whitter's "Dollar and the Devil" is a relative rarity today, which suggests that it did not sell well. There is also little reason to believe that Whitter's record was sold "all over the country." His records, particularly his early solo recordings, were sold throughout the South but they were not generally marketed outside that region.

With Pearson's threat of a lawsuit for copyright infringement coming to naught, the way was now open for other recordings, and there were at least two. In November 1928 the blind duo of Lester McFarland and Robert Gardner, known as Mac and Bob, recorded the song for Vocalion. This record, probably released in March 1929, is even closer to Pearson's original text than the Whitter version. "Where" and "there" are substituted for "when and "then" as in Whitter's text. Pearson's second verse is used as a recurring refrain, although it is slightly different from both the original and Whitter's rendition. The notable change is in the fifth and sixth line of Pearson's second stanza. In Whitter's recording, "Job" is the Dutchman rather than the "Joe" of Pearson's 1911 poem; Mac and Bob's version, however, retains Pearson's "Joe" but substitutes the name "Sherlock" for the Jew. This recording also uses almost verbatim the fifth and sixth lines of Pearson's fourth stanza. The original poem's "Then the faithful old believers,/They are getting mighty few" appears in Whitter's version as

"There's a people—old believers—they are getting mighty few" and in Mac and Bob's lyrics as "Where the faithful old believers—they are getting mighty few."[18]

There is no evidence that Mac and Bob attempted to copyright the song. This is not so with the third act to record the number, the McCravy Brothers. Natives of Laurens, South Carolina, Frank and James McCravy recorded the song at least twice, first in late 1928 or early 1929 for the Brunswick label, which was released as Brunswick 424 in the latter half of 1929. On July 15, 1929, the McCravys made a second recording in New York City for the Victor label. This rendition, which featured the backup work of Carson Robison on harmonica and guitar, was released in October 1930 as Victor 40312. On April 9, 1930, the McCravys secured a copyright on the song; their text and tune appeared in 1933 in the Southern Music Publishing Company's folio, *The Frank & Jim McCravy Album of Fireside Songs* (1933:8–9). The head of Southern Music at the time was the same Ralph Peer who, in 1926, had been in charge of Okeh's country records and had corresponded with Pearson's lawyers concerning copyright violations.[19] Peer's publication of "The Dollar and the Devil" five years after the threatened lawsuit, with an attribution to the McCravys, is further evidence that Pearson's prior claim to the lyrics was never accepted by Okeh or, apparently, anyone else in the country music industry.

The McCravy lyrics follow the Pearson text closely but there are a couple of interesting changes. As in Mac and Bob's recording, Pearson's second stanza is used as a refrain but without the references to the Dutchman and the Jew. Instead, the line reads "But as sure as I'm a-talkin' and your taxes will come due" (McCravy 1933:9). The only other significant change is the substitution of the word "Devil" for "Satan." As in the other recorded versions, "where" and "there" are generally substituted for "when" and "then." Otherwise, the McCravy lyrics are an exact copy of the 1911 original.

Apparently, neither the Mac and Bob nor the McCravy recordings sold well. The former was issued as Vocalion 5322, a high number for Vocalion country records, which suggests its rarity as well as probable limited sales. The McCravy Brunswick release was in that company's 400 series, none of which sold well, and their Victor release sold only 1,800 copies. By October 1930, when the Victor recording was released, the Depression was in full bloom and profoundly affecting record sales but, even by the lower standards of that era, a total sale of 1,800 copies was poor.

Thus, it seems that none of the several recordings of "The Dollar and the Devil" was even a moderately good seller. Why was it recorded so much? Why did a song that, as far as cash registers were concerned, flopped abysmally, get recorded four times by three different acts? Perhaps the recording company executives liked it and knew it to be a crowd pleaser at live performances. Reportedly it was the most popular song the McCravys did at personal appearances.[20] In the 1920s and early 1930s marketing techniques of the fledgling country music business were certainly less sophisticated than those of today, and at the time there was a greater degree of risk-taking in the recording industry than there is now.

Following the three publications and four recordings of "The Dollar and the Devil," it made a further appearance in 1936.[21] Lillian Crabtree's George Peabody College master's thesis, "Songs and Ballads Sung in Overton County, Tennessee," includes the song, apparently taken from oral tradition.[22] Crabtree's version, titled "The Two Rulers," is given below.

THE TWO RULERS

In this world of frills and fashions
Where the churches are so fine,
And the trade marks are religion,
As a classic dollar sign.
There's a rule that never faileth,
You will always find it true:
Where the dollar rules the pulpit,
The devil rules the pew.

There may be lots of singing,
And an awful lot of prayer,
And the sermon may be answered
With an Amen, here and there,
But as sure as Joe's a Dutchman,
And old Shylock is a Few [sic],
Where the dollar rules the pulpit,
There the devil rules the pew.

When the money gets to talking,
And the Master's voice is still,
And the preacher swaps his sermon
For a twenty dollar bill,
It is then old Master Satan
Gets the churches in a stew.
Where the dollar rules the pulpit,
The devil rules the pew.

When religion goes a-begging,
And the Bible is forgot,
And the preacher preaches nothing,
But a scientific rot,
There the faithful old believers,
They are getting mighty few,
Where the dollar rules the pulpit,
And the devil rules the pew.

Like the Jews in ancient temple,
When the Lord was here on earth.
They had ceased to obey God's orders
And joined in greed and mirth,
While Jesus was on earth,
What he said to them was true.
Where the dollar ruled the pulpit,
And the devil ruled the pew.

You may not get the idea,
But I've watched it from my youth,
The people they are growing
More opposed to Gospel truth.
Their ears seem to be itching,
They are seeking something new.
The dollar rules the pulpit,
And the devil rules the pew.

In the days of truth and honor,
Back fifty years ago,
The preacher preached the Gospel,
Not for greed, or graft, or show,
But times have changed orders.

You must pay your monthly dues.
Where the dollar rules the pulpit,
And the devil rules the pew.

Our widows and our orphans
Are seemingly forgot.
While the preacher preaches nothing,
But a foreign mission rot.
His greed for filthy lucre
Has got things in a stew,
And the dollar rules the pulpit,
And the devil rules the pew. [Crabtree 1936:93–95]

Unfortunately, Crabtree was casual about documentation, so her exact source is unknown, as are the circumstances by which she acquired the text. She provides no information about the song other than the prefatory comment that it "probably came through the Holy Roller harbingers" (Crabtree 1936:93). The Crabtree text consists of eight eight-line stanzas, double the length of Pearson's poem. "Mister Satan" becomes "Master Satan" and "where" and "there" are substituted for "when" and "then" as in the commercially recorded versions. Other minor discrepancies are found in the four stanzas the two texts share; where Pearson says "the trade-mark of religion is the classic dollar sign," the Crabtree text has "the trade marks are religion, as a classic dollar sign." "The Two Rulers" also omits some words found in the Pearson poem. For example, Pearson's "And you'll always find it true" becomes in Crabtree's first stanza "You will always find it true"; Pearson's second stanza changes "There may be a heap of singing, And an awful sight of prayer" to "There may be lots of singing, and an awful lot of prayer"; in Pearson's third stanza "the preacher swaps a sermon" is in Crabtree's text "the preacher swaps his sermon"; Pearson's fourth stanza talks of "only scientific rot" whereas Crabtree's text refers to "a scientific rot." And the reference to Shylock as a "Few" is obviously a typo; almost certainly the intended word was "Jew." All of these changes are minor and seem to be the sort a text would undergo if learned orally by Crabtree's unidentified source.

Clearly, someone other than Pearson composed the last four stanzas. Although generally keeping the tone of the 1911 poem, the final stanzas of "The Two Rulers" do show slight shifts in emphasis.

Whereas Pearson's lines talk about the present without reference to the past the last four lines make great use of the past, mentioning the "Jews in ancient temple" and talking about the days of truth and honor "back fifty years ago." There are also other noteworthy differences. One suspects that Pearson wrote his lines tongue-in-check complaining about ministers who were more interested in their financial well-being than their spiritual well-being. The unknown author of the additional stanzas, however, spends much of his verbiage carping about those who are becoming "more opposed to Gospel truth." He also takes additional swipes at those who overlook widows, orphans, and other needy people while preaching "a foreign mission rot." The tongue is perhaps still in cheek but at the same time the intent is in a sense more serious.

The four additional eight-line stanzas are by someone who was less skilled at crafting lyrics than Pearson. The latter prided himself on producing poetry that rhymed; he had little use for blank verse, "incorrect rhyme," and similar forms (Wood 1936:25–38 and Williams 1986:128–30). Thus, it is not only improbable but virtually impossible that he would have produced a rhyme as forced as that in the next to last stanza of "The Two Rulers" where "dues" is made to rhyme with "pew." Generally, though, the unknown lyricist succeeds fairly well in aping the Pearson original; indeed, he or she even uses three of the same rhymes in the original; "true" and "stew" are made to rhyme with "pew" and "forgot" is rhymed with "rot."

Nothing in the eight stanzas of "The Two Rulers," or in the 1911 poem, is inconsistent with fundamentalist Christian dogma, but the antimission statement in Crabtree's text is especially typical of the more emotional fundamentalist groups, those sometimes called "Holy Rollers." Antimissionism began in the early nineteenth century, and in some frontier communities few persons or churches dared oppose this trend. Many factors accounted for the rise of this attitude. Many people felt that missionaries and missionary organizations were contrary to Scriptural authority, and that the church was the only ecclesiastical body sanctioned by the Bible. Others held to an orthodox Calvinist position that maintained God needed no help in bringing his elect to salvation; all the missionary activity in the world could not save those who were not among the chosen. For these people it was almost sacrilegious to suggest that missionaries could change the preordained pattern of events. A deep-seated objection to authority and an even greater dislike of taxing churches for the support of missionaries also contributed to antimission sentiments (Olmsted 1960:271–74). By the twentieth century antimissionism had a long, unbroken history and still appealed strongly to many fundamentalist Christians; this attitude is effectively conveyed in "The Two Rulers" by the three words, "foreign mission rot."

It could be reasoned that the extra length suggests that "The Two Rulers" is the original rather than a troped version of Pearson's poem. This possibility is problematic, though, on several counts. First, it makes Pearson a plagiarist without showing cause for such a charge. Moreover, there is much evidence favoring Pearson's claim to be the original author, the most important being his two publications of the poem that predate any other known publication. Moreover, Crabtree makes no claims for "The Two Rulers" beyond the comment that the song "probably came through the Holy Roller harbingers." Her comment gives the impression that she felt the song was of some age, but just how old is impossible to determine.

In 1949 Pearson published "When the Dollar Rules the Pulpit" for the final time in his volume *Plowed Ground: Humorous and Dialect Poems*. By this time the popularity of Henry Whitter, Mac and Bob, and the McCravy Brothers was past and readers of Pearson's 1949 collection were probably unaware that the poem had once been part of early country music. Not even the author himself considered the fact worthy of mention which, considering the history of the recording controversy, is understandable.

This brief chronicle of the transformation of James Larkin Pearson's poem into a song illustrates that the story behind an individual song is often more complex than it may appear on the surface. For that reason, one should be cautious about attributing lyrics or themes to "the folk" or any other group, unless there is solid evidence to support the imputation. The history of "The Dollar and the Devil" also demonstrates a matter that some folklorists—including Bill Nicolaisen—have called attention to, namely that there is a considerable link between popular poetry and popular and folk song (see Nicolaisen 1983, Cohen 1981, Green 1972, and Logsdon 1989).[23] In this instance the lyrics were the work of a person who wasn't particularly interested in music and certainly did not write the text with its potential as a song in mind, yet the fact that his poem was taken up by others bears witness to its appeal to a widespread audience. The history of "The Dollar and the Devil" is a classic illustration of the need to understand the difference between a folk creation and a production that found considerable favor with the folk. Making that determination is often more difficult than it initially seems.

NOTES
1. Despite the subtitle of Pearson 1971, the book is by no means a complete collection of Pearson's work.
2. The entire poem runs:
    Absolute knowledge have I none,
    But my aunt's washer-woman's sister's son
    Heard a policeman on his beat
    Say to a laborer on the street
    That he had a letter just last week,
    Written in Latin—(or maybe Greek)
    From a Chinese coolie in Timbucktoo
    Who said that the Negroes in Cuba knew
    Of a colored man in a Texas town
    Who got it straight from a circus clown
    That a man in Klondike heard the news
    From a gang of South American Jews
    About somebody in Borneo
    Who heard of a man who claimed to know
    Of a swell society female fake
    Whose mother-in-law will undertake
    To prove that her seventh husband's niece
    Has stated in a printed piece
    That she has a son who has a friend
    Who knows when the war is going to end.
3. In this lengthy letter Pearson says, among other things, "I am the mute inglorious Milton who fathered that famous fugitive fragment of fine and fancy foolishness."
4. This is the total circulation claimed by Pearson in the letter of December 22, 1944.
5. Harlan Daniel has told me that the song appeared in at least two gospel songbooks published during the 1920s. He could not recall the titles of the songbooks or their exact year of publication. The version he recalled seeing may well be the same as that collected by Lillian Crabtree.
6. Telephone conversation with Pearson's daughter, Agnes Fox, North Wilkesboro, North Carolina, April 21, 1985.
7. Mrs. Fox said that Pearson did not like the fact that his poem had been set to music without his permission, but he did not pay much attention to the matter initially.

8. The date of release is an estimate based on the discography in Cohen 1975:62–66. The date of Whitter's recording, however, is well documented.
9. Letter from James Larkin Pearson to Register of Copyrights, Library of Congress, dated January 6, 1926. For this and other letters cited in this article I am indebted to Janet Atwood, Librarian, James Larkin Pearson Library, Wilkes Community College, Wilkesboro, North Carolina.
10. Letter from Ralph S. Peer, General Sales Manager, Okeh Record Division, General Phonograph Corporation, to Hayes & Jones, Lawyers, North Wilkesboro, North Carolina, January 9, 1926.
11. Letter to James Larkin Pearson from Robert H. McNeill, Attorney at Law, Washington, D.C., August 3, 1926.
12. Ibid., August 27, 1926.
13. Ibid., September 26, 1926.
14. Ibid., December 8, 1926.
15. Ibid., March 3, 1928.
16. Letter to James Larkin Pearson from Walter C. Darby, New York, March 16, 1928.
17. James Larkin Pearson, "When to Get a Copyright." I have found no evidence that this undated manuscript was ever published, but on page two Pearson says, "Believing that the incident may be of interest to other writers I am writing this brief account of it for The Writer's Monthly."
18. Some of the recorded lines are a bit difficult to understand but there is no problem with those cited here.
19. Although the songbook has a copyright date of 1933, this version of "The Dollar and the Devil" has a copyright of 1932 listed. As already stated, the McCravy's filed for copyright in 1930. Possibly the copyright was taken out in their behalf by Peer.
20. I have this information from Charles Wolfe in a telephone conversation of May 13, 1985. Wolfe interviewed a member of the McCravy family several years ago who made a comment to this effect. Frank and Jim are both dead.
21. Had I been able to locate any of the songbooks in which the number reportedly appeared, the number of printings would of course be greater.
22. Nashville, 1936.
23. These three books and an article, written by folklorists, deal at some length with the relationship between popular poetry and popular song, yet the relationship is still overlooked by many folk song scholars.

REFERENCES

Cohen, Norm

    1975   Henry Whitter: His Life and Music. John Edwards Memorial Foundation Quarterly 2 (Summer):57–66.

    1981   Long Steel Rail: The Railroad in American Folksong. Urbana: University of Illinois Press.

Green, Archie
- 1970 Hear These Beautiful Sacred Selections. Yearbook of the International Folk Music Council. Urbana: University of Illinois Press.
- 1972 Only a Miner: Studies in Recorded Coal-Mining Songs. Urbana: University of Illinois Press.

Logsdon, Guy
- 1989 "The Whorehouse Bells Were Ringing" and Other Songs Cowboys Sing. Urbana: University of Illinois Press.

McCravy, Frank; McCravy, Jim
- 1933 The Frank and Jim McCravy Album of Fireside Songs. New York: Southern Music Publishing Company, Inc.

Nicolaisen, W. F. H.
- 1983 Theodor Fontane's "Sir Patrick Spens." *In* James Porter, ed., The Ballad Image: Essays Presented to Bertrand Harris Bronson. Los Angeles: Center for the Study of Comparative Folklore and Mythology, University of California, pp. 3–19.

Olmsted, Clifton E.
- 1960 History of Religion in the United States. Englewood Cliffs, N.J.: Prentice-Hall.

Pearson, James Larkin
- 1971 Autobiographical Sketch of James Larkin Pearson. *In* My Fingers and My Toes: Complete Poems of James Larkin Pearson. Nashville: Ingram Book Company.
- 1924 Pearson's Poems. Wilkesboro, N.C.: Pearson Publishing Company.
- 1949 Plowed Ground: Humorous and Dialect Poems. Guilford College, N.C.: Pearson Publishing Company.

Williams, Miller
- 1986 Patterns of Poetry: An Encyclopedia of Forms. Baton Rouge and London: Louisiana State University Press.

Wood, Clement
- 1936 The Complete Rhyming Dictionary and Poet's Craft Book. Garden City, N.Y.: Garden City Books.

NARRATIVE

5

PEARL BRYAN IN LEGEND

RONALD L. BAKER

On February 1, 1896, the headless body of Pearl Bryan was discovered near Fort Thomas, Kentucky. Pearl was the daughter of Alexander S. Bryan, a prominent farmer in Putnam County, Indiana, who lived a half-mile south of Greencastle. Pearl's second cousin, William Wood, son of a local minister, introduced Pearl to Scott Jackson in 1894, the year Jackson and his mother moved from Jersey City, New Jersey, to Greencastle, where Jackson's brother-in-law taught at DePauw University. In the fall of 1895, Jackson moved to Cincinnati to attend the Ohio College of Dental Surgery, where he roomed with Alonzo Walling, whom he had met earlier in Indianapolis.

The details of Pearl's last days are sketchy, but apparently when Pearl informed Jackson that she was carrying his child, Jackson, through William Wood, arranged for Pearl to meet him in Cincinnati. In late January 1896, Pearl told her parents she was visiting a friend in Indianapolis, but instead she went to Cincinnati, where Jackson housed her in the tenderloin area and allegedly attempted to induce an abortion with a drug. According to other accounts, Jackson previously had sent William Wood instructions for preparing abortifacients and administering them to Pearl in Greencastle; however, the home remedies were unsuccessful, so Pearl went to Cincinnati for a surgical abortion. It was also reported that an attempted surgical abortion killed Pearl and that she was decapitated to prevent identification of the body.

Although there appears to be some truth to the reports that Pearl or someone else attempted to induce an abortion with drugs or home remedies, a "criminal operation," as newspapers of that day called a surgical abortion, apparently was not attempted, for the coroner's report of February 2, 1896, revealed that Pearl was carrying a healthy fetus in its fifth month and that Pearl and the fetus were alive when she was beheaded. At the site of the murder the volume of blood spilled and pattern of bloodstains indicated that Pearl's heart was still beating when her head was severed.

At Newport, Kentucky, Scott Jackson and Alonzo Walling were tried and convicted of murdering Pearl, and were hanged from the same gallows on March 20, 1897. During the trial, Jackson and Walling each professed his own innocence, accused each other of murdering Pearl, implicated other people, including William Wood, and changed their stories right up until the executions. Walling and Jackson were convicted largely through circumstantial evidence, notably the testimony of a hackie, George Jackson, who said he drove Pearl, Jackson, and Walling from Cincinnati across the Ohio River to the secluded spot near Fort Thomas, Kentucky, where Pearl was murdered. According to George Jackson, Pearl appeared to be drugged when he drove them to Kentucky, and the coroner's preliminary examination confirmed that cocaine was present in Pearl's system.

Pearl's head was never found in spite of extensive searches by officials and dramatic pleas by her family. Walling testified that Jackson had planned to cut up Pearl's entire body and dispose of the pieces in Cincinnati sewers, but he claimed Jackson succeeded only in severing the head and disposing of it to prevent identification. Pearl's body was identified anyway by her dress, which her sister said she helped make, and by her shoes, which had the imprint of a Greencastle shoe store, Louis and Hays. The fact that Pearl was webfooted also assisted in the identification.*

In *American Folklore and the Historian,* Richard M. Dorson (1971:

---

*This account of Pearl Bryan's murder and the trial of Jackson and Walling comes mainly from newspaper sources, notably the *Daily Banner Times* (Greencastle, Indiana), February 1, 1896, to March 21, 1897, and the *Daily Banner* (Greencastle, Indiana), July 26, 1969. See also Cohen (1973:8–38) and Wilson (1939:15–16).

170) claims that "murder is one of the complex events in community life most apt to generate local traditions." He notes that "ballads inspired by murders have been gathered together by Olive Woolley Burt in *American Murder Ballads and Their Stories* (New York, 1958), but folk legends of murders have not been assembled or much investigated." Dorson's generalization still holds true in the case of Pearl Bryan, for ballads inspired by her murder have received considerable attention, yet legends generated by the murder have not been examined.

The details of Pearl's murder and the subsequent trial and execution of her convicted murderers were widely publicized in newspapers over a thirteen-month period and became a lively topic of conversation, especially among people living in Indiana, Ohio, and Kentucky—the three states in which the tragedy unfolded. The sensational newspaper accounts of the murder of Pearl Bryan and the subsequent trial inspired several ballad types—three, according to Laws (1964:191–93); six, according to Cohen (1973:45). As John Vlach shows, however, there were basically two forms of Pearl Bryan ballads popular in tradition between 1913 and 1935: the historical form, "which closely follows the events of Pearl's murder," and the nonhistorical form, which, with "few major differences," conforms to the popular "Jealous Lover" (Laws FI) type of murder ballad (Vlach 1972:48–54).

Cohen compares newspaper and ballad accounts of Pearl Bryan's story and concludes that newspapers gave ballad makers ready-made material for two different ballad formulas: the murdered-girl formula, which concentrates on the crime, and the criminal-brought-to-justice formula, which concentrates on the punishment. "Given the nature of the crime," she says, "the ballad muse could choose only the murdered-girl formula" (Cohen 1973:113), which she encapsulates as, "Artful man seduces innocent girl; when he learns she is pregnant he lures her to a secluded spot; she offers little resistance to being murdered; he abandons her body" (Cohen 1973:39). This kind of murder story appeared frequently in American newspapers in the late nineteenth and early twentieth centuries, so the pattern was well established in American journalism as well as in American balladry. For example, in New York in 1891, Carlyle Harris, a medical student, had an affair with Helen Potts and poisoned her when she became a threat to his ambition of becoming a physician. In 1906 in Cortland, New

York, Chester Gillette seduced Grace Brown, and when she became pregnant he drowned her in Big Moose Lake. In 1911 in Hyannis, Massachusetts, the Reverend Clarence Richson courted Avis Linnell, who also was pregnant when he poisoned her. This same formula was developed in well over 800 pages by Theodore Dreiser, who based his popular 1925 novel, *An American Tragedy,* on the Gillette case (Swanberg 1965:253–54).

Although the heyday of Pearl Bryan ballads in oral tradition has passed, legends of Pearl Bryan have continued to be reported in Indiana from the 1930s through the 1970s. The earliest legend text is from the Indiana WPA collection, and nine texts and five fragments are in the Indiana State University Folklore Archives. In addition, the Indiana University Folklore Archives has two legendary accounts of Pearl's murder in letters (Shore 1963a, b) written in 1963 by a retired public school music teacher to Joe Hickerson, then folklore archivist at Indiana University. Some legend informants recalled hearing a Pearl Bryan ballad, but none could remember any words of the song. For instance, the music teacher wrote to Hickerson that "a song was written regarding the event and existed in several forms. I have heard it sung many times as late as 1910 when I attended college [DePauw] over there [Greencastle]. But I can remember neither the words nor the music as it was sung by the [N]egro employe[e]s at the sorority house where I worked" (Shore 1963b).

Pearl Bryan legends follow neither the murdered-girl nor the criminal-brought-to-justice pattern. Whereas in Pearl Bryan ballads, details from newspaper accounts of the murder and trial were selected and reshaped to conform to a common ballad formula, Pearl Bryan legends have details selected and reshaped to conform to common legend conventions. For example, Cohen (1973:105) notes that one "example of the influence of the murdered-girl formula" on the Pearl Bryan ballads is "in the increasing tendency, in time, for the ballads to suppress the fact that Pearl was beheaded. In other murdered-girl ballads victims are stabbed, beaten, drowned, and poisoned, but beheading is not in the repertoire of allowable methods. Thus, a sensational feature of a story, which one might expect to be memorable and hence retained, is quick to disappear." Accordingly, in one Pearl Bryan ballad type, Cohen's Pearl Bryan II, "Headlessness appears in eleven out of twenty-four texts up to 1927, in two out of seven between 1928 and 1938, and not at all after 1938" (Cohen 1973:73).

Half of the legend tellers, however, stress that Pearl's body was found headless, and generally they develop familiar legend motifs: a headless ghost looking for her head in two versions, a misty form that screams and becomes a half-rotted face in one version, and a "white thing" that screams in another. Pearl's ghost does not haunt the scene of the tragedy, though, as ghosts often do; it walks closer to the locale where the legend was collected. For example, the earliest Pearl Bryan legend text from Indiana, collected by WPA workers in the 1930s, had Pearl Bryan's ghost searching for her head in Mooresville, Indiana, approximately 150 miles from Fort Thomas, where Pearl literally lost her head over Scott Jackson, and at least thirty miles from Greencastle, where Pearl was born and buried:

> Traditionally, there is a ghost story that has survived in Mooresville for the last forty-four years. It was in the year 1892 [sic] that Pearl Bryan of Greencastle was murdered and beheaded; her head was never found, so she was buried headless. Many communities for miles around that point reported seeing a white, headless, will-o'-the-wisp appear in marshes and lowlands or other dark and lonely places. Many of the younger folks of Mooresville and vicinity were no exception to that rule.
>
> At a point where the road—now State Road 267—made a sharp turn immediately after crossing a little stream, every so often, especially on dark, foggy, and rainy nights, a headless woman dressed in white could be seen in the center of the road at this lonely, dark spot and could be heard to exclaim in a weird, piercing shriek, "Oh, I've lost my head." When anyone tried to approach the apparition, it would suddenly disappear.... [Baker 1982:130–31]

In a text collected more recently in Greencastle, Pearl's ghost has moved closer to her home:

> Pearl Bryan was a student at Depauw [University, in Greencastle, Indiana]. She had two male medical students as two of her many friends. Somehow Pearl got pregnant, so the two medical students offered to give her an abortion. They ended up killing her and disposed of her body in Kentucky. Somehow the body got sent back to her home. One legend has it that her head was on, and another has it that it was off. In this situation, the family decided to

bury her without a funeral in Forest Hill Cemetery. People started to ruin her gravestone by chipping off pieces. But even today people see her [ghost] walking across the road in front of her house; some say with her head, and others say without her head. [Baker 1982:131]

In an attempt to give the Pearl Bryan legends more immediacy, a tendency is to set the crime closer to the home of the storyteller and his or her audience. The setting of the crime is Greencastle in seven texts, though in two of these texts the body is disposed of in either Kentucky or Ohio. Only two versions are set in Kentucky, and single versions are set in Mooresville, Indiana, and Bloomfield, Indiana. In one account the crime is committed in Ohio and the body is disposed of in Kentucky. Thus, a version in the Indiana State University Folklore Archives collected from an elderly Linton woman in August 1974 is set in nearby Bloomfield rather than 60 miles away in Greencastle, where Pearl lived, or 160 miles away in Kentucky, where Pearl died. Moreover, the dental students from Cincinnati become a local physician:

Her name was Pearl Bryant. And they hunted for her and hunted for her, and they suspected a doctor over there.... She was pregnant, and... they all suspected an old man, an old doctor over there. And there was a song about that; there was a song. I couldn't think of what it would be, but... it ought to be someplace. It was Pearl, Pearl Bryant. And there should be a song about that. And people around Bloomfield should know about that. Lot more than I do. Never found her body; never found anything. But there was a song about it. I think it was in... more in Bloomfield. The girl might have lived out in there someplace, but the doctor was at Bloomfield, I believe—an old doctor. 'Course, you couldn't use any names or anything. That's as much as [I know]... That's not a legend; that's the truth!

In other texts, however, the villain in Pearl Bryan legends is not an "old doctor." In three accounts, the villains are two medical students, and in two accounts, they are three DePauw students—theological students in one of these texts. In two other texts, the villains are a student and a cab driver. In single versions, the villains are two college students or simply "these fellas."

Following Pearl's murder, a rumor that Scott Jackson raped Pearl when he worked in a local dentist's office made the rounds in Greencastle. Supposedly, when Pearl complained of a toothache, Jackson invited her to the office when the dentist was away, drugged her with cocaine, and raped her. According to an article in the Greencastle *Star Press* on March 2, 1896:

> Miss Bryan was in the office, in an unconscious condition, for almost two hours.
> People here are of the opinion that it was there that Scott Jackson ruined the girl whom he is now alleged to have murdered. It is stated, on quite reliable authority, that this story will be told on the witness stand at the proper time. [Cohen 1973:18]

The story, however, was not told on the witness stand, probably because the coroner's report stated that Pearl had not been raped (Cohen 1973:10) and because the dentist, Dr. Gillespie, maintained that Jackson did not have the keys to his office on the date that the alleged rape occurred. Although the rape rumor did not find its way into any of the Pearl Bryan ballads, apparently because it does not comply with the ballad formulas, it does appear in two legend texts. Here is one account collected in Greencastle in 1968 (Indiana State University Folklore Archives) and set in a more recent decade as well as in a more familiar locale:

> Back in the 1940s, after the war, there was a famous murder around Greencastle. A DePauw coed was picked up by a taxi driver and a student from ISU [Indiana State University], or probably it was Indiana Central Normal then. The taxi driver was from Terre Haute, too. This girl was really wealthy. It was sort of mysterious. No one knew if she was dating this student or not. They took her out to this covered bridge with intent of rape. They got her out, tore her clothes off, and raped her. They were going to kill her, but she broke loose and ran across the bridge screaming. They chased her and caught her at the other side of the bridge. They killed her with knives and took her apart. They strung the pieces out, hoping they wouldn't be found.
> To this day, once a month or so, on the day of her death she runs back through the bridge. Some have seen a white misty form running through the bridge screaming. Reputable people have seen it.

John Torr saw it. He said it was like a cloud; it floats through, screaming. When it got to the car window, he said it was like a girl's face, half-rotted. One time it caused an accident. Some people won't go through the bridge, even though it is a shortcut.

Both men were caught and got the death penalty. The remains of the girl are buried in Forest Hill Cemetery. They had to take the tombstone down because tourists came to see the grave and took chips as souvenirs. Now it's an unmarked grave. They are supposed to put the marker back up in 50 years.

In most versions (nine), however, the crime is murder without rape, and the date, when it is mentioned (only four other times), is closer to the 1896 date of the murder: 1892, 1893, 1895–97, and "about 1897" in single versions.

In newspapers and ballads, Pearl is portrayed as a young, simple, innocent, trusting, and helpless victim—the stereotypical murdered girl. In legends, however, her youth and innocence are not stressed, and in one text she appears to be an older woman who delivers and murders illegitimate children of DePauw coeds:

> There was this woman who lived in Greencastle, and her name was Pearl Bryan. College girls who went to DePauw [University] and who got pregnant would go to see Pearl when the baby was about to be born. Pearl would deliver the babies, and she would keep them. A few years ago under Pearl's house there were a bunch of baby skeletons found, and nobody could explain this. [Baker 1982:130]

Other Pearl Bryan legends, unlike Pearl Bryan ballads, stress Pearl's pregnancy and the attempted abortion, as in the following text from the Indiana State University Folklore Archives collected near Greencastle in Cloverdale in May 1972:

> I don't know how many tombstones they had to put up. People would come and chip off a piece of the tombstone for a souvenir. Then they had to put up another, and pretty soon it'd be chipped away. She was pregnant, and they was a couple of medical students. They was gonna get rid of it some way or another, but she died. It killed her.

A few legends deal more factually with the murder and stress realistic motifs, such as souvenir hunters who chip off pieces of Pearl's tombstone. One informant who claimed she "didn't know the story well enough to tell it" gives a fairly concise account of the Pearl Bryan story:

> I was only five years old then. I remember everyone talking about it. I can't make much of a story out of it. How they did it . . . she went away with these fellas, and they went on a trip to . . . I think it was Kentucky . . . and she was murdered. But I don't know the story well enough to tell it. That's been so long ago. They found her body in a river somewhere in Kentucky, but her head was gone. They never did find her head. They identified her by the shoes she was wearing, which was from Allen Brothers store in Greencastle, and that store was right over there on the corner where Penney's are now.
>
> They put up monuments to her grave, good-sized ones. And the first one they chipped it away, and they put up another one, and anybody that would come to Greencastle . . . that was such an unusual story . . . that any stranger that would come to Greencastle would inquire about it and find that her grave was here, and they'd go out and chip off the monument. After they chipped the second one away, they quit puttin' 'em up and haven't put anymore up since. She was distantly related to me. [Baker 1982:129–30]

As we have seen, four of the legend informants mention that souvenir hunters chipped away pieces of the headstone, but supernatural motifs also cluster around Pearl's grave. One informant said that grass would never grow on Pearl's grave (Shore 1963b), and in April 1971 a thirty-two-year-old housewife from Greencastle said in a text now in the Indiana State University Folklore Archives that when she was in high school in the early 1950s members of her class performed rituals over Pearl's grave in Forest Hill Cemetery. She said the rituals were performed during the day because students weren't allowed in the cemetery after dark. She explained that the rituals were like seances, an attempt to communicate with the dead. She couldn't remember what was said at these rituals because the words changed with each ritual performance.

Newspapers continued to nourish the Pearl Bryan material in the oral tradition, for after the publication of a front-page article on Pearl Bryan in the *Greencastle Daily Banner* on July 26, 1969, several traditions about Pearl circulated in the Greencastle area. The article featured a 5½–x–7½–inch photo of the Bryan burial plot, with an umbrella stuck in the ground to mark Pearl's grave. The caption read: "Pearl Bryan's headless remains lie in Forest Hill Cemetery without the headstone, which was the victim of souvenir hunters. She was interred there March 26, 1896, the victim of two men who committed one of the most infamous crimes of the era. The grave was marked for the photograph by the umbrella." Following publication of the article, a belief circulated that the stone had mysteriously disappeared because a headless body should not have a headstone (Indiana State University Folklore Archives). Tales about Pearl's ghost also were revived after the appearance of the newspaper article in 1969, for people who happened to be in the cemetery on dark nights claimed they saw a headless ghost near Pearl's grave. People also tried to locate Pearl's house. According to one account in the Indiana State University Folklore Archives, Pearl lived in a house on U.S. 231. Following Pearl's death, her parents kept Pearl's room just as she left it, and no one entered Pearl's room. Later, according to the informant, a fire totally destroyed Pearl's house.

Although Pearl Bryan ballads and Pearl Bryan legends are different in style and narrative content, they may share at least one common function. Pearl Bryan ballads, typical of the "Jealous Lover" type, often end with a moral, as in the following example from Indiana:

> Young ladies, now take warning; young men are so unjust;
> It may be your best lover, but you know not whom to trust.
> Pearl died away from home and friends, out on the lonely spot;
> Take heed; take heed! believe me, girls; don't let this be your lot!
> [Leach 1955:790]

Although the legends are not so overtly moralistic, apparently young women in Greencastle were often reminded of Pearl's fate as a warning to be good. In April 1971 a retired Greencastle schoolteacher and native of Putnam County, Indiana, recalled in a text in the Indiana State University Folklore Archives that when she was a schoolgirl, teachers warned young women to remain virtuous and told them the story of Pearl Bryan to illustrate what happened to girls who were "too familiar with boys."

A major question in folk genre research is "whether folklore genres have specific properties that attract certain subject matters and reject others" (Roth 1980:141). Since the ballad usually is defined as a narrative folk song and since the legend is generally considered a genre of narrative folk literature, it would appear that the narrative content in ballads and legends would be similar, but I have attempted to show that ballad makers and legend makers who drew on common newspaper accounts of the murder of Pearl Bryan selected, reshaped, and added different details to the story to conform to the respective conventions of ballad and legend. Accordingly, as Vilmos Voigt (1976: 493) has noted, "even the most creative storyteller has to follow the principles of the genre.... This means, any individual storyteller (as long as he follows the rules of the genre) has some room for his personal innovations, but only within the existing structural esthetic framework." In other words, as Nicolaisen has written, "The folkcultural response offers the expected but—and this is important—while shunning startling and disconcerting innovation, leaves room for judicious improvement and personal creativity" (1984:269).

REFERENCES

Baker, Ronald L.
    1982   Hoosier Folk Legends. Bloomington: Indiana University Press.
Cohen, Anne B.
    1973   Poor Pearl, Poor Girl! The Murdered Girl Stereotype in Ballad and Newspaper. Austin: The University of Texas Press.
Dorson, Richard M.
    1971   American Folklore and the Historian. Chicago: The University of Chicago Press.
Indiana State University Folklore Archives
    1968–78   Nine texts and five fragments of legends about Pearl Bryan collected over a ten-year period. Department of English, Indiana State University, Terre Haute, Indiana.
Laws, G. Malcolm, Jr.
    1964   Native American Balladry: A Descriptive Study and a Bibliographical Syllabus. Philadelphia: The American Folklore Society.

Leach, MacEdward
    1955   (ed.) The Ballad Book. New York: A. A. Barnes and Company.

Nicolaisen, W. F. H.
    1984   Names and Narratives. Journal of American Folklore 97:259–72.

Roth, Klaus
    1980   Genre, Subject Matter, and Culture: A Comparative Study of English and German Jocular Ballads and Tales. *In* Nikolai Burlakoff and Carl Lindahl, eds., Folklore on Two Continents: Essays in Honor of Linda Dégh. Bloomington, Indiana: Trickster Press.

Shore, Eddie B.
    1963a   Letter to Joe Hickerson, February 20, 1963. Bloomington: Indiana University Folklore Archives.
    1963b   Letter to Joe Hickerson, February 27, 1963. Bloomington: Indiana University Folklore Archives.
    1963c   Letter to Joe Hickerson, March 7, 1963. Bloomington: Indiana University Folklore Archives.

Swanberg, W. A.
    1965   Dreiser. New York: Charles Scribner's Sons.

Vlach, John M.
    1972   "Pearl Bryan": Two Ballads in One Tradition. Journal of Country Music 3:45–61.

Voigt, Vilmos
    1976   Towards a Theory of Genres in Folklore. *In* Linda Dégh, Henry Glassie, and Felix J. Oinas, eds., Folklore Today: A Festschrift for Richard M. Dorson. Bloomington, Indiana: Research Center for Language and Semiotic Studies, Indiana University, pp. 485–96.

Wilson, Ann Scott
    1939   Pearl Bryan. Southern Folklore Quarterly 3:15–19.

Works Progress Administration
    1935–39 Indiana Files of the Federal Writers' Project, Cunningham Memorial Library, Indiana State University, Terre Haute, Indiana.

6

THE LEGEND CONDUIT

LINDA DÉGH

A conversation in Hungarian occurred in Kakasd, County Tolna, Hungary, on July 17, 1986, at the home of Mátyás ("Matyi") Szentes, 67 years old, grandson of János, son of József, nephew of János and Mrs. Zsuzsanna (Palkó) Zaicz, all venerated community storytellers.[1] Present were his wife Mári, 65, and three guests: Mr. Ambrus Ágoston, 76, a tailor specializing in traditional costumes (he now makes costumes for the Kakasd Székely Folk Ensemble); Mrs. István (Anna) Kerekes, 69, a neighbor; and Mr. Ádám Sebestyén, 61, church singer, bank director, founder and head of the Folklore Ensemble, native folklorist, author of several collections and a book of local history. As he usually did when socializing or seeing clients in his office, Ádám carried his tape recorder to fulfill his mission "to save the Székely culture." The sixth participant was Emma, 59, Ádám's wife and partner in ensemble work, a self-consciously active bearer of tradition.[2]

It was Sunday afternoon, time for a relaxed get-together for old-timers who preferred a chat—gossip and remembrance—about olden times to a ballgame on TV. As had been my custom since 1980, I was staying with the Sebestyéns, whose hospitality is unsurpassable and whose cultural knowledge is inexhaustible. Living in their home gave me a fairly complete picture of their views, politics, likes and dislikes, as well as their relationships with other villagers, but at the same time it deprived me of hearing other voices. Like all communities, Kakasd had its factions and rivalries, and the Sebestyéns are too prominent and powerful not to antagonize some members of the community. The Sebestyéns influenced friends to take their view of community affairs, and to form opinions on the basis of their version of information about people and their acts. Once the family had to leave town for a week while I stayed alone in the house. Before they left, Emma told me, "Well, I'm sorry for you because now that we will be gone, people will not talk to you. It is because of us that folks are so friendly. Remember the woman who turned around when she saw you coming? She did not want to meet you." As soon as they left and I walked across the street to take a picture, the woman in question came forward to the fence. "You are avoiding us? How could you forget us?" she reproached me. Indeed, the situation was the reverse of what Emma led me to believe would happen. I saw many others during their absence with whom I could not have renewed our friendships had they been there. For years Ádám never succeeded in tape recording Mrs. Palkó's cousin's tales—the 86-year-old illiterate woman always was busy when he visited. Yet, this woman told me two long, elaborate magic tales without any persuasion when she dropped in at her daughter's house where I happened to be.

People knew me and were open with me because I published the tales of their beloved storyteller, Zsuzsanna Palkó. Her book (Dégh 1955) went hand to hand in the community, and her printed stories became the source of new variants. I was an old friend they remembered from Kakasd. They recalled that I was there during the miserable years of hunger, deprivation, and humiliation; they told little anecdotes about how they saw me back then and what they thought of other folklorists and students who came with me. People in Kakasd thought that by my publishing Aunt Zsuzsa's book, I had a role in their ethnic survival. Rozália Kóka, a native grade-school teacher turned professional folklore performer, found my address in Bloomington, Indiana, and sent a letter to me thanking me for "saving the precious Székely folk tradition."

The people of Kakasd met many other folklorists during the years and came to understand what they were doing. They themselves became active collectors, preservers, popularizers, and propagandists of their own culture. The modern bearers of this culture—archaic and modern at the same time—view themselves as insiders but are able to distance themselves and take the outsider's position to create a new ethnic identity (Dégh 1989:290–95).

That Sunday afternoon my presence was no handicap to the formation of a "legend-conduit."[3] I have used this term to draw attention to the way that legends are transmitted through a conduit composed of people of shared interest, distinct from those for other kinds of folklore expressions. As I conceived it, the line of transmission of legends which is created by affinities between certain people forms a legend conduit: by this term it is understood that contact is established between individuals who qualify as legend receivers or transmitters. But this definition also assumes that there are persons who qualify neither as receivers nor transmitters of legends. These individuals may be the "passive bearers" of legends, or else they simply may not choose to communicate legends. The same persons, however, might prefer to narrate other genres and participate as "active bearers" in different communicative sequences. The forms of oral transmission are extremely diverse, and the eventualities of affinity between people and folklore are just as multifarious (Dégh and Vázsonyi 1975:211).

The six people who gathered for this chat were all old-timers. All were born in the Bucovinian village of Andrásfalva and remembered the traumatic flight and relocation to Hungary; they were neighbors and relatives by blood, kinship or godparentship. They shared a common world view that includes devout Catholicism, trust in God's providence, and belief in evil supernatural forces. Nevertheless, new experiences made them adapt to the modern world and question the persistence of traditional knowledge about consequences of misconduct and the reciprocity of crime and punishment. As elderly people, they also shared a concern about proper behavior to win God's mercy at the time of death.

With everyone participating, the conversation was lively and solidified at points into thirteen legends. Typically, the stories—some told by one person, some by two coproponents, most supported by additional information or questions from the others—were well known and probably often repeated in the community. The numerous referents mentioned by name also show that speakers brought well-established experiences into the conversation, although not all the experiences were developed into legends.

Small talk preceded the telling of legends. The participants discussed Matyi's health; he was treated for ulcers and just returned from the hospital. Then the discussion shifted to eternal themes: young people do not listen to their elders, boys date the wrong girls.... Emma's youngest son just did. This brought up the first story by Mári. Then, after two legends were recited, a break came. Fulfilling an old promise to Ádám, Mrs. Szentes told three tales she learned from her father-in-law. Another shift in the conversation occurred after the third story. It was a spin-off from the story of a jealous husband who became possessed by an incubus, reminding participants of a local scandal ending in tragedy, the death of a wife beater and the wife's descent into lunacy. It was then easy to return to the previous theme, picking up the thread of accounts regarding wise women and luminous evil spirits. The legend exchange ended when the last string of stories about the controversial church-oriented ritual of fasting, praying, and confessing to destroy a human being led into talks about people who achieved a "good death" without suffering because of constant fasting and praying with the rosary.

Under the given conditions, the presence of a folklorist known as culturally distant did not prevent the airing of embarrassing social conflicts or practices of magic and countermagic in the context of devout Catholicism. My translation from the recording of the Hungarian conversation follows.

THE CONVERSATION

1. Playing Ghost[4]

MÁRI: The Fábiáns, the old fox and his boys. All gigantic, big men. So tall. It was the second son. The first was Pál, then came Andy, and the others after. Well, this András dated Anna Kalinka—I really don't know what their other name was....[5]

MATYI: That's how they called them, okay?

MÁRI: I know them by *this* name. No... it was not Kalinka, it was Kocziba. Mrs. Miska Kocziba. Miska Kocziba was the father.

MATYI: It was Miska, ya.

MÁRI: He was so much into this dating that he went to see her early in the evening and it was midnight when he came home. Old Fábián did not want to let him, he was against his son's dating. But this went on for long. He did not listen no matter what they said. He left early in the evening and who knows when he came back? "Well," said his father, "I'll scare him good." "Oh, no," said the woman, "you can't. It's not possible." They had a stable with a roof that was high in front but low in the back so that the cart could haul up the hay. And the old man took a white sheet and wrapped it around himself. It got dark, there was no moon. He waited until András showed up at the end of the street. He came as far as the gate but did not dare to come in. He ran back from the gate. And his mother called after him: "What's the matter? Why are you standing there? What is the matter?" "Well," he said, "there is a big ghost on the roof of the stable," he said, "it may be two meters tall." "Gee," she said, "we haven't seen it, we were asleep." All right. She brought a lamp. He never dared again to stay that long. He went home early. "Yes, yes," said uncle Miska, "after eleven the ghosts walk. From eleven till midnight, one o'clock, this is their time," he said, "that's when they walk." They did not tell him that he did it, he was the ghost. They laughed at him; after he got married, they told him. "That's how the ghosts are." Uncle Fábián was some character.

2. *Towel Mistaken for Ghost*[6]
MATYI: Oh, our neighbor is also something. He said they went to bed—he was still with his first wife, not this Márta who is now his wife. Well, he says, they went to bed. They weren't paying attention, he said, there was a full moon. Once they see that at the corner of the door, there is a man standing. I was looking, but I didn't dare to get out of bed, not for the mercy of the Lord. It's a ghost, on the door. There was a candleholder, he said, and he threw it that direction to have the ghost leave, to scare it away. But, he said, it just stayed there. Until morning, he said, "we did not dare sleep or get up, we just stayed under the comforter. "Then," he said, "in the morning, the cocks began to crow," he said, "thank God, it's morning." It still did not leave. "This must be something... I got out of bed, took one of the candles and lit it—what is it? Oh Lord, Creator," he said, "it was a towel on a nail, folded halfway down [laughs]. I didn't sleep all night." The old man could tell some stories.

(There followed three tales by Mári.)

3. *The Lüdércburján*[7]
MATYI: In the war of [19]14 they dug trenches. There were many. There was a man among them, had a beautiful wife. He wasn't ugly either, but his wife was a beautiful woman. And his friends

constantly teased him [about this and that]. Because they could not go home, they had to work at the trenches, dig. My father was also there. They said to him: "Your wife is sleeping with a soldier." He took it so much to his heart that they joked with him; he ultimately imagined that they are right, that it is true. Then, when he went home, he believed that while he was away his wife slept with another man; he visits her... this was her... whatever. The war came to its end, but this was still constantly on his mind. Finally what happened was that the *lüdérc* began to haunt him. So that at night, during the day they did not bother him, but when evening came, the *lüdérc* was always there. Others did not see it, but he did. Wherever he went, he went with him, this spirit. They called it *lüdérc*. Well, time passed, much time. They told him to put a rosary to his neck and pray. It was all in vain, the *lüdérc* was always with him. No matter what he did, he could not get rid of it. So, there was an old woman, well, she was already 80 years old and she has learned from one even older. They used to collect herbs in the fields before, how to say it, they picked all sorts of crabgrasses and leaves and made medicine of them.

EMMA: They do it still.

MATYI: So she went there, this old woman, she said she will find the *lüdércburján*. She picked half a sack full and took the *lüdércburján* home: "Don't worry my son, this will chase the spirit away; it will never come again." So, she put it into a big cauldron, she cooked it for so long that it could have been eaten as a salad. They took it off the fire to cool, not to... to cool it. When it cooled down she put it into a vat and poured it on the young man. She washed him. Once the *lüdérc* comes to the window he screams and groans through the window so that he almost fell into despair.[8] They drove him away from the man, because they bathed him in the *lüdércburján*. It could not get to him because he was washed off from him; this *lüdércburján* washed the spirit off him. So the *lüdérc* split. But when they did not treat him with the *lüdércburján*, did not give him the bath, the spirit came every night, he could not rest. The man had it always on his mind.

ÁDÁM: It followed him everywhere?

MATYI: Yes, every evening... true or not? But he saw him all the time.

EMMA: What did it look like?

MATYI: I don't know because I have only heard about it, I did not see it.
EMMA: And what did this *lüdércburján* look like?
MATYI: I don't know, I just heard about it. I asked Mrs. Barabás. She said that it was true. What it looked like she didn't know either. Aunt Erzsi, she only heard about it. This is how they chase the *lüdérc* away, with picking the *lüdércburján* and having the victim bathe in it.
ANNA: And there are things like this, just the same.
ÁDÁM: Not in Kakasd; that is, I haven't heard about it. But for sure, there are in County Tolna.
MÁRI: Very likely there are.
MATYI: There are those who believe in this and there are those who can heal it. In County Tolna, they did not say which village. I heard that there is a man or a woman who does this and can heal it.
EMMA: The daughter of Péter Ráfi was it...
ÁDÁM: Near Kalocsa... or where? The same place where this folklorist lives.

4. *The Woman Who Can Talk to the Dead*[9]
EMMA: They talk to the dead. They still do it. Zsuzsika, the daughter of Mári Lengyel, told me, her son hanged himself, the brother of Tera. On a tree. And this hurt his mother so much, so much that she heard it in Szekszárd, from whomever I don't know, that this woman can talk to the dead. The mother went to see her with Mári, oh, she told me where it was....
ANNA: I know where she was. I heard about her, they mentioned her on TV. And what did she say?
EMMA: Well, and then they got there, they didn't let them in. That she is busy...
ANNA: This was the mother-in-law of Zsuzsika...
EMMA: Well, and then, he hung himself. And she said she will go because she suffers so much from the pain. She had three sons, all died, one by one. And she became mentally sick...
MÁRI: This Zsuzsi remarried...
ÁDÁM: Her husband died. One of the sons had lung cancer. The other son had colon cancer, and the third hung himself.
MÁRI: Oh, oh... what pain a mother has to endure!
EMMA: So then she went there and she said there were so many people

in front of the house—there aren't so many at a funeral. But, she said, the police were already there.

ANNA: We saw it on TV, long ago...

AMBRUS: She is a seer.

EMMA: I know where she lives. I saw her address.

ANNA: And she had the guts to go and speak to her.

EMMA: Zsuzsika told me that her mother-in-law will accompany her. They did go but they weren't let in.

ÁDÁM: This seer, she made lots of money.

EMMA: There were two women who went to see her, one took her daughter along. And one of the two did not believe. And when they got there, "Don't come in, you don't believe." And then, the other woman was allowed in. And she started to talk, and as she talked, it was recorded on a tape. And the flower came out from the vase, and the dead appeared and they conversed. The woman cried terribly on the tape, we just listened.

MÁRI: Wasn't that horrible?

ÁDÁM: They play these at national conventions.[10]

EMMA: Oh dear!

[Long conversation about family violence. Heated discussion about sex life and the decline of decency and morality in the community.]

EMMA: Listen, pardon me for saying this, but there is much dirt around the church. Once this, then that, first it was the trouble with Jóska Ferenc, then with Mrs. Márton, with Laci, with Jóska Kák...

MÁRI: Whew, really too much...

EMMA: I am telling you, this neighborhood is damned; all drunks, cocks, and whores.

5. *Fishing Adventure*[11]

MATYI: My grandfather...

MÁRI: No, I didn't know him. He was my godfather. I didn't know him, only heard of him.

MATYI: He went fishing, the old Zaicz. And I don't know, maybe you remember... here in the... there were some houses, there was an old straw-roofed house, and an old woman lived there. Well, they found this old woman dead. She had nothing but a cat and the cat was found there dead. Of course nobody went there for long before they found her. Well, she had no relative and they buried her. Then they tore the house down. And this smoky reed that covered the roof was there, in a heap. Old Kozma and my grandfather, they were fishing there. They put the net down. They fished all night, they stayed out there. They made fire, they burned this... smoked their Miska-pipe. I remember, this was a pipe made of clay, burned black. They took out a little tobacco, spit into it, squeezed it into the pipe, and placed it into the fire to bake it a little. This was so strongly baked that it became one hard lump. It was so strong that if a fly came by, it fell into it. And they sat there, smoking. But then the fire needed more fuel. And my grandfather told him: "I am getting some of this reed, pal." He took his jacket, walked to the heap, and picked up as much as he could cover with his jacket and threw it on the fire. This smoky reed was better than dry straw; it burned slow and kept the amber glowing. They sat down and talked. He said that the flame was gone, only the amber glowed. Once my grandfather said to the old man that the amber was rising up. Old Kozma was staring at it. He said, "Pal, what is lifting off the ashes?" and he backed up, "What is it?" And, he said, suddenly a big frog came out from the ashes. But he, he said, they were already jumping up and started to run toward the hill. (The women laugh.) And he said, "I took this fishing axe. I said, 'I'll get this frog.' And when I wanted to hit it," he said, "it jumped and turned into some kind of black bird. It flew towards Kostich. Because there Kostich was not far." (The women groan.) "It flew away high and threw sparks, fire," he said. Well, "it was a *lüdérc*," he said. This is what they told, these old men. But this was true. "Then, my pal came back. The other night," he said, "I went again. But when I reached the hill, there was a balloon there. Like the ball of an ox." In front of him, as he walked on the road. And he said, he had this fishermen's axe with him to scare animals away from him. Well, he said, "I grabbed the axe and threw it toward the ball. The ball transformed into a bird and threw sparks after him—it was a *lüdérc*." Well, that's what they said. How come they were then and they aren't now?

AMBRUS: I can't understand why don't they exist now?

6. *The Candle*[12]
MÁRI: They were brothers.
EMMA: Sure?

MÁRI: With the brother of my father, this thin old man.
EMMA: Yes, yes. I knew him. And then he died. Then Gizi came to my mother in the evening—Sunday evening, I'll never forget—to ask for a sheet.
MÁRI: Wasn't this the father of Jóska Daradics?
EMMA: They wanted to make a wake and they did not have enough bedsheets. Then my mother took an embroidered sheet[13] out of the trunk—we still have it—and gave it to Gizi. And when my mother walked with her to the door, she said: "Look Aunt Mári, up there, there is a candle." But then we also dashed out, because... we went to see it... and it was a little light that floated. Our János was already gone...
MATYI: He died earlier.
EMMA: No, he died in '42, your grandfather, the year we got married.
MÁRI: I was still a little girl.
ÁDÁM: It was in '43, the year I was drafted.
EMMA: He was almost 100 years old.
MATYI: Yes, yes, I remember him, he was 98 years old.
ÁDÁM: He served twelve years and two months.
MATYI: I also saw the candle, and told it to Péter Benda; he didn't say it is not true. I saw it at the Ágoston's [house], you know where it is.
EMMA: Yes, sure, I know.

7. *Another Candle*[14]

ÁDÁM: Buriáns were their neighbors, behind them there was a...
EMMA: Big empty house.
ÁDÁM: And we talked there in the gate, a few houses below, us young people. And suddenly it came down behind the house nicely, down the window of the shed. There it stopped for a while, then it flared up and went down into the shed. That is, it disappeared. It was there for about 10 to 15 minutes. And we watched: Now, what next? Then, after a while it got tired of it and left the same route it came. But it was around midnight. Then—not a grain of oat could be put into my ass as I walked home.[15] I did not dare to go places.
MATYI: There is no such thing now?
ÁDÁM: Yes. They also call it a firebug but that's different.

8. *White Woman Ghost*[16]

MÁRI: He, our Márton, used to date a girl in the big village. And it always took him late to come home. It struck midnight when he reached the rectory. "And as I walked home," he said, "there is a white clothed woman coming across. But her dress rustled loudly, but it was pure white. And then, I even greeted her 'good evening' but she did not call back. Neither did she speak, she just walked on." And he said: "When I went further, it occurred to me that this is a dead woman who came out of the grave, that's what it is." And he said, "It may be the spirit, because the dead cannot come out of the body," he said. "And I went home so... I never stayed out until twelve, never."

9. *The Bouncing Frog*[17]

MÁRI: And once, they started a fight at Mátyás Begyi's. On a Sunday. I was a little girl then. But I could pay attention to everything. They sat down to talk but the talk ended in a squabble. Then, when he was leaving, on the way home he noticed that a frog is bumming in front of him. He said that he kicked the frog and the frog disappeared. He fell into despair and started to scream from fear: "Uncle Mátyás, Uncle Mátyás, please help." They were already in bed. "What is it, what do you want?" "Please come because I am falling into despair." And my godfather didn't see anything, but he had to take him home to save him from desperation. And he also made peace between the two.

ÁDÁM: That was the good side of it (laughs).

MÁRI: Yes. Well, the world is full of these things.

10. *Frog That Turns into a Dog*[18]

MATYI: István Barna told me that he went home from Jóska Gyurkacska and as he was on his way, he dated Erzsi. And they talked until midnight, and he said that when he went home, a big frog jumped on the side of the street. It was brown, frog-shaped, it jumped. When he reached home, it turned itself into a big dog at the gate, it accompanied him all the way. But he didn't dare to stay out after midnight after that. I think he also kicked it. I think the man would tell about this anytime.

11. *Fasting on Rózsi Diszke*[19]

EMMA: And then, they fasted on the mother of Jani Fábián.

MÁRI: Who? Who fasted on her?

EMMA: You know who it was.

MÁRI: Her aunt.

EMMA: Yes, her aunt.

MÁRI: I know that. 'Cause Rózsi Diszke was an old maid. And she lived across grandmother's.

EMMA: Yes.

MÁRI: I heard it from Mommy.

ANNA: Yes, I heard it too.

MARY: And then, she, the first wife of Gergely Fábián...

ANNA: Yes, yes.

MARY: Her aunt. Someone was dead and there was the funeral. In the rear side of the house there was a little window and she knew the way, because she used to go there, and took those many bedsheets, the decorative woven ones, and I don't know what else.

EMMA: She stole...

MÁRI: I don't know what, but a lot. But no one knew who was doing this. And she pledged a fast on Rózsi Diszke. And before the fasting was completed, the woman...

EMMA: She was well, only she began to have headaches, but suddenly she dropped down and died.

MÁRI: Kicked the bucket.

EMMA: And then they made a wake and many people went.

ANNA: I heard it, we were neighbors.

EMMA: But Mrs. Dobondi also came as she heard the news that Rózsi... they told that they caught that woman who stole. They told her that Rózsi died, she had no sickness, she was a big, fat, healthy, pretty blond, young, and she died all of a sudden. And all the women came. They bathed her and made a vigil. Once, she said, they were about to go home. Mrs. Dobondi told me this. Yes. She said that they did not gather enough courage to go home. "Wait, Boris, I'll see you home if you are afraid." 'Cause she said that she is terrified. Because she knew that she was involved (laughs), not lily white. Red. She did not want to go and Manyi went with her. And she says that at a big meadow, all along the way, a frog leaped after them. But she did not see it, only Aunt Bori saw it. Then she spelled it out. "Bori, say it after me, say it: If God is with me, nobody is against me." And Bori said it, but, she said, "I did not dare enter her house." "Come in Aunt Erzsók, please, come, sleep here with me." Well, she went in and Bori made a bed for her. And they closed doors and windows. And a big black... I don't know what went on the window. Aunt Bori saw it but Erzsók didn't. And it made her fall into despair. "Oh my, I'm dying, I'm falling into despair"—she kept wailing. Mrs. Dobondi told me all this, she said: "Had your mother not been with me I would have died of fright." Then, she said, she prayed there with her. They prayed and prayed until they both fell asleep. Nothing happened then. "I stayed until daylight with her," she said. "Oh my," she said, "if András comes home he will spank me if he finds out that I got home at dawn." So Boriné took her home. She was a little guilty. She bought the stolen goods from Rózsi, she knew well, why this woman had died. That's why she was scared.

MÁRI: I heard it from Mom because we were neighbors...

ÁDÁM: They said Rózsi Diszke was an old maid, or a widow?

MATYI: An old maid. She picked up much stuff.

12. Pledge on Mrs. Fazakas[20]

EMMA: You know what? There is such a thing in Kakasd still. I just heard it. That's what this Anna Sebestyén told me. It's Mrs. Lajos Fazakas, the thief, that's why she cannot die.

MÁRI: Why?

EMMA: Because Anna's goose down was lost. And the police were after it. They investigated, and she was charged. And it came to nothing. And then she, Mrs. Sebestyén, pledged a fast. Aunt Anna told me that herself when I went to see her. A very quiet woman. She did not learn the truth until she did not do it. She is a regular churchgoer, she, I am sure, confessed it to the priest.

ÁDÁM: Really?

EMMA: The priest would not tell what someone confessed. But Anna told us that she told the priest that she did the pledge. Since that time she does not attend services.

ÁDÁM: She hasn't been in church for long.

MÁRI: I heard it from Kicsi András Jóskáné, from Erzsi.

EMMA: I heard it from the mouth of Aunt Anna herself. But God beware, one does pass on such a thing. I would not tempt the Lord. I was so shocked when I heard about it. Half of her head was gone, half of her skull; it is a miracle that she still lives. Oh, you haven't seen her?

MÁRI: No, I haven't.

ANNA: It's a wonder that she still lives.

EMMA: You see, because she cannot die.

MÁRI: No.

EMMA: And this whole thing came up that you told us how sick Mrs. Lajos Fazakas is, that she was gone. Because Anna Sebestyén asked whether she died. And she cannot die because she is cursed. Because Mrs. Sebestyén put a curse on her.

MATYI: Is it true or not?

EMMA: It is true. Aunt Anna told me. She told where she went and how she did it, that she committed herself to the pledge that God enlightens. But she did not tell me more. That God enlightens. And the police caught her.

ÁDÁM: And the pledge she did for God to enlighten her first, but that she resisted and did not confess, it made her suffer.

EMMA: And you know what? She went around to borrow, or to buy feathers. And Teri Kovács, who she asked, told her: "Máriné, do you hear me? What kind of an idea is this? I saved my down for so many years, for myself, for my grandchildren, how should I give it away?" She wanted much, for a whole bed, as a load. And she said: "No, I won't give, neither will I sell it; there are people to whom to give." She would never return it to me, never. Well then, soon enough, a few weeks or a month later, she took sick. She was cursed. Her whole body was covered with wounds. And she told everybody that it was because she did not give her feathers. And then, Máriné's (Aunt Mári's) daughter wanted to get rid of the feathers. She offered it to me. I needed them badly, for the girls, you know, I could have also used some to renew my bed, but I wouldn't buy this. It was cheap and beautiful, incredibly clean, swan-white but...

MÁRI: I wouldn't have touched it, no matter what.

EMMA: They took it to the market and the Gypsies bought it for an incredible low price. God beware... who wants that stuff with the curse on it? They got a good bargain but I wouldn't have anything to do with it. Ten kilos, 800 forints the whole stuff.

MÁRI: Oh my!

EMMA: I needed it, but... no, no, that someone should put a curse on me? This was tampered with, who knows what token was among the feathers? Not for money, let alone for free, she wanted to give it to me. Then Laci (her son) told me: "Mother, why didn't you buy it, we also need new filling." Then Erzsi came, she wanted to take it too. No-no-no! Then, she wanted me to store it for her, in the attic. But I didn't want to have anything to do with it. Somebody would have accused me of taking something out of it. You understand? She brought a huge sack and asked if I can keep it for her. "What is in there?" I asked. "Sheets, some pillowcases, stuff." "Take it away, don't leave it here, get out of here as fast as you can walk! Go!" I didn't want to be suspected and cursed. Am I right?

13. Son Cursed by Father for Stealing[21]
AMBRUS: Yea, they really put curses on people. It's dangerous. This man's eye flowed out...
EMMA: Sure, because he stole from his father.
ÁDÁM: It was the Berkóci boy.
EMMA: Right.
AMBRUS: I knew the son and the old man. I know where they lived.
ÁDÁM: Then you know how it happened.
AMBRUS: Yea. The son took something from him and the old man fasted him out. As I heard it, he confessed it to the priest and he had to do penitence. He had to pray at the grave of his father every night at twelve o'clock. If it was true or not, I don't know. I tell you sincerely, as far as I'm concerned, I don't believe in this fasting.
MÁRI: But the fasting is true. And the good Lord answers to the prayer.
ÁDÁM: In desperate situations. I don't know, I can't answer the question.

☙ ☙ ☙

At this point I threw in the question: how does one do the fasting? All five answered and the response was so intense that the tape recorder could not make it intelligible. Only Ádám's voice came through.

☙ ☙ ☙

ÁDÁM: They have their animals fast with them. Once a week you do it for six but mostly seven weeks, each time, on the following day. You take a candle to the church and pray that God enlightens you about who did the ill to you. When this person is identified—in vision or dream—he can be confronted and if he doesn't repent, the curse takes full effect.

❧ ❧ ❧

From there the conversation took a new direction, picking up the idea of praying and fasting. The group felt it was important for God to bless them with a "good death." Participants mentioned people who prayed every day with the rosary and fasted once a week at least, or, in general, fasted every day by refraining from eating meat and rich delicacies. They commented that these people were deeply religious and never suffered from torturous sicknesses but died by falling asleep in old age.

THE CONDUIT AND ITS CONTENT

The conversation of six people in the presence of a mostly listening seventh on this summer afternoon had the potential to form a legend conduit. They were talking about general concerns, not "folklore." As folklore informants they were used to being interviewed on diverse genres and topics. This time, however, it was only Aunt Mári who offered tales (as folklore) to Ádám's tape recorder. Otherwise, the discourse addressed not folklore, as they knew it, but problems that excited them in the past and continue to create social conflicts in the present. They were concerned about the decline of morality, particularly in the neighborhood of the church (the center of the community, where the most prominent families live), distrust between marriage partners, adultery, family violence, disobedience of children, thievery, magical manipulation, and misuse of religious rituals. Based on a deep religiosity and on a profound belief in witchcraft, evil spirits, and the return of the dead that constitute the pillars of the folk religion of the Bucovnia Székelys, the legends emerged as illustrative examples.

Not all stories were rounded out and polished: several remained brief, sometimes merely a statement, a question, or an unfinished sentence, as they deal with familiar matters known to everyone in the village. The immediate relevance provides a common frame of reference which keeps the statements intelligible. Therefore, I would not feel comfortable forcing the finished and unfinished stories into the artificial categories we create to distinguish the ways they are narrated. The folklorist's knowledge of "more complete" variants—memorates, fabulates—should not interfere with the native sense of story. More importantly in this conversation, the broader social and cultural and the closer intertextual contexts along with the speakers' personalities and relationships to one another reveal how legends emerge as the conduit is activated.

The participants were not telling legends *qua* legends (folklorists did not teach them what a legend is). They talked, gossiped, and created an atmosphere that accommodated the climate of the legend. The exchange was lively: many people were named—those who knew about the occurrence, saw something, were involved closely or distantly, or just talked about the occurrence—and perpetrators and victims were also identified. Through introductory, connective, and conclusive dialogues, speakers revealed community affairs, personal relationships, world view, and formal and informal religiosity. All speakers were well educated in supernatural belief by experience and by knowledge of tradition. All were good speakers, intelligent, and interested in formulating speech when it comes to reciting folklore, yet none of the stories seemed to be artistically polished. Speakers retold communally known "events" about diverse kinds of hauntings, first to prevent young people from staying away from home at night and second to show that misconduct results in haunting by evil spirits. This legend exchange showed that legends that are so relevant to reality, as in the case of the Kakasd people, cannot become polished and standardized texts distanced from actual concerns.

The sequence of stories displayed smooth logical connections. The first, Mári's negative legend, was based on positive belief, that is, firm knowledge of ghosts or evil spirits that follow, haunt, and cause people to fall into "despair," as is shown in numbers 3, 4, 7, 8, 9, 10, and 11. Playing ghost reminded Matyi of a laughable incident (no. 2) a couple experienced when they realized that their ghost was imaginary. In no. 3, following Mári's three tales, Matyi brought up a story about the expulsion of the *lüdérc*, the most feared incubus figure of the Bucovina Székely folk religion. This figure is usually described as a male or female demon who sleeps with and tortures people who have lost their marriage partner. The figure appears as a chicken, turns itself into human shape, but travels as a candle, a ball of fire, or a burning shaft, trailing sparks as it flies (see Hoppál 1969:402–17; Dégh 1965: 83–85). It was the first time that I heard about the *lüdércburján* and the administration of a bath by a wise woman. The story provoked questions that Matyi could not answer. He had no firsthand knowledge but rather had heard it from others. The theme raised interest in wise women, and the conversation switched to the healer-seer, in connection with a Kakasd suicide case and the quest of the bereaved mother who wanted to talk to the dead son.

In no. 4, a visit to the nationally known, media-propagated seer, commonly known as the *putnoki asszony* (woman from Putnok), was related in the conversation that continues the theme of family violence and community morality with reference back to no. 3, also a story of jealousy. With no. 5, the incubus theme continued with Matyi's version of an incident told to me by Mrs. Palkó in 1949 and again in 1954, and by György Andrásfalvi in 1948. This version, more than 30 years later, was a faint reflection of the earlier ones by two master storytellers who happened to be daughter and grandson of the experienced old János Zaicz. If names were missing and the real cause of the *lüdérc*'s appearance—the woman was a witch with a spook-cat—was not mentioned, the story in this skeleton form still raised interest and was worth retelling. In no. 6, Emma mentioned a candle (the incubus flies looking for its victim), and in no. 7 Ádám tells about seeing one. In no. 8 Mári told about a white woman revenant scaring her brother; in no. 9 Mári again brought up the ghost-frog's stalking as punishment for fighting, and in no. 10, told by Matyi, the frog turns into a dog as scarer of the late dater.

Here the talk shifted to another emphasis: "pledging" for divine revenge. Spooks continue to appear, this time as punishment for the pledge. Emma and Mári were the proponents of the first fasting story (no. 11), which Emma has referred to when mentioning in no. 6 that she loaned a sheet for the wake because the thief took the woman's linen. Emma (with involved comments from the others) continued with the case of Mrs. Lajos Fazakas (whom I knew personally, and visited during her nine-year-long sickness). The great complexity of fasting was also shown in the final brief story by Ambrus. I should add that the practice (or talk about it) continues to this day in Kakasd. According to local gossip, untimely death is never accidental but someone's "secret pledge." Victims of fasting plague the faster as ghosts (or *lüdérc*) and return to complete unfinished business.

The conduit as presented here illustrates an approach to folklore from the viewpoint of human creativity. It was developed in field ethnography, based on the study of individual performers, their audiences, communities, and encompassing traditions. It is encouraging to know that I can agree with Bill Nicolaisen that "... creativity and tradition, individual and community, together produce vital variability thus keeping alive the very items that their integrated forces help to shape" (Nicolaisen 1990:45).

I want to close with a quotation that neatly summarizes all that has been stated by me and by other students of narrating in many diverse ways: "No story exists out there by itself. The story takes life from two of us: the teller and the listener, writer and reader, actor and watcher, each a necessary participant in the creation of the space in which the utterance takes life, in which all our utterances take life" (Jackson 1990:416).

NOTES

1. Szentes is an assumed name Matyi chose to replace the German-sounding family name Zaicz. As a gesture of loyalty, others with foreign names also Magyarized their names: another Zaicz, the storyteller Andrásfalvi, memorialized the name of his beloved native village, Lajos Rancz became Lajos Rózsa (Rose); and Károly Daradics became Károly Derék (honest, brave).
2. For details on the Sebestyén family see Dégh 1989:302–3.
3. Although the term "conduit" in its lexical usage refers to a man-made channel for the conveyance of a substance, I proposed its application to denote a spontaneous way of oral transmission. It was especially important to distinguish the transmission sequence from what is known as "channel" in several disciplines. See Dégh and Vázsonyi 1975 and 1976, and Dégh 1979. I have also pointed out that if the legend is transmitted by members of the legend conduit, we might as well assume that jokes, for example, are dispensed through the joke conduit by a sequence of witty people; riddles pass through the riddle conduit made up of riddle fans; and tales progress through the tale conduit shaped by different types of storytellers, and so forth. This assumption is logically plausible and may be supported by careful observation of the social transmission of folklore. Furthermore, within a single genre—as the tale, for example—different types, type clusters, episodes, minor incidents, and even motifs and formulas have their own conduit, as they are all subject to transmission (Dégh and Vázsonyi 1975:212).
4. Playing Ghost (Mrs. Szentes. For easier reading and reference, I have given titles to each narrative). I call this a negative legend because it negates the belief in revenants but is told in a legend climate. An antilegend, with its rational emphasis, intends to attack and destroy the legend as a whole; the negative legend substitutes one belief for another (see Dégh and Vázsonyi 1978:254–57). This particular negative legend is

based on a belief in revenants. The father assumed the role of the ghost as a disciplinary measure to make his son give up his date. The father's effective imitation of a ghost must mean that he conformed to the community's belief in ghosts; his masquerading did not preclude the possibility that at other places and on other occasions ghosts may appear.

5. The frequent reference to names in this transcribed text reflects the cultural practice of name-giving among these people: use of nicknames and informal names showing descent and both maternal and paternal lineage to identify individuals. There is also a ritual and supernatural aspect to replacing a name earned at baptism (Lörincze 1948).

6. Towel Mistaken for Ghost (Mrs. Szentes). This story is an addition to other innumerable scares people had at night, on the road, on the village street, near mills and cemeteries, or at home in bed mistakenly identifying shadows and sounds as supernatural agencies culturally known to them. Realizing that the vision was not a ghost is a relief, indeed, and a contributing factor to a tellable story for amusement, without undermining the belief in the existence of revenants.

7. The *Lüdércburján* (Mr. Szentes). An unusual version of the widespread legend complex prominent in the Hungarian language territory about the incubus figure (MI F.491, Bihari 1980:135–39). The male or female demon who sleeps with and tortures people who have lost their marriage partners appears as a chicken, turns itself into human shape, and travels as a candle, a ball of fire, or a burning shaft, shooting sparks as it flies. For the semantic model of the legend, see Hoppál 1969:402–17; for the developmental process, see Dégh 1965:83–85.

8. *Kétségbeesés* ("desperation, to fall into despair") is equivalent to "his heart broke" and appears as a general concept in the sense of causing sudden, unexpected collapse and death by a scare or shock from an evil spirit through magic manipulation.

9. The Woman Who Can Talk to the Dead (Mrs. Sebestyén). Bihari, 1980: 96–98. The famous fortune-teller and seer was fined several times for her quackery and fraudulent dealings with gullible clients. She also became the subject of folklore research: the story of her life and activities was made into a film documentary and published in a book by Domokos Moldován (1982).

10. Reference to the annual convention of the Hungarian Ethnographic Society that Ádám attended.

11. Fishing Adventure (Mr. Szentes). Bihari 1980:138. This is a late variant of an adventure Mrs. Palkó's father had in 1927, fishing in the Suceava River with his buddy, Orbán Kozma. Mrs. Berétyi, the Romanian widow who lived alone with her cat beyond village boundaries, was a witch who was buried by a charitable Romanian peasant. The appearance of evil spirits (frog, bird, burning shaft, or a fiery ball: *lüdérc*) was caused by the disturbance and the use of the witch's remains. Mrs. Palkó's two texts (Dégh 1955, 1989:135–37) and Andrásfalvi's version (Dégh 1960, 1989, no. 75)

in which he included himself as a participant, are elaborate, masterful accounts of skilled narrators.
12. The Candle (Mrs. Emma Sebestyén). Bihari 1980:139. A widespread concept known as foxfire is referred to here as the *lüdérc* that travels in the air (Dégh 1965:84).
13. Called *ablakos lepedö*, made particularly for the bier.
14. Another Candle (Ádám Sebestyén). Bihari 1980:139. This is also a *lüdérc* story: young people spot it traveling to someone's place. Even the innocent bystanders are scared out of their wits.
15. A common Hungarian proverbial expression for being scared.
16. White Woman Ghost (Mrs. Szentes). Bihari 1980:28, 32 [MI E 425.1., 424.1.3].
17. The Bouncing Frog (Mrs. Szentes). Frog pursues quarrelers [MI 211.13].
18. Frog That Turns into a Dog (Mrs. Szentes). Bihari, 25.
19. Fasting on Rózsi Diszke (Mrs. Szentes and Mrs. Sebestyén). See Mrs. Palkó's story and comments about current practices (Dégh 1989:13, 300). According to belief, the dead are rendered restless because the survivors force them to return by fasting. A narrative collected in 1954 bears this belief out. "The woman began fasting so as to harm her husband. The man had beaten the woman badly and she was very bitter about it and then started to fast, and then he had to stay in bed for twenty years" (Dégh 1989:300).
20. Pledge on Mrs. Fazakas (Mrs. Sebestyén). This story's personalization is remarkable. The homemaker's treasury, particularly the highly valued goose down, is at stake. The whole household, the domain of women, may be destroyed by such tampering.
21. Son Cursed by Father for Stealing (Mr. Ágoston) [MI E 415].

REFERENCES
Bihari, Anna
    1980   Magyar Népmonda Katalógus (A Catalogue of Hungarian Folk Belief Legends). Budapest: MTA Néprajzi Kutatócsoport.
Dégh, Linda
    1955   Kakasdi népmesék. Budapest: Akadémiai Kiadó (1960).
    1965   Processes of Legend Formation. Laographia 13:77–87.
    1979   "Conduit." *In* Kurt Ranke, ed., Enzykopädie des Märchens. Handwörterbuch zur historischen und vergleichenden Erzählforschung, vol. 3. Berlin: Gruyter, pp. 124–26.
    1989   Folktales and Society: Story-Telling in a Hungarian Peasant Community. Expanded Edition with a New Afterword. Translated by Emily M. Schossberger. Bloomington: Indiana University Press.

Dégh, Linda; Vázsonyi, Andrew
- 1975 The Hypothesis of Multi-Conduit Transmission in Folklore. *In* Dan Ben-Amos and Kenneth Goldstein, eds., Folklore: Performance and Communication. The Hague: Mouton, pp. 207–52.
- 1976 Legend and Belief. *In* Dan Ben-Amos, ed., Folklore Genres. Austin: University of Texas Press, pp. 93–124.
- 1978 The Crack on the Red Goblet, or Truth and Modern Legend. *In* Richard M. Dorson, ed., Folklore in the Modern World. The Hague: Mouton, pp. 253–72.

Hoppál, Mihály
- 1969 Adalékok a lidérc hiedelemmondakör szemantikai modelljéhez. Ethnographia 80:402–17.

Jackson, Bruce
- 1990 The Perfect Informant. Journal of American Folklore 103:400–16.

Lörincze, Lajos
- 1948 A tolna-baranyai (volt bukovinai) székelyek névadási szokásaihoz. Ethnographia 59:36–47.

Moldován, Domokos
- 1982 A halottlátó. Filmek, dokumentumok. Budapest: Gondolat.

Nicolaisen, W. F. H.
- 1990 Variability and Creativity in Folk-Narrative. *In* Veronika Görög-Karady, ed., D'un conte... à l'autre: La variabilité dans la littérature orale. Paris: Editions du Centre National de la Recherche Scientifique, pp. 39–46.

7

NARRATING IN SOCIALIST EVERYDAY LIFE:
Observations on Strategies of Life Management in Southeast Europe

KLAUS ROTH

Discussing localized narrative humor in his presidential address to the American Folklore Society, Bill Nicolaisen drew attention to its power "to cope with a puzzlesome, sometimes threatening past" (1984:267). Nicolaisen's consideration of everyday narrating as a behavioral "register," commenting on appropriate occasions and conditions for a folk-cultural response, is a significant contribution to analyzing the meaning of emergent modern folklore in various national and local settings (see Nicolaisen 1970, 1980). My concern here is examining narrating as a creative folk-cultural response in the socialist settings of Southeast Europe, particularly Bulgaria.[1]

When Alan Dundes published an edition of Romanian political jokes in 1986, he identified a number of parallel motifs in the joke traditions of other socialist countries and the Third Reich, and confirmed some important observations on function and meaning which other scholars had gained from the materials of totalitarian countries.[2] Political jokes, Dundes wrote, "provide a much-needed outlet for any people forced to be silent" (Dundes 1986:10). A decade earlier, Lutz Röhrich wrote that the political jokes of the Third Reich functioned as "a mental outlet and regulator for the reestablishment of emotional balance" and thereby indicated "a kind of escape into a world of illusion" (1977:211). On the one hand, political jokes as a "substitute of . . . free speech" gave expression to "inner resistance to the totalitarian state," but on the other hand the laughter about the joke also gave "pleasure, satisfaction, relief" (1977:211).

Dundes (1986) holds additionally that political jokes give "an unrivaled view of the daily conditions prevailing behind the Iron Curtain." Their satirizing caricature of reality often presents "a clearer account of living conditions than what is customarily reported in conventional political and economic studies" (Dundes 1986:10), and Röhrich even suggests that on the basis of jokes "one could write the history of a whole era" (1977:215). An even more intimate relationship between the everyday reality of totalitarian states and the necessity of political jokes is pointed out by Dundes who suggests that telling political jokes can often provide vital and indispensable emotional help: "In fact, it is partly these jokes which make it possible for oppressed people to survive" (1986:13).

The observations made by Dundes, Röhrich, and other scholars are undoubtedly essential and useful. However, by limiting their studies to just one narrative genre, the joke, they are able to grasp only one segment of the far more complex reality of everyday narrating in totalitarian countries.[3] The scholar visiting one of the socialist countries in Europe will soon realize that jokes are only the tip of the iceberg, that they are only the most prominent expression of a phenomenon that might be called the "narratization" of everyday life. To an extent hardly comparable in Western industrialized countries, socialist societies are characterized by the narrative representation and transformation of everyday life. The recordings of local folklorists, as well as my own observations and field recordings in southeast Europe, indicate that this transformation of everyday experience into oral communication occurs in a fascinating variety of forms and expressions and with an impressive degree of re-creativity. These materials further show that in this narrative tradition, which has developed over four decades of real socialism, new forms and contents have developed alongside old ones, and modified traditional genres exist side by side with new genres that have already grown traditional.

Apart from humorous genres like the joke, the anecdote, the jest, and the parody, we find such forms in everyday narrating as
- fairy tales and parodies of fairy tales;
- legends, particularly modern urban legends;
- narratives of extranormal events and superstitions;

- "horror stories" told by children and adolescents, in recent years as the retelling of the plots of horror movies;
- rumors, gossip, news, and information;
- didactic and illustrative stories (exempla);
- proverbs, sayings, aphorisms, and riddles;
- graffiti and slogans;
- biographical and autobiographical stories;
- poems and songs;
- public obituaries (as printed narratives).[4]

Not only is the variety of genres striking, but also the realism and the topicality of the narratives as well as the speed of their creation and the rapidity of their diffusion. Jokes and stories, rumors and sayings about topical events, crimes, or catastrophes usually appear within hours after the event and are known by everyone only days later. They are told by members of all social groups, especially by urban dwellers. Direct face-to-face communication dominates in all narrative situations, but, depending on the contents, indirect communication over the telephone can also play an important role.

The social contexts of this everyday narrating are almost exclusively informal ones. Depending on the genre as well as the degree of familiarity and trustworthiness of the participants, one can differentiate three kinds of contexts; each of them determines different narrative contents and strategies of narration. The *private,* intimate context, i.e., the family or the circle of close relations and friends, plays the most important role. A similar degree of intimacy and narrative interaction can be established after a phase of mutual testing in *semipublic* informal contexts, such as among neighbors and colleagues, in schools and universities, in work brigades, and in the military. *Public* informal contexts used to be less significant, because narrating in the streets, in buses and streetcars, in restaurants and cafes, in lines in front of shops and department stores, at sports events, and in other public places was risky. A whole series of jokes makes it clear that the teller must beware of unknown persons. Since the fall of 1989, however, this attitude has changed considerably. People talk freely in public, and they discuss and tell stories without any restrictions.

What is needed in view of this impressive abundance and creativity of storytelling is the inclusion into narrative research of the entire field of everyday narrating in socialist countries. If we want to gain a deeper understanding of the psychological, social, and cultural problems that find expression in everyday narrating, it is no longer sufficient to limit the scope of research to a few prominent genres. For the narrators, the question of genre is in most cases irrelevant, anyway; what counts for them are the intentions and meanings of their stories, their functions in everyday life. Accordingly, I will concentrate on the function and meaning of this intense, "thick" everyday narrating as well as on the tightly knit networks of verbal interaction in Bulgaria.

Before discussing the more serious aspects of everyday narrating, however, its relevance and function as *entertainment* has to be emphasized, the pleasure of storytelling and the need for diversity and excitement, for laughter and comedy, are strong even under unfavorable political conditions. The innumerable jokes, anecdotes, rumors, and other narratives told every day are evidence of this human need. Another basic and obvious function of everyday narrating is emotional and social *relief*. The telling of a political joke or a rumor about political leaders provokes liberating laughter and may thus provide emotional relief to the individual; this kind of laughter has serious undertones, though, for "if man laughs to keep from crying, then the more he laughs, the more he needs to cry" (Dundes 1986:14). On the other hand, storytelling may provide social relief and may thus function as a social or political safety valve and as a substitute for political action; in these cases it serves as an "escape into...inward emigration," as Röhrich has shown for the political jokes of the Third Reich (1977: 211).

Another decisive function of everyday narrating is the representation, interpretation, and *management of reality*. In socialist countries, people have to cope with two different kinds of reality: the promised or faked reality presented by the state through the official media and the harsh reality of socialist everyday life. The two realities are represented, interpreted, and managed with different narrative forms and strategies. The attitude toward the "official" reality is characterized not so much by direct opposition or criticism, by anger or aggression toward "them," but rather by unmasking irony and satirizing "correction." The humorous narratives,[5] rumors, or even poems[6] give unofficial interpretations of, and make ironical or even extremely cynical comments on, political, social, and economic reality. They thereby ridicule and symbolically reduce the totalitarian power of the state. The following joke ridicules an earlier attempt at economic reform in Bulgaria:

In a village a man returns from a political meeting and his wife asks him what the meeting was about. "It was about the 'New Economic Mechanism' and the neutron bomb," he tells her. She asks him for an explanation. "That is very easy to explain. We are sitting around the table and the table is set. With the neutron bomb, we are gone and the food will remain. And with the 'New Economic Mechanism' it is the other way 'round." [Collected in Sofia, December 1989]

The narrative treatment of "real" everyday reality differs considerably from the treatment of "official" reality, because here the stories must help people cope with the unsaid and the unspeakable, with political taboos, fear, and the daily experience of shortages and scarcity. The problems of daily subsistence, the dread of the encroachments of the state, the dangers of technical innovations and urban life, and the fear of many children being left alone at home while both parents are at work—all these anxieties find their expression and outlet in a frightening wealth of "horror stories" of children and adolescents as well as in modern urban legends and in stories of grisly experiences (cf. Brunvand 1981, 1984). Over the last few years there has been a marked increase in stories about supernatural events and beings and in prophecies of catastrophes and political upheavals. These stories have only recently caught the attention of some Bulgarian folklorists (Savova 1987). The following example serves as an illustration of the popular genre of "horror stories":

A girl buys herself a blue piano. She had wanted such a blue piano for a long time. The first night she lies down to sleep and the next morning they find her strangled. The following night her sister lies down to sleep (in the room where the piano stood) strangled as well. The third night their mother. Finally only the father remained. He lay down, but he did not sleep and saw a hand coming out of the piano. And he cut it off. The next morning he went to take the piano back to the shop, and he notices that the salesman is without hands. [Savova 1987:142]

Adolescents commonly tell the preceding contemporary legend along with many others, but the legendry is not exclusive to this age group (cf. Brunvand 1981, 1984). Adults have their share of contemporary legends in everyday narrating. An example is the following legend told by a woman who insisted that the story had been reported on the radio:

> A family moved into a new apartment in "Mladost 4" (one of the new suburban residential areas with high-rise blocks in Sofia) and the first night they laid their child to sleep on a sofa. In the morning they found it dead. No traces were to be found, only some small spots on the child's neck. They called the police and searched, but nothing could be found. A unique murder. But what came out in the end: the parents finally found out with the help of an investigating commission that in one of the partitions of a newly bought cupboard there was hidden a polecat or a badger who had bitten and killed the child. [Recorded by E. Savova in Sofia; cf. Brunvand 1981:90–98 and 160–71]

Before the beginning of communist rule, the southeast European societies were largely closed peasant societies based on the family and on informal groups as social units. Social groups with a high degree of inner cohesion, or "high context groups," dominated economic, social, and cultural life. After 1944, the socialist economy, the dissolution of the few formal associations and groups, and the continuous threat posed by the secret police and other institutions further strengthened the role of the family and of informal groups and even turned them into a means of survival. Apart from the exchange of material goods and mutual aid, the steady flow of information through intense everyday narrating plays an essential role in the maintenance of these vital networks of "connections" with relatives, friends, neighbors, and colleagues. In a recent study of the consequences of kindred relations in Bulgaria, Eleanor Smollett has emphasized the social and psychological relevance of informal private communication. "Within households," she writes, "there is a good deal of concerned, emotional conversation about...relatives and their affairs" (1989:129), because "relatives rely heavily on each other for finding appropriate contacts to help unravel some of life's complexities—information is needed...about apartments, or about job possibilities..." (1989: 130). The cohesion among relatives and friends is continually maintained by the passing on of news, by talks and discussions, and by the telling of jokes, anecdotes, autobiographical stories, or other narratives, which of course mean a considerable investment of time and emotion.

These informal communicative networks show that everyday narrating serves another important function in socialist societies, namely the dissemination of *information* and instruction about real life. In view of the fact that the censored mass media are largely restricted in their ability to cover the problems of socialist life, everyday narrating acquires a pivotal role in the transmission of important and often vital information. This informal flow of information, based largely on hearsay, usually takes the form of rumor and gossip, but frequently information is passed on in such traditional forms as sayings and exempla, jokes, anecdotes, parodies, and riddles. Every person is woven into networks in which informal and unofficial information about all matters relevant to everyday life travels rapidly from mouth to mouth. In the first place, information is handed on about the availability of scarce goods and services, about job possibilities and "connections," and about successful ways to deal with the authorities or about officials who can be "influenced." Second, news and rumors are passed on about economic measures of the government (like price hikes or currency devaluations), about laws proposed by the Party or the State (like those on the treatment of the Turkish minority), or about political events (like the removal of politicians). Third, the members of the "nomenklatura" (the privileged elite in socialist countries) are a permanent object of storytelling: in the form of rumors, jokes, and anecdotes and in the guise of fairy-tale-type stories the narrators comment on the actions, the abilities, and the lifestyles of the political elite. Ludmila Zhivkova, daughter of the former party chief Todor Zhivkov and former minister of culture in Bulgaria, was an extremely popular object of stories that were always told as true. I heard the following in 1981, the year of her death:

> In an airplane crash only Ludmila survives but loses all the clothes, shoes, and jewelry she needs for an important international social event the next day. Immediately she calls the best tailors, shoemakers, and jewelers from all over Bulgaria and orders them to make her a new dress, shoes, and jewelry in one night. At the reception she is the best-dressed lady of all. [Sofia 1981, heard by the author]

This story carries the Cinderella motif; in other versions Ludmila takes the government jet and orders her dress from Pierre Cardin, who tailors her the most beautiful dress overnight. The recent revelations in the media about the actual lifestyles of the nomenklatura made known to the world what the people, through folk narrative, have known for a long time. These stories seem to lag behind reality, whereas the stories about crimes, accidents, and catastrophes (like the nuclear catastrophe at Chernobyl) move in the opposite direction. As a consequence of the restrictive informational policy of the state-controlled media, the rumors, urban legends, and jokes usually exaggerate such events. The numbers of victims or casualties, the heinousness of the crimes, and the wickedness of the criminals grow in oral tradition from day to day and from town to town, as I was able to observe after a bomb attempt in Plovdiv in 1984. Rumors and reports about a Bulgarian Jack-the-Ripper provide another illustration of this tendency. During the 1970s, a series of stories circulated about "Zhoro-Paveto" (George-the-Paving-Stone), who roamed the streets of Sofia by night and killed women walking alone by hitting them over their heads with a paving stone. He was finally apprehended and sentenced. Popular imagination invented a female equivalent, "Mara-Tukhlata" (Mara-the-Brickstone), who was said to have killed men the same way. The fact that only days after the Chernobyl disaster dozens of jokes and cynical riddle questions circulated about the "accident" and its consequences was a result of the official policy of concealment and appeasement.

The functions of everyday narrating mentioned so far are all directed at the present or the future. It is, however, another important task of storytelling to keep alive individual and collective remembrance. According to my observations, individual (auto)biographical storytelling can take on three forms. First and most frequently, it occurs as a narrative rendering of the sufferings of an individual or a family, as the story of injustice inflicted by the "system," of persecution and humiliation, of deprivation and imprisonment; these stories were formerly told in private contexts only, but today one may also hear them in public.[7] Second, autobiographical storytelling can serve to justify a person's actions (cf. Lehmann 1980) or his membership in the Party or in the secret police. This kind of autobiographical storytelling will certainly grow in importance in the future. Third, autobiographical or biographical storytelling may have the form of success stories presenting exemplary life histories and heroic actions (e.g., of Active Fighters against Fascism) as models for imitation; such stories have become rare, however.

It is precisely with the correction of the "official" interpretation of history propagated in the schools and in the media that the unofficial remembrance, the preservation of the people's view of (national) history in their *collective memory,* begins. "Folk history" finds its verbal expression in jokes and anecdotes as well as in eyewitness accounts of historical events. The large number of narratives about the Communist takeover in 1944 and especially about the guerilla and the "Active Fighters" is a case in point. The popular riddle question, "Why is the Bulgarian forest the thickest in the world? Because guerilla fighters still keep coming out of it," ridicules the highly exaggerated number and historic relevance of these fighters and thus reduces the legitimization of communist rule to truer proportions.

Everyday narrating in the socialist countries fulfills many functions that in pluralistic industrialized societies find their expression in other media, institutions, communicative patterns, and forms. In Bulgaria (and in other socialist countries), the system of oral communicative interaction has, over the years, gained a strength and dynamism that render it an almost uncontrollable obstacle to modernization and at the same time easy prey for manipulation. For example, out of distrust and habit, even printed information (like timetables or newspaper reports) is often passed on orally and thus becomes subject to the laws of oral transmission—with all their consequences in a modern, urban, industrialized society. Furthermore, this system of informal everyday narrating is exploited by the Party and the State for their own purposes. Rumors were spread about an imminent currency devaluation a few years ago to persuade Bulgarian residents to deposit their cash, commonly hoarded at home in mattresses and other hiding places, into savings accounts. Further, rumors about minorities (e.g., Turks and Gypsies) were spread to evoke nationalist emotions in support of the Party's policy.

How do we interpret the significance, the meaning, and the consequences of this phenomenon? To what extent can everyday storytelling be a reliable indicator of social, cultural, and psychological processes in the socialist countries? From the folklorist's viewpoint, the existence of such a ubiquitous, dynamic, creative, and uncensored narrative culture as part of present-day folk culture is certainly to be hailed. This storytelling tradition, with its old and new forms and genres, signals human closeness, solidarity, and intense relations and connections. The creativity in the slogans on posters and wall newspapers in the streets of many socialist countries during the revolutionary events of late 1989 may seem surprising to many but for anyone familiar with the situation it was only the most visible expression of a well-functioning system of communication. But are these forms of popular creativity in the modern world a source for unmitigated delight?

Our pleasure with this strong narrative tradition is reduced considerably when we consider the price these societies pay because of the defects of the socialist system. The prevalence of informal oral communication in almost all spheres of life indicates grave social and cultural problems in countries which, by their demographic and economic data, are apparently industrialized and urbanized.[8] It indicates the preservation of a closed tradition-oriented society, instead of the establishment of an open and pluralistic one; the dominance of informal groups with high cohesion and the privatization of social and cultural life, instead of the evolution of the institutions and rational relations of a modern industrialized society; the reliance on small social networks, especially affective kin relations, instead of formal associations and predictable relations; the return to a subsistence and barter economy and the development of a "parallel economy" instead of rational economic planning; and, in southeast Europe, the continued existence of rural lifestyles in urban centers, a phenomenon known as "peasantization" or "rurbanization" of the city (Roth 1985). The backwardness of socialist countries is thus, at least in part, a consequence of the traditionalizing effects of real socialism, i.e., its tendency to preserve basic structures of traditional peasant society.

What conclusions can be drawn from these observations for contemporary, problem-oriented narrative research? In the socialist countries themselves, particularly in southeast Europe, ethnology and folklore must acknowledge that storytelling is not restricted to old people in remote villages, but is an integral part, a register, of contemporary urban life. Its significance for the narrative researcher derives not only from its formal and thematic variety but from its social, cultural, and emotional functions, and from its function as an indicator of continuity or change in social and communicative structures. The specific historical situation of the socialist countries thus makes them one of the most important and fascinating areas of future narrative research.

The relevance of our findings for folkloristic narrative research exceeds the bounds of the socialist countries, however. The very fact that the intensity, the meaningfulness, and the creativity of everyday narrating in these societies are responses to specific political situations emphasizes the necessity of taking political, economic, social, and cultural contexts far more seriously than traditional narrative research is wont to do. The analysis of everyday narrating in its macro (and micro) contexts offers the chance of further proceeding from a literary emphasis to a social narrative research that can contribute to the diagnosis and possibly even the solution of problems of the individual and of contemporary society. Everyday narrating has its place in real life and is a sensitive seismograph of that life and its changes.

NOTES

1. For a version of this contribution in German, see Roth 1991. In light of recent political changes in southeast Europe, some of the information in my contribution is historical (hence the past tense in many of my references), but the cultural relevance of that history still continues into the present.
2. I refer to Alan Dundes here because he wrote the preface and the text of *First Prize: Fifteen Years!;* he collected the jokes from an unidentified Romanian friend who adopted the pseudonym C. Banc (see Dundes 1986: 12). *Banc* in Romanian means joke. The authors of *First Prize: Fifteen Years!* are listed as C. Banc and A. Dundes (1986).
3. The term "everyday narrating" is a rendering of the term *alltägliches Erzählen,* which Bausinger proposed (Bausinger 1958).
4. For discussions of such forms in everyday narrating, see Anchev 1984; Angelova-Georgiera 1987; Ivanova 1986; Karastojcheva 1987; Roth and Roth 1990.
5. Afanasieva-Koleva (1987:135) points out that two-thirds of the jokes presently told in Bulgaria treat either political or sexual themes.
6. In late 1989, a sixty-eight-line poem in the style of traditional narrative songs, allegedly composed by a group of workers in the city of Radomir, spread by typewritten copies throughout Bulgaria. The poem mocks and criticizes the deposed leader Todor ("Tosho") Zhivkov. The first lines read:
    Grandad Tosho, grandad Tosho / you ruled us badly.
    You've gone out of your mind / and made us the laughter of Europe.
    Your "April" line in politics / is now cursed by the whole people.
    Your fat volumes / are filled with nonsense.
    You told us that we will enter / communism tomorrow,
    And you cheated us with temptations / but our purses are empty.
    Instead of full democracy / you filled us up with bureaucracy...

7. In late December 1989, I witnessed an elderly man giving a full account of his life since the war to the passengers in a streetcar in Sofia, the Bulgarian capital.
8. Bulgaria is often considered industrialized on the basis of economic data, but cultural collection provides a different view of the country's basis of life. There is a contrast between the country's outward appearance as an industrialized society and its inner reality based on the basic structures of traditional peasant society.

REFERENCES

Afanasieva-Koleva, Antonina
    1987   Vicăt folklor li e? (Is the joke folklore?) Smehăt văv folklora:132–38. Sofia.

Anchev, Anatol
    1984   Nablyudeniya vărhu folklora v edno zveno na rabotnicheska stroitelna brigada (Observations on the folklore in a construction brigade). Bălgarski folklor 10,1:90–102.

Angelova-Georgieva, Rosica
    1987   Kontinyuitet i promeni văv folklornata proza (Continuity and change in narrative prose). Bălgarski folklor 13, 1:17–25.

Banc, C.; Dundes, Alan
    1986   First Prize: Fifteen Years! An Annotated Collection of Romanian Political Jokes. Rutherford New Jersey: Fairleigh Dickinson University Press.

Bausinger, Hermann
    1958   Strukturen des alltäglichen Erzählens. Fabula 1:239–54.

Brunvand, Jan H.
    1981   The Vanishing Hitchhiker. American Urban Legends and Their Meanings. New York, London: W. W. Norton.
    1984   The Choking Doberman and Other "New" Urban Legends. New York, London: W. W. Norton.

Dundes, Alan
    1986   Preface. In C. Banc and A. Dundes, First Prize: Fifteen Years! An Annotated Collection of Romanian Political Jokes. Rutherford: Fairleigh Dickinson University Press, pp. 9–14.
    1987   Laughter Behind the Iron Curtain: A Sample of Rumanian Political Jokes. In Cracking Jokes. Berkeley: Ten Speed Press, pp. 159–68.

Ivanova, Radost
    1986   Folklornite yavleniya v nashi dni (The folklore phenomena in our days). Bălgarski etnografija 12,3:3–9.

Karastojcheva, Cvetana
    1987   Aforizmite v mladezhkiya sleng (The aphorisms in the slang of adolescents). Smehăt văv folklora:83–90. Sofia.

Lehmann, Albrecht
   1980   Rechtfertigungsgeschichten. Über eine Funktion des Erzählens eigener Erlebnisse im Alltag. Fabula 21:56–69.
   1983   Erzählstruktur und Lebenslauf. Autobiographische Untersuchungen. Frankfurt/M.: Campus.

Nicolaisen, W. F. H.
   1970   National and International Folklore. Bulletin of the Pennsylvania Modern Language Association 49:17–24.
   1980   Variant, Dialect, and Region. New York Folklore 6:137–49.
   1984   Names and Narratives. Journal of American Folklore 97:259–72.

Röhrich, Lutz
   1977   Der Witz: Seine Formen und Funktionen. Stuttgart: Metzler.

Roth, Klaus
   1985   Großstädtische Kultur und dörfliche Lebensweise. Bulgarische Großstädte im 19. und 20. Jh. *In* H. Bausinger, ed., Großstadt. Aspekte empirischer Kulturforschung. Berlin: Staatliche Museen, pp. 363–76.
   1991   Erzählen im sozialistischen Alltag: Beobachtungen zu Strategien der Lebensbewältigung in Südosteuropa. Zeitschrift für Volkskunde 87:181–95.

Roth, Klaus; Roth, Juliana
   1990   Public Obituaries in Southeast Europe. A Study of Attitudes Toward Death and Mourning. International Folklore Review 7:80–87.

Savova, Elena
   1987   Detskite strashni istorii i nyakoi tehni transformacii (The cruel stories of children and some of their transformations). Smehǎt vǎv folklora: 139–45. Sofia.

Shturman, Dora; Tictin, Sergei
   1987   The Soviet Union through the Prism of the Political Anecdote. Jerusalem: Express.

Smollett, Eleanor W.
   1989   The Economy of Jars: Kindred Relationships in Bulgaria—An Exploration. Ethnologia Europaea 19:125–40.

8

"I SAW THE TREES HAD SOULS":
Personal Experience Narratives of Contemporary Witches*

ELIZABETH TUCKER

All of us have personal experience stories to tell: stories from our own lives that illustrate or illuminate who we are and what we have accomplished. Sometimes our stories tell of significant realizations and turning points in which, for example, a career is chosen, a courtship is launched, or a catastrophe is avoided. For contemporary witches—participants in the neopagan belief system that stands on the outskirts of mainstream American religion—the story of personal revelation offers an important means of communication with those who are not (or not yet) witches. It gives the listener a sense of what witchcraft is while presenting the storyteller as a strong, powerful individual with extranormal perceptions and abilities. In analyzing witches' stories collected between 1979 and 1982 in Binghamton, New York, I found the narrators' presentations of themselves to the listener are closely related to their common understanding of heroic behavior in the magic tale. Since witches and those who seek contact with witches are often enthusiastic readers of folktales, myths, and fantasy literature, the linkage is not difficult to establish. Analysis of witches' stories demonstrates that the magic-tale hero thrives within the context of artfully constructed personal experience.

---

*An earlier version of this paper was presented at the American Folklore Society meeting in Nashville, Tennessee, in 1983. I would like to thank Bill Nicolaisen for his encouragement of this research, as well as my other work at SUNY-Binghamton.

Folklore scholarship on mixed or transitional forms of folk narrative has developed since the publication of Hermann Bausinger's "Strukturen des alltäglichen Erzählens" in 1958. Bausinger describes three primary connections between formularized traditional stories and current "everyday" narratives: stories of happy events related to the magic tale, stories of merry events related to the *Schwank,* and stories of sinister events related to the belief legend. Kurt Ranke, further developing these insights in his "Kategorienprobleme der Volkprosa" (1967), finds that mixed forms such as a combination of the magic tale and the *Schwank* are common and quite variable. Of particular relevance to my study is Linda Dégh's *People in the Tobacco Belt: Four Lives* (1975). In examining the life stories of four individuals, Dégh explores how narrators portray themselves as quasi-heroic characters through the selective heightening and downplaying of experiences. "Epic" qualities emerge from a story in which the teller perceives himself or herself as a hero (Dégh 1975). This does not mean that the storyteller deliberately imposes the pattern of the hero tale onto the story; on the contrary, the mixing of narrative forms seems to happen naturally and gradually. Such is the case in the stories I have collected from witches; there is little evidence of deliberate exaggeration or self-promotion.

The study of personal-experience narratives has been enriched by Bill Nicolaisen's seminal concepts of individual inviolability and of cultural register. Nicolaisen has strongly advocated "a new awareness of the inviolability of all individual texts and, above all, of all individual narrators, artisans, tradition bearers, active and creative agents in the realm of folk culture" (Nicolaisen 1984:268). Respect for the integrity of each narrator is crucial for effective analysis. Nicolaisen's concept of cultural register, with its articulation of situational folk-cultural behavior, is also highly relevant to the understanding of witches' personal experience stories (Nicolaisen 1980).[1] In some situations individuals can identify themselves as witches and feel free to tell stories; in others, these individuals will not feel free to express themselves openly. Prejudice against witchcraft has driven many witches to keep their identities secret from all but a trusted few. The researcher must understand witchcraft within its folk-cultural register, always being careful to exercise sensitivity and discretion toward those who must live in a wider, frequently intolerant society.

One might ask whether or not contemporary witches really express themselves within the folk-cultural register. Is it possible that popular culture is a more appropriate framework for their narratives? Certainly numerous books and pamphlets on witchcraft have been published within the past thirty years; newsletters have circulated, and individuals have used such materials to shape their own beliefs and rituals. I find, however, that witches' membership in groups—usually small groups of believers in their religion—gives them a forum for developing their own versions of traditional beliefs and rituals. Most witches have a "Book of Shadows," a personal collection of rituals that includes both traditional and creative elements. And the telling of tales is an act of creation, even if it is strongly influenced by folk tradition. In my dissertation research with pre-adolescent girls (1977), I found that even the most markedly traditional tales showed some evidence of creative embellishment. In witches' narratives as well, the interplay of creativity and tradition is well worth exploring.

Before turning to the analysis of witches' narratives, it is necessary to clarify the origins of contemporary witchcraft and the prejudices that have developed against it. Many witches believe Margaret Murray's hypothesis, advanced in *The Witch-Cult in Western Europe* (1921), that a pagan matriarchal religion has existed in a continuous line of descent since ancient times, antedating Christianity. Although this theory has been largely rejected by scholars, it offers the attractive image of an immensely long, unbroken chain of underground religious tradition. Depending upon one's viewpoint, contemporary witchcraft either emerged or experienced a revival in the early 1950s through the work of Gerald B. Gardner in England. Gardner, the author of *Witchcraft Today* (1955) and other books, vividly describes a form of worship in which members of a coven, led by a high priestess and a high priest, perform rituals in honor of the Mother Goddess and her consort, the horned god. Herbalism, solstice celebration, and "skyclad" (unclothed) worship outdoors are all elements of the original Gardnerian format. Witches today acknowledge Raymond Buckland, author of *Witchcraft from the Inside* (1971), as the bringer of the Gardnerian movement to America in the 1960s, a period when witchcraft was an attractive religious alternative that gained numerous converts. An excellent explanation of the Wiccan revival in America is found in Margot Adler's *Drawing Down the Moon* (1979). Adler describes, in addition to the Gardnerian tradition, the Alexandrian, Georgian, and Dianic forms of worship, among others. Most recently, T. M. Luhrmann's important study, *Persuasions of the Witch's*

Craft: Ritual Magic in Contemporary England (1989), has provided fresh insight into the philosophical and psychological roots of witchcraft. As serious scholarly studies continue to emerge, contemporary witchcraft will be better understood by those who are not followers of the craft.

For the present, however, the general public seems to know little about witchcraft. Many people who hear the term "witchcraft" assume that it means Satanism or another form of devil worship; others see the stereotypically old, ugly, malevolent witch of our Halloween tradition. My witchcraft research in Binghamton, an industrial city of about 56,000 citizens, has given me ample evidence of non-witches' hostility toward what they perceive as evil and threatening. Witches in Binghamton take a serious risk if they reveal their religious identities to outsiders; if so, they may lose their jobs or suddenly discover that their leases are nonrenewable. On the SUNY-Binghamton campus, there is less hostility toward witchcraft than in town. I have found that a significant number of students are interested in witchcraft; a much smaller number actively seek to join a coven. Whenever I have taught a witchcraft course, I have heard the rumor that I myself am a witch, recruiting students for my own nefarious purposes. (By coincidence, my first witchcraft class had thirteen students, the traditional number recommended for a coven.) Such is the mystique of witchcraft and the mistrust that people feel. It is necessary to take these attitudes into account when analyzing witches' stories, because their modes of self-presentation are closely related to the reactions they expect to receive from outsiders.

In all the stories I have chosen to analyze here, the narrators characterize themselves as unpromising or unusual persons who, through witchcraft, become extraordinarily perceptive and powerful. In this respect, they conform to the characterization of typical magic tale heroes. Magic tales, as Linda Dégh says, "tell about an ordinary human being's encounter with the suprahuman world and his becoming endowed with qualities that enable him to perform supernatural acts" (Dégh 1972:62–63). Along with this characterization, there is a plot pattern that lends consistency to these stories of eventful realization: discovery, dramatic proof of new powers, and often wondrous help for others. Not all stories chosen by witches conform to this pattern; I have chosen to focus upon narratives told to non-witches interested in learning about the craft. Perhaps these accounts of early discovery are told so that listeners, as yet non-witches, can learn that similar opportunities are possible for them also.

My first text comes from the life history of Noble Star, a witch who, at the time of my interviews, was in his mid-thirties and worked in a Binghamton factory. Noble Star began to learn about witchcraft when he was a student at SUNY-Binghamton; his teacher was a fellow student who claimed to have learned about witchcraft from her deceased grandmother in dreams and visions. Under this young woman's guidance, Noble Star meditated and studied books of the widespread Gardnerian tradition. His first understanding of witchcraft predated this formal instruction, however; it came while, as a boy, he was walking in the woods near his parents' cottage. Noble Star had always been a lonely child, partly because his parents brought him to the country every weekend, but also because he felt different from the other children in a way that he found hard to understand. As he walked in the woods, feeling lonely and sad, a flash of understanding came to him:

> It was in the middle of a big thunderstorm, when I was out in the forest. I looked up and [pause] I saw the trees had souls. The Baptist church always treated me as if I had no brain, but now I knew they were wrong about life. Every tree had a being inside it, and every stump was like a castle. I didn't really understand *why* then, but it was comforting to see that was the way it was.

This moment of revelation, which Noble Star described frequently to me and other non-witches, was clearly a crucial turning point in his life. From that point on, even before he knew the name of the Mother Goddess, Noble Star knew there was a directing force in his life. After a while, he discovered that he could make things happen; one day he even hurt someone by accident. By then, he was fully aware that a spiritual power was in charge of everything he did.

It is difficult to convey the flavor of Noble Star's narrative with this brief excerpt and summary, but one can see a definite selectivity in the telling of this much of his life story. The narrator stresses his own growing perceptions: his sensitivity to nature, his spirituality, and his realization of the falseness of Baptist values. Instead of dwelling on his loneliness and unhappiness, he makes these feelings serve as a prelude to his exciting discovery.

As a character in his own story, Noble Star bears a resemblance to the hero of the magic tale. Like this hero, he has an ordinary and rather unpromising early life. He is lonely and isolated from his peers; like the youngest of three sons in so many folktales, he is not well respected and seems out of harmony with his environment. When his moment of revelation arrives, it is in the forest. The magic tale's hero frequently discovers something that will change the course of his life when he is out in the forest, which represents wildness and freedom from societal restraint. In many narratives, from Dante's *Inferno* to "Hansel and Gretel" (AT 327A), the forest is a menacing environment to which the hero responds with confusion and fear. The witch in "Hansel and Gretel" personifies the danger and lawlessness of the environment in which she lives. On the other hand, the forest can be a place of delightful discovery, as in the suitor's recognition of silver, golden, and diamond trees in "The Twelve Dancing Princesses" (AT 306). The wildness of the forest is not only threatening, but also replete with opportunities for understanding and enrichment.

The mode of Noble Star's revelation also fits the pattern of the hero's development in epic and folktale. In the midst of a thunderstorm, Noble Star suddenly sees a new world. Similarly, Siegfried hears the singing of a bird and suddenly understands its meaning as he goes off to rescue the princess. Many other examples of sudden insight or illumination can be cited from folktale tradition. In AT 326, "The Youth Who Wanted to Learn What Fear Is," a young man abruptly learns how to shiver when cold water is thrown on his back. The darker, more serious tale of "Bluebeard" (AT 312) grips the reader's imagination with the sudden revelation to the young bride of what lies behind the door of her husband's secret room. Numerous other tales give us, in one form or another, the same kind of episode: a dramatic revelation that alters the hero's life in a significant way.

A comparable experience is described in Adler's *Drawing Down the Moon* (1979); a woman recalls singing in the choir at church on Christmas Eve and looking out at a full moon over a lake. She felt "something very special happening" and climbed the hill behind the church:

> Suddenly I felt a "presence." It seemed very ancient and wise and definitely female. I can't describe it any closer than that, but I felt that this presence, this being, was looking down on me, on this church and these people and saying, "The poor little ones! They mean so well and they understand so little." [Adler 1979:14–15]

This personal experience story conveys well the image of the benevolent, powerful Mother Goddess. Like Noble Star, the teller of this story looks out at the natural world and sees the strength of the spirit within it. Such an experience, we hear from both tellers, would never occur inside a church or another enclosed space.

A similar emphasis on nature and newly discovered power is evident in narratives that I collected from two other witches in Binghamton. The first of these stories comes from Frank, who, at the time of my interview with him, was a graduate student in his late thirties who served as unofficial leader of the Pagan Studies Group at SUNY-Binghamton. Frank is a tall, imposing person with a forceful personality. During the time that I was getting to know him, he was aggressive in making contact with students and townspeople to explain his beliefs as a pagan and a witch. His brand of witchcraft is eclectic, with a strong emphasis on psychic phenomena as well as worship of the Mother Goddess. In this respect he differs considerably from Noble Star and other witches of my acquaintance who have tended to be rather quiet, shy, and elusive. As Adler points out, witchcraft is not generally a proselytizing religion (1979:14). But Frank, a gregarious and self-confident individual, found great delight in discussing and promoting paganism. He and his wife, also a witch who has done palm readings at home, have even risked public exposure by appearing on local television and radio shows to discuss witchcraft. Fortunately, the public appearances resulted in no serious adverse effects.

In telling several students and me about his conversion to witchcraft, Frank told the following story about an incident that occurred when he was twelve years old:

> My first experience was with weather-working. I was moving some clouds around in the name of Jesus, and it worked. I was moving some clouds around in the name of Mary, and it worked. I tried moving some clouds in the name of Joe the Barber . . . and that worked too, which was kind of an interesting piece of knowledge.

One surprising aspect of Frank's story is that, although he was not yet a witch at the age of twelve, he describes himself as able to move clouds around in the sky—a sharp contrast to the traditional children's pastime of watching clouds, perceiving the shape of animals, humans, or buildings, and predicting which way the clouds are going to move. Frank's approach—invoking the names of Jesus and Mary to make the clouds move—is related to his rearing as a Christian. He may have been experimenting with the powers of his religion, or he may have embellished his story with these details for the purpose of humorous contrast. In any case, the listener receives the impression of unusual capability that exists well before the teller's conversion to witchcraft.

Frank's moment of revelation contrasts interestingly with Noble Star's; while both boys are outside, realizing something very important about their worlds, the roles taken by each of them are quite different. Noble Star is a sensitive observer, suddenly noticing beings and castles in the forest, while Frank is a nonchalant manipulator of his environment. Like the raisers of storms mentioned in the fifteenth-century *Malleus Maleficarum* (Summers 1971), Frank is interested in influencing what goes on in the sky. As a character in his own story he is active, strong, and self-assured; Noble Star, in contrast, is relatively passive and oriented toward observation rather than action.

Since Frank presents himself as such a strong character, he fits the pattern of the successful folktale hero quite well. One hero that resembles him behaviorally is young John in "John the Bear" (AT 301). Even as a small child, John is unusually strong and active; he rescues his mother from the bear's cave, subdues his schoolmaster, and then goes on to have supernatural adventures with his extraordinary companions. John is, like Frank, an action-oriented hero whose destiny stems from unusual capabilities revealed to him in childhood. This kind of hero is markedly different from his peers, aware early on of an unusual destiny.

A somewhat different pattern of heroism emerges in a story told by Mary, a high priestess of Celtic witchcraft. In her early thirties at the time of my interview with her, Mary suffered from an ailment that had left her crippled and wheelchair-bound since early childhood. Up to the age of sixteen, she had lived in a hospital, with regular visits home. Her first encounter with witchcraft, she told me, had occurred when she found a small group of witches celebrating a seasonal ritual outside. Although she felt an immediate kinship with them, this discovery was not her most important moment of revelation. That came later, when she was able to take an active role as witch and healer. Her hospitalization, Mary explained, had made her fearful of active participation. She told me:

> I didn't officiate until I was about sixteen because in the hospital, everything was very closed. You never went outside, you never

had windows open, so I was terrified of the outside. In fact, now, if I go into the middle of the field, if there's not trees, I feel kind of scared.

Mary's honest admission of her fear and insecurity evokes sympathy in the listener; she certainly doesn't sound like a woman of particular power or promise. And yet, in the tradition of unprepossessing folktale heroes, we see her stature changing as the story unfolds:

A friend of mine slipped and broke her kneecap in about six million places and was told she would never walk again. Just out of curiosity, I was about twelve, I wanted to see what I could do and I just put my hand over her knee. I *didn't touch it* and I told her to *concentrate* and feel the pain leaving. So I said, "Let me try it and see," and I did that for a while, about ten minutes. So then I said, "It's going to be sore for a while but it's going to be all right." And sure enough, she stood up and went back to the doctor a week later and there was about *three months' worth of healing* on it. And he asked her how she did it and she said she didn't know. Nobody knows how it really works. It seems to be a transfer of energy.

Since Mary's story begins with the extreme pronouncement that her friend will "never walk again," the sudden revelation of her healing power brings about a dramatic reversal of expectations. Neither the doctor nor the healer herself understands what has happened, though the power of the Mother Goddess is one way to explain it. The mysteriousness of this cure adds a significant dimension to Mary's narrative; as in the magical processes of the folktale, there is no rational explanation for what has happened.

As a character in her own story, Mary is certainly an unpromising hero. Her early suffering and isolation in the hospital make her feel helpless and frightened and her wheelchair marks her as an outsider. But her success at mending a broken knee leads her to become much more powerful and self-confident, though in comparison to Noble Star and Frank, she still seems more vulnerable and more sensitive to other people. Her development as a hero resembles that of the young girl in the Grimms' "The Six Swans" (AT 451), who works so hard to save her brothers from their enchantment by the wicked queen. There is also a resemblance to the hero's deeds in "The Healing Fruits" (AT 610), in which the hero receives healing power as a gift from an old woman to whom he has been kind and is able to cure a sick princess. Other folktales could be mentioned as well; the tradition of the hero as healer and restorer is strong in folk narrative.

In conclusion, what we find in witches' personal experience stories is just the opposite of the sinister witch figure from folktales. It is a portrait of the witch as hero, as a perceptive, strong, and altruistic character. Through unpromising origins, isolation, and closeness to nature, the contemporary witch figure gains a close kinship to the magic-tale hero. Perhaps it is poetic justice that, after so many years of witches' suffering from persecution and misunderstanding, the "Hansel and Gretel" witch is now being replaced by a more admirable personage. As more witches grow comfortable enough to share their stories with noninitiates, it is possible that the green skin and warty nose of the public image will fall away to reveal a kind, gentle person who sees living souls in the forest.

NOTES

1. The personal experience narrative relates an event "endured, performed, witnessed, remembered, and cast into story form by the teller" (Stahl 1977a:6). Stahl argues that "the traditional aspects of the personal narrative will require looking at 'tradition' as a function of continuing time (past, present, and future, not simply past) and as a quality tied to a wide range of substance (process and its components as well as plot and its motifs)" (Stahl 1977b:10). Although recognizing the character of innovation in personal experience narratives, folklorists analyze the stories as a folk narrative genre. See the special double issue of the *Journal of the Folklore Institute* 14, nos. 1–2, on "Stories of Personal Experiences," and Stahl 1977b, 1989. For analysis of personal-experience narratives related to identity formation and values clarification among members of religious groups, see Titon 1988, Lawless 1988. Von Sydow proposed the terms *Memorat* and *Fabulat* to distinguish first-person experience stories of actual events from invented narrations of imagined occurrences (Von Sydow 1977:73–77), but as Nicolaisen (1990) points out, the distinction is artificial. "Even in our autobiographical recollections," Nicolaisen states, "we continually invent ourselves, and the stories of our personal pasts are therefore as much intoxicated fabulation as sober memory, however genuinely portrayed as nothing but the truth (1990:6). Nicolaisen adds: "We tell stories because, in order to cope with the present and to face the future, we have to create the past, both as time and space, through narrating it. If these stories are autobiographical in nature and sometimes if they are

not, we create, in the process, the illusion of identity and of a continuous self by inventing ourselves in true stories of a past that never was" (1990:10).

REFERENCES

Adler, Margot
    1979   Drawing Down the Moon. Boston: Beacon Press.

Bausinger, Hermann
    1958   Strukturen des alltäglichen Erzählens. Fabula 1:239–54.

Buckland, Raymond
    1971   Witchcraft from the Inside. St. Paul: Lewellyn Press.

Dégh, Linda
    1972   Folk Narrative. *In* Richard M. Dorson, ed., Folklore and Folklife. Chicago: University of Chicago Press, pp. 54–83.
    1975   People in the Tobacco Belt: Four Lives. Ottawa: National Museums of Canada.

Gardner, Gerald B.
    1955   Witchcraft Today. New York: The Citadel Press. Originally published in 1954 by Rider and Co. in England.

Lawless, Elaine J.
    1988   God's Peculiar People: Women's Voices and Folk Tradition in a Pentecostal Church. Lexington: University Press of Kentucky.

Luhrmann, T. M.
    1989   Persuasions of the Witch's Craft: Ritual Magic in Contemporary England. Cambridge, Mass.: Harvard University Press.

Murray, Margaret A.
    1921   The Witch-Cult in Western Europe. Oxford: Oxford University Press.

Nicolaisen, W. F. H.
    1980   Variant, Dialect, and Region: An Exploration in the Geography of Tradition. New York Folklore 6:137–49.
    1984   Names and Narratives. Journal of American Folklore 97:259–72.
    1990   Why Tell Stories? Fabula 31:5–10.

Ranke, Kurt
    1967   Kategorienprobleme dre Volksprosa. Fabula 9:4–12.

Stahl, Sandra D.
    1977a   Introduction. Journal of the Folklore Institute 14:5–8.
    1977b   The Personal Narrative as Folklore. Journal of the Folklore Institute 14:9–30.
    1989   Literary Folkloristics and the Personal Narrative. Bloomington: Indiana University Press.

Summers, Montague
    1971   (ed.) Malleus Maleficarum. New York: Dover.

Titon, Jeff Todd
    1988   Powerhouse for God: Speech, Chant, and Song in an Appalachian Baptist Church. Austin: University of Texas Press.

Tucker, Elizabeth
    1977   Tradition and Creativity in the Storytelling of Pre-Adolescent Girls. Ph.D. Dissertation, Indiana University.

Von Sydow, C. W.
    1977   Selected Papers on Folklore. 1948 repr. New York: Arno Press.

THE FRUIT OF THE WOMB:
Creative Uses of a Naturalizing Tradition in Folktales*

CRISTINA BACCHILEGA

Are women at one with nature? Folktales, as they are frequently collected, edited, and reported would seem to imply that they are. In doing so, the tales participate in a figurative process—one with many folkloric and literary manifestations—which serves to mask "the cultural construction of the feminine" (Ebert 1988:19) and finds an especially potent example in the discourse of pregnancy. While reading pregnancy books, for instance, I find:

> The uterus... is an organ shaped like an upside-down pear. [Samuels and Samuels 1986:24–25]
> Week 6. Your uterus is now the size of a plum.
> Week 10. Your uterus has expanded to the size of an orange.
> Week 14. Your uterus is the size of a large grapefruit.
> At 20 weeks. The baby is... as heavy as a medium-sized Spanish onion (8 oz. or 250 grams). [Kitzinger 1985:323, 324, 325, 66]
>   "Cristina," exclaims a male colleague, looking appreciatively at my swelling body, "you are blossoming." No wonder I shop at

---

*This essay is a revision of a paper presented at the 1989 American Folklore Society meeting in Philadelphia as part of the panel "Rethinking Female Initiation: The Innocent Persecuted Heroine" with Ruth Bottigheimer, Steve Jones, Bill Nicolaisen, and Elizabeth Tucker.

"In Bloom," I remind myself as I go home to practice "butterfly" and "sheep's" breathing.
Week 39. Your cervix is ripening in preparation for labor. [Kitzinger 1985:331]
"I feel ripe," I say.

This same naturalizing discourse, I want to argue, scripts the tales of the "innocent persecuted heroine" and confines the heroine's experiences—in particular her being mothered and her becoming a mother—to a quasi-"natural" world that is the necessary premise of both her innocence and persecution. This essay by no means advocates the simple rejection of these tales as sexist; rather it questions some of their appeal—for appealing indeed they are. By focusing on a selection of Italo Calvino's *Italian Folktales* (1980 translation of *Fiabe Italiane*, 1956), I wish to map the production of the feminine in the "Innocent Persecuted Heroine" subgenre (Dan 1977 and Jones 1986) as well as address Calvino's own creative use of the naturalizing tradition in its ideological, stylistic, and effectual implications.[1]

Naturalizing the heroine's experience and identity is yet another manifestation of what Max Lüthi calls the "one-dimensionality" and the "universal interconnection" of the folktale (1982). There is no fear or surprise when the folktale hero encounters the otherworld, receives magic gifts, holds conversations with animals, experiences miraculous transformations. The numinous is artfully made to appear natural. Further, the hero's isolation from a specific community allows him to form "all-encompassing relationships" and the folktale to exercise its stylistic unity. What would require explaining in a culturally grounded legend, for instance, is perceived in the folktale not as mysterious or accidental but natural. These and other features of the folktale's abstract style produce that effortlessness which Mircea Eliade remarks on when he describes the folktale as "a lighthearted doublet of myth and initiation rite" (see Lüthi 1982:116). Consenting to the rules of one's community is represented as a natural process. The stylistic and thematic projects of the folktale, then, are one: to disguise its artifice.

When this disguise applies to tales which center upon the experiences of women, it seems to me to be doubly persuasive as well as ideologically insidious. A long tradition of representing woman both as nature and as concealed artifice contributes to the success and power of such images in the folktale. Anthropological and historical research has shown how women are more often than not "identified as being closer to nature than to culture" which, in a patriarchal system, makes them "symbolic of an inferior, intermediate order of being" (Lerner 1986:25). As Simone de Beauvoir wrote, woman—as he represents her—incarnates man's dream: "She is the wished-for intermediary between nature, the stranger to man, and the fellow being who is too closely identical" and therefore competitive and possibly hostile (1972:172). Within the framework of this dream, woman is exalted as passive matter, earthy fecundity; yet, if she attracts man because she is perceived as close to nature (especially in her role as mother), she also repels him because she is too close to nature, the bearer and reminder of his mortality:

Woman becomes plant, panther, diamond, mother-of-pearl, by blending flowers, furs, jewels, shells, feathers with her body; she perfumes herself to spread the aroma of the lily and the rose. But feathers, silk, pearls, and perfumes also help to hide the animal crudity of her flesh, her odour. [de Beauvoir 1972:190]

De Beauvoir's analysis of ornaments and of women's transformation into what she calls "idols" beautifully exemplifies how "man, wishing to find nature in woman, but nature transfigured, dooms woman to artifice" (de Beauvoir 1972:191).

Thus, while it is not innocent, the metamorphosis of woman from/into plant, fruit, or animal in folktales appears all the more natural as it gains strength from a long tradition of thought. "Why can't I bear children the same as the apple tree bears apples?" asks one queen, while another exclaims, seeing the many seedlings growing around a rosemary bush, "A mere rosemary has all those children, while I am a queen and childless!" (Calvino 1980:308, 583). In these two versions of "The Myrtle Child" (AT 407A), the queens respectively give birth to an apple and a bush of rosemary, each the enchanted refuge of a beautiful maiden, who immediately becomes the object of male desire and is then persecuted because of it. It is true that queens also give birth to, for instance, male pigs in folktales (see "King Crin"); yet these offspring are not wholeheartedly welcomed by their families nor are they actively sought after by loving princesses. Furthermore, neither prince in the "Myrtle Child" versions thinks of disenchanting the girl, who in both stories is a successful metaphor of the "disguised artifice" I previously described. The first girl comes out of the apple only to bathe and comb her hair; she never talks, and the prince simply enjoys looking at her as a quasi- or pseudonatural spectacle. The other girl does hold conversations with the prince but mostly dances to his flute, stepping "naturally" as it were from the rosemary bush into his aura.

La ragazza mela, the Apple Girl, and *Rosmarina,* Rosemary, are but two examples of the woman-as-nature metaphor that other innocent and persecuted heroines embody, often in their very names. *Erbabianca,* literally "white grass" but much less poetically "Wormwood" in English, is named after the bush by which she was abandoned as an infant; *Prezzemolina*'s name is a constant reminder of her mother's craving for parsley; and, it almost goes without saying, *Belsole* is as beautiful as the sun and *Biancaneve* is as innocently white as snow.

To reinforce the metaphor, descriptions of these heroines' exceptional beauty call upon nature as a term of comparison. Belsole's brother asks, "Is this my sister? My sister with eyes like stars? My sister whose mouth is like a flower?" (Calvino, 1971:429; my translation) when he sees the impostor in a Roman version of "The Black and White Bride" (AT 403). "I will marry only when I've found a girl as white as ricotta and rosy as a rose" (Calvino 1980:568) states the young prince in "The King of Spain and the English Milord" (AT 881, related to AT 712). This wish evokes the more famous "I would like a wife white like milk and red like blood" (1980:389), where once again beautiful maidens spring out of pomegranates or citrons (AT 408). And if we expect the Apple Girl to be "as fair and rosy as an apple" (1980:308), Sleeping Beauty's complexion is quite stunning in a seemingly dead woman: "At the sight of the beautiful maiden lying among the flowers with her face as fresh as a rose and her cheeks looking like milk and blood, [the prince] almost swooned away" (Calvino 1971:563; my translation). Can one blame him if—touched by such portent—he loves her so intensely that she gives birth to twins in her sleep? Nature and "love" displace the issues of consent and rape.

And, of course, it is in nature that these innocent heroines often find help and refuge when unnatural fathers, wicked stepmothers, or envious mothers-in-law persecute them. In "Uliva" (AT 706) a pear tree bends down its branches so as to allow the hungry handless girl to bite into its fruits (Calvino 1980:257). In another version of "The Handless Maiden" (this time from Piedmont and not edited by Calvino), the poor girl finds refuge in a hollow tree which closes around her leaving only a hole large enough for the loaf of bread that the king's dogs bring her every day (Beccaria and Arpino 1982:143). In "The King of the Peacocks" (AT 403) it is the heroine's little dog which saves her: his barking gets the attention of a poor sailor who, using his harpoon, draws in the mattress with the sleeping girl and her dog from the ocean (Calvino 1980:341). And in a Roman version of the same tale, a whale and ducklings contribute to the maiden's rescue (1980:370–73).

These ties with nature—artfully marked by the heroine's miraculous birth, name, physical appearance, and helpers—contribute to the audience's awareness of her innocence, especially when she is being persecuted in the beginning and ending stages of initiation from childhood into motherhood. A child is innocent tautologically, but the persecuted heroine's prolonged state of grace seems to be further "guaranteed" by her association with nature and her complementary isolation from the world of men. The heroine's frequent confinement to a tower or palace in these tales, while it prevents her from having human relationships, does not in fact contradict her capability for "universal interconnection" as discussed by Lüthi. What the woman-as-nature metaphor adds to the heroine's innocence is that listeners/readers are further encouraged to think of the heroine in precultural, unchangeable terms. It will seem "natural," for instance, for one child to grow up without ever leaving the palace, "gazing out of the window at the countryside, singing softly, chatting with the nursemaid..., and embroidering" (Calvino 1980:338), if another leaves her apple only to bathe and comb her hair. Perceiving these processes as metaphorically equivalent works in both cases to naturalize patriarchal training for marriage (admittedly of the royal category) and also the protection of the heroine's virginity, a necessary premise to that marriage.

When the heroine is subjected to repeated persecution, it is usually after marriage and motherhood that she is attacked the second time. In a tale from Calabria, "The Turkey Hen," the handless protagonist is accused of having given birth to two dogs (Calvino 1980:498) and in a Florentine version of AT 707—with an overstatement I particularly enjoy—it is first a monkey, then a dog, and finally a tiger cub (Calvino, "The Fine Greenbird" 1980:315–17). Again the ambiguity of the woman-as-nature metaphor is relevant, for in every case the villain—be it the devil, the king's minister, his mother or sister—seeks to show that there is something "unnatural" about the young bride precisely by carrying her association with nature to an extreme. On the one hand, the audience knows and the husband in the tale wants to believe that the heroine is too naturally beautiful and good to be guilty; on the other hand, the villain's accusation implies that she is *not* innocent because she is natural to the excess and therefore unnatural: one or several monstrous couplings have allegedly occurred. As Simone de Beauvoir argues, woman's closeness to nature is perceived as both asset and threat. Furthermore, by pointing to the natural/unnatural dichotomy, the animal imagery shifts the audience's attention away from the king's need for paternity, a socially and economically based concern. However, that need is overt in "The Fine Greenbird" when the King marries the baker's daughter because she promised, "I [will] give [the king] two rosy-faced, golden-haired sons, and a rosy-faced, golden-haired daughter with a star on her brow" (Calvino 1980:315). Since the girl is eventually rewarded for having kept that promise, the bargaining power of childbearing within an exclusively monogamous couple overtly appears to be a dynamic element of the plot.

Ultimately—and not exclusively in Calvino's collection—it is by proving herself to be a "naturally" good mother (and implicitly a "naturally" monogamous wife) that the heroine finally reaches the happy ending of her story. In the version of "the Handless Maiden" from Piedmont, for example, Filomena is happy to live in a hut eating roots and herbs just as long as she can rear her children in peace; when her husband comes looking for her after several years, all she needs to say to him is, "Look at [these children] carefully, and you'll see whether you are their father or not!" (Beccaria and Arpino 1982:145; my translation). He happily takes the three of them home with him. And before this last trial—the long stay in the wilderness with her children—the heroine's absolute innocence is symbolically proven when she miraculously regains her hands in order to save her babies from drowning. I say "miraculously" because in some versions a religious agent is responsible for the wondrous growth, but in many other versions the tale simply plays on the audience's belief that a mother, handless or not, would "naturally" find a way of saving her children simply because she is a mother. Talented storytellers such as

Susan Gordon have proved many a time that the episode is, in fact, just as powerful without any religious intervention to explain it.

Being a child, being with child. The beginning and ending stages of the "innocent persecuted" heroine's initiation process symbolically and physically assert her ties with nature; they are also the stages on which the narrative dwells. In "Filomena dalle mani mozze," the king finds Filomena in a hollow tree when she is but a beautiful child. The next sentence tells us that she is almost twenty and the king wants to marry her. Right after that the king goes to war and she has twins (Beccaria and Arpino 1982:143). The initiation process apparently takes her from childhood to childbearing and childrearing with a wedding in between, the wedding which is the make-believe happy ending of so many other tales of female persecution. The artful naturalizing of this initiation process conceals the fact that these female characters never grow up to attain identities of their own. They "mature," but they never develop. As an innocent child, a rosemary bush, or a mother, the heroine depends on someone else for her survival, cultivation, and identity. What these tales forbid—and thus never represent—is the independent, grown woman. Even the very active protagonist of a Piedmontese "Rapunzel" (AT 310) remains true to this path. In order to save her wounded lover, she finds her way out of her high tower, listens in on witch-talk, and magically cures the prince while pretending to be an old doctor; having succeeded in all this, she returns to her tower where she waits for the prince, the man she will eventually marry (Calvino 1980:52–57).

A semiotic square provides a visual representation of how the tales of the "Innocent Persecuted Heroine" map the process of female initiation and ideologically constitute the feminine within them (Figure 1).[2]

What is desirable, then, in our heroine? For her to be and remain a child, thereby preserving her innocence and her reliance on patriarchy (the father figure and/or the prince figure). In more abstract terms, the narrative prescribes *dependence;* what it forbids, then, is *independence,* the independence of a (childless) woman who as a sexual, psychological, and social subject would not be subordinate to man. This position is possible for women, but it is not articulated in these tales. Rather, the narrative shifts our attention to the negations of both the prescribed and the forbidden so as to create false oppositions and tasks. The not-prescribed is *not-dependence,* which in the form of the evil,

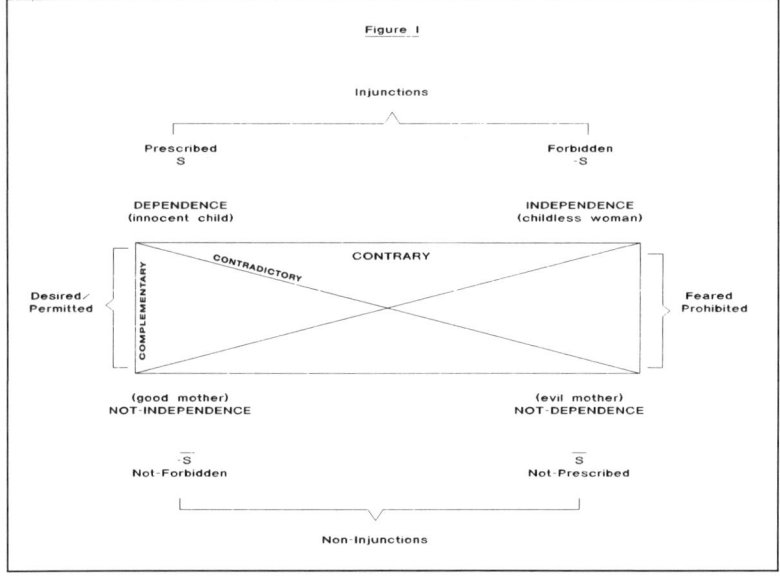

Figure 1

crafty mother figure is opposed to the innocent child. While this false opposition reinforces rivalry among women, it poses no serious threat to the system of injunctions set up by the narrative discourse. The not-forbidden term is *not-independence,* as represented by the "good" mother, the one who remains symbolically innocent and dependent on her children for her identity. Dependence and not-independence complement and implicate each other: good mothers give birth to innocent children and good children mature into symbolically innocent mothers. By presenting these two positions and their interaction as "natural," the narrative strengthens its internally persuasive discourse and conceals its reduction of female initiation to one pattern alone—an ideologically set one.

From a feminist perspective, this hypothesis holds valuable interpretive implications: first, by emphasizing women's ties with nature and motherhood, these tales implicitly prescribe and forbid specific forms of gendered identity to female characters as well as listeners/readers; second, the traditional categories of initiation used to analyze these tales participate in that same discourse. For instance, in analyzing "Innocent Persecuted Heroine" tales, Jones explains: "the sequence of episodes is structured to correspond to the basic trials and transitions of the maturing young woman in order to illustrate for the audience the process of maturation"; furthermore, "the successive acts of the persecution pattern coincide with what may be considered three of the most crucial transitions in the heroine's life—puberty, marriage, and childbirth" (1986:177). But what makes these "the most crucial transitions in the heroine's life"? I am not objecting to the structural and thematic observations that Jones makes while focusing on the heroine's journey; I am pointing out that "maturation" is not equivalent to development and that the woman-as-nature metaphor in these tales has the effect, among others, of cultivating women to remain uncultivated.³

My discussion has for the most part drawn on Calvino's collection for examples, but I believe that anyone familiar with tales of magic would have tales to add to my selection. What makes Calvino's *Italian Folktales* provocative is its creative and ambivalent use of this naturalizing tradition. On the one hand, Calvino's stylistic and ideological choices enact this tradition to an extreme; on the other, his collection as a whole transcends the limitations of the "woman-as-nature" metaphor.

A most self-conscious participant in the tradition of folktale editors, Calvino takes the Brothers Grimm as his model but makes his main editorial and stylistic changes explicit in his introduction and notes, wishing to be more "scientific" than the Grimms (see Bacchilega 1989). All the tales he includes and translates from a variety of dialects into standard Italian come from written/printed sources, and Calvino attempts to work as a modern researcher sensitive to the editors' and the storytellers' interplay. Yet he takes the Tuscan proverb "La novella nun è bella, se sopra nun ci si rappella" ("The tale is not beautiful if nothing is added to it"; 1980:xxi) to heart and states that he has selected "the most unusual, beautiful, and original texts" (1980:xix) and "enriched" them "when it is possible to do so without altering [their] character or unity, in order to shape them more fully and articulately" (1971:xix; my translation).

The woman-as-nature metaphor seems to embody Calvino's idea of what makes a tale "unusual, beautiful, and original." For instance, in his rendition of Giuseppe Pitrè's "La mela," Calvino further naturalizes the Apple Girl by having the queen give birth to an apple following her wish to be as fertile as the apple tree rather than relying on the intervention of an old woman helper (for a fuller analysis of Calvino's manipulation of Pitrè's Tuscan tales, see Beckwith 1987). The change is, of course, consistent with other folktale wondrous births, but it is also a symptom of Calvino's attraction to simple, elegant metaphors.[4] As he puts it in the introduction, "There is a genuine feeling of beauty in the communions or metamorphoses of woman and fruit, of woman and plant.... The secret lies in the metaphorical link" (1980:xxix). No wonder the key tale for Calvino in Basile's *Pentamerone* is that of the three citrons (Calvino 1988a:144–46). This metaphor/metamorphosis of woman and plant/fruit is perhaps the metaphor of metaphors in Calvino's collection, which seeks to represent the Italian folktale as enacting the "precise rhythm" and "joyous logic" of transformations, the "continuous quiver of love" and eroticism, and yet the "realistic" needs and work of the peasants (1980:introduction).

In his essay "The Nature of Italian Folktales," Marc Beckwith suggests that "misogyny" might be at work in the editorial changes made by Calvino (1987:257). Arguing such a point would require a more thorough analysis than his or mine. Calvino's privileging of the woman-as-nature metaphor would seem to provide some evidence in that direction; nevertheless, of the 200 tales edited by Calvino, a great many present active, smart, bold heroines who do not follow the narrow initiatory path of the "innocent persecuted heroine" ("Catherine, Sly Country Lass" AT 875, "Catherine the Wise" AT 891, "The Handmade King" AT 425). And even within the subgenre of the "Innocent Persecuted Heroine," Calvino takes care to choose less passive protagonists, as is clearly the case with his Prezzemolina (1980:310–14) or his Cinderella "who wasn't used to being ordered around" ("Rosina in the Oven" 1980:226). The range of behaviors, wishes, and personalities offered by female characters in Calvino's tales is invigorating, and it marks, it seems to me, the writer's awareness of the sexist potential of fairy tales—an awareness also evident in his own fiction, especially when it draws on fairy-tale structures.[5]

In Calvino's use of the woman-as-nature metaphor I see showcased the tension between the modern folklore editor, attentive to performance, and the stylist, the author who wishes to capture the best voice. And gender is at the heart of such creative tension (see Weigle 1989). For instance, Calvino's favorite storytellers are forceful, active women.[6] He considers Raffaella Dreini, the teller of "Apple Girl," to be the "best storyteller" recorded by Siciliano (Calvino 1980:733) and he praises Agatuzza Messia, an illiterate Sicilian teller, for her dramatic flair ("One minute she is talking like a sailor; the next, her tone is very genteel" Calvino 1980:748) as well as her "enterprising and courageous" female characters who defy the stereotype of Sicilian women (Calvino 1980:xxiii). When editing "The Apple Girl," however, he deletes some of the dialogue that in Dreini's version portrays an articulate, assertive old woman helper: " 'You will give birth, Your Majesty, but to an apple.' 'An apple? What am I to do with an apple?' 'Be content with it for now, Your Majesty. Put it in the best spot you have on your terrace' " (Pitrè 1941:44). Calvino seems to appreciate these women's lively storytelling, yet his task, as he sees it, is to help us hear the special quality of their voices, the "precise rhythm" and "joyous logic" he values (Calvino 1980:xxix). In doing so, he frames these female narrators in ways that parallel the representation of "innocent persecuted heroines" in fairy tales: he valorizes them, but somewhat paternalistically limits their independence.

Focusing on Calvino's use of the woman-as-nature metaphor in his *Italian Folktales*, then, serves to caution against an essentializing rejection of this metaphor and of the "Innocent Persecuted Heroine" tales that privilege it. At the same time this focus provides an elegant case study of the naturalization of women in this subgenre. What Calvino finds fascinating in the tale of magic and what sustains his interest in it throughout his career is the genre's gift of transforming metaphor into story (Calvino 1980, 1988). As edited by Calvino, these stories show that the relation of metaphor to narrative is never simple or predictable. In Calvino's transformative use of the woman-as-nature metaphor, we can see yet another instance of his acting both as anonymous storyteller and author—always wishing to add to the tale—rather than an editor.

NOTES

1. When quoting from Calvino, in some cases I will not be using the 1980 English translation of Calvino's collection; rather, I will translate more literally from a 1971 reprint of the 1956 Italian edition. For this essay, I am interpreting the "Innocent Persecuted Heroine" tale more broadly than, but along the same lines as, Ilana Dan and Steve Jones indicate. For an extended discussion of the metaphor of Snow White, see Bacchilega 1988.

2. "The semiotic square, at its most abstract, is a schematic representation of

what Greimas calls 'the elementary structure of signification' which is the fundamental network of contrary, contradictory, and complementary relations between value terms necessary for the production and apprehension of meaning" (Ebert 1988:28). Doing away with the logical formalism of this model and its exclusive focus on options available in the plot, Ebert—like Fredric Jameson—uses the square to show how "the elementary structure of signification" describes "ideological relations (the historical conditions of possibility) organizing the symbolic order and its signifying practices." Her revision of Greimas' square strengthens Jameson's political restructuring of it by emphasizing "the suppression and concealment of oppositional elements just as ideology attempts to repress its incongruities and prevent those aspects that challenge its hegemony from being articulated in discourse" (Ebert 1988:29). Ebert's semiotic square also explicitly shows how sociocultural rules inform Greimas's typology of rules. Thus, her square marks the significance of the forbidden as well as the crucially ambiguous "not-forbidden" and presents itself explicitly not as a truth-finding apparatus, but as an ideologically constructed signifying practice.

3. The 1989 American Folklore Society meeting offered two important panels entitled "A Cackling of Crones: The Crone and Tradition." What emerged from discussions of aging, its rituals, and its narratives is the richness of this transition for women and its dismissal or rejection by dominant ideology and social practice. Jo Radner's paper, in particular, explored the complex function of the "creative rituals of older women," rituals which celebrate a "coming of age" and at the same time temporarily exorcise the social stigma associated with it.

As the fundamental distinction between sex and gender is being actively questioned by feminists, who are beginning to see how "male" and "female" are not simply biological universals, it becomes harder to posit the "objectivity" of scientific categories used to break down human experience. For some recent explorations of this controversial issue in various fields, see Rosi Braidotti, "Organs Without Bodies," *Differences* 1 (1989): 147–61; Donna Haraway, "A Manifesto for Cyborgs," *Socialist Review* 80 (1985):65–107; and "Monkeys, Aliens, and Women: Love, Science, and Politics at the Intersection of Feminist Theory and Colonial Discourse," *Women's Studies International Forum* 12 (1989):295–312; Sandra Harding, *The Science Question in Feminism* (Ithaca: Cornell University Press, 1986).

Steven Swann Jones develops his observations on gender and initiation in his essay, "Female Initiation in the Innocent Persecuted Heroine Genre," in *"Mirror, Mirror": Women's Initiation in Folklore,* ed. Bacchilega and Jones (forthcoming).

4. See Calvino's "La mappa delle metafore" ("The map of metaphors") originally published in 1974 as an introduction to Basile's collection, for an example of his interest in metaphor as fulfilled by the fairy tale (Calvino 1988:129–46).

5. Calvino's reworking of fairy tales never came to a stop, as his observations in *Six Memos for the Next Millennium* show (posthumous, 1988b).
6. Most of Calvino's tellers were women and most of the tales were collected in the late nineteenth century. In his notes, Calvino provides information on the collections he used and on some of the changes he made. Many tales are from Giuseppe Pitrè's collections of Tuscan and Sicilian lore (see *Opere Complete di Giuseppe Pitrè*, Firenze: Barbera); I discuss some of them: "The Apple Girl," "Rosemary," and "The King of Spain and the English Milord." Pitrè's Tuscan tales were collected by his friend and collaborator Giovanni Siciliano in 1876; all tellers were women and with the exception of Raffaella Dreini illiterate. Among other collections Calvino draws from are Vittorio Imbriani, *La Novellaja Fiorentina* (1877) for "The Fine Greenbird" and part of "Belsole"; Gherardo Nerucci, *Sessanta novelle popolari montalesi* (1880), his favorite Tuscan source, for "Olive" told by the widow Luisa Ginanni; Letterio Di Francia, *Fiabe e ovelle calabresi* (1929–31) for the "Turkey Hen" told by Annunziata Palermo.

REFERENCES

Bacchilega, Cristina
    1988   Cracking the Mirror: Three Re-Visions of "Snow White." boundary 2 15–16:1–25.
    1989   Calvino's Journey: Modern Transformations of Folktale, Story, and Myth. Journal of Folklore Research 26:81–98.

Bacchilega, Cristina, and Steven Swann Jones
    Under consideration, (eds.) "Mirror, Mirror": Women's Initiation in Folklore.

Basile, Giambattista
    1986   Lo cunto de li cunti. 1634–36 repr. Michele Rak, ed. Milano: Garzanti.

Beccaria, Gian Luigi; Arpino, Giovanni
    1982   (ed.) Fiabe piemontesi. Milano: Mondarori.

Beckwith, Marc
    1987   Italo Calvino and the Nature of Italian Folktales. Italica 64:244-62.

Calvino, Italo
    1971   Fiabe italiane. 1956 repr. Torino: Einaudi.
    1980   Italian Folktales. George Martin, trans. New York: Pantheon.
    1988a   Sulla fiaba. Mario Lavagetto, ed. Torino: Einaudi.
    1988b   Six Memos for the Next Millenium. Cambridge: Harvard University Press.

Dan, Ilana
    1977   The Innocent Persecuted Heroine: An Attempt at a Model for the Surface Level of the Narrative Structure of the Female Fairy Tale. *In* Heda Jason, ed., Patterns in Oral Literature. Paris: Mouton, pp. 13–30.

de Beauvoir, Simone
    1972   The Second Sex. H. M. Parshley, trans. and ed. London: Penguin.
Di Francia, Letterio
    1929–1931   Fiabe e novelle calabresi. Torino: "Pallante," fasc. 3–4, Dec. 1929, and fasc. 7–8, October 1931.
Ebert, Teresa L.
    1988   The Romance of Patriarchy: Ideology, Subjectivity, and Postmodern Feminist Cultural Theory. Cultural Critique, no. 10 (Fall): 19–57.
Imbriani, Vittorio
    1877   La Novellaja Fiorentina. Livorno: Vigo
Jones, Steven Swann
    1986   The Structure of "Snow White." *In* Ruth B. Bottigheimer, ed., Fairy Tales and Society. Philadelphia: University of Pennsylvania Press, pp. 165–86.
Kitzinger, Sheila
    1985   The Complete Book of Pregnancy and Childbirth. New York: Knopf.
Lerner, Gerda
    1986   The Creation of Patriarchy. New York: Oxford University Press.
Lüthi, Max
    1982   The European Folktale. John D. Niles, trans. Bloomington: Indiana University Press.
Nerucci, Gherhardo
    1880   Sessanta novelle popolari montalesi. Firenze: Le Monnier.
Pitrè, Giuseppe
    1941   Novelle popolari toscane. Opere complete di Giuseppe Pitre. vol. xxx. Firenze: Barbera.
Samuels, Mike, M.D.; Samuels, Nancy
    1986   The Well Pregnancy Book. New York: Summit Books.
Weigle, Marta
    1989   Creation and Procreation. Philadelphia: University of Pennsylvania Press.

LANGUAGE
AND
CULTURAL
KNOWLEDGE

10

ON THE NAMING OF PLACES AND KINDRED THINGS

WILBUR ZELINSKY

What is a place-name? At first glance such a question seems too simple-minded to justify any sort of reaction. Places are places, after all, and place-names are certain words inscribed on maps that label those various points, lines, and two- and three-dimensional features that merit cartographic notice. Why not end the discussion here and now?

My argument is just the opposite, that to date the discussion has not really begun and that, more to the point, the universe of place-names is vast, varied, and fertile with some of the loveliest of intellectual challenges—a terra incognita whose barest outlines we only dimly apprehend. Wild though it may sound, my claim is that a thoughtful examination of place-names and the place-naming process, one broadened and deepened beyond the usual approaches, will yield major insights into that greatest of enterprises, one in which we are all players, the creation of reality.

The time-honored custom in dedicating scholarly work is to absolve the dedicatees from any blame for the shortcomings of the work at hand while thanking them lavishly for help or inspiration. Bill Nicolaisen will not get off so easily. The ideas or suggestions herein would not have germinated if I had not read and been infected by a number of wonderfully venturesome Nicolaisen essays on the nature of names and naming and the interconnections between places and names (see Nicolaisen 1976, 1984, 1988).

I begin by dismembering the term "place-name" into its two components. "Places" are much more complicated creatures than any such lexical definition as "a particular portion of space" would lead one to suspect. In fact, human geographers and their fellow travelers have only recently begun to explore and grasp the meaning of placefulness and place-making, to comprehend the truth that places are totally human constructs, not just chunks of a Newtonian cosmos, with all the complications and paradoxes such a genesis implies. An elemental consequence is that the great majority of explicitly, as well as implicitly, space-related objects are hard to pin down within sharp territorial bounds for any extended time. For the purpose of this essay, I shall argue for a rather relaxed conceptualization of place, and will squeeze as much scholarly juice as possible from the inherent spatial, or placeful, qualities of most types of names.

In order to keep matters from getting out of hand, I confine my conception of place as associated, however tightly or loosely, with some sort of physical territory. In actuality, of course, the world contains many varieties of space, since any phenomenon that is dimensional inhabits a kind of space. Examples include the continua occupied by temperature, musical pitch, color and the electromagnetic spectrum, genealogical charts, chromosomal maps, crystals and molecules, graphs, and narratives; but perhaps nothing is more interesting than social space.

The discussion turns much murkier when we try to define "name" with precision, a task that continues to agonize philosophers and students of language. In an effort to make life simple, let us confine ourselves to signs that can be rendered alphabetically or numerically or via appropriate equivalents in nonalphabetic writing systems. That means ignoring, *inter alia,* graphic items such as the brands used to identify cattle and other livestock, personal monograms, business logos, or certain musical motifs—all devices that strongly resist verbalization.

The essential difficulty is that, try as we might, it is highly unlikely that we can ever hit upon a formula with which to draw a sharp line between common and proper nouns. Indeed, the messy truth is that these two classes of terms interdigitate and melt one into the other, with many nouns and adjectives alternating as names and ordinary words, e.g., *center, square, buffalo, jewel, acme, faith, lance, providence.* Let me suggest a pragmatic escape from the dilemma, a way to maneuver around a philosophical quagmire that is both deep and muddy, even though this makeshift solution will not fully satisfy anyone, including me. Suppose then we accept as a name: "Any combination of letters and numerals wittingly applied by some presumably identifiable individual or group to a specific new or unfamiliar object of any description." This formula sets aside most of our everyday vocabulary, including words such as *hand* or *baby,* that must have been worked out more or less subconsciously as our remote ancestors learned to speak. To illustrate the practical application of the definition, I would classify *oxygen* and *plutonium* as names but not *gold* or *lead;* similarly *Vitamin C* merits namehood but not *fat* or *starch.* The key elements in the definition, please note, are conscious deliberation and an encounter with something novel.

A virtue of this working definition is that it enables us to sail past the reef of the Singularity Problem. It matters not how many Springfields, Jimmy Johnsons, or Dew Drop Inns are at large in the world today or yesterday or that *the* Bible abounds in all its countless incarnations. In every case, it is an initial or local decision that counts, however large or small or nonexistent the amount of originality. The decisive consideration is: Did someone have to stop and think about what to call the thing in question? If so, naming has occurred. If the labeling is automatic, the answer is no.

The canny reader will have noted how my definition sweeps under the rug another less tractable problem: the status of generic terms. They are, of course, common nouns, and although each generic term may enfold a multiplicity of specific, authentic names, the category fails to meet fully my criteria for namehood. On the other hand, as happens so often with other common nouns, a number of generics derive from specific names, and vice versa, as in the case of *monadnock, meander,* and *podunk.* There is a crucial distinction between generic and specific place-terms and for other classes of terms for that matter. For the great majority of the former, we must attribute an origin to some sort of unconscious spontaneity, a collective exercise in word coinage, not a discrete act we can assign to particular persons cerebrating at identifiable times and places. Consider, for example, the obscure germination of *whistlestop, speakeasy, ghost town, sitcom, white-collar occupation, senior citizen,* the (musical) *blues, banana republic,* or *theme park.*

But it must be confessed that in a few instances, such as *pulsar, skid row,* or *Central Business District,* we might be able to document the invention. The most convenient way to dispose of the annoyance of generics is to set them aside as another class of words, one emphatically deserving monographic treatment elsewhere.

Also left unconsidered here is the phenomenon of anonymity, or rather namelessness. We perceive many objects that, wittingly or not, we decide to ignore or else remark casually without bothering to attach meaningful names to them beyond such tags as *it, thingamajig, gizmo, whatchamacallit,* or perhaps *Jane Doe.* The universe of nameless things, the lexically unborn, could well be the subject of another essay.

If we can agree on the considerable overlap between names and words in general, we next confront the fact that every name, like every word, vibrates within its own special, multidimensional field of attributes. Most of these traits are common to both names and the general run of words, such as pronunciation; orthography; etymology; variability; function; social status; class, gender, ethnic, and other human correlates; subconscious overtones; degree of popularity or acceptance within the community—and temporality and spatiality! Of peculiar importance to this discussion is the fact that every word of whatever description, like every language, exists only within a unique bubble of time and space, that words are born, live, and die (perhaps leaving their ghosts behind) only within certain parts of the inhabited world during certain periods.

What sets the name apart from every other verbal form is its mode of origin, as already argued, and another characteristic that devolves from that specialness: the existence of codes governing the making or choice of names, a set of rules that is highly specific to each species and subspecies of names and which, like names, can vary markedly over time and space. These codes run the gamut from the utterly simplistic to those of byzantine intricacy. Furthermore, there is an equally wide spread in the level of consciousness among the namers, from those who are completely alert to and/or absolutely constrained by the rules, to those who follow the guidelines faithfully without ever realizing what they are doing.

A few examples can clarify these points. At the simple but rigidly ordered end of the spectrum we find the surveyors who plotted the various townships, ranges, and sections of the American public domain by means of the rectangular survey system and knew ahead of time just which alphanumeric tag to apply to each parcel. In Table 1, which is largely based on the American scene, I have listed this system along with a number of other classes of objects for which numerals and/or letters of the alphabet, often sequentially ordered, may suffice for naming purposes.

There are other interesting formulaic devices besides the use of numbers and letters for designating clusters of objects, perhaps most notably for city streets (but sometimes for children, as in Faith, Hope, and Charity). For example, many American towns have their historically sequential procession of parallel streets named after presidents, beginning with Washington. I have also encountered neighborhoods where the prevailing street-naming theme is famous colleges or American battles. The District of Columbia's diagonal avenues bear the names of the fifty states, and the fourth alphabetic series of its east-west streets is floral in character. Perhaps the most imaginative system is that of Columbia, Maryland, most of whose street signs contain titles or phrases from the works of eminent American poets and novelists. At the world scale, though, Mexico City may well be the champion with its many neighborhood clusters of street names spelling out a common concept, e.g., famous rivers or foreign cities.

But there are other naming formulae that are not sequential in character. As an example, every competent research chemist knows precisely what to dub whatever new compound he may happen upon since the formula for devising new nomenclature is preordained. Almost as rule bound is the biologist who comes across a hitherto unknown organism, although there is some leeway for her imagination. At the other extreme, we espy the organizers of rock groups who, it would seem at first, enjoy absolute anarchic freedom in deciding what to call themselves. But even there certain unspoken principles prevail, so that it is highly unlikely, though not unthinkable, that we will ever hear of an aggregation known as *Mary Frances* or the *U.S.S. Constitution*.

The batch of codes used in conventional place-naming leans toward the elaborate pole of the continuum. When it is a matter of naming settlements, political jurisdictions, roads, major physical features, and other items of consequence in the American public domain, duly constituted bodies—such as the Board on Geographical Names, the postal service, city councils, railroad companies, real estate firms, and other

TABLE 1: Classes of Named Objects Designated in Alphanumeric Terms

Wholly alphanumeric and sequential:

Alumni, classes of	Musical scales
Auto license plates	Musical opuses
Congresses	Nonrectangular land survey parcels
Congressional districts	Offices & apartments
Convicts (?)*	Olympiads
Dynasties (as in Egypt)	Patents
Experimental plants & animals	Rectangular land survey parcels
Highway interchanges	Social Security numbers (?)*
Legislation	Superbowls
Library cataloging systems	Theater seats
Lockers	Vitamins
Meridians & parallels	Zip codes
Military serial numbers	Zoning districts

Wholly alphanumeric and nonsequential:

Fraternities & sororities	Telephones
Telephone area codes	Television & radio stations, ham radio operations

Partly alphanumeric:

Academic regions (as in climactic classification systems, or in "First World," "Second World," and so on.)	
Archaeological sequences	Monarchs, popes, noblemen
Bus routes	Movie sequels
Catalog items	Oil & gas wells
College courses	Personal names
Conventions	Political regimes (as in Fifth Republic)
Floors of buildings & theaters	Schools (as in New York City)
Highways	Street addresses
Military units	Tropical storms

*Numbers may not be entirely sequential

corporate entities—either initiate or pass upon prospective names, observing rather explicit, if not always written, principles that are too numerous or subtle to yield to simple summary. But in the vernacular naming of highly localized features and those within the personal realm, there is much ampler scope for fantasy, idiosyncracy, humor, and irreverence.

Perhaps the most rewarding example of complexity in naming codes, and also probably the one best studied, is that set of rules, mostly unwritten and largely unaffected by legislation or the judiciary, followed in bestowing given names on American infants. (The rule concerning surnames is nearly absolute: the inheritance of the father's, with the only notable exceptions involving adoption, divorce, or remarriage of parent, change of nationality, or uncertain paternity.) However, the increasingly common decision to give children hyphenated surnames derived from both parents reflects changing social attitudes in contemporary America. It is taken for granted that the child will have only one or two forenames, that none will contain more than four syllables, and that none will duplicate the name of a living sibling. Other givens include: the names(s) will be verbal (except for the appending of a II, III, etc., on an inherited name); it will be pronounceable and not be excessively cacophonous; that ludicrous, vulgar, and other offensive words are to be avoided (a notion that, ideally, should also apply to the derived acronym); and that, despite the growing stock of androgynous items, names that are gender-bound should be confined to the appropriate sex. All these rules are subject to regional, ethnic, and religious modification, not to mention specific family traditions, and evolve over time. A conspicuous example of the ethnic factor is the recent penchant among African Americans to adopt authentic African names or African-sounding coinages. In any case, the rather volatile patterns followed today in conferring specific given-names on infants are a far cry from staid nineteenth-century practices.

But, to this point, we have considered only the decisions leading to the legal or formal name. Making things more interesting is an ancillary clutch of practices—codas to the code, so to speak. Thus we have had certain time-honored procedures regarding changes in the wife's name upon marriage or divorce, a subcode currently in a state of rapid flux, with some involvement of husbands' names as well. Individuals may acquire official or honorific titles to set before the name or precious initials to affix to the rear. There are certain rather loosely defined patterns having to do with nicknames and other name transformations, terms of endearment (and abuse), or CB handles for those who indulge in such practices. Many individuals have occasion to acquire a nom de plume, alias, stage or professional name, or religious name, all affected by various unwritten codes. There are additional namelike ways to identify individuals beyond the formal verbal name and its variants: Social Security number, telephone number, vanity plate, and the quantified fingerprint pattern.

Standing apart from the more or less formal naming acts emphasized above—decisions that are usually or routinely recorded in some type of document—we have the wonderful world of folk naming. It is a major component of the realm of folklore, a field best defined concisely as intimate, informal communication and where what is said or done is all too seldom preserved or reduced to written form. When we contrive nicknames for persons (whether openly or behind their backs), for new foods, body parts, landscape features, towns, highways, railroads, business firms, makes of autos, commercial products, or other items in our quotidian world, we are being our most completely human selves. Folk naming is the most effervescent sort of creativity, the kind no school can teach, forever fresh and topical but also intensely traditional, certainly as venerable as any other activity that has endured since our prehistoric beginnings.

But, to return to the initial query, are we any closer to answering the riddle of the identity of place-names? Yes, in a rather roundabout way, we are. By stating that their loci in space and time are intrinsic qualities of all words and, more particularly, of all names, we can begin focusing on the truly vital spatiotemporality of names.

The central thesis of this essay is that the overwhelming majority of all names, as previously defined, have a geography, that they interact with place, or space, to a greater or lesser degree and in a variety of ways that are intellectually provocative. Even the small excluded minority, as listed in Table 2, of names for chemical compounds, subatomic particles, or the named bands within the electromagnetic spectrum have a geography of sorts, albeit a rather uninteresting one. We can discuss where and how such names originated, and their diffusion to the entire client community throughout the world, but thereafter these terms remain quite planetary in scope and indeed now extend outward to the entire observable universe and, as far as we can tell, will remain valid and unchanged in perpetuity.

The contention that most names are place-names of sorts, that they fall along a continuum stretching from the indubitable, map-anointed, officially acknowledged place-name down to items that have only the faintest whiff of spatiality, is certain to arouse initial skepticism. All I ask is careful cogitation and temporary suspension of disbelief. And to that end I have assembled Table 2. In it every class of named objects I can think of is listed, some 178 in all, within eight categories, which, in turn, are arrayed in order of decreasing spatial relevance. (Within each of seven groupings I have arranged the generic classes in order of increasing level of freedom and imagination in the naming process as best as I can estimate it from casual observation.) The final category, that of the unclassifiable, contains only a single entry: the captivating world of imaginary places. Note that I have indicated those classes of things, well over 40 in all, whose qualifications as place-names few would be inclined to doubt. With the exception of the imaginary places, all the conventionally recognized place-names fall within the upper three categories. In addition, I have flagged several other sets of phenomena that are occasionally mapped by geographers and others but whose titles are not universally regarded as place-names.

The fact that each class of named objects carries with it its own private code for the naming process, that indeed there are subcodes within the various subdivisions of many of these classes, bears repetition. (Furthermore, each of these codes merits close study.) The observation is especially germane whenever we consider three remarkably populous classes of objects and their names: commercial establishments, commercial products, and business firms. The spartan code for labeling the offices of attorneys and accountants is a far cry from the usages of hi-tech industries; the whimsicality so often found in the names of restaurants, beauty shops, or boutiques would never do for feed merchants, morticians, or banks; and there is little overlap in the vocabularies exploited by perfumers for their wares and purveyors of screwdrivers, fertilizer, or carbon paper.

In considering how difficult, or even impossible, it is to draw a tight cordon around the concept of place-names, let us look again at the attributes of place, but in the narrowest geometric sense—that of a sharply delimited portion of the earth's surface. Admittedly there are

TABLE 2: Classes of Named or Numbered Objects Arrayed in Terms of Spatial Attributes and Level of Imagination in Naming Process[1]

I. Fixed, relatively permanent objects with strictly defined dimensions:
Meridians and parallels[2]	Subway stations
Map coordinates for point locations	**Oil & gas wells**[3]
Lockers	*Castles*
Rectangular land survey parcels	*Church buildings*
Other real estate parcels	Famous trees
Stars & galaxies	Geodetic survey points
Theater seats	Hotel meeting rooms & suites
Offices & apartments	Apartment buildings
Floors of buildings and theaters	Vacation homes

II. Fixed spaces with well-defined dimensions but subject to change:
Country & area telephone codes	Schools
Postal zip code areas	*Reservoirs*
Congressional districts; city wards	*Academic regions*
Voting districts	Outer planets & their moons,
Zoning districts	asteroids, and comets
Bus routes	*Cities, towns & other*
New nations	*municipalities*
Political jurisdictions	*Parks*
Prisons	Interstate highway rest areas
Public buildings	*Retirement homes*
College buildings	*Farms & ranches*
Military establishments	*Marinas*
Libraries	*Country clubs*
Hospitals	Houses
Pipelines	*Industrial & office parks*
Airports	*Resorts*
Business & administrative territories	Office buildings
Scientific stations & observatories	*Amusement parks*
Railroads	*Cemeteries*
Railroad & subway stations	*Shopping centers*
	Residential subdivisions

III. Spatially fixed entities with boundaries imperfectly defined and perhaps subject to change:

Highway interchanges
Telephone exchanges
Political regimes
Historical events & eras
Canals
Archaeological epochs
Dams
Bridges

Plazas, squares, corners, etc.
Neighborhoods
Stadia
Mines & quarries
Natural physical features
Extraterrestrial features on planets & their satellites
Ski runs
Streets

IV. Spatially variable or mobile entities with uncertain or changeable dimensions:

Airplane & train seats; ship cabins
Airplane flights, scheduled bus and train runs (as in the 4:55 to New Haven)
Superbowls
Olympiads
Radio & television stations, ham radio & CB operations
Comets
Symphony orchestras, opera & ballet companies
Conventions
Business regions and districts
Highways

Tropical storms
Athletic tournaments
Vernacular regions (as in "Sun "Sun Belt")
Factories and warehouses
Newspapers
College courses
Street & criminal gangs
Athletic teams
Military operations
Business firms[4]
Commercial establishments[4]

V. Spatial fields strongly implied but not clearly specified:

Social Security numbers
Convicts
Auto license plates
Dynasties
Monarchs, popes, noblemen
Legislative acts & referenda
Endowed chairs
Geological eras
Racial classifications
Currency

Nuns & monks
National figures (as in John Bull, Marianne, Uncle Sam, Johnny Reb)
Scientific terms for biological genera, species, etc.
Soil types
Minerals
Military units
Wines & varieties thereof
Commercial products[4]

VI. *Spatial fields weakly implied:*

Alumni, classes of
Military serial numbers
Experimental plants & animals
Library cataloging systems
Numbered commercial catalog items
Opus numbers
Musical scales & notes
Congresses
Legal cases
Movie sequels
Fraternities & sororities
Chess strategies
Gymnastic maneuvers
Football plays & formations
Famous gems
Governmental bureaus
Units of measurement
Prizes & awards
Holidays
Political parties & factions
Religious denominations
Diseases
Renowned violins, organs, and other instruments
Nonprofit associations
Mechanical inventions & parts thereof
Chamber music groups & dance bands
Personal terms of endearment

Hairdos
Aliases
Musical compositions
Magazines
Quilt patterns
Dances & dance steps
Recipes & dishes
Mixed drinks
Weapon systems
Individual vehicles
Noms de plume
Stage names
Characters in fiction
Personal names
Nicknames
Code names for public figures
Chapters in books
Plays, films, ballets, operas
Radio & television programs
Books & articles
Paintings & other graphic works
Phonograph records & albums
Varieties of fruit, roses, orchids, lilies, etc.
Vanity plates
CB handles
Pets
Race horses
Rock groups

VII. *No spatial connotations:*

Patents
Chemical compounds
Vitamins
Isotopes of chemical elements
Metric system of measurement
Map projections

Electromagnetic spectrum
Scientific laws, theorems, formulae
Scientific devices procedures
Chemical elements
Subatomic particles

VIII. Unclassifiable:
Imaginary places

1. Within each category, items are arranged in order of increasing level of imagination.
2. Italic items bear conventional place-names, and have also been mapped.
3. Bold items have been mapped by geographers and others.
4. There is such great variety in naming practice among the many subgroups within this class that it is impossible to rank them by level of imagination.

mappable, nameable spaces (whether all of them constitute real places is another matter) we can neatly delineate and which are seemingly immutable—those listed under Category I in Table 2. But if I were playing devil's advocate, I could point out that even those tracts surveyed precisely in two-dimensional space usually have indeterminate upper and lower bounds. How far up does Libya extend? And how far down is Oklahoma Oklahoma?

But then we encounter other entities that are unquestionably places but whose horizontal extent is debatable or elastic and subject to revision over time, such as congressional and school districts, cemeteries, ranches, municipalities, college campuses, a metropolis' milkshed. Does anyone know where to mark off the Pacific from the Indian Ocean or what precisely comprises the Middle East? To plot the whereabouts of the Gulf Stream one must specify day and hour. Or, to be a real stickler for cartographic perfection, just where, down to the meter, is the outer edge of Times Square, Pike's Peak, Death Valley, the Brooklyn Bridge, or Lake Chad?

Given such fuzziness of physical dimensionality in standard places, perhaps I can persuade you that such ephemeral or loosely packaged affairs as Hurricane Agnes, Operation Overlord, the Aurignacian, Mormonism, the Ordovician, the Know-Nothings, Butterfield 8, Woodstock, the Second Crusade, or sherry have certain claims to place-namehood. Or at least that they have some intermediate grade of placefulness? Allow me to illustrate with a trio of seemingly outlandish possibilities.

Can we regard the names of college courses as place-names? We certainly could because they have specific, often unique names and numbers, may have a fixed location in a given chamber in a given building on a given campus, and, of course, are rigidly packaged timewise. Thus, to take a fictitious (I hope!) example, announcing Phys Ed 355, "Eurythmics of Jai Alai," might be the equivalent of mapping a place. Or, turning to the realm of popular culture, don't the terms *bluegrass, bebop, zydeco, scrabble,* and *hula hoop* (which may or may not fully meet my criteria for names) have a distinct spatial resonance? Another telling example is that of library classification systems. With a few interesting exceptions, they may not be unique to given institutions, but they are maplike in nature within a given setting. If I know the Library of Congress (LC) catalog number of a wanted item, I can lay hands upon it readily, almost blindfolded, with a little experience, for the number gives me its horizontal and vertical spatial coordinates in my university library, i.e., stack level and a reasonable guess as to which aisle or even shelf. In essence, then, that LC number is a veritable place-name.

Perhaps the best way to clinch the case is to return to the relatively well-trodden field of personal names. Are they place-names? More so than one would suspect at first. At the very minimum, there is the most intimate sort of interplay between personal names and place-terms. Within cultures in which surnames have been adopted, one of the more popular categories tends to be the resident's village, city, valley, or other locality. In the English-speaking world, names with such suffixes as *-ton* and *-field* signal ancestral if not present habitation. Indeed many a nobleman, past and present, is recognizable simply as Kent, Windsor, Burgundy, Milan, or Nevski. Need I mention the profusion of famous personalities on the map? Lenin, Victoria, Alexander the Great, Jefferson, Bolivar, Christ, St. Francis, and many others have spawned their own constellations of place-names. On a humbler scale, houses, farms, ranches, cemeteries, mills, ponds, general stores, rural roads, bridges, ferries, streams, hills, and urban shops as well as grander enterprises often bear the name of a current or former proprietor, while many an otherwise forgotten local notable is memorialized in the names of city streets.

But even if we do not bequeath a cartographic legacy, every single one of us is a spatial entity performing within a unique action-space ranging through every imaginable degree of simplicity and convolution, so that whenever one mentions a person's name, one is also, in a quite genuine sense, summoning up at least subliminal thoughts of a certain geography. The relationship is especially keen for some extraordinary place-besotted creative individuals. Utter the names James

Joyce, William Faulkner, Robert Frost, Robinson Jeffers, Thomas Hardy, Eudora Welty, James Agee, James T. Farrell, Johann Strauss, Peter Breughel, Vincent Van Gogh, or Martin Anderson Nexö, and immediately certain vivid landscapes flash onto our mental screen. But the most potent evidence comes from all those full-fledged, intensely humanized places, however miniature in scale: the countless graves and gravestones on which personal name and place are merged in the firmest, most inseparable of ways for as long as the inscription endures.

I could offer similar observations about many of the other classes of names appearing in Categories V and VI, for example, those for newspapers, racial groups, or diseases, though with less onomastic scholarship to back up the argument. Admittedly the connection between names and places is not immediately obvious for most of the items listed in those categories. But that is the whole point. Since location is somehow an attribute of all names, the relationships do exist in however tenuous a shape, falling somewhere within that long continuum from the spectrally spatial to names riveted to rigorously fixed terrestrial plots of ground or lines thereon. But we dwell in worlds, both human and physical, that are in constant flux. Even those most absolute of place-names at the uppermost end of the scale, those for parallels and meridians, refer to a planet of finite duration and fluctuating shape. Indeed there is an infinitesimal, shift from hour to hour in the location of these lines—one that would be impractical to monitor—because of the wobbling of the poles.

To return to my initial argument, the theme pulsing beneath all the foregoing statements is that the peculiarly human exercises of naming things and place-making, which, I must insist, are opposite faces of the same coin, are indispensable acts in our fabrication of reality. Consequently, we cannot comprehend the world adequately unless we take place-making into serious account. If I have drawn nearly all my examples from the English language and the pan-European experience in which I am, willy-nilly, a participant, I have little doubt that the ideas promulgated above are universal and apply cross-culturally as well as diachronically. But the ways in which they are applied most likely will vary perceptibly and in interesting ways among different cultures and eras that could reveal hidden realities about the mindsets of other peoples and other times.

The moral in all this? Only that the reader continue the author's work by pondering further the enormous amplitude and the ambiguities implicit in the concept of place-naming and what such considerations imply concerning the task of being human. This is really an invitation to continue, or think about, Adam's work. Isn't it remarkable that our putative ancestor's very first chore was onomastic? "...and whatsoever Adam called every living creature that was the name thereof. And Adam gave names to the cattle, to the fowl of the air, and to every beast of the field..." (Genesis 2:19–20). Is there any doubt that soon after he and his helpmate were evicted from Eden they began naming places and kindred things? The job is not finished.

REFERENCES

Nicolaisen, W. F. H.
- 1976 Words as Names. Onoma 20:142–63.
- 1984 Names and Narrative. Journal of American Folklore 97:259–72.
- 1988 Once Upon a Place, or Where Is the World of the Folktale? In Albrecht Lehmann and Andreas Kuntz, eds., Sichtweisen der Volkskunde. Berlin-Hamburg: Dietrich Reivner, pp. 359–66.

ও II ও

PAREMIOLOGICAL MINIMUM AND CULTURAL LITERACY

WOLFGANG MIEDER

By recognizing the linguistic nature of basic verbal items such as names, and by studying the psychological and cultural uses of names in different communities, Bill Nicolaisen has observed that "so much is usually made of the naming process, the creation of names, that it is easy to forget that in the vast majority of instances we are called upon not to name but to know names" (Nicolaisen 1980:41). As a result, he has contributed the concept of an "onomasticon," a conventionally accepted repertoire of names, which is used "appropriately in recognition, in thinking, and in talking." Although all individuals have distinctive name repertoires, they are influenced by "a community of name users and name givers, who make up an onomastic dialect area that is also culturally and socially stratified" (Nicolaisen 1980:42). The issue that Nicolaisen has identified is part of a more general field of study, that of comprehending the range of traditional knowledge relative to a society (Nicolaisen 1976). The issue can be carried further into the study of proverbs, especially as proverbs traditionally connote conventional wisdom within a society.

Recent theoretical research on proverbs and proverbial expressions has been primarily linguistically oriented, emphasizing in particular structural and semiotic aspects of proverbs on a comparative basis. The Soviet linguist and folklorist Grigorii L'vovich Permiakov (1919–83) published his now classic study *Ot pogovorki do skazki* in 1970, the English translation of which, *From Proverb to Folk-Tale* (1979), has had an important influence on international paremiological scholarship. Matti Kuusi in Finland continues to work *Towards an International Type-System of Proverbs* (1972), and Alan Dundes' article, "On the Structure of the Proverb" (1975), and Shirley L. Arora's article, "The Perception of Proverbiality" (1984), have established a solid foundation for modern paremiology. It must suffice to mention from among dozens of articles, dissertations, essay volumes, and books[1] three additional studies: Zoltan Kanyo, *Sprichwörter-Analyse einer Einfachen Form* (1981), Peter Grzybek and Wolfgang Eismann (eds.), *Semiotische Studien zum Sprichwort* (1984), and Neal R. Norrick, *How Proverbs Mean: Semantic Studies in English Proverbs* (1985).

Although these contributions represent major advances concerning the definition, language, structure, and meaning of proverbs, they fail for the most part to consider two extremely important questions that go beyond purely linguistic aspects of proverbial texts. One deals with the diachronic problem of traditionality, i.e., the fact that any text to qualify as a proverb must have (or have had) some currency for a time. Related to this is the synchronic question of frequency of occurrence or familiarity of a given text at a certain time. None of the dozens of proverb definitions addresses these questions, and yet any proverb must "prove" a certain traditionality and frequency in order to be considered verbal folklore.

As far as proverbs from past generations are concerned, questions as to their true proverbiality can be and have been ascertained by historical proverb dictionaries that amass references and variants for particular proverbs from written sources. Paremiographers around the world have assembled superb diachronic collections, the model being the massive work in English and American proverbs by Bartlett Jere Whiting (1968, 1977, 1989). With the aid of modern computers, such historically oriented volumes will continue to be published for various nations and languages, but this type of paremiographical work usually stops short of answering some extremely important questions: How about proverbs right now? Which texts from former generations are still current today? What are the truly new proverbs of the modern age? How familiar are people with proverbs today?

These questions are not new, but they need to be addressed in a more scientific fashion using modern means of statistical research. The

American sociologist William Albig (1931) was one of the first scholars to use demographic methods with proverbs. While his conclusion that proverbs have little use in complex cultures with rapid social change is not valid in light of newer research, he did include a list of the thirteen most popular proverbs in 1930 based on the answers of 68 university students who were asked to list all the proverbs they could think of during a thirty-minute period. A total of 1,443 proverbs or 21.2 proverbs per student were written down. Of these, 442 were different, and the most frequently cited was "A stitch in time saves nine" with 47 of the 68 students listing it. Table 1 shows the frequency of the top thirteen proverbs (Albig 1931:532):

TABLE 1: Most Popular Proverbs in 1930

TIMES MENTIONED	PROVERB
47	A stitch in time saves nine.
40	A rolling stone gathers no moss.
39	A bird in the hand is worth two in the bush.
37	Early to bed and early to rise, makes a man healthy, wealthy and wise.
30	Never put off till tomorrow what you can do today.
27	Haste makes waste.
26	An apple a day keeps the doctor away.
23	All that glitters is not gold.
23	Do unto others as you would have them do unto you.
21	Laugh and the world laughs with you.
21	Birds of a feather flock together.
20	There's no fool like an old fool.
20	Make hay while the sun shines.

Eight years later another American sociologist, Read Bain, had similar results using almost twice the number of students. He asked 133 first-year college students to write down all the proverbs they could. A total of 3,654 proverbs or 27.5 texts per student were listed (Bain 1939:436, Table I). Unfortunately Bain did not cite any of the proverbs, but we may assume that they included those found by Albig among American university students a few years earlier. What is of special interest is that on the average students could *only* cite between 21.2 and 27.5 proverbs in the 1930s. Admittedly, the sample was relatively small, and we know today that it is difficult to quote proverbs out of context, but this number is nevertheless surprisingly low from the point of view of cultural literacy, let alone folklore.

Unfortunately this type of research was not continued. It took some thirty years before the Soviet folklorist and paremiologist Isidor Levin (1968–69) called for detailed demographic research by paremiologists, especially if they wanted to reach conclusions about the national character or world view of certain peoples via proverbs. He refers to a survey which a German Institute of Demography undertook in 1968 that included a list of 24 German proverbs and asked the informants to indicate whether they totally agreed with their stated ideas. The greatest agreement, 69 percent, occurred with the proverb *"Es ist nicht alles Gold, was glänzt"* (All that glitters is not gold). *"Reden ist Silber, Schweigen ist Gold"* (Speech is silver, silence is gold) received 61 percent, but *"Gut Ding will Weile haben"* (A good thing needs time, i.e., Haste makes waste) received only 36 percent (Levin 1968:291). Levin concluded that much more demographic research is needed about the popularity and acceptance of certain proverbs before they can be interpreted as indicators of commonly held attitudes.

A year after the second part of Levin's essay appeared in the international journal *Proverbium*, the same journal published a small but significant study by the Swedish folklorist Carl-Herman Tillhagen in which he discusses the proverb repertoire of several inhabitants of a small Swedish village in the 1930s. From his field research with informants he was able to conclude that a good elderly informant had knowledge of about a thousand proverbs, proverbial expressions, proverbial comparisons, and other phraseological units. In an accompanying statistical table representing the frequency of the different genres of these fixed phrases, Tillhagen shows that his informants varied in their knowledge of proverbs from a mere 21 texts all the way to 575 (Tillhagen 1970:539). Again it must be remembered that these texts were collected out of context, but this rural population of retirement age certainly "knew" its proverbs (an average of about 134 proverbs per informant) better than the American college students.

These articles probably influenced G. L. Permiakov, an ardent reader of and contributor to *Proverbium*, to conduct a major paremiological experiment with the help of folklore students in Moscow. They presented 300 Muscovites with a large list of proverbs, proverbial expressions, proverbial comparisons, and other types of fixed phrases. The informants were asked to mark those texts which they knew, and the result was that all informants were acquainted with about a thousand of the texts. Permiakov considers them the basic stock of fixed phrases among native Russian speakers, referring to the thousand texts as a *paremiological minimum* in his short monograph (Permiakov 1971). This was followed by a short summary statement in English in *Proverbium* (Permiakov 1973) that was not published in Russian until eleven years later (Permiakov 1984).[2] A list of 75 of the most frequent Russian proverbial comparisons also appeared in *Proverbium* (Permiakov 1975), to which Matti Kuusi added an appendix of English, French, and Finnish equivalents, showing that many of these common comparisons have general currency throughout Europe (Kuusi 1975). Permiakov's most complete essay on the idea of the paremiological minimum appeared in Russian in 1982, and its English translation by Kevin J. McKenna, "On the Question of a Russian Paremiological Minimum," has recently been published in *Proverbium* (Permiakov 1989).[3] Since the short English-language note of 1973 on the need for establishing paremiological minima for Russian and other languages did not draw the expected scholarly reaction, it is now to be hoped that his longer English essay in the new *Proverbium* will encourage scholars to begin working on the establishment of paremiological minima in other nations and languages.

Permiakov's aim of establishing the Russian paremiological minimum was anything but merely academic. He had definite pragmatic ideas in mind and discussed them in the publications mentioned above. On the one hand, he was interested in the lexicographical problem of getting the most frequent phraseological units into foreign language dictionaries, and on the other, he was committed to the idea that the paremiological minimum was of important consequence in the instruction and learning of foreign languages.[4] Toward the end of his life he finished the manuscript for a small book that combines these two interests for 300 of the best-known Russian proverbs and proverbial expressions. The book appeared posthumously with a splendid introduction and variants and cultural notes for the texts as *300 obshcheupotrebitel'nykh russkikh poslovits i pogovorok (dlia govoriashchikh na nemetskom iazyke)* (Permiakov 1985a). For German students studying Russian as a foreign language, a German edition appeared in the same year (Permiakov 1985b),[5] and a Bulgarian edition came out one year later (Permiakov 1986). It was Permiakov's wish that this book would be translated into many other languages to help those studying Russian to gain a knowledge of the paremiological minimum, to become proverbially literate in a foreign language, as it were. Given the resurgence of Russian studies in the Anglo-American world, it is indeed high time that an English version of this standard work be made available to students of Russian. As Permiakov would have argued, no student of a foreign language can hope to gain cultural literacy in the target language without the knowledge of its paremiological minimum.

Two friends of G. L. Permiakov are keeping his insistence on demographic research toward paremiological minima alive. Matti Kuusi, in a short laudatory essay about Permiakov, stressed that he was the first to do systematic frequency analysis in order to establish the Russian paremiological minimum (Kuusi 1981). And the German linguist and paremiologist Peter Grzybek published a longer paper on Permiakov's accomplishments with the bilingual title "How to Do Things with Some Proverbs: Zur Frage eines parömischen Minimums" (Grzybek 1984:351–58). Three additional German papers (Daniels 1985, Schellbach-Kopra 1987, and Ruef 1989) have also touched upon the importance of paremiological or phraseological minima for foreign language instruction and dictionaries.

But this is not to say that other scholars have not independently pursued questions of frequency and currency of proverbs in their societies using statistical research methods. The American psychologist Stanley S. Marzolf, for example, presented 159 college students with a list of fifty-five "common sayings" (i.e., proverbs), asking them which of the texts were familiar to them. The proverb most frequently reported to be familiar (by 87.4 percent) was "If at first you don't succeed try, try again." Next in familiarity were "Where there's a will there's a way" (73.0 percent) and "Actions speak louder than words" (69.2 percent). Unfortunately Marzolf did not include his list of proverbs, but if the above percentages already seem a bit alarming, then what follows indeed indicates a rather low familiarity with proverbs by American students: "Only 16 of the 55 sayings were familiar to more than 50%, 6 were familiar to less than 10%. 'Act in haste, repent at leisure' (6.3%) and 'One bad apple spoils the whole bushel' (5.0%) were least familiar" (Marzolf 1974:202).

Another study used a standard psychological proverbs test to ascertain the familiarity which 278 African American students had with its forty proverbs.[6] The following table shows the five most and least familiar proverbs with percentages of respondents (Penn, Jacob, and Brown 1988:852):

TABLE 2: Proverb Familiarity among African American Students

Five most familiar proverbs	Known by (%)
Where there's a will there's a way	90
Don't judge a book by its cover	89
Quickly come, quickly go	89
When the cat's away the mice will play	86
All's well that ends well	86
Five least familiar proverbs	Known by (%)
One swallow doesn't make a summer	12
A golden hammer breaks an iron door	14
The used key is always bright	15
The hot coal burns, the cold one blackens	17
The good is the enemy of the best	18

A larger familiarity test based on 203 "sayings" (i.e., proverbs) was given to 50 students who were asked to rate the proverbs on a seven-point scale ranging from low familiarity (1, defined as "sayings that you have never heard or read") to high familiarity (7, defined as "sayings that you have heard or read many times") also showed that not a single proverb was well known to every student. Others, like "One swallow does not make a summer," had a very low level of familiarity. Listed in Table 3 are the 15 most familiar and the 15 most unfamiliar texts with their average scores (Higbee and Millard 1983:216–19).

These findings certainly show that some old proverbial standbys—"One swallow does not make a summer" and even "Make hay while the sun shines"—have a surprisingly low familiarity level among today's college students. While it is perhaps understandable that such "literary" proverbs as "Beware of Greeks bearing gifts" or "Brevity is the soul of wit" are less well known owing to the steady decline of cultural literacy, it is amazing to see such "simple" proverbs as "Hope springs eternal" or "Handsome is as handsome does" fall by the wayside. Certainly these small psychological tests are clear indicators that some of the hitherto commonly known proverbs are definitely declin-

TABLE 3: Proverb Familiarity among American Students

Most familiar	mean value
Practice makes perfect	6.92
Better late than never	6.90
If at first you don't succeed, try, try, again	6.88
Like father, like son	6.84
A place for everything and everything in its place	6.76
Two wrongs do not make a right	6.76
Two's company, three's a crowd	6.72
Where there's a will, there's a way	6.72
All's well that ends well	6.70
Don't count your chickens before they're hatched	6.70
Easier said than done	6.70
Practice what you preach	6.70
An apple a day keeps the doctor away	6.68
You can't tell a book by its cover	6.68
A penny saved is a penny earned	6.64

Most unfamiliar	mean value
One swallow does not make a summer	1.22
Little pitchers have big ears	1.32
It's better to be right than president	1.44
Vows made in storms are forgotten in calms	1.50
It's an ill wind that blows nobody good	1.54
There's many a slip, 'twixt the cup and the lip	1.68
A drowning man will clutch at a straw	1.74
Beware of Greeks bearing gifts	1.78
Make haste slowly	1.78
Brevity is the soul of wit	1.82
Rats desert a sinking ship	1.90
He who pays the piper can call the tune	1.94
Hope springs eternal	2.00
Handsome is as handsome does	2.04
Make hay while the sun shines	2.06

ing in popularity and currency. This in itself is nothing new. Proverbs have always come and gone, with others hanging on, but we appear to live in an age where even the paremiological minimum seems to be shrinking.

But perhaps this is not happening as much as one might think. How about new proverbs that may be replacing some of the overused and outdated proverbs of past times? Have the psychologists listed such new twentieth-century proverbs as "Different strokes for different folks," "It takes two to tango," "A picture is worth a thousand words," or "Garbage in, garbage out"? Of course not, for they have used almost entirely texts from standard proverb collections, many of which have questionable currency today. A German survey of young students concerning their familiarity with modern slogans, graffiti, and certain antiproverbs revealed astonishingly high ratings for some of them. Even the English language slogan "Make love, not war!" reached a familiarity rating of 85 percent among young Germans, a clear sign that such subcultures have their own repertoire of fixed phrases (Zinnecker 1981).

Furthermore, since the above-mentioned familiarity tests by psychologists were based on only a limited sample of young college students, they have questionable validity as far as actual familiarity levels of proverbs are concerned for a cross section according to education and age of the American population. There is no doubt in my mind that familiarity ratings for some of the standard proverbs used in these tests would be considerably higher if addressed to the total spectrum of American society. A fascinating study by the German polling company Intermarket (Düsseldorf) reports in dozens of statistical tables about the familiarity and use of proverbs by 203 males and 201 females from all walks of life, ages, and professions (Hattemer and Scheuch 1983). The study was based on an extensive questionnaire of 27 questions, among them "Which proverb do you use most frequently?", "How often do you use proverbs?", "What kind of people use proverbs a lot?", "When do you use proverbs in particular?", "Do proverbs help to cope with certain difficult situations?", "Do proverbs contain a lot of practical wisdom?", "Do you think that men or women use more proverbs?", "How did you learn most of your proverbs?", and "What is the educational level of people who use a lot of proverbs?" (see Mieder 1985 and 1989c:189–94 for a detailed analysis of this unpublished 198-page study).

Permiakov's pioneering paremiological experiment didn't include such questions, but this German study contains invaluable statistical information concerning attitudes toward, familiarity with, and use of proverbs by native speakers in a modern technological society. Of especial interest for the discussion at hand are the responses to the first question: "Which proverb do you use most frequently?" Of the 404 subjects, 363 answered this question. The answers contained 167 different proverbs, of which 114 texts were mentioned only once, while the other 53 texts were recorded between 2 and 26 times for a total of 249 citations. The most frequent and by implication the most popular German proverb was *"Morgenstund hat Gold im Mund"* (The morning hour has gold in the mouth, i.e., The early bird catches the worm) with 26 informants citing it as their most commonly used proverb.[7] Next comes the biblical proverb *"Wer andern eine Grube gräbt, fällt selbst hinein"* (He who digs a pit for others falls in himself) with 21 references, followed by 16 recordings of "Zeit ist Geld" (Time is money). These three most popular proverbs certainly belong to the German paremiological minimum (all the texts are listed on pp. 161–75 of Hattemar and Scheuch 1983).

What is now needed is for a team of scholars from such disciplines as folklore, linguistics, sociology, psychology, anthropology, paremiology, and demography to work out an even more elaborate questionnaire to be used with several thousand German citizens. The result of such an integrated study would in turn give us a precise idea of how proverbs are used and viewed today and which proverbs belong to the German paremiological minimum. Once national paremiological minima are established, we will also be able to determine the most frequently used international proverb types through comparative proverb collections (see Kuusi 1985:22–28). Such work will eventually lead to an international paremiological minimum for the world's proverbial wisdom.

Much work is required before this scholarly dream becomes reality. After all, we are only at the early stages of establishing paremiological minima for some national languages. Regarding the Anglo-American scene, it must be stated that the few psychological studies already mentioned represent but a meager beginning. Their purpose never was to establish a paremiological minimum, and in order to accomplish that task, major cross-cultural demographic research will be necessary. But what can be said today—at least speculatively—about the Anglo-American paremiological minimum? Ever since E. D. Hirsch published his best-selling book *Cultural Literacy: What Every American Needs to Know* (1987), educators, intellectuals, and citizens at large have in fact been discussing a kind of minimum of cultural knowledge for the average educated person. With the help of Joseph Kett and James Trefil, the author added a controversial appendix, "What Literate Americans Know: A Preliminary List" (pp. 146–215). Among this list are plenty of references to folklore in general and to proverbs in particular. Under the letter "A" alone appear the proverbs "Absence makes the heart grow fonder," "Actions speak louder than words," "All roads lead to Rome," "All's fair in love and war," "All's well that ends well," "All that glitters is not gold," "Any port in a storm," "April showers bring May flowers," "As you make your bed so must you lie in it" (pp. 152–56). In other words, proverbs figure prominently in what Hirsch and his co-authors consider American cultural literacy.

In the meantime the three authors have published their massive annotated *Dictionary of Cultural Literacy: What Every American Needs to Know* (1988), which after chapters on "The Bible" and "Mythology and Folklore" contains as its third chapter a major list of approximately 265 "Proverbs" (pp. 46–57). Hirsch takes credit for authorship of this chapter (p. 46), but unfortunately he is not always sure about the difference between a proverb and a proverbial expression. Thus his "Don't throw out the baby with the bath water" (p. 56) would surely be better placed in the following chapter on "Idioms" (pp. 58–80), which contains numerous proverbial expressions like "To throw out the baby with the bath water." Every paremiologist would obviously disagree with Hirsch for including "Carpe diem" (p. 48) or "Yes, Virginia, there is a Santa Claus" (p. 57) in a chapter on proverbs. Another problem is, of course, the alphabetical arrangement of the texts according to the first significant word, when alphabetizing by subject noun would be more useful.

More importantly, Hirsch does not state how he came up with his list of 265 essential proverbs. In the introduction to the volume, he merely states that entries were tested "to determine how widely known an item is in our culture.... Therefore, in selecting entries, we drew upon a wide range of national periodicals. We reasoned that if a major daily newspaper refers to an event, person, or thing without defining it, we assume that the majority of the readers of that periodical will know what that item is. If this is true, that event, person, or thing is probably part of our common knowledge, and therefore part of our cultural literacy" (p. ix). Perhaps proverbs fall under "things" in this statement, but I doubt that Hirsch got all of these texts out of newspapers or magazines. Besides, this statement says nothing about the general frequency of appearance necessary for *any* item to have been included in the dictionary. In any case, Hirsch most likely gleaned his list from one or more of the standard Anglo-American proverb dictionaries and perhaps discussed a somewhat longer list with friends and colleagues before deciding on these particular texts. Realizing that no studies on the Anglo-American paremiological minimum exist, Hirsch really had not much choice but to compile this "unscientific" list.

Lest my statements seem too harsh, permit me to admit that I was faced with much the same problem at the same time that Hirsch worked on his proverb list. I had been asked by the Philipp Reclam publishing house in Germany to put together a collection of *English Proverbs* (1988) and was given enough space to include 1,200 texts with English-German vocabulary and some annotations at the bottom of each page. How else was I to come up with these 1,200 texts but to go to some of the historical English and Anglo-American proverb collections and let my scholarly knowledge of proverbs together with my subjective feelings guide my decisions on whether any given text had enough currency (frequency, traditionality, familiarity, etc.) to be included? And my task was easier than Hirsch's, for I probably was able to include most of the texts in the Anglo-American paremiological minimum, in contrast to Hirsch and his much shorter list. I stuck out my proverbial neck at times and marked some proverbs as particularly "popular," but I remember a certain scholarly unease since I was not really basing this judgment on demographic research (see my introduction, pp. 3–19).

So much for scholarly honesty. Were I today in a position of having to reduce my list of 1,200 proverbs to Permiakov's 300 or even Hirsch's 265, and were I to be restricted to listing texts that have a proven familiarity among Anglo-American speakers of the twentieth century, I would now be able to enlist Barlett Jere Whiting's large new collection of *Modern Proverbs and Proverbial Sayings* (1989). This book contains 5,567 main entries based on materials that avid reader Whiting discovered in over 6,000 books and countless magazines and newspapers published in this century. Of special importance is that these publications range from serious literary works to mysteries and other light reading that represent a true cross section of Anglo-American written communication in the twentieth century. Under each entry, the proverbs and their many variants are listed in chronological order, some entries of the more popular proverbs amounting to short monographs. Those entries with the most texts obviously represent the proverbs with high frequency and belong by implication to the paremiological minimum of the Anglo-American language. What follows in Table 4 is a list of such high-frequency proverbs listing 13 or more references and having key words that start with the letters A, B, or C.[8] Both Hirsch and I missed "Crime does not pay"; I also somehow failed to register "Let bygones be bygones," and Hirsch did not include "Charity begins at home," "Appearances are deceitful," "Unlucky at cards, lucky in love," "The bird that fouls its own nest," and "Children should be seen and not heard." Alas, Whiting is not foolproof either. It is amazing that he did not come across the American proverb "One picture is worth a thousand words," which originated in 1921 (see Mieder 1989b) and which both Hirsch and I have included in our lists. And how about the quite modern, but nevertheless very common, American proverb "Different strokes for different folks," which was coined in the South around 1950? Neither Whiting nor Hirsch have registered it. At the time I put my 1,200 texts together, it luckily came to mind because I had just completed a chapter on this proverb for my book, *American Proverbs: A Study of Texts and Contexts* (1989a:317–32).

What this short comparison of Hirsch, Whiting, and Mieder has shown is, of course, that the study of the larger idea of cultural literacy and the narrower concept of a paremiological minimum must be based on scientific demographic research. Especially for the Anglo-American language, it is critical that today's paremiological minimum of native speakers be ascertained through a widely distributed questionnaire. Although such a study has obvious benefits for national and international paremiographers and paremiologists, it will also assure that the most frequently used proverbs of the modern age will be included in foreign language dictionaries and textbooks. This in turn will enable new immigrants and foreign visitors to communicate effectively with Anglo-American native speakers. Proverbs continue to be effective verbal devices, and culturally literate persons, both native

TABLE 4: Anglo-American High Frequency Proverbs

WHITING'S NUMBER	PROVERB TEXT	NUMBER OF REFERENCES
C257	Every *Cloud* has a silver lining	28
B229	A *Bird* in the hand is worth two in the bush	26
B291	*Blood* is thicker than water	24
B236	The early *Bird* catches the worm	23
C164	*Chickens* come home to roost	22
B136	One had made his *Bed* and must lie on it	21
C11	One cannot have his *Cake* and eat it	21
C141	*Charity* begins at home	21
C318	Too many *Cooks* spoil the broth	21
C236	*Cleanliness* is next to godliness	20
A99	*Appearances* are deceitful	19
B235	*Birds* of a feather flock together	19
C42	Unlucky at *Cards*, lucky in love	19
B432	New *Brooms* sweep clean	18
C302	Easy *Come*, easy go	18
C404	*Crime* does not pay	17
B135	Early to *Bed* and early to rise, makes a man healthy, wealthy and wise	16
C115	When the *Cat's* away the mice will play	16
B234	It is an ill *Bird* that fouls its own nest	15
B488	*Business* before pleasure	15
C180	*Children* should be seen and not heard	15
C275	Let the *Cobbler* stick to his last	15
C318	*Confession* is good for the soul	15
C360	The *Course* of true love never did run smoothly	15
C449	*Curiosity* killed the cat	15
C82	A *Cat* has nine lives	14
A12	*Absence* makes the heart grow fonder	13
A110	One rotten *Apple* can spoil the whole barrel	13
B162	*Beggars* cannot be choosers	13
B206	The *Bigger* they are, the harder they fall	13
B525	Let *Bygones* be bygones	13
C175	The *Child* is father to the man	13
C218	*Circumstances* alter cases	13

and foreign, must have a certain paremiological minimum at their disposal to participate in meaningful oral and written communication.

NOTES

1. For additional bibliographical references, see my international proverb bibliographies (Mieder 1982 and 1984).
2. The Russian title of this short paper is "O paremiologicheskom urovne iazyka i russkom paremiologicheskom minimume." It has recently been reprinted (Permiakov 1988:143–44).
3. A shortened version of the Russian text with the same title has been reprinted twice (Permiakov 1984:265–68 and Permiakov 1988:145–49).
4. A colleague of Permiakov, A. Barulin, also delivered a lecture in 1973 in Varna (Bulgaria) with the title "Russkii paremiologicheskii minimum i ego rol' v prepodavanii russkogo iazyka" of which a summary has subsequently been published (see Permiakov 1984:264–65). Following Permiakov, Barulin stresses the importance of teaching proverbs, proverbial expressions and other phraseological units to students studying Russian as a foreign language. He refers to Permiakov's paremiological minimum of about a thousand texts and argues that the learning and active oral and written use of proverbial materials should be part of all foreign language instruction.
5. It should be noted that A. M. Bushui from Samarkand quite independently from G. L. Permiakov published an article in 1979 on the minimum German proverbs that should be part of the curriculum of secondary schools in the Soviet Union. The major part of the article (pp. 9–28) presents a bilingual list of German proverbs in alphabetical order. Comments on the frequency and linguistic level of these proverbs as well as important considerations for the teaching of folk speech in foreign language classes are included.
6. For a review of the use of proverbs in psychological testing, see Mieder 1978.
7. For a discussion of this German proverb, see Mieder 1983:105–12.
8. I thank Janet Sobieski for her help in putting together these statistics by counting the references in Whiting's collection.

REFERENCES

Albig, William
    1931   Proverbs and Social Control. Sociology and Social Research 15: 527–35.

Arora, Shirley L.
    1984   The Perception of Proverbiality. Proverbium 1:1–38.

Bain, Read
1939 Verbal Stereotypes and Social Control. Sociology and Social Research 23:431–46.
Bushui, A. M.
1979 Paremiologicheskii minimum po nemetskomu iazyku dlia srednei shkoly. *In* Kh. M. Ikramova, ed., Problemy metodiki prepodavaniia razlichnykh distsiplin v shkole i vuze. Samarkand: Samarkandskii gosudarstvennyi universitet, pp. 4–28.
Daniels, Karlheinz
1985 "Idiomatische Kompetenz" in der Zielsprache Deutsch. Voraussetzungen, Möglichkeiten, Folgerungen. Wirkendes Wort 35: 145–57.
Dundes, Alan
1975 On the Structure of the Proverb. Proverbium 25:961–73.
Grzybek, Peter; Eismann, Wolfgang
1984 (eds.) Semiotische Studien zum Sprichwort. Simple Forms Reconsidered I. Tübingen: Gunter Narr.
Hattemer, K.; Scheuch, E. K.
1983 Sprichwörter: Einstellung und Verwendung. Düsseldorf: Intermarket. Gesellschaft für internationale Markt- und Meinungsforschung.
Higbee, Kenneth L.; Millard, Richard
1983 Visual Imagery and Familiarity Ratings for 203 Sayings. American Journal of Psychology 96:211–22.
Hirsch, E. D.
1987 Cultural Literacy. What Every American Needs to Know. With an Appendix, What Literate Americans Know, by E. D. Hirsch, Joseph Kett, and James Trefil. Boston: Houghton Mifflin Company.
Hirsch, E. D.; Kett, Joseph; Trefil, James
1988 The Dictionary of Cultural Literacy: What Every American Needs to Know. Boston: Houghton Mifflin Company.
Kanyo, Zoltan
1981 Sprichwörter-Analyse einer Einfachen Form. Ein Beitrag zur generativen Poetik. The Hague: Mouton.
Kuusi, Matti
1972 Towards an International Type-System of Proverbs. Helsinki: Suomalainen Tiedeakatemia. Reprinted in Proverbium 19 (1972): 699–736.
1975 Nachtrag [to Permiakov: 75 naibolee...]. Proverbium 25:975–78.
1981 Zur Frequenzanalyse. Proverbium Paratun 2:119–20.
1985 Proverbia septentrionalia. 900 Balto-Finnic Proverb Types with Russian, Baltic, German and Scandinavian Parallels. Helsinki: Suomalainen Tiedeakatemia.

Levin, Isidor
  1968–69 Überlegungen zur demoskopischen Parömiologie. Proverbium 11:289–93 and 13:361–66.
Marzolf, Stanley S.
  1974 Common Sayings and 16PF [Personality Factor] Traits. Journal of Clinical Psychology 30:202–4.
Mieder, Wolfgang
  1978 The Use of Proverbs in Psychological Testing. Journal of the Folklore Institute 15:45–55.
  1982 International Proverb Scholarship: An Annotated Bibliography. New York: Garland Publishing.
  1983 Deutsche Sprichwörter in Literatur, Politik, Presse und Werbung. Hamburg: Helmut Buske.
  1984 International Proverb Scholarship: An Updated Bibliography. Proverbium: Yearbook of International Proverb Scholarship, 1 ff.
  1985 Neues zur demoskopischen Sprichwörterkunde. Proverbium 2: 307–28.
  1988 English Proverbs. Stuttgart: Philipp Reclam.
  1989a American Proverbs: A Study of Texts and Contexts. Bern: Peter Lang.
  1989b "Ein Bild sagt mehr als tausend Worte": Ursprung und Überlieferung eines amerikanischen Lehnsprichworts. Proverbium 6:25–37.
  1989c Moderne Sprichwörterforschung zwischen Mündlichkeit und Schriftlichkeit. In Lutz Röhrich and Erika Lindig, eds., Volksdichtung zwischen Mündlichkeit und Schriftlichkeit. Tübingen: Gunter Narr, pp. 187–208.
Nicolaisen, W. F. H.
  1976 Folk and Habitat. Studia Fennica 20:324–30.
  1980 Onomastic Dialects. American Speech 55:36–45.
Norrick, Neal R.
  1985 How Proverbs Mean: Semantic Studies in English Proverbs. Amsterdam: Mouton.
Penn, Nolan E.; Jacob, Teresa C.; Brown, Malrie
  1988 Familiarity with Proverbs and Performance of a Black Population on Gorham's Proverbs Test. Perceptual and Motor Skills 66: 847–54.
Permiakov, Grigorii L'vovich
  1970 Ot pogovorki do skazki (Zametki po obshchei teorii klishe). Moskva: Nauka. English translation by Y.N. Filippov, From Proverb to Folk-Tale. Notes on the General Theory of Cliché. Moscow: Nauka, 1979.
  1971 Paremiologicheskii eksperiment. Materialy dlia paremiologicheskogo minimuma. Moskva: Nauka.

1973 On the Paremiological Level and Paremiological Minimum of Language. Proverbium 22:862–863.
1975 75 naibolee upotrebitel'nykh russkikh sravitel'nykh oborotov. Proverbium 25:974–975.
1979 From Proverb to Folk-Tale. Notes on the General Theory of Cliché. Translated by Y. N. Filippov. Moscow: Nauka.
1982 K voprosu o russkom paremiologicheskom minimume. In E. M. Vereshchagina, ed., Slovari i lingvostranovedenie. Moskva: Russkii iazyk, pp. 131–37. English translation by Kevin J. McKenna, On the Question of a Russian Paremiological Minimum, in Proverbium 6 (1989):91–102.
1984 Paremiologicheskie issledovaniia. Sbornik statei. Moskva: Nauka.
1985a 300 obshcheupotrebitel'nykh russkikh poslovits i pogovorok (dlia govoriashchikh na nemetskom iazyke). Moskva: Nauka.
1985b 300 allgemeingebräuchliche russische Sprichwörter und sprichwörtliche Redensarten. Ein illustriertes Nachschlagewerk für Deutschsprechende. Leipzig: VEB Verlag Enzyklopädie.
1986 300 obshcheupotrebitel'nykh russkikh poslovits i pogovorok (dlia govoriashchikh na bolgarskom iazyke). Sofia: Narodna prosveta.
1988 Osnovy strukturnoi paremiologii. I. L. Elevich, ed. Moskva: Nauka.
1989 On the Question of a Russian Paremiological Minimum. Kevin J. McKenna, trans. Proverbium 6:91–102.

Ruef, Hans
1989 Zusatzsprichwörter und das Problem des Parömischen Minimums. In Gertrud Gréciano, ed., Europhras 88. Phraséologie contrastive. Actes du Colloque International Klingenthal—Strasbourg, 12–16 mai 1988. Strasbourg: Université des Sciences Humaines, Département d'Etudes Allemandes, pp. 379–85.

Schellbach-Kopra, Ingrid
1987 Parömisches Minimum und Phraseodidaktik im finnisch-deutschen Bereich. In Jarmo Korhonen, ed., Beiträge zur allgemeinen und germanistischen Phraseologieforschung. Oulu: Oulun Yliopisto, pp. 245–55.

Tillhagen, Carl-Herman
1970 Die Sprichwörterfrequenz in einigen nordschwedischen Dörfern. Proverbium 15:538–40.

Whiting, Bartlett Jere
1968 Proverbs, Sentences, and Proverbial Phrases from English Writings Mainly Before 1500. Cambridge, Massachusetts: Harvard University Press.
1977 Early American Proverbs and Proverbial Phrases. Cambridge, Massachusetts: Harvard University Press.
1989 Modern Proverbs and Proverbial Sayings. Cambridge, Massachusetts: Harvard University Press.

Zinnecker, Jürgen
   1981   Wandsprüche. *In* Arthur Fischer, ed., Jugend '81. Lebensentwürfe, Alltagskulturen, Zukunftsbilder. Hamburg: Jugendwerk der Deutschen Shell, vol. 1, pp. 430–76.

❧ 12 ❧

WHAT, IF ANYTHING, IS A SCOTTICISM?

J. DERRICK MCCLURE

A polymath like Bill Nicolaisen will readily recognize the occasional temptation to browse in subjects far removed from our fields of expertise. In such a mood, I once happened upon an article with the intriguing title "What, if anything, is a zebra?" (Gould 1981), from which I learned that this deceptively familiar word refers to three distinct species of equine mammals which, stripes apart, are not self-evidently more closely related to each other than to other members of the horse tribe, and one of which has (on at least one zoologist's showing) more in common with true horses than with its striped kin. This, of course, calls into question the whole practice of classifying and categorizing entities. Such a procedure must, clearly, be conducted by abstracting from an infinite complexity of features certain salient ones with reference to which disparate specimens are grouped together, and therefore of necessity ignoring many others which, had they been preferentially selected, could have given rise to a different system of classification.

Classification of entities has occupied the attention of Bill Nicolaisen throughout his career: not mammalian species, certainly, but folktale motifs according to such factors as type, frequency, and provenance, and place-name elements according to distribution, field of reference, and language of origin. It is no denigration of his work in other fields to suggest that the contribution to scholarship for which he will be principally remembered is his exposition of the ordering principles behind the almost terrifyingly intricate toponymic map of Scotland (Nicolaisen 1976). This has naturally entailed much work on the Scottish languages: not only the still-living Scots and Gaelic, but languages no longer heard within the bounds of Scotland. If folktales are the stuff of creative language use, so too is the giving of place-names, every instance being in its origin a miniature exercise of the creative spirit. What, if anything, is a place-name? Nicolaisen could readily answer that: he has expounded in fascinating detail on the nature of names as a special class of words. Linguistic items are, on the face of it, less complex phenomena than living organisms, and their classification would seem to raise fewer difficulties. Yet the field is by no means free of pitfalls. What, if anything, is a noun? It is common knowledge that even as anciently and universally recognized a category-word as this presents grave problems of definition. And if it is not always, perhaps not ever, possible to devise foolproof definitions for terms referring to intra-linguistic items and their relationships, no more is it to be expected that terms invoking extra-linguistic criteria will be easier to pin down. The expert categorizer of folklore motifs and place-name elements is now invited to consider what precisely should come under the heading of *Scotticism.*

The word, spelled with one or with two t's, came into general currency in the eighteenth century. It is defined in the Oxford English Dictionary as "An idiom or mode of expression characteristic of Scots; esp. as used by a writer of English"; its first use recorded there is by Daniel Defoe in his *Memoirs of the Church of Scotland,* referring to the expression "to ride the marches" (used by James VI in a rebuke to the ministers of the Kirk, which Defoe quotes thus: "(T)here could be no agreement between him and them till the Marches of their Jurisdiction were ridden"). Later, David Hume in 1752 produced a list of "Scotticisms" in his *Political Discourses* and saw it reprinted eight years later in Vol. XXII of the *Scots Magazine* (pp. 686–87). Further lists of Scotticisms, each drawing on its predecessors, appeared from James Beattie in *Scoticisms Arranged in Alphabetical Order, Designed to Correct Improprieties of Speech and Writing* (1779, a revised, rearranged and expanded version following in 1787), from John Sinclair in 1782 (the title of his work is *Observations on the Scottish Dialect,* but the opening paragraph of the Advertisement states: "It was the full persuasion that a collection of Scoticisms would be of use to my countrymen, not the vanity of being thought an author, which gave rise to the following publication"), and from Hugh Mitchell in 1799.

What kind of material do these lists contain? What, if anything, is a Scotticism; or at least what did Hume, Beattie, Sinclair, and Mitchell think it was? Even more obvious than the fact that a zebra is striped is the fact that a Scotticism is heard in Scotland. Before beginning to examine the lists, however, our expectation of what they will contain must be based on more refined criteria than this. First, though a contemporary linguist can use the word "Scotticism" as a more or less neutral descriptive term (cf. Romaine 1980: "Scotticisms exist at all linguistic levels"), this was not to be expected in the eighteenth century. In the period following the abolition of the Scottish parliament in 1707, and more particularly in the second half of the century, an assumption had arisen that educated Scotsmen should abandon their native vernacular and adopt the vocabulary and idiom, if not necessarily the pronunciation, of London English (for the most recent discussion, with particular reference to Beattie, see Hewitt 1987). Bilingualism in Scots and English had been commonplace in Scotland, and not only among the upper classes, for decades before this, but an intention actually to discontinue the use of Scots was a new phenomenon. The pathetic self-abnegation and provincialism which Scotsmen were now assuming in regard to their own language are shown by quite innocent comments on the parts of the list-makers. Sinclair, for example, writes: "There is no colloquial idiom more common with Scotchmen, or more disagreeable to the English, than *What's your will*" (p. 31), the parenthetical phrase suggesting that it is simply natural that the Scots should wish to shape their language to please the English instead of themselves.

A Scotticism, then, is something undesirable by definition. The full title of Mitchell's collection is *Scotticisms, Vulgar Anglicisms and Grammatical Improprieties Corrected,* and though he distinguishes these (as he perceives them) by abbreviations, they are all listed together in alphabetical order. In the first version of his list Beattie selects six expressions: "He came *again* him, I *see'd* him, I will wait *of* you, this *here* and that *there,* I said none of *them* things, he *lays* in bed": of which he says "[These] are not properly Scoticisms; being common in England among people of the lower class, from whom illiterate Scotchmen take them, on the supposition that they are good English." He is entirely right, at least to the extent of denying that these are historically

Scottish usages: as to the last, far from using *lay* for *lie* a not uncommon Scottish habit is to do the reverse, and likewise to use *sit* for *set* ("Sit the pan on the cooker"). Yet even being perfectly aware that these forms are substandard English and not Scots, he includes them in what by its title is a list of Scotticisms. His "I will not go *without* I am paid for it" is in the same category: the criterion of impropriety outweighs that of Scottishness. Even more extreme sensitivity is shown by Sinclair, who regards "He is ten years old next May" as an expression to avoid—one should say, "He was ten years old last May"—since it is "asserting a circumstance which, by the death of the person, may never happen" (p. 33): but this is hardly a peculiarly Scottish habit. Sinclair, however, to his credit, ends his book with the observation: "If England were to be ransacked, as numerous a list of improprieties as is contained in this collection, might be exhibited to the world," and demonstrates this in part by a short list of "absurd and ridiculous" *English* idioms (pp. 229–30).

Secondly, the criterion of Scottishness alone is not sufficient to qualify a form for inclusion in a list. As an obvious example, only Sinclair includes any selection from the common Scots vocabulary items characteristic of the eighteenth-century revival of poetry in vernacular Scots, which culminated in the work of Robert Burns: *biggin, fash, lowe, blate, clarty, douce, horse-couper, oxter, thrapple*. The lists, with the partial exception of Sinclair's, are far from being accounts of Scottish *popular* speech: on the contrary, many of the words which they contain are clearly from an educated register. This lack is explained by Beattie: "His (Sinclair's) plan and mine are different. Mine is nothing more, than to put young writers and speakers on their guard against some of the Scotch idioms, which, in this country, are liable to be mistaken for English. With respect to broad Scotch words I do not think any caution requisite, as they are easily known, and the necessity of avoiding them is obvious" (pp. 2–3). Scots usages, that is, are of two kinds: those which are generally recognized in Scotland as being distinctively Scottish and those which are not. This distinction is still recognized as a valid and useful one, though the sociolinguistic situation has changed since the eighteenth century in two important respects. On the one hand, common speech in Scotland is much more closely assimilated (except in pronunciation) to that of England than it was then; on the other, social prejudice against Scottish linguistic features among the educated classes in Scotland is much less strong. The two groups are now referred to, in terminology introduced by Aitken (1979), as *overt* and *covert* Scotticisms. It is the latter which Hume, Beattie, and Mitchell thought it necessary to include: those which a native Scot might—significant phrase—"mistake for English," or, more accurately, use in the innocent assumption that they are simply how everybody speaks.

A Scotticism then, for the purposes of Hume, Beattie, and Mitchell, is an expression which is Scottish but not necessarily obviously so, and (perhaps *and/or*) is not in conformity with the canons of eighteenth-century prescriptive grammar (Dr. Johnson and Bishop Lowth are appealed to on several occasions in the lists). The compilers were men of learning and culture, and there is no doubt that they had heard all the forms they cited in the mouths of Scotsmen and that they recognized them as "ungrammatical" or otherwise improper by the literary standards of their time. Yet controversy attended the lists from their first appearance. A small indication is that a first edition of Beattie's second collection in Aberdeen University Library has, in the margin opposite the entry for *compete* (which Beattie regards as a mistake for *contend*), a note in pencil by an unknown hand: "Compete is good English, and if you do not think so you are under a horrible delusion."

Even more interesting is the reception of David Hume's list. Sylvester Douglas, in a letter to Beattie (29 October 1777), remarked that "... he (Hume) suppressed [it] in the subsequent impressions, and very wisely I think as it contained, short as it was, several mistakes."[1] A skeptical and ironical response to the list, by one signing himself Philologus, was published in Vol. XXVI of the *Scots Magazine,* March 1764, "to warn our countrymen equally against fancying all Scoticisms to be there contained, or all there contained to be Scoticisms" (pp. 187–89). "Philologus" queries Hume's prescriptions on the use of *shall* and *will, these* and *those* (in which, incidentally, Hume does not specify what he regards as Scotticisms but merely states the canonical usage: one wonders whether he simply considered anything else to be ipso facto both Scottish and wrong), points out several cases where Hume's alleged Scotticisms are attested in respectable English authors or current in English speech, and in response to Hume's remarkable suggestion that (for example) *butter and bread, pepper and vinegar* and *paper, pen and ink* are Scotticisms for *bread and butter, vinegar and pepper* and *pen, ink and paper* comments "Nor can she (England) forbear smiling, when ... she hears her sister taught, that *paper pen and ink, a pretty enough girl,* and *as ever I saw,* are become the monopoly of North Britain."

Hume's list, in fact, though certainly demonstrating his awareness of Scots as contrasted with English usages, demonstrates still more clearly his excessive fear of linguistic impropriety and his unexamined assumption that solecisms and Scotticisms were virtually the same thing. Beattie, in his turn, recognized the morbid timidity regarding the native idiom which had come to affect many Scotsmen with deleterious effect on their writing: "Our style is stately, and unwieldy, and clogs the tongue in pronunciation, and smells confoundedly of the lamp... and when an easy, familiar, idiomatical phrase occurs, dare not adopt it, if we recollect no authority, for fear of Scoticism" (letter to Lord Glenbervie, 5 January 1778).[2] Yet in the preface to his *Scoticisms,* he acknowledges: "It is possible I may have marked as improper some words for which good authority might be produced. But, where the purity of language is concerned, it is, in *my* opinion, more safe to be too scrupulous, than too little so" (p. 3).

Beattie's list of Scotticisms, in fact, is a remarkably mixed selection. Naturally it contains a goodly number of what are Scotticisms in the simplest, most obvious and most genuine sense—usages which had arisen in Scotland as part of the centuries-long independent development of Northumbrian Anglo-Saxon north of the Tweed; many are of considerable interest both in themselves and in Beattie's attempts to supply English equivalents. Some are vocabulary items unknown, or virtually so, in what he would have thought of as "English," i.e., the standard literary language and the spoken dialect of the landowning class and the London social elite: because of his desire to exclude "broad Scotch words," these are few in number. They include *ashet* (defined simply as "a plate, at table," though actually its use is generally restricted to a large serving-dish), *airt* ("direction": he describes this word as "Erse," i.e., Gaelic; but though it may in fact be derived from the Gaelic word *aird,* for "compass point," this is not certain), *allenarly* (only), *anent* (concerning), *dure* (hard, difficult) and *trance* (passage), besides some Latin-derived words suggestive of legal or other formal contexts: *preses* (chairman), *cognosce* (take cognizance of), *demit* (resign), *delate* (accuse before a court), *exeem* (exempt), *depone* (declare upon oath). *Deponent* he acknowledges to be English but notes the Scots habit of accenting it on the first syllable. Philologus for his part lists over forty words of which the stress-patterning in Scotland differs from that used in England: some are still heard among Scots, either occasionally or regularly, with the pronunciation he cites (*AprIL* [or *AprILE*], *JUly, commitTEE, harRASS, INquiry, interEST*).

One term of the Treaty of Union was that the distinctive legal system of Scotland should be retained, and the established (and still surviving) terminology of Scots law furnished Beattie with numerous examples of Scotticisms for his list. It should be borne in mind that the legal profession was a popular means of advancement in eighteenth-century Scotland and that a large proportion of Edinburgh's social and intellectual leaders were men who had undergone the rigorous discipline of legal studies: the vocabulary of the law was therefore far more widely known and used than it now is. Beattie lists several words that have special senses in Scots law, words frequent in their more familiar senses: *instruct* (prove), *panel* (prisoner at the bar), *repeat* (repay), *subjects* (effects, i.e., property), *writer* (advocate); as well as specialized technical terms: *homologate* (ratify), *interlocutor* ("interlocutory sentence," i.e., judgment or order of a court), *onerous* (of a contract, for the mutual benefit of both parties). He illustrates the Scots sense of *mortification* (fund bequeathed for a charitable purpose) by an anecdote: " 'We have lately got a mortification here,' said a northern burgess to a gentleman from England... 'an old miser died the other day, and left us ten thousand pounds to build an hospital.' 'And call you that a mortification?' said the stranger" (p. 56). Beattie's explanation of *designation* is erroneous: "a title given to a man over and above his Christian name and surname, showing his estate, degree, occupation, trade, place of dwelling, etc." (p. 28). This usage is not particularly Scottish, and the meaning which the word has in Scots law, "the setting apart of manses and glebes for the clergy from the church lands by the presbytery of the bounds" (OED), is not mentioned.

Beattie's motives in including these and other legal terms in what is avowedly a list of expressions to be avoided are somewhat confused. In his entry for "Sheriff depute" (a Scotticism, according to him, for "deputy sheriff"), he concedes that "words peculiar to the law of Scotland must be used by Scotch lawyers. But in history, and in all elegant writing, they should be avoided; or, if unavoidable, explained, and printed in a different character, as if they were words of a foreign tongue" (pp. 29–30). Yet an edifice of the scale, antiquity, and venerability of the Scots legal system necessarily had its own terminology which could scarcely be avoided by its practitioners; nor did they wish to, for the distinctive law of Scotland was (and is) regarded with pride as one of the remaining independent national institutions. Philologus in his answer to Hume observes that "many Scottish law-terms, from the French or Latin, have never been known in England," citing several from Hume's list including *forfaulture* (forfeiture), *notour* (notorious), *adduce* (produce, of proof), *evite* (avoid), and *superplus* (surplus), and adding some of his own including *decreet* (decree), *relevant* (amounting or sufficient), and *assoilzie* (acquit). Neither Beattie nor Hume has the legalisms in a separate section of his list, but Sinclair treats the issue in far more detail, including nearly 100 entries of which some of the most distinctive are *to hold blench* ("to hold lands for the payment of a small quitrent"), *mails and duties* (rents), *liege poustie* (legal power), *thirlage, socome, and multure* (regulations or dues relating to mills), and *reply, duply, triply, quadruply, quintuply, etc.* ("to answer, reply, rejoin, rebut, sur-rebut, etc."). He also argues in an introductory essay for "the wisdom and policy of incorporating our laws [i.e., those of Scotland and England] together, and of digesting them into one complete and regular system" (p. 203).

The genuine Scotticisms in Beattie's collection are not only vocabulary items. We find distinctive usages of articles, prepositions, and adverbs, most of which are still widely used as covert Scotticisms: *the day* (today), *he has got the cold, the fever, say the grace, go to the school, the church, going to my bed, my dinner, angry at him, I stuck among the snow, married on such a person, he spoke through his sleep, a bit bread, I rose whenever I heard the clock strike eight*. Sinclair has several more such examples: *to come into the fire, to profit from experience, to set off on a journey, I gave him a pen for till write with*. A few cases are cited of words holding different class membership in Scotland from England: *conform to agreement, he is cripple, difficulted*. Examples are numerous of words having distinctively Scottish senses: *flower* (nosegay), *gutter* (mud), *kitchen* (tea-urn), *misgive* (fail or miscarry, often used of crops), *fog* (moss) and *moss* (marshy ground), *victual* (corn) and *corn* (oats), *spice* (pepper), *storm* (lying snow), *shore* (quay), *wright* (joiner), *bursar* ("a student who, for a small number of years, enjoys a small exhibition or allowance"), *policy* ("a gentleman's pleasure gardens we call his policy"), *park* (though Beattie does not specify the Scottish use of the word implicitly contrasted with the English sense of a "piece of ground enclosed for the purpose of keeping deer," he is presumably referring to the meaning "field"), *factor* (steward), *fee* (wages), *stipend* (a minister's salary), *to crave a man for debt* (dun), *I find no pain* (feel), *to mandate* (commit to memory), *he rests me nothing* (owes), *weaving* (knitting). In all these cases Beattie has cited an authentically and peculiarly Scots usage.

By no means do all his so-called Scotticisms have so incontrovertible a claim to the title. Beattie and the other compilers were presenting an account specifically of the usages of their own time; it was not germane to their purpose to discuss *how long* a particular usage had laid claim to the status of Scotticism. Sinclair in his introduction observes that "the two languages [Scots and English] originally were so nearly the same, that the principal differences at present between them, are owing to the Scotch having retained many words and phrases which have fallen into disuse among the English" (p. 4). It is indeed true that many items in the lists—some of which, again, still survive in Scottish speech—are simply conservative retentions of idioms formerly current throughout the Anglo-Saxon language area. Hume, and Beattie and Sinclair following him, remark that though Milton wrote "Hindered not Satan to pervert the mind," the idiom "hinder to" is now obsolete in England though still current in Scotland. Spenser's *ken* (know), Spenser's and Shakespeare's *out of hand* (immediately), Shakespeare's *have with you* (I'll go with you), *bygone* (past), and *bairn* (child: though this word, spelt *barne,* occurs in only two speeches, both assigned to "low-class" characters),[3] and the Bible's *young man* (bachelor) and *meat* (food) are similarly cited by one or another of the compilers. Mitchell also lists numerous examples of confusion between past tense and past participle forms from reputable English writers such as Shakespeare, Milton, Dryden, Swift, Pope, and Addison, while denouncing this practice as a Scotticism.

But examples of Scotticisms in this negative sense—forms which have become Scottish merely by going out of fashion in England—are far more abundant in the lists than the compilers show any sign of realizing. Beattie's *misfortunate* and *wrongous, behind* meaning "late," *challenge* (reprove or rebuke, the original sense of the word), *cautioner and caution* (security and bail), *feel* (perceive by smell or taste), *marrow* (one of a pair), *napkin* (handkerchief), *prognostication* (almanac), *timber* (wooden), *tradesman* (craftsman), and *widow* used of a man as well as a woman: all these have attestations in the works of English writers until the seventeenth or even the eighteenth century. *Shirt* referring to a woman's shift as well as a man's shirt is not originally a Scotticism, though it may have acquired an extended lease of life in eighteenth-century Scottish usage through the word's being adopted as an equivalent for the native *sark,* which had always been used of male or female garments. Shakespeare bears witness to *friend* meaning kinsman and *lime* meaning mortar, Drayton to *stair* meaning staircase, Milton to *mind* meaning remember, Dryden to *pull* meaning pluck (a flower). Words which had gone out of common use in the south at an earlier period of English are *morn* (morrow), *purchase* (procure, not necessarily by buying), and *yard* (garden). The use of *behove* as a personal verb ("I behoved to go") is singled out for Sinclair's special disapproval, but it was not disdained by Chaucer, or later Caxton. A similar grammatical change resulted in an eighteenth-century Scotticism in *He thinks long for summer, he thinks long when alone* (Beattie), basically a misunderstanding of the impersonal use of *think* to mean seem, but neither the original nor the secondary construction was first attested in Scotland: Chaucer and later English writers use the form criticized by Beattie.

Not only do the list-makers overlook the fact that numerous words had only recently become Scotticisms: on a truly culpable scale, they include words that were current in colloquial speech on both sides of the Border and some that were entirely acceptable even in the literary English of their time. *Iniquous* (iniquitous), though a rare word, does not appear to be peculiarly Scots. The existence of *iniquity* as a technical term in Scots law, the trespass of a judge who passes sentence contrary to law, may have led to the related word's being wrongly classed as a Scotticism. *Abort* is also a rare word, but not Scots: one is tempted to surmise that it was the indelicacy of the word rather than any other factor that prompted its inclusion in Beattie's list. *Burial* for "funeral service" may likewise have been seen as dysphemistic, but it is not a Scotticism. *Beast* meaning any kind of creature except man—"The cock is a noisy beast, the spider, a filthy beast, the shark, a terrible beast"—can scarcely be described as a uniquely Scottish usage, given the frequency and the semantic variability of the word. *Badly* meaning "unwell" may not have been standard literary English in the eighteenth century, but it was certainly frequent in regionally and socially marked language in England as well as Scotland. The same is true of *coarse* (bad, of weather), "*cast up* a fault to one—To upbraid one with a fault," *hog* (young sheep), *hook* (sickle), *learn* (teach), *mother-in-law* (stepmother), *milk-cow* (to which Beattie preferred "milch-cow"), *presently* (at present), *reckon* ("think, conjecture, am of opinion, apprehend, etc."), *shearers* (reapers), and *summons* as a verb either in the legal sense of "present a summons" or meaning simply "summon." *Clattering* meaning "talking carelessly or familiarly" could have been heard south of the Tweed, although it was developing a special Scottish sense unremarked by Beattie, talking slander or scandal. (Cf. Burns: "What tho' they ca' me fornicator,/ An' tease my name in kintra clatter?"[4]) In one or two other cases he likewise misses a possible point. *Tender* meaning "sickly, weakly, valetudinary" if not standard in English is not peculiarly Scots, but the word had a unique Scots sense, though obsolete by Beattie's time, of "closely related"; *tutor* in the sense of "guardian" (the original meaning of the word) was common to Scotland and England, but in the northern kingdom it had a special application to one who administered an estate in the event of the owner's being legally incapable. Beattie's suggestion that the correct (i.e., English) sense of *chapman* is "not a seller, but a buyer" (in Scotland the word means an itinerant peddler) is misguided; both senses were current in England and if anything it was that of "buyer" that was becoming obsolete.

Account (for *bill*, which Beattie and Sinclair consider more proper), *curt*, *compliment* meaning "gift," *chamberlain* in the historical sense of "steward," *deduce* (deduct) and *detract* (take away), *debit* and *debitor*, *desuetude* (albeit "very rare" in English, according to Beattie), *extinguish* (pay off a debt), *indweller*, *liberate*, *labour* in the sense of "till the soil" (though *labourer* for "farmer" and *labouring* for "farm" are Scots usages), *militate* (against a doctrine), *ornate*, *simply* as an intensifier meaning "absolutely," *sustain* an excuse (admit), *subsist* (support, maintain), *tell* (bid), *turn* (become), *witness* (behold): all these words could have been heard from Englishmen, or found in English writings, in the eighteenth century. *Take on* meaning "enlist" is attributed by Beattie to the Scottish novelist Tobias Smollett, but it is not restricted either to him or to his compatriots. *Here* for "hither" and *where* for "whither" are quite understandably criticized by Beattie and Mitchell in view of the prescriptions of Latin-based grammar, but they were never exclusively Scots, and had been current in literary as well as colloquial English since well before their time. In suggesting that *autumn* should be used instead of *harvest*, Beattie and Sinclair seem unaware that the original sense of the word *harvest* was the season, and that this was still current in both countries. The only distinction between Scottish and English practice, besides the presence of the Scots cognate *hairst,* was that the older word was in almost exclusive use in Scotland for the season as well as for its associated activity or produce, *autumn* never having come into widespread currency. *Throng* meaning "crowded" likewise had a distinctive Scots cognate *thrang,* but the Scotsmen who adopted the English form and retained its familiar meaning were not in error, despite Beattie's pronouncement that "throng is never an adjective"; it had been used in this sense since at least the Middle English period, and still was in England as well as Scotland.

Scots cognates of English words, incidentally, provided the list-makers with a few examples. "The Scots confuse *boar* and *bear,*" Beattie complains; but this is for the straightforward reason that as *home, stone, oak, rope,* etc., are *hame, stane, aik, raip* in Scots, so the Scots cognate of *boar* is pronounced identically to *bear.* "He *roves* in a fever," for *raves,* is clearly a reference to a hypercorrection.

A different category of Scotticisms, from a twentieth-century perspective, are the words adopted from Scots into the common English language, a phenomenon that would no doubt have astonished Beattie and his colleagues could they have foreseen it. Somewhat later than the period of the lists, Walter Scott introduced substantial numbers of Scots words to English. Even among the eighteenth-century collections of Scotticisms, however, can be found several words which, though once predominantly or exclusively Scottish, were rapidly coming into use in the southern dialect. *Greed* is an unexpected but genuine example. Another is *bygone:* early attestations for the word are Scottish and Dr. Johnson in his dictionary calls it "a Scotch word," but it was available to Beattie's English contemporaries (Swift has it, for example), and of course was to become popular as a poetic word in Victorian times. A possible case is *expiry,* first recorded in a letter by Robert Burns. *Incarcerate,* used in Scotland before England to mean "imprison," acquired some currency in eighteenth-century England as a medical term before becoming naturalized, at least in educated speech and writing, in its original sense. The meaning of "fulfil" (a promise or obligation) for *implement* is derived from the use of the noun as a Scots law term meaning "fulfilment": though cited as a Scotticism by Beattie and later Mitchell, it was shortly to become acceptable in English formal usage. *Plenish* for "furnish," a French loan word of long standing in Scots, and its derivative *plenishing* for "furniture," were adopted into English usage in the nineteenth century. Beattie contrasts with Scots practice the English use of *pretty* to mean "beautiful without dignity" but acknowledges that the more serious and complimentary meaning given to the word in Scots has been in use "of late" in England. He also condemns the use of *faint* as a noun meaning "swoon," for which the OED's first attestation is from Walter Scott. A notable example of a mistaken prophecy is Mitchell's comment on *restrict*, a word first attested in sixteenth-century Scotland and condemned by Dr. Johnson as "scarce English": "To *restrict* is used by Arbuthnot, but seems now to be gone into disuse." (Still more ironical is Mitchell's comment on *vivres* for "provisions," a word taken into Scots from French—though much less recently than he evidently supposed—and given a short-lived currency in English by Scott: "Vivres is a French word . . . about forty other French words and phrases have, without the smallest necessity, been introduced into the English language. The French have been very sparing in taking English words in exchange.") *Relevant* (originally a Scots law term meaning "sufficient") and *superplus* (surplus) are former Scots words which had become current in English even before the period of the lists.

Still another group of words cited as Scotticisms prove on investigation to be in fact neologisms, equally current, and perhaps equally suspect, in both countries. Beattie in the introduction to his second edition clearly expresses his opinion of such usages:

> I knew a gentleman, who thought the coining of a new word a proof of genius. This opinion seems to have become prevalent. If it be true, Horace was a dull fellow, who coined only one; and Virgil not much better, who made but three or four. . . . They thought they did their country a service, by speaking the language of their fathers, and discouraging the introduction of a new one. When greater writers and speakers arise in this country, I shall not object to their taking greater liberties. [pp. 4-5]

This is certainly a respectable opinion, but Beattie's disapproval of neologisms led him into the error of listing several of them as Scotticisms. *Appreciate* has only one attestation in the *Scottish National Dictionary* (SND) (s.v. *appretiate*), that being its entry in Sinclair's list, where it is included in his section headed "legal words and phrases."

Its meaning in Scots law is "appraise, estimate the value of," and according to the SND it is "rare in St. Eng. in this sense." But in fact it was notably rare in *any* sense in English before the mid-eighteenth century: its first attestation in the OED is its entry in Nathan Bailey's Dictionary of 1742. *Compete* (contend) is unattested before the seventeenth century, though related forms such as *competition* appear earlier; it has no entry in the SND and its earliest quotations in the OED are not Scottish. The first three attestations for *maltreat* are from eighteenth-century English writers: Collier, Cibber, and Sterne. The first use of *dubiety* cited by the OED is from Richardson; the same is true of *narrate,* eliminating a special use of it in a translation: Richardson describes it as a "Scottish phrase," but it is also attested for mid-eighteenth-century English writers. "*Narrate,* and *to notice,* have of late been used by some English writers, but it is best to avoid them," according to Beattie, but *notice* as a verb had recently become current in England and there is no evidence that it had reached there from Scotland. Two words rooted much less securely in the language, *versant* (conversant) and *vocable* (word), are also cited as Scotticisms, but the strongest claim that can be made for the first ("in frequent use from c.1700 to c.1860"—OED) is the SND's "most early instances are from Scottish writers," and the second was evidently more often criticized as a recent adoption than as an alleged Scotticism. Its first attested user after 1638, Alexander Geddes, wrote: "Some have approved it, as a term we wanted; others have objected to it, as an innovation."

Finally, a dubious category of alleged Scotticisms is cases in which Beattie or a colleague appears to be aware of a subtle national distinction between the Scots and the English usages of a given word. An instance from Beattie (repeated verbatim, as often, by Mitchell) is "Chimney, in English, is the fire-place, or the passage for the smoke, but never means, as in Scot. the grate, or iron frame that holds the fire." (Hume also gives a one-word equivalence of *grate* for *chimney.*) Given that this word since its first adoption into English has meant the ornamental surrounds of a fireplace, the projection on the roof, and everything in between, Beattie is scarcely justified in saying that it *never* has the cited meaning in England (assuredly it had in the past) nor in suggesting that it *always* meant this in Scotland; though it is true that the presence in Scots of the word *lum,* with a closely overlapping range of meanings, had led to a possible distinction between *chimney* (or often *chimley*) for "fireplace" and *lum* for "flue and/or chimney-pot." The proverb "it's best to sit next the chumley when the lum reeks" illustrates this. To *operate* payment meaning to procure or force it, if it is a Scotticism, is illustrated in the SND only by this particular reference; and though the OED does not cite its use as applied specifically to payment, its regular meaning of "To effect or produce by action or the execution of force or influence, to bring about, accomplish, work," could certainly include this. *Pointed,* Beattie suggests, is misused frequently in Scots to mean "exact and concise," whereas in English it "conveys the idea of wit or conceit." Ignoring the debatable assumption that one *figurative* use of a word may be less proper than another, it may be observed that since the SND gives as applied uses for *pointed* "precise, punctilious, (over-)attentive to detail, fussy, demanding, punctual, exact, accurate," and the OED, "having the quality of penetrating or piercing the sensations, feelings or mind; piercing, cutting, stinging, pungent, 'sharp,' having point," it is rash to say that the two wide ranges of meaning could not have overlapped. *Roar* of a baby's cry was, and is, common in Scotland; but if (as the OED confirms) the word could formerly be used in England of sheep, birds and bees, besides more obvious candidates, it is unlikely that its use in Beattie's sense was never known outside Scotland; though again, perhaps it is a certain imagined coarseness in the word that is the real ground for his objection. *Seek* for "beg" is hardly sufficiently distinguished from the well-attested sense of "ask for, demand, request" to qualify for special mention as a usage to be avoided. *Close* the door as a Scotticism for *shut* indicates a pedantic preference for the strict historical distinction between *closing* the entrance passage and *shutting* the wooden barrier, but the distinction was not regularly observed, certainly not as a national habit. Still more pedantic and, though referring to actually conceivable distinctions, unwarranted in respect of his assumption that Scottish as distinct from English practices are represented, are his objections to *I weary when I walk alone* ("become weary"—the word has been much more freely used in Scotland than in England, but the grammatical construction has never been distinctively Scottish), *he took a fever* ("was taken, or seized, with a fever"), and *give me a drink.* "Drink (noun) means liquor to be swallowed, but not the quantity of liquor that is swallowed at once," and the "correct" expression is "give me drink, or some drink, or something to drink" or "a draught," though "a drink" in this sense has been acceptable throughout the history of the language.

The eighteenth-century lists of Scotticisms cannot, clearly, be regarded as forerunners to more recent studies of the nature of Walter Gregor's *The Dialect of Banffshire*[5] or William Graham's *The Scots Word Book*.[6] They are prescriptive rather than descriptive in purpose, and are written in accordance with the assumptions of linguistic propriety current in their time. Their value is as evidence not only of actual usages but of attitudes: specifically, they demonstrate the almost morbid sensitivity among men of high intellectual distinction to their national origins, and their tendency to use their Scottish nationality as a scapegoat for all linguistic traits that they viewed, rightly or wrongly, as open to disapproval—disapproval, of course, by the external standards of London, Oxford, and Cambridge. A Scotticism in the time of Hume and Beattie was, roughly defined, a linguistic usage for which a Scotsman might fear an Englishman's ridicule—a category much more broad and heterogeneous than that of "zebra."

NOTES

1. MS 30/2/298 in Aberdeen University Library's Beattie archive.
2. MS 30/1/135. Quoted extensively in Mossner 1980, ch. 27, which contains a detailed account of the language situation.
3. All's Well I.iii.28, Winter's Tale III.iii.70.
4. "Welcome to a Bastart Wean," 7–8.
5. London: Asher, 1866.
6. Edinburgh: Ramsay Head Press, 1977, rev. ed. 1980.

REFERENCES

Aitken, Adam J.
    1979   Scottish Speech: A Historical View with Special Reference to the Standard English of Scotland. *In* A. J. Aitken and T. McArthur, eds., Languages of Scotland. Edinburgh: Chambers, pp. 85–118.

Beattie, James
    1787   Scoticisms Arranged in Alphabetical Order, Designed to Correct Improprieties of Speech and Writing. Edinburgh.

Gould, Stephen J.
    1981   What, If Anything, Is a Zebra? Natural History 90, 7:6–12.

Graham, William
    1980   The Scots Word Book. 1977, revised ed. Edinburgh: Ramsay Head Press.
Gregor, Walter
    1866   The Dialect of Banffshire. London: Asher.
Hewitt, David S.
    1987   James Beattie and the Languages of Scotland. *In* J. J. Carter and J. H. Pittock, eds., Aberdeen and the Enlightenment. Aberdeen: Aberdeen University Press, pp. 251–60.
Mitchell, Hugh
    1799   Scotticisms, Vulgar Anglicisms and Grammatical Improprieties Corrected. Glasgow.
Mossner, Ernest C.
    1980   The Life of David Hume. Second Edition. Oxford: Oxford University Press.
Nicolaisen, W. F. H.
    1976   Scottish Place-Names: Their Study and Significance. London: B. T. Batsford.
Romaine, Suzanne
    1980   The English Language in Scotland. *In* R. W. Bailey and M. Görlach, eds., English as a World Language. Ann Arbor: University of Michigan, pp. 56–83.
Sinclair, John
    1782   Observations on the Scottish Dialect. London.

WORDS AND THINGS IN GAELIC SCOTLAND*

ALEXANDER FENTON

The science of linguistics spread its wings from the 1880s beyond its specific domain into the realm of cultural history. At first the Indo-Germanic scholars in Vienna and then the Germans quickly adopted the new approach. They used the study of words and their meanings to throw light on historical change seen through the distribution of objects and their variant forms at earlier periods; among their first concerns was the terminology of dwelling house features and their traditional contents (cf. Fenton 1978). It is this general relation of words and things that has influenced Bill Nicolaisen's work and commands my attention in this essay.

Using words and things as an organizing principle, the influential journal *Wörter und Sachen. Kulturhistorische Zeitschrift für Sprach- und Sachforschung* was founded in 1909 and ran until 1943. The editors believed that reconstructions on the basis of the laws of language were not enough, and that the history of language was needed to explain the terminology of material culture, and vice versa. They considered that the future of cultural history lay in a union of language and material culture studies. This concept became, and remains, one of the most

---

*This contribution, now expanded, was first presented as the O'Donnell Lecture in the Department of Celtic of the University of Edinburgh on 7 May 1984.

important adjuncts to cultural-historical research (cf. Graebner 1966: 71; Wiegelmann, Zender, and Heilfürth 1977:25–26).

The concept of "Words and Things" may carry a slightly old-fashioned echo, for the "Wörter und Sachen" approach to cultural history became a creature of political attitudes in Germany in the years leading up to the Second World War. Nevertheless it remains a valid and invaluable approach, as I learned—really from first principles, and then in ignorance of this background—when working as senior assistant editor of the Scottish National Dictionary, under the guidance of David Murison, who provided me with four years of education in the very roots of the heritage of the country.

Though this was not directly an education in the culture of Gaelic Scotland, it allowed the development of principles of approach which are generally valid. Even so, as a speaker of a Scots dialect, I approach the subject of words and things in Gaelic Scotland with diffidence, well aware of the dangers that can attend the speculations of those untutored in Gaelic.

Let me mention, with a lack of gentlemanly courtesy, the example of a lady, Miss Russell of Ashiestell, who published an article on the "Gaelic Element in the Spoken Language of the South of Scotland" in 1892. She listed forty-six terms, and got some right, though more by luck than good management simply because they had an ultimately Celtic origin. Those she got wrong are also of interest, since they reflect the speculations of educated nonspecialists of the period. They include: *maud,* a shepherd's plaid; *cruive,* an enclosure or salmon trap; *geens,* wild cherries; *grieve,* a farm bailiff; *tee,* the starting point at golf and the goal in curling; *cadie,* the attendant in golfing; *kirn,* harvest-home.

Some of her words have Gaelic parallels: *plaid,* G. *plaide; bannock,* G. *bannag, bannach, bonnach; bonnet,* G. *bonaid, boinead; airt,* point of the compass, G. *aird.* The direction of movement, however, is here not from Gaelic into Scots but from Scots into Gaelic.

A third group consists of words with genuine Gaelic links: *ingle,* hearth, G. *aingeal,* fire, in Old Scots from c. 1500; *brat,* an apron, G. *brat,* a mantle or cloak, in Islay having the sense of an apron. (Since the word occurs in Old Scots from c. 1470–80, and probably came into Old English from Celtic, the Islay sense is likely to be a reborrowing from Lowland Scots.) Other words with Gaelic links include *craig,* a cliff, G. *creag,* known as an Old Scots place-name element from c.

1145 and Celtic in origin; *loch,* G. *loch,* in Old Scots from 1375, probably also Celtic in origin; *fank,* a sheepfold, is from G. *fang; grue,* ice floating on a river, is an odd one, thought to be an adaptation of G. *gruth,* curds, and *clachan,* a small village or hamlet in which there is a parish church, inn, and smithy, ultimately from G. *clach,* stone (Russell 1892:1–11).

What can Miss Russell's list tell us? Setting aside the spurious examples, we are left with two groups of words: in one the Gaelic connection owes more to early common links with the Celtic languages; in the other, the movement is at least in part from Lowland Scots into Gaelic.

The first needs no special explanation, and I shall look at Miss Russell's *plaid* as my example for the second. Both Scottish and English writers tend to associate the plaid with the Scottish Highlands. The earliest reference, however, is to the dyeing of plaids in Dunkeld in 1510. Other sixteenth-century references are from Selkirk, Ayrshire, Moray, Aberdeen, Angus, Fife, and other lowland counties; the same is true of the derivative *plaiding,* the kind of cloth from which plaids were made. If from the Highlands, they could be called "heland plaidis" (c. 1500); if from Galloway, "Galloway plaiden" (1692) (Dictionary of the Older Scottish Tongue [DOST]: heland, plaid, plaiding). Older Scots has various spellings that indicate both simple and diphthongised vowels. The latter suggests that the term is a past participle form from the verb *ply,* to fold, and that G. *plaide* is a borrowing into Gaelic, from Lowland Scotland, of the simple vowel form. G. *plaide* normally refers to a blanket, however, and in general it has a more limited use in Gaelic. It is likely, therefore, that we are dealing with only a partial diffusion from Lowland Scots into Gaelic.

The Gaelic terms for a plaid as such are *breacan,* with *breacan-anfheilidh* or *feileadh-bhreacan* for the belted plaid and *filleag* for a shawl or little plaid. Martin Martin's late seventeenth-century *Description of the Western Islands* refers to the "arisad" as a white plaid with a few small stripes of black, blue, and red worn by women (Martin 1716:208–9). So there are Gaelic names enough, and though the Scots *plaid* penetrated to some degree, there was equally a movement from Gaelic into Scots, for already by 1546 there were references to "ane braikane plaid" and "ane brekin cote," in 1587 to "brechane zarne" (DOST: sv brakane), and in 1596, in a charter granted by Sir Duncan Campbell of Glenorchy to one of his sons, an "optimam chlamidem coloratum vulgo ane fyne hewd brakane" (I am indebted to Hugh Cheape for this reference). Clearly, therefore, there was a two-way flow and this must have something to say about the nature of the item of dress itself.

The *Dictionary of the Older Scottish Tongue* and the *Scottish National Dictionary* tell us, on the basis of numerous quoted sources, that "plaid" refers chiefly to a garment or bedcovering. As a garment it was worn by men and women throughout much of Scotland. Women wore it like a shawl; men, in the form of a mantle. Only in the Highlands did it come to refer to the belted plaid worn as the principal article of dress. In this form, it survives as part of the ceremonial dress of members of the pipe bands of Scottish regiments. Thus, the concept of "plaid" has never been static; it involves changes relating to both place and time as well as variant forms, including those owing to wearing by men or women.

Among the earliest descriptions of dress that appear to include forms of plaids is that of John Major in 1521, who wrote that the wealthier "Wild Scots," or Highlanders, wore a loose plaid for an overgarment and a saffron dyed shirt: "chlamyde pro veste superiore, camisia, croco tincta, amiciuntur." The ordinary run of Highlanders wore a linen garment sewn and painted or daubed with pitch, with a covering of deerskins, when rushing into battle: "in panno lineo multipliciter intersuto caerato aut picato cooperatura vulgus sylvestrium Scotorum corpus tectume cum cervinae pellis habens in praelium prosilit." The domestic Scots and English, however, fought in woolen garments (Major 1521:41–61).

In his book on *Old Irish and Highland Dress*, McClintock noted that "intersuto" had been variously translated by interpreters of this passage as patched, pleated, or quilted, and favored the last on the analogy of the padded acton or *cotun* worn as armor in Ireland (McClintock 1943:123; Grant and Cheape 1987:126–27). This could be an overinterpretation. Since the plaid was apparently known throughout Scotland by Major's time, and since the word seems to derive from *ply*, to fold, is it not possible that all we are concerned with here is a form of plaid, pleated to increase warmth, sewn to hold the pleats in place, and adapted to the rough conditions of war by a waterproofing of pitch to convert it into battle dress? We know also that plaids could be of flax as well as of wool.

There is no doubt, however, that by the first half of the sixteenth century, Lowland Scots were seeing something distinctive about Highland dress and were even being influenced by it. The infiltration of the term "brakane" is one example. In 1538, James V ordered a "short Heland Coit" in velvet of various colors, trews for which three ells of "Heland tertane to be hoiss" were required, and "Heland Sarkis" of Holland cloth, with ribbons sewn around the wrists. Variation in color is a regular motif. The combination of colors and stripes was no doubt one of the criteria for Highlandness, though colors—perhaps of a lesser range—were also present in the Lowlands. In the late sixteenth century, Fynes Moryson said of the use of tartan in the Lowlands that "the inferior sort of Citizen wives, and the women of the Country, did wear cloaks made of coarse stuffe, of two or three colors in Checker worke, vulgarly called "Plodan" (Moryson 1617: 33). It was this kind of checked pattern with two or three colors to which the term "tartan," a word of French origin, was being applied from the end of the fifteenth century. *Tartan* was a name for a form of check, and its production kept the litsters busy where color was wanted. What distinguishes it as "Highland" or "Galloway" or anything else appears to be the form of check, and it is probably the use of color combinations among those who could afford the extra cost that led in the long run to the image of "tartan" as we now conceive it.

By the early seventeenth century distinct attitudes toward Highland dress were becoming evident. Sir Robert Gordon wrote about 1620 to his nephew John, Earl of Sutherland, giving him a whole series of pieces of good advice and admonitions. Among other things, he said:

> Vse your diligence to take away the reliques of the country, to wit, the Irishe language, and the habit. Purge your country peice and peice from that vnciwill kynd of cloithes, such as plaids, mantels, truses and blew bonnets. Mak sewre acts against those that shall weare them. Cause the inhabitants of the country to cloith them selfs as the most ciwill prowinces of the kingdome do, with doublet, hoise, cloiks and hats, which they may do with less charge then the other. It is no excuse which some wold pretend alledgeing that vnciwill habit to be lightest among the montanes. They may cloith them selfs (if they list) with coats and breiches of one color, as light and handsome as plaid and truses. The Ireishe language cannot so soon be extinguished. [Fraser 1892:III,359].

Such views hardened into proscription of Highland dress, with its component elements of "Plaid, Philebeg, or little kilt, Trowse...," and so on, following the Jacobite Rising of 1745 (Dunbar 1962). The proscription was lifted thirty-seven years later, in 1782, though the use and indeed development of Highland dress for military purposes kept a link going. When the visit of George IV to Scotland took place in 1882, largely organized as a tartan invasion by Sir Walter Scott and David Stewart of Garth because of the quantity of tartan worn, it was the military dress that formed the basis of the civilian revival of Highland dress. The consequences of this occasion are still with us. Lexicographer and exponent of *Wörter und Sachen* alike must find a definition of the word *plaid* and its Gaelic equivalents that can take into account this variety of shifts in meaning brought about by changes in culture owing to the passage of time, political pressures, fashion, and whimsical accidents of fate like the coincidence of George IV's visit with Scott's romanticism. Words and things must work together in establishing the course of cultural history, its regional variety, and the interaction between the regions.

The plaid provides one kind of pointer. For later periods, other phenomena could be studied, such as the effects of the introduction of sheep farming, stone dyking, draining, fencing, and other agricultural improvements. Indeed, the more recent terminology of clothing and adornments could be developed far beyond the specific example of the plaid and is a rich field for such study. In Glendale in Skye, for example, James Ross (1962:64) noted the following adopted English and Lowland Scots words in the 1960s:

Jacket [ˈʃahxkɛtˈ]	Gravat [kərəˈvahtə]
Scarf [ˈskarfə]	Buckle [ˈbuxkəɫ]
Brooch [ˈbrɔtʃə]	Frock [ˈfrɔɡə]
Worn-out shoes [ˈbaxəls]	Cloth shoelaces [ˈlisɛr]

Already in the mid-1840s, numerous references in the *New (Second) Statistical Account* (1845) pinpoint the strength of Lowland influence on dress, due, inter alia, to regular intercourse with the south by fashion-conscious young folk, especially women, who travelled annually as migrant workers to shear the harvest in the Lothians and in southeast and east-central Scotland from at least the late seventeenth century (Howatson 1982:18). There was movement for other reasons too, such as droving, the East Coast fishing, and domestic service.

My second theme relates to land use and to the fact that not all the phenomena of Gaelic Scotland have Gaelic names. The word *horsegang* first appears in 1720 (Grievances 1720:31). It has a limited distribution. It occurs in Islay, in eighteenth-century rentals. For legal purposes an Islay *horsegang* paralleled a Lowland *oxgang* at one-eighth of a full ploughland, though the Islay ploughland unit seems to have been set at half that of a Lowland one (Lamont 1957:196–99; 1958:88–90).

At Kilmartin, Argyll, eighteenth-century farms usually had four tenants, though some of the larger had six or eight, getting closer to Lowland levels. The four-tenant farm was served by one plough drawn by four horses abreast. Each tenant's portion was a horsegang (Old [First] Statistical Account [OSA] 1793:VIII,97). In the Shotts area of Lanarkshire, a source of 1772 listed ploughgates and horsegangs, noting that the ploughgate was equal to four horsegangs (Grossart 1880:108). In a survey of Lochtayside carried out in 1769, the ploughlands were divided into four horsegang units and represented that amount of arable land for which a plough team of four animals was necessary.

The world of our ancestors was not, of course, carefully organized according to the best mathematical principles, for though the simple equation "four horsegangs = four tenants = one plough" may have been the case in Kilmartin, in Lochtayside the farm of Blarliargan had ten tenants, and Etramuckie had nine, each tenant holding a horsegang. In Kenmore parish, Wester Carawhin had four ploughs and was divided into four units; Marraguaha, four horsegangs and three tenants; Marragphuil, two tenants; Marragdow, two tenants; and Tombour, two tenants (McArthur 1936:xxxiii–xxxix, 18, 21, 25, 27). The equation, therefore, does not always work on the ground, but can be treated as a legal device—like the seed-yield ratio of 3:1 for oats and 4:1 for barley in testamentary lists—for calculations of rental in the estate management of the period.

This interesting word, horsegang, goes to the heart of the social and work organization of the eighteenth century in four neighboring areas of Scotland. It makes a West Central and southern Inner Hebridean horsegang enclave, surrounded, at least on the mainland, by a solid phalanx of oxgangs. We are dealing with a kind of interface between Lowland and Highland in which grazing played an equal part with arable agriculture. The half-ploughland horsegang is an acknowledgment of such conditions, though oxen were not excluded from this enclave, for the *Breadalbane Account Books* refer to "plow oxen" long before the 1769 survey (McArthur 1936:xl). This may indicate their use on the home farm, but horses, not oxen, were the everyday plough animals.

We have seen that tenants joined forces, four horses to a plough. The horses were yoked four abreast. This no doubt led to the term horsegang, but was there also a special form of plough? There is in the National Museums of Scotland a particular type of plough, generally called a *crann-nan-gad* in Gaelic, alleged to have come from Islay. It has a single stilt or handle, and the beam curves down in front so that it runs on the ground like a skid (Fenton 1969:I, 2, 124–27). On mainland Scotland, in a crescent running along the Highland-Lowland edges from northeast to southwest, and including the horsegang enclave, a light form of the old Scotch plough was in use, with two rather steeply set short stilts. It is like the one illustrated by Dwelly (1949:11) under the name *crann Gaidhealach*. The enclave, therefore, had two plough types, neither of which was indigenous to it, for the *crann-nan-gad* was more at home in the Outer Hebrides and the lighter type of Old Scotch plough was widely distributed. However, each used the team of four horses abreast, and each was involved in the kind of communal plough work that marked the joint-tenancy farms of the period.

What makes the horsegang enclave different, therefore, is not the equipment or the team, but the fact that a group of neighboring estates chose to adopt a management device that acknowledged both the nature of the ground with its half-grazing, half-arable potential, and the needs of the tenants and the kind of work animals they used. To define horsegang properly, therefore, is to make a contribution to the study of early estate management and its regional variations on the edge of the Highlands—a topic about which little has yet been said.

I want to touch on another form of culture contact, in which Gaelic Scotland was the undoubted giver (Fenton 1980:5–16; Fenton and Pálsson 1984:137). In Faroese and Icelandic, there are several terms that can hardly have anything other than a Scots Gaelic source. Examples are Faroese *cadlåamor*, left-hand or left-handed, compounded of G. *làmh*, a hand, and *cearr*, left; Faroese *soppur*, G. *sop*, a wisp or loose bundle of straw or hay; F. *blak*, G. *blathach*, buttermilk; F. *køkja*, G. *caigeann*, a pair of animals, especially sheep, tethered to one stick but kept separate by a wooden swivel that has two holes in the Faroes and usually three in the Hebrides; F. *drunner*, G. *dronn*, tail of an animal; and so on.

Such links point to a flow out of Gaelic Scotland at a time when parts of Gaelic Scotland were tightly bound in with the Scandinavian north. The words that have been pinpointed are not prestigious terms that reflect imposing aspects of cultural transmission. Instead, they exemplify the small details of everyday life. Hardly any scholars have paid attention to them except those like Christian Matras in the Faroe Islands, who looks at them as a linguist. It is of much interest to look at them in this way, but I also want to make the words speak, to examine their stories of the lives and living conditions of men and women in the past, to point to the objects they used and worked with.

So far, I have looked at three categories of phenomena:

1. Lowland Scots and Gaelic terminology for the plaid, which developed a range of connotations, especially in Gaelic-speaking areas, but which can only be fully interpreted by maintaining an awareness of the runs of sense in both Highland and Lowland Scotland.

2. The legal term *horsegang,* with no Gaelic equivalent, but which nevertheless significantly comments on a limited area on the fringe of the Highlands. It would not be included in a Gaelic dictionary. Dictionaries of Scots and dictionaries of Gaelic must be used complementarily.

3. A selection of words relating to everyday life with no prestigious connotations, yet which are still capable of pinpointing the movements of people and ideas, whether from Lowland into Gaelic Scotland or vice versa, or from Gaelic-speaking areas into those of Norse speech.

To look at other categories of terms would produce in turn other ways of examining the phenomena they represent, through time, in space, and for their social significance. This is a function of the *Wörter und Sachen* approach, There is, however, an aspect of the exercise that cannot be strongly enough emphasized for the culture of Gaelic Scotland, one that is also part of the heritage of Scotland and of Europe and beyond.

When Thomson wrote about Gaelic in Scotland (Thomson 1981), he represented, as a reviewer put it:

> an astonishingly ambivalent situation, contrasting the secure establishment of Gaelic in some fields (notably religion and the arts), and the practical support given by the bilingual policy of the Western Isles Region, with its chronic political and educational weakness, and the determined and altogether admirable work being done in

the academic and literary spheres with a dangerous tendency among speakers to parochialism and acquiescence in the progressive Anglicisation of the language. [McClure 1983:3]

Thomson spoke of the place of Gaelic in public life and education, in the media, in music, in entertainment, in literature, and of the construction of Gaelic terms to cover, e.g., literary criticism, current affairs, and aspects of technology. He commented that

> there are still people often leading ordinary lives for whom Gaelic is fully alive and healthy, a finely honed instrument for the portrayal of a particular kind of Christian experience; the vehicle for an ancient tradition of story-telling or song, or for the art of the raconteur; a subtle tongue of infinite possibilities for the making of poetry.

He went on to identify a range of strands in Gaelic culture, with professional and intellectual as well as folk-traditional aspects, and to look at the creation of structures in the society designed to strengthen and perpetuate aspects of Gaelic culture (Thomson 1981:16–17).

All this is fine, and he is not alone in saying these things. But there is another aspect that tends to be ignored, and yet it is the richest lode into which any Gaelic scholar can quarry. It is simply the language itself, as spoken by all manners and classes of men, with its numerous regional varieties, its social and work-oriented variations, its living vocabulary that covers every detail of the work and interactions of everyday life. However laudable it is to invent Gaelic words for the speedometer (*astar-chleòc*), the switchboard (*suids-chlàr*), and surtax (*for-chàin*) (cf. MacDonald 1968:196), this remains an artificial exercise. In the meantime, because of the pressures of modern times, many examples of what were once standard everyday activities are dying out. When the need for kilns and mills goes, there is no longer a living need for the names of their parts. The end of the horse plough will lead to the loss of its terminology in little more than a generation. Without a base in *Sachen*, the *Wörter* may disappear. In spite of the good work already done in dictionaries and glossaries, I am sure that concentrated effort by Gaelic scholars can retrieve much more. I would urge the recording of the great deal that exists, in its functional contexts, theme by theme, rather than using time on inventing new words. It is the more natural language of the people, even if affected by English or Scots or any other tongue—such as Norse in past ages—that can provide a sound and realistic base for study and even—why not?—further inspiration to literary endeavor. This language can never be replaced once the objects and work to which it relates have vanished, and this is where the weakness of current educational policies lies. A culture will not be preserved simply by preserving a language artificially, or by making a cult of the personalities who have used it, but every culture and the historical changes that have affected it are important for mankind in general. If we can gain a knowledge not only of the literature and music and the art of making and ornamenting guns and targets and powder horns, but also of the everyday activities of the past as well as of the present, on land and at sea, we will be doing much for the preservation and in part perpetuation of the culture in a more fully rounded way. It is this culture of the everyday that has stayed firm through centuries of change—not necessarily always unhealthy—as induced by related cultures, Scottish, English, Irish, or Scandinavian.

In the *Companion to Gaelic Scotland,* out of 450 entries by subject, only about 7 percent touch on aspects of material culture—i.e., archaeology, art and architecture, and activities included under economic and geographical headings. I am well aware that the culture of a people covers the creations of the spirit as well as artifacts, but I am in no doubt that the latter are being in some degree neglected. If those teaching Gaelic in our universities would encourage their students to produce dissertations and doctorates on the plaid, to take an example—and I have earlier tried just to lift the tail of the topic—or the localized terminology of settlement patterns with special reference to, e.g., shieling equipment and activities (about which a great deal is still remembered in Lewis, where the shieling tradition lingered longer than in any other part of Britain) or of cultivating implements like the plough, we would soon be satisfyingly better off in terms of knowledge of our national culture and of its adaptations as past leads into present. And the related Scots or English *Wörter und Sachen* should be taken into account, too, to make a more level balance.

I am reminded of a riddle current in the Arnol district of Lewis:

> Cha'n eil e muigh
> 's cha'n eil e stigh

ach cha'n eil tigh
as eugmhais
de a tha'nn?

"It's not without and it's not within, and there's no house without it, what is it?" "The earthen core of a blackhouse wall."

Such a riddle could not exist outside an area that did not have blackhouses, which are characterized by walls of double thickness with a packing of peaty earth between the two faces. For another, it suggests how unthinkable it was to the inventors of the riddle that there could be any other kinds of houses. Not only does it point to a localized and vanishing form of material culture in relation to vernacular buildings, but also to the implicit attitudes of the people who lived there.

It is this enduring earthen core, which can stand when all other parts of the structure have fallen or been taken away, the unknown, invisible, scarcely acknowledged internal *Wörter und Sachen* mechanisms of Gaelic Scotland that we should now examine with our fullest attention, both for their own sake and as part of our European culture. The possibility of doing so is still with us on the tongues and in the heads of all those brought up naturally to speak the Gaelic language. And as Bill Nicolaisen would certainly agree, careful attention to the recording of such aspects of tradition and their sensitive interpretation will undoubtedly point to new kinds of creativity for the future. In the ultimate analysis, tradition lives through change.

REFERENCES

Carmichael, Alexander
    1941–76 Carmina Gadelica. Edinburgh: Scottish Academic Press (Vols. 1–3, 6); Oliver & Boyd (Vols. 4–5).
Dictionary of the Older Scottish Tongue [DOST]
    1937   London: University of Chicago Press, Oxford University Press, and Aberdeen University Press.
Dunbar, John Telfer
    1962   History of the Highland Dress. Edinburgh and London: B. T. Batsford, Ltd.
Dwelly, Edward
    1949   The Illustrated Gaelic-English Dictionary. Glasgow: Alec Maclaren & Sons.

Fenton, Alexander
    1969   A Plough Type from the Outer Isles of Scotland. Tools and Tillage I, 2:117–28.
    1978   The Island Blackhouse. Reprint 1989. Edinburgh: Her Majesty's Stationery Office.
    1980   Northern Links. Northern Studies 16:5–16.
Fenton, Alexander; Pálsson, Hermann
    1984   Northern Links: Continuity and Change. The Northern and Western Isles in the Viking World. Edinburgh: John Donald Publishers Ltd.
Fraser, William
    1892   The Sutherland Book, 3 Vols. Edinburgh: privately published.
Graebner, Fritz
    1966   Methode der Ethnologie. 1911 repr. Oosterhuit NB: Anthropological Publications.
Grant, Isabel F.; Cheape, Hugh
    1987   Periods in Highland History. London: Shepheard-Walwyn.
Grievances...
    1720   Some of the Grievances and Complaints of the Poor Commonality of Scotland. Glasgow.
Grossart, William
    1880   Historic Notices and Domestic History of the Parish of Shotts. Glasgow: Aird & Coghill.
Howatson, William
    1982   The Scottish Hairst and Seasonal Labour 1600–1870. Scottish Studies 26:13–36.
Lamont, W. D.
    1957–58   Old Land Denominations and 'Old Extent' in Islay. Part 1 and 2. Scottish Studies 2(1957):183–204; 2:1(1958):86–106.
McArthur, Margaret M.
    1936   (ed.) Survey of Lochtayside 1769. Edinburgh: Scottish History Society.
MacDonald, Father Allan
    1958   Gaelic Words and Expressions from South Uist and Eriskay. Dublin: Dublin Institute for Advanced Studies.
MacDonald, Kenneth D.
    1968   The Gaelic Language, Its Study and Development. In D. S. Thomson and Ian Grimble, eds., The Future of the Highlands. London: Routledge and Kegan Paul, pp. 177–201.
McClintock, Henry F.
    1943   Old Irish and Highland Dress. Dundalk: W. Tempest.
McClure, J. Derrick
    1983   The Year's Work in Scottish Literary and Linguistic Studies, (1) Language. Scottish Literary Journal 19 (Winter):1–7.
Major, John
    1521   Historia Majoris Britanniae, Tam Angliae quam Scotiae. Second

edition. Quoted in P. H. Brown, ed., Scotland before 1700 from Contemporary Documents. Edinburgh: Hamilton, 1893, pp. 41–61.

Martin, Martin
   1716   A Description of the Western Islands of Scotland. 1981 repr., 2d ed. Edinburgh: James Thin.

Moryson, Fynes
   1617   An Itinerary. Quoted in J. T. Dunbar, 1962, History of Highland Dress.

New (Second) Statistical Account [NSA]
   1845   Edinburgh: William Blackwood & Sons.

Old (First) Statistical Account [OSA]
   1791–99 Edinburgh: William Blackwood & Sons.

Ross, James
   1962   Bilingualism and Folk Life. Scottish Studies 6, 1:60–70.

Russell, Miss
   1892   The Gaelic Element in the Spoken Language of the South of Scotland. Transactions of the Berwickshire Naturalist's Club, pp. 1–11.

Thomson, Derick S.
   1983   (ed.) The Companion to Gaelic Scotland. Oxford: Blackwell Reference.

   1981   Gaelic in Scotland: Assessment and Prognosis. *In* Einar Haugen, J. Derrick McClure, and Derick Thomson, eds., Minority Languages Today. Edinburgh: Edinburgh University Press, pp. 10–20.

Wiegelmann, Gunter; Zender Matthias; Heilfurth, G.
   1977   Volkskunde Eine Einfuhrung (Grundlagen der Germanistik 12). Berlin: Erich Schmidt Verlag.

COMMUNITY
AND
IDENTITY

❧ 14 ❧

THE FORGOTTEN MAKARS:
The Scottish Local Poet Tradition*

MARY ELLEN BROWN

One remarkable thing about the new four-volume *History of Scottish Literature* (Craig 1987) is the inclusion of chapters on oral and local literature—the ephemeral and regional, the noncanonical. Inclusion of these long-overlooked topics owes much to the lobbying efforts of scholars like Bill Nicolaisen, and this essay honors his example, touching on ballad and folk song, the relationship of folklore and literature, Scottish artistic culture, even place-names—all in the service of expanding knowledge of partially recognized, noncanonical literatures. In doing so I hope to delineate more clearly one kind of overlooked literature, to show its links to earlier and simultaneous literary cultures, oral and written, and to reinscribe one aspect of artistic culture ignored, implicitly denigrated, certainly forgotten: the Scottish local poet tradition.

Popular chroniclers of Scottish cultural history are fond of referring to Scotland as the land of song, a nation of poets; numerous local, regional, and national anthologists have assembled collections to confirm that contention. Sometimes anthologists place canonical works

---

*Research for this project was made possible by a Research Fellowship at the Institute for Advanced Studies in the Humanities, University of Edinburgh, and by a Grant-in-Aid from the American Council of Learned Societies. I gratefully acknowledge their support.

and authors adjacent to unknown works and minor authors to illustrate the breadth and depth of Scottish literary output. While much has justly been written of the medieval makars, the later vernacular writers—of the great works of Scottish literature—the canon, far less has been written about the minor poets, often because their work fails to measure up to accepted aesthetic standards understood, if not explicitly articulated, by the literati, the "ideal audience," those elusive arbiters of cultural taste and values. The work of some minor poets, however, has met local—if not national—aesthetic standards, and the poets and their productions have been recognized, even acclaimed, within a circumscribed environment.

The local poet tradition, while a widespread, grassroots phenomenon, is but one of many creative traditions operating simultaneously within the Scottish cultural landscape. And the local poet tradition shares general influences, participants, and media with all of them. Nonetheless, the tradition *is* distinct and has its own history, its own qualities, which enable identification and isolation.

The local poet tradition emerged as a widespread phenomenon only after literacy had spread to many portions of society, when print had become accessible and cheap, about the mid-eighteenth century. Building on earlier and simultaneous forms of literary expression, oral and written, the local poet tradition may well be an extension of Scotland's great oral ballad and song tradition, but it also has affinities with the written vernacular tradition. As with a news story or current joke, the passage of time may dull the message of the poetry and promote oblivion, for the content of the poetry is, at least overtly, significantly local and limited, appealing to and written for a particular audience whose values and concerns in large measure shape the poetry. Thus the local poet is a chronicler, often a barometer, of the community's events, concerns, aesthetic values, and through poetry—and song— plays an integral role in the life of a locale or region. James Thomson of Kenleith combined his roles as local poet and general factotum on the Malleny estate when he versified the rules governing hunting:

> A' ye wha liberty hae got
> To course the lands o' General Scott,
> The following rules observe ilk ane,
> Or faith ye'll ne'er get leave again.

> I'm authorised, gentlemen,
> By my good Laird, to let you ken.[1]

The poem ends with the seventh rule:

> Three deaths we grant, nae mair, a-day,
> These are our laws, you must obey;
> And tho' ye think them rather hard,
> Ye manna gang to blame the Bard. [1819:162–64]

Similarly, Robert Tannahill encapsulated community opinion in poetic maxims:

> Of all the ills with which mankind is curst,
> An envious, discontented mind's the worst.
> [1876:110]

Such poetry and poets enjoyed considerable popularity. Even today, for example, at least five place names in and around Currie, a suburb of Edinburgh, honor the Kenleith Bard. Several local poets had poems or songs circulating about them, Charles Leslie's in two versions, beginning:

> O dolefu' rings the bell o' Raine!
>   Bonny Laddie, Highland Laddie,
> For Charlie ne'er will sing again,
>   My bonnie Highland Laddie. [National Library of
>   Scotland][2]

And Robert Tannahill's life and works were long celebrated in a spring festival and concert and continue to be celebrated today by a select club of men in his hometown of Paisley. Records survive, then, of countless local poets and poetry which once had its day, playing an important role in the artistic, expressive lives of many people. Regional anthologies, privately published editions, newspapers, and periodicals—all attest to the vitality of local poets while preserving only a small portion of their productions.

The volume of extant examples of local poetry is staggering and attests to the breadth and persistence of the tradition. Yet local poets and their poetry have received little notice save in regional, occupational, or class contexts. The regional factor is of primary importance: because most of the poetry deals with local matters, the bulk of it never leaves the neighborhood of its origin, being meaningful only to the local audience. Recognition, acceptance, and relevance within a loosely delineated region or area are defining qualities of the local poet tradition and separate the local poet from the far more numerous minor poets who often write for themselves, have no audience to speak of, and for whom poetic production is largely a private, individual affair.

Few discussions have been particularly laudatory of local poets or of their works; the poetry is often seen as imitative. Wonder is often expressed that the local poets are able to write at all, given their presumed lack of education and poverty. Yet the local acceptance and popularity of the poets and their poetry and the pervasiveness of the tradition suggest that it deserves discussion in both cultural and literary terms—in terms of audience, place, and time and in terms of the tradition's links with other Scottish literature, oral and written. More generally, the local poet tradition deserves attention because it beautifully illustrates the residual orality, continuing into the age of literacy and print, that Walter Ong (1982) describes: additive, formulaic, copious, conservative, familiar, participatory, present-oriented. Additionally, the tradition deserves recognition for continuity with the past, as a widespread expressive form of popular art. Examination of local poets, their poetry, and their audiences also offers a perspective on the aesthetic sensibilities of ordinary individuals, providing insight into the values, interests, and concerns of local constituencies. Consideration of the local poet tradition is important for a holistic view of culture and of art.

1. The local poet is a leisure-time poet, an artist by avocation. And he (the majority of the remembered local poets have been men) is recognized within the community as poet or bard. Often referred to as the poet of a locale such as "Methven poet" or "Paisley bard," the poet is in some ways an unofficial poet laureate, the group's artistic voice. It follows that the local poet's work is usually conservative, adhering to the accepted and expected in form and context. James VI's interesting advice—"Ze man also beware with composing anything in the same manner as hes been ower oft vsit of before" (Henderson 1910:334)—contradicts the implied aesthetic sensibilities of the local

poet and his poetic aims. The local poet suffers little "anxiety of influence." Much of the poetry, whether narrative or lyric, deals with local events, places, characters, and attitudes known to and representative of the poet's loose-knit constituency. James Thomson's poem "On Raising and Selling the Dead" (1894:221–28), for example, describes a local event, the capture of body snatchers who had exhumed two bodies in Lanark and were on their way to Edinburgh to seek financial gain for their nocturnal activity.

Many of the poems have been set to music, and some of these songs, such as the Paisley-centered songs of Robert Tannahill, have received wide and lasting circulation. For the most part the language of the poems and songs reflects the local speech, though standard orthography—increasingly through time in English—obscures this. Hearing rather than silently reading a song or poem, however, reveals the local linguistic coloration, the contemporary vernacular (Purvis 1979:62–76), despite recurrent laments over the supposed decline or death of the vernacular from poets and scholars alike:

> To suit our fashionable times,
> A Bard maun now compose his rhymes
> In what is ca'd a pompous style,
> Or else they're nae thought worth the while.
> Wi' foreign phrases, now we're loaded,
> The plain braid Scots is maist exploded,
> And unco' little's said or sung,
> In honour o' our mither tongue. [Ingram 1812:54]

The poet's primary audience is local and known and the poet addresses it specifically. When removed from place and audience, the poetic voice may fail as it did for Robert Tannahill during his absence from Paisley and for William Thom, the Inverurie poet, when he went to London. While the local poet tradition is primarily a literate tradition, many songs and poems are communicated verbally and aurally rather than by silent reading; that is, they are recited from memory or read aloud from manuscript or print in formal and informal groups for family or friends at home, in clubs, pubs, and bothies, at weddings, and on other convivial occasions. Many works, no doubt, languish at this point; some few are picked up and widely circulated orally. Others reach print and sometimes wider audiences through magazines, newspapers, chap publications, anthologies, and editions of individual poets. The latter was often facilitated in the eighteenth and nineteenth centuries by a subscription taken prior to publication from among one's friends and family, the local audience. A poet's work might thus circulate orally, scribally, and typographically, and today, electronically.

2. Poet and audience share to some extent both physical and perceptual worlds: the poet and his artistry depend on the community. Without such connectedness, there is no community. Charles Leslie, unofficial poet laureate of Aberdeen, whose death at 105 was recorded in the periodical press, was so popular that the ballad about his life referred to earlier circulated posthumously in several versions. Leslie's popularity was no doubt derived from the nature of the material, both traditional and original, which he chose to sing and sell, his favorite topics being sex and politics. In fact, his pro-Jacobite songs at least once landed him in jail after the judge asked why he didn't sing less offensive songs. The reply—"They winna buy them"—attests to the close relationship of poet and community (National Library of Scotland ms. 912).

James Thomson of Kenleith left a permanent mark on his community, for the standard map of Edinburgh lists five place names in the village of Currie that recall him (Brown 1989). Thomson's popularity in his own day probably derived from his poetic celebration of shared events, known characters, and community views, as in the stanza:

> Our neighbor's fau'ts are often shewn
> Without attending to our own,
> Which if we did wi' candid e'e,
> Far less censorious would we be. [1819:42]

He also used his poetry for practical reasons as in the rules of hunting mentioned earlier.

Thomson reached his audience orally, in manuscript, and in print: these three means of communicating enabled an expanding circle of potential audiences. The printed subscription lists that appear in his volumes represent the fullest extent of his audience in the greater Edinburgh area and include individuals of various classes and social statuses. The closer one lived to Thomson and the nearer in social status, the greater the chance of face-to-face encounter; the farther away, the greater the likelihood of printed communication. There is evidence that Thomson had a very vocal, very local fan club that visited him periodically, certainly yearly on his birthday. Called the Kent Club after the kent or shepherd's crook they each carried in imitation of Thomson, they paraded to his house behind a piper. Many other individuals came as well, both to show their esteem for his work and to hear him recite. He kept a visitor's book that had been signed by 1,500 persons by 1827, five years before his death. And the dedication of his first volume recognizes the audience as necessary coparticipants in artistic communication:

> Come, tell me, lads when you let slip
> Frae out your port a dainty ship,
> Dinna ye get a pilot stout,
> To guid her right, and steer her out?
> Sae should an author 'bout him look,
> For patrons to protect his book. [1801:xxi]

Robert Tannahill, the Paisley poet, also encapsulated community opinion in his poetry; his chief lasting artistic contributions to his community were his numerous songs, often set to traditional tunes. By using the medium of song, he was able to tap into the still flourishing song culture of Scotland, which circulated the old beside the changed and the new. Weavers picked up and sang his songs; a local pubman specialized in them; popular musicians sang his works in concert. A variously told anecdote describes Tannahill's own delight at hearing by chance one of his songs sung by a young woman about her work. For a time, then, it is possible that the songs had an oral circulation and were selected for performance by members of the community. Formal concert performances moved some of his songs into an alien milieu where they were popular for a moment and then forgotten. But they were not so quickly discarded in the local area largely because, in addition to their absorption into the song culture, they so explicitly spoke of Paisley and environs—names in several instances coined or made familiar by Tannahill himself, like Gleniffer Braes, Stanely Castle, the Woods of Craigielee.

Tannahill actually became *the* local poet after his death; his songs particularly contributed through their often memorable traditional tunes but particularly because of their mention of specific places in and around Paisley. The area itself was large enough and prosperous enough to support memory of an obscure poet because he celebrated their own identifiable spots, still extant, in such lyric generalities that they were not outdated by the passage of time. As the town grew, he, and more particularly his songs, became a means of fostering local pride. The way this happened is in some measure analogous on the local level to the development of the Burns "cult" and the raising of Burns to symbolic significance on the national scene.

Tannahill belonged during his lifetime to a select club, the Paisley Literary and Convivial Association. At the time of his death, members and other local poets paid tribute to him in countless memorial poems. The Club ceased to exist in 1856, but, to fill the vacuum, a Tannahill Club was established in 1858. A purpose of the club—modeled on the successful Burns Club—was to keep Tannahill's memory alive as a focal point for local pride, to place a sign on his house, to raise a tombstone over his grave, and otherwise to proclaim the existence of a local poet who once sang of the beauty of specific spots in the adjacent environment. It was not, however, until the centenary celebration in 1874 that recollection of Tannahill moved beyond a select, self-chosen few. That celebration, intensified by being joined with the celebration of the Queen's birthday, raised Tannahill to altogether new heights as the town decked itself in floral arches, planned and executed a massive procession by spots significant in his life, heard his songs performed by a choir in the Glen, and culminated with banquets and soirees whose pattern of toasts and memorial poems followed—in modified form—the by-then established ritual of the Burns Suppers.

Members of the Tannahill Club were so heartened by the turnout for the centenary that they urged the establishment of yearly concerts in the Glen to celebrate Tannahill's birthday, the proceeds to go toward the purchase of a statue of the bard to be placed in the Abbey Church grounds, and later to help put up a monument to Robert Burns and to support the work of the Royal Alexander Infirmary. The dual focus on poets and civic institutions illustrates the place of the local poet as a focal point for civic pride. A large choir—the Tannahill Choir—was formed, in one year having as many as 700 members, to perform Tannahill's songs, in later years adding other Scottish materials. The concerts continued until 1936, in their latter days poorly attended, though in peak years as many as 30,000 persons had been present. Undoubtedly, Tannahill and sentiments in his works became increasingly out of phase with Paisley's rapid urbanization and sophistication, not to mention the mobility that took some natives away and brought in strangers unacquainted with the bard and owing more loyalty to business or job than to the town of Paisley.

While the mass of people no longer recall Tannahill, the club continues as the Tannahill-Macdonald Club, jointly honoring two local poets. The club seeks to keep these poets' memories alive and to do civic service, retaining the close connection between the poets and the town. Now limited to twenty-five members, all men, the club meets perhaps seven times a year, with special celebrations on the anniversaries of the poets' birthdays.

3. This grassroots poetic movement did not spring up suddenly out of nowhere, for it built on, and developed naturally from, earlier artistic traditions. Its emergence both reflects and resulted from a radical alteration of Scottish society in the eighteenth century precipitated by modifications of agricultural practices, the rise of machine industries, and of printing, which in turn facilitated literacy and spread material rapidly to an expanded audience. The local poet tradition arose at the point of change from one kind of society to another, when the oral world was being altered by the world of print. The local poet served as mediator between the two worlds, and the poetry provided some of the first reading materials for the emerging literate populace because it was often rooted in the oral materials and was, thus, generally familiar in form and content.

The primary oral influence on the local poet tradition, certainly at the point of its origin, was balladry and folksong. The first local poets may well have been one and the same as the creators of ballads and songs, composing orally. Others may have had their work written down by another, as did the New Cumnock Bard David Wood (Macintosh 1910:48). William Cadenhead "had acquired great facility in throwing into metrical form any subject which struck his fancy, through practicing composing aloud, while travelling along our more lonely highways during his business journeys" (Walker 1887:538). James Thomson, the Kenleith Bard, composed some songs mentally, never bothering to write them out because a portion of his audience could not read. Others he wrote out and circulated in manuscript (1894:v–vi). Authorship was not always an issue; pen names and initials might hide the real identity of the creator, and acceptance into oral tradition often obliterated awareness of authorship. As the print-oriented world with its visual and spatial sense became dominant, the attitude of both author and audience shifted: the individual wanted recognition as author; the audience felt a concomitant obligation to replicate material accurately, to avoid change, if it were learned at all.

Like the ballads and folksongs, the local poets' songs and poems were initially performed for a local, known audience at informal and formal gatherings such as clubs, like the one attended weekly by Robert Tannahill and his musical friend R. A. Smith. Sometimes the poetry and songs were communicated orally and no visual aid was used; alternately, the works might be read. Traditional orally transmitted material might well have been performed at the same gatherings. In fact, some local poets, like Charles Leslie, were also recognized transmitters of traditional material. And local poets, like redactors of traditional materials, sometimes ran in families.

There are other, more demonstrably evident continuities between the two artistic traditions in the areas of content and form and in the stylistic and aesthetic preference for repetition. Since the oral medium continues and oral literature persists after writing and print are introduced, ballads and songs as well as other traditional material naturally continue to provide a readily available model for creating individual works, especially, but not exclusively, when they are songs.

Tunes for songs are primarily taken from the traditional fund, are designated by name—usually derived from the traditional text with which the tune is most often associated—but are not written or printed with the new text. The assumption is, as in most ballad and song collections, that the traditional tunes are common knowledge. Favorites for local poets include "Dainty Davie," "Jock o' Hazeldean," "Bonny House o' Airlie," "Chevy Chace," "Gilderoy," and "The Battle of Sheriff Muir." Local poets, like makers of ballads and songs, have played an important role in renewing and revitalizing the ballad and song tradition by using traditional tunes with contemporaneously relevant texts. No doubt the use of traditional tunes often predisposes an audience to respond favorably to a new song and to select it for recirculation, providing the new text meets group standards.

The themes of love and death and legendary material, belief and custom, all widely found in traditional ballad and song, provide the basis of many local poetic compositions: "How early his spirit has been touched by the legendary lore, the ballads and tales—which stood in the place of literature to the rustic mind of his generation—it is impossible to tell, but as early as his fourteenth year he had begun to embody some of them in verse" (Walker 1887:435). Many a local poet will call his work a ballad, implying its narrative point of view and its use of ballad stanza forms as in Charles Leslie's "Macleod's Defeat at Inverury," beginning:

> Come Country man and sit a while
> and listen to my sang man
> I'll gie my aith twill gar yair smile
> and winna keep you lang man. [National Library of
>   Scotland]

Both the oral ballad and song tradition, as well as its more literary descendant, the local poet tradition, might be appropriately subsumed under the larger category of vernacular literature.[3] Both are created by and for local persons in a familiar language approximating that of everyday speech; and both deal with topics of common, sometimes current, interest. The local poet, however, could read, and this facility enabled acquaintance with written, published, permanent literary accomplishments. Authors—which included those educated, elite and/or court-connected poets who early wrote in Scots, such as Lindsay of the Mount, Dunbar, and Henryson, seventeenth-century writers such as Hamilton of Gilbertfield, and eighteenth-century poets including Ramsay, Fergusson, and Burns—have had an enormous impact on the local poets, invigorating an already rich creative tradition and stimulating innovations in form and content. Print made the contact possible, and print potentially expanded the possible audience of many local poets' work.

The verse form with the greatest impact was the form traditionally referred to as Standard Habbie after a poem by Robert Sempill of Beltrees, "The Life and Death of Habbie Simson, the Piper of Kilbarchan." The lines written "On the Times, in 1799" by James Thomson, which might well have been penned only yesterday, provide an example:

> What will poor bodies do ava,
> For ev'ry thing's grown prices twa',
> The like o' this we never saw,
>   Or ever kent,

>   They'll tak our very life awa'
>   Or e'er they stent. [1801:23]

Other uses of Standard Habbie also illustrate another written precedent—the verse epistle—as in James Duff's "Epistle to Andrew Scot, A Border Bard, on reading his book of Poems, 1810":

>   Had I the gifts o' ROBIE BURNS,
>   Or FERGUSSON, wham Scotland mourns,
>   Or canty ALLAN's crafty turns
>   For poetry,
>   I'd drap a tear o'er a' their urns,
>   An' crack wi' thee. [Duff 1816:30]

Epistles employ a variety of verse forms such as rhymed couplets in stanzas with lengths dependent on content rather than on formal demands.

4. As a participatory, local, ephemeral movement, the local poet tradition flourished in the nineteenth century. From the great fund of balladry and song, local poets took themes, content, form, and style, borrowing compositional techniques as well as audiences. Literacy enabled the local poet to know and be influenced by the written literary tradition, to adapt forms, to use reflective compositional techniques, and, above all, to use an additional means of dissemination—print.

Obviously much has changed since the local poet tradition emerged with the rise of literacy; the conditions of life have altered and the tradition itself has changed. The rise of literacy, which initially made the tradition possible and influenced it so effectively could, simultaneously, by its potential to isolate the individual, undermine the very tradition it had enabled. Print has through time become a more dominant mode of communicating the local poet's work: a small pamphlet, privately printed and sold in the local shop, may have replaced the earlier oral reading or recitation to assembled friends and family. In a sense, then, the face-to-face contact of poet and audience, which goes back to the oral world of the past, has, over time, diminished. The more recent introduction of yet another technology—various electronic media—has heralded a new era that further expands communicative potentialities, making them global in scope, and returning to orality—but aurality that is technologically transmitted. Along with the broadened communicative field is a correspondingly extended area for discussion and perception. The values, concerns, and sentiments of the local poet may be too local and too provincial to thrive under changed media conditions which themselves reflect a further remove from individuals *qua* individuals in communicating and nurturing groups.

The increased mobility of the twentieth century, taking individuals more or less permanently away from the region of birth and its traditional, poetic associations, has contributed, too, to the decline of interest in local poetry. Place, however, remains an important factor in Scotland; "where do you belong?" is a common question reflecting the importance of region, of locality, of ascribed rather than acquired status. Where place remains an important factor, the local poet tradition has the potential to continue, to develop, to thrive.

Wherever genuine local poets are found, wherever the tradition flourishes, the dual influence of oral and written antecedents continues. The local poets then are genuine inheritors of what T. C. Smout has called "a magnificent double heritage"—the ballad makers and the "makaris" of the court circle who gave "the Scottish tongue a literary force and sweetness" (Smout 1970:188). Taking aspects from both, the local poet tradition is a combination, perhaps a synthesis, precipitated by the age of print. Beginning in the eighteenth century, thriving in the nineteenth century, the tradition continues today.

Such marginal literary traditions deserve the critical scrutiny they are just beginning to receive; they have much to tell about art and creativity and life itself. The poet is involved in cultural reportage, commenting on events, characters, and locales reflexively. The poet makes a social text of material shared with the audience, filters it through poetic form, heightens the record, and *re*-presents it to the coparticipants for agreement, nodding acceptance, selection, dismissal. In a sense, the community comes to know itself better through the poetry, and the poetry is at once a reflection of aesthetic values held in common and a metalanguage about ordinary language, thoughts, and experiences. The local poet tradition offers evidence of a communicative and artistic process which converts the everyday to art.

NOTES

1. For an extended discussion of Thomson, see my study in Walls and Shoemaker (Brown 1989).

2. For extended discussions of Charles Leslie, see George Ritchie Kinloch and Mary Ellen Brown (1985). Leslie was by profession a peddler of songs, singing to stimulate interest in the broadsides, chapbooks, and garlands he had for sale. His wares included traditional and original ballads and songs, especially those dealing with seduction, impotency, suspicion of extramarital relations, adultery, and politics, especially pro-Jacobite accounts, implicitly favoring the restoration of the Stewarts.

3. The concept of Vernacular Literature—note capital V and L—has not always been used so inclusively. T. F. Henderson (1910) defined it for the Scottish context as a term "not used to denote merely a common, vulgar, provincial or dialect literature, but what, in a loose form, may be termed native or national Scottish literature, as distinguished from the Scottish literature for which the medium of expression is modern English" (v). Clearly his concerns are primarily with linguistic attributes and with the culture drift he sees as increasingly corrosive of the Scots language, and less with audience, author, or content. Henderson's criteria are limiting and antiquarian; they enable him to claim that the vernacular is dead and Vernacular Literature a thing of the past. He includes material generally labeled "national" by literary critics, reflecting in printed form an early method of representing dialect by using a variable orthography unconfined by modern principles of standardization. He ignores the fact that language changes, that printed standardization encouraged by the growth of print and its ability to disseminate material beyond linguistic barriers often obscures a work's vernacular origins, evident in recitation if not in orthography, although typographical and electronic media may well work for standardization. On the basis of Henderson's definition, few works of local poets, considering their combined corpora, would qualify.

However, Henderson does include a chapter late in his study which deals with "Traditional Ballads and Songs." He ignores the differences between this material and the other material with which he deals: when traditional balladry and song are an active form of artistic communication, they exhibit variation, constant change from performance to performance. Henderson admits eighteenth- and nineteenth-century texts to his canon of Vernacular Literature, but following his linguistic criterion would exclude versions in English or those recorded and printed in a more standardized orthography. He further fails to realize that many of the ballads and songs he would include, though Scottish versions, are part of an international body of material held in common with other parts of the British Isles and areas of Europe, as Child's collection of material so amply illustrates. They are not then "national" in a pure sense, nor can one truncate a tradition by limiting it only to those versions in Scots, recorded in variable orthography.

Henderson's focus is on written literature; properly speaking, this excludes ballads and songs which were created orally and exist dynamically in oral tradition in the language commonly spoken—Scots. The development of literature using the spoken language is, of course, of utmost importance and is, undoubtedly, one prior condition for the development of nationalism. Henderson, however, goes too far in claiming that the Scots language and vernacular literature are dead; people continue to write and create in the language of everyday speech. Local poets did and do. The definition of Vernacular Literature given by Henderson is too restrictive, ignores the role of print and literacy in standardizing spelling, ignores language change, and fails to understand the qualities of traditional balladry and song. Surely a more inclusive view of vernacular literature would offer a positive and dynamic perspective on Scottish literature and would find a place for all versions of traditional ballads and songs recorded in Scotland—in Scots or English, Henderson's Vernacular Literature, and the local poet tradition, which is indebted to both.

REFERENCES

Brown, Mary Ellen
 1985 The Street Laureate of Aberdeen: Charles Leslie, alias Musle Mou'd Charlie, 1677–1783. *In* Carol Edwards and Kathleen Manley, eds., Narrative Folksong: New Directions. Boulder, Colorado: Westview Press.
 1989 Jamie Tamson's Legacy. *In* Robert E. Walls and George H. Shoemaker, eds., The Old Traditional Way of Life. Bloomington: The Trickster Press, pp. 367–81.
Craig, Cairns
 1987 (ed.) The History of Scottish Literature. Aberdeen: Aberdeen University Press.
Duff, James
 1816 A Collection of Poems, Songs & Chiefly Scottish. Perth: R. Morison.
Henderson, T. F.
 1910 Scottish Vernacular Literature. Edinburgh: John Grant.
Ingram, William
 1812 Poems in English and Scottish Dialects. Aberdeen: D. Chalmers.
Kinloch, George Ritchie
 1827 The Ballad Book. Edinburgh.
Macintosh, John
 1910 (comp. and ed.) The Poets of Ayrshire from the Fourteenth Century Till the Present Day, with Selections from their Writings. Dumfries: Thos. Hunter.

National Library of Scotland
- 1825 Letter of James Troup, Lochead Skene, to Alexander Irvine of Drum, with an account of the bard Charles Leslie, with a song by him, Ms. 912, ff. 277–80.

Ong, Walter J.
- 1982 Orality and Literacy: The Technologizing of the Word. London: Methuen.

Purvis, D.
- 1979 A Scots Orthography. Scottish Literary Journal, Supplement No. 9, 62–76.

Smout, T. C.
- 1970 A History of the Scottish People 1560–1830. 2d ed. London: Collins.

Tannahill, Robert
- 1876 The Poems and Songs and Correspondence of Robert Tannahill with Life and Notes, David Semple, ed. Paisley: Alex. Gardner.

Thomson, James
- 1801 Poems, in the Scottish Dialect. Edinburgh: J. Pillans/Leith: W. Reid.
- 1819 Poems, in the Scottish Dialect. Edinburgh: Leith/William Reid.
- 1894 Poems by James Thomson Weaver of Kenleith, R. B. Langwill, ed. London: Archibald Constable.

Walker, William
- 1887 The Bards of Bon-Accord 1375–1860. Aberdeen: J. & J. P. Edmond & Spark.

15

CELEBRATION OF THE *SLAVA* BY A SERBIAN FAMILY IN ENGLAND*

VENETIA NEWALL

Thinking about the interrelationship of foodways and social events, I offer a prologue to this essay by referring to my first meeting with Bill Nicolaisen. It was some twenty-five years ago at a delightful folklore luncheon, in a restaurant which alas no longer exists, not far from University College. The traditional introductions took a creative twist when Bill vaulted across a table on one hand, shouting, "just to show you I'm still young at forty!" He denies the story, but I can vouch for its authenticity. I shall always be grateful for that memorable introduction and the years of dialogue since on creativity and tradition. Bill has been a source of inspiration on these topics to a whole generation of scholars. His ideas of cultural register, and his work on adaptive ethnic traditions are particularly relevant to this account of a Serbian family celebration in England.

Slava or *Krsna Slava*, the feast of the patron saint of the family, is an

---

*I am greatly indebted to the kindness of Dr. Aleksandar Lopašić of the University of Reading who generously placed at my disposal his report on the *Slava* prepared for the University of Cologne. Dr. Lopašić, an anthropologist of Yugoslav origin, is a specialist on the *Slava,* and the general remarks made in this paper are based on his published report. Any errors in interpretation are my own. I am also deeply grateful to Dr. Lopašić for introducing me to the Novaković family and sharing with me their celebration and understanding of the *Slava*. I am also grateful to Sava Peic, then Assistant Librarian at the School of Slavonic Studies, University of London, for help in obtaining certain references.

important festival among the southern Slavs. Associated with the great patriarchal communities based on family kinship, it has been known in various parts of Yugoslavia—Serbia, Macedonia, Montenegro, Boka Kotorska, Bosnia and Herzegovina, Dalmatia, Baranja, and the Voivodina.

Slava is an Orthodox feast, although it is also occasionally celebrated by Catholics and even Muslims. Rumanians in the Banat, Wallachians in Serbia and Macedonia, and even Gypsies have adopted the feast under Yugoslav influence. So have northern Albanians, probably because, for a period during the Middle Ages, their land was under the control of the Serbs. The feast of *Slava* is not observed by other Slavs, nor by the Greek Orthodox, and today it is regarded as a Serbian institution, hence the saying "Where there's a *Slava*, there's a Serb," for it is their most important ritual observance (Halpern 1972:110). Other types of *Slava*, which will not concern us here, include the *Slava* of the saint of the parish church; the monastery *Slava*; the guild *Slava*, a town phenomenon; the school *Slava*, a later ceremony originating from 1827; the *Slava* of the patron saint of the regiment, and so on.

There are indications that *Slava* is partially pre-Christian, dating from the time that the Slavs were converted. There are traces of an ancestor cult; names of ancestors are recited during mass and their graves are visited during the period of the *Slava*. The first historical written reference is from eleventh-century Macedonia and the area surrounding Ohrid. In 1018 the Byzantines imprisoned and blinded a Macedonian prince, Ivac, on the day of his *Slava*, the Assumption of the Blessed Virgin. Other references date from Herzegovina (1391), the Dubrovnik Republic (1466), Boka Kotorska (1772), Serbs in Hungary (eighteenth century), and Croats in Slavonia (1840). There is a great wealth of nineteenth-century material from Herzegovina, Montenegro, Serbia, Dalmatia, and Macedonia, as well as several folk songs dating back to the Middle Ages.

Krsna Slava means literally baptismal celebration. It refers to the first ancestor of the family who was baptized and adopted the name of a patron saint. The holy person then became patron saint of the family and is specially venerated, invoked in times of need, and called to witness the swearing of oaths. Any slighting of this name is regarded as a great insult.

Slava is a festival not of a person but of the home, so it is celebrated by the head of the household. The patron saint and the observance are passed down through the male line; if there is no son, they transfer to the eldest daughter (Lodge 1941:228). A widow celebrates the *Slava* of her dead husband. If, as eldest daughter, she had inherited a patron saint from her father at his death, she will also celebrate his *Slava*.

The patron saint himself is believed to be present at the feast, so traditionally the host entertained his guests standing. Preparations began several days in advance when the priest came and blessed the water used to prepare the festival loaves, which are thus made with holy water. Various dishes were cooked, the house cleaned, and friends and relations invited. The celebration usually lasted for three days, sometimes as long as a week. Typical dishes were stuffed cabbage (*sarma*), fish soup, different kinds of fish, both boiled and fried, sour cabbage, beans, bean salad, suckling-pig, and the *kolač*, a festival loaf of specially prepared sweet bread decorated with symbolic motifs in dough —the dove, the cross, flowers, ears of corn, and so on (Lodge 1941: 229).

Žito, a dish of boiled, sweetened wheat, is cooked only for the *Slava* of saints who have died. Thus it is never offered at the *Slava* of the Archangel Michael.** As a foodstuff it is also prepared for the deceased and is an important element in the cult of the dead. In Serbia and Macedonia it is served at funerals and placed on the graves of dead relatives on the anniversaries of their deaths.

Of course there are variations but, generally speaking, according to Dr. Lopašić, the typical pattern is as follows: the head of the household goes to church with wine, oil, incense, a candle, *žito*, and several festival loaves. The candle is stuck into the *žito* and burns during the service. When the ceremony is over, the loaf is taken to the priest for blessing. He prays and makes four cuts on the underside in the shape of the cross, pours a few drops of wine into the cuts and blesses the bread. He reserves a piece for himself and returns the rest. Congratulations are offered afterwards outside the church.

At home the festive loaf is ritually broken at the midday meal by the host. He lights the *Slava* candle and pours wine over the *kolač*, praying that his house may never lack wheat and wine. The bread is then cut or broken either above the head or over the knee and shared among the guests. Toasts and a festive meal follow. The guests stay until late at night, eating and drinking; the young sing and dance. The

---

**Information kindly provided by Đorđe Novaković.

dead are remembered in prayer and by the lighting of candles and the loaf is shared for the repose of their souls. On the second day, when neighbors come, there is more eating and drinking. The third day, which is seldom made much of, is a time for eating leftovers.

On January 20, 1979, I was invited to attend the *Slava* of Đorđe (George) Novaković and his family in Caversham, Reading. Đorđe is a Serb from Dalmatia, who was then in his early fifties. He had come to England in 1946–47 to study theology under an agreement between the Anglican and Orthodox churches dating from the First World War, enabling a few theology students to receive scholarships. Đorđe settled in England, but changed his mind about his career and took a job with the BBC; later he became head of his department.

Seka, his wife, is from Valjevo, a town in the heart of Serbia. A woman then in her early fifties, she taught languages, including Russian, at a secondary school in Slough. In the early 1970s, as a mature student, she read Russian at London University's School of Slavonic Studies and received a first-class honors degree. Her father was an officer, her mother a teacher.

Zoran, their son, was then in his early twenties. His name, which means "dawn," originates in medieval Dalmatia. Zoran graduated in languages and works for a well-known travel agency. He speaks perfect English without a discernible foreign accent; his girlfriend, who is English, attended the *Slava* for part of the evening.

Vesna, the Novakovićs' daughter, then in her mid-twenties, is named after an old Slavonic goddess of spring. Vesna graduated in Russian and Slavonic Languages. Her political views, subsequently modified, used to be left-wing, and this caused some friction with her émigré parents. She teaches in a school half an hour from Reading.

Micha, Vesna's Russian husband, is several years older than his wife. They met when she spent a year studying literature at the University of Moscow for her M.A. He was also studying literature. Micha is from Leningrad and was expelled from his Soviet university for dissident activities. His mother is Russian, but his father was a Volga German who "disappeared" after the Nazis invaded the Soviet Union in World War II; the Russians sent him to Siberia and he is presumed dead. Micha came to England in 1978 and was learning English with the intention of becoming a university lecturer.

Đorđe's mother, who was then eighty-three, was born in Sibenik and lives in Belgrade. She always comes for the *Slava* if she can, helps to prepare the food, and stays for several months. On this occasion she stayed for six months.

When the family is together at home they speak Serbian. Đorđe and Seka handle the language fairly well, while Vesna speaks rather oddly, despite a year in Belgrade in connection with her academic work; her brother, who never studied the language, is more proficient. Serbian family friends at the *Slava* tended to use English expressions like "trade union" and spoke a sort of bastard language.

There were twenty-one people in the small house at various times during the course of the celebration, but all the intended guests could not be accommodated, and a second party was therefore planned for the following evening. Sometimes guests come from abroad, from Yugoslavia or Germany for instance, and one family group, headed by a Serbian émigré leader, had travelled up from London. Zoran's girlfriend and I were the only non-Serbian-speaking guests present. Several hundred Yugoslavs live in Reading, many of them Serbs; some work for the BBC, and the other guests were all drawn from this local Yugoslav community.

The religious ceremony took place in the morning. Guests were not invited and only the immediate family members were present. The community in Reading cannot afford to support a priest, so arrangements were made for one to travel from the Serbian church in London. In an emergency (if there is a blizzard, for example, and the priest is prevented from coming), the head of the family is permitted to conduct the service himself.

The ceremony, which is characterized by special prayers and lasts for half an hour, was later described to me by the family. Đorđe had prepared a list of immediate family members—parents, brothers, sisters, and close relatives—and prayers were said for them as well as for the dead. A round *kolač* of sweet bread had been prepared, decorated with appliqué motifs of a sheaf of wheat symbolizing harvest, a dove, a rose, and a stamp incorporating Old Church Slavonic motifs. The appliqué which results from using this stamp is called *slovo*, meaning "letters," and must include the name of the *Slava* saint, in this case John the Baptist.

In the course of the ceremony, the men gathered round the *kolač*, grasping it with their thumbs pointing upwards and moving in a circle, singing a prayer. Women as a rule do not perform this ritual. The priest then took the bread, broke it in half, and poured a little wine on the bottom. Everyone who took part in the ceremony kissed the bread three times, the priest said "Christ is with us," and those present replied "So be it." The names of the living and the dead in the family were then read aloud.

Several items used during this ceremony remained on display with the *kolač* on the sideboard: an icon of John the Baptist and a beeswax candle with oak leaves around the base. The leaves had been blessed by the priest and given to the congregation on Christmas Eve. A few are then used to decorate the *Slava* candle. Seka had also added a ribbon, but this is "phony" according to Đorđe: it should be a small Serbian flag. In the sitting room a candle in a red glass was lit beneath the icon. This is only done for special occasions such as Easter, Christmas, and *Slava*. Normally the sitting room is decorated with various icons and reproductions of Yugoslav "naive" painters.

Traditionally visitors do not bring gifts, as this is taken to mean that the hospitality is inadequate. At Đorđe's *Slava*, however, it is customary to bring gifts of wine, cakes, and fruit. I arrived with a bottle of Serbian *slivovitz* (plum brandy) and my Yugoslav friend gave a bottle of wine to Đorđe and expensive German cakes to Seka. Another visitor brought a presentation basket containing a pineapple and a bunch of grapes.

When the guests arrived, they greeted Đorđe and Seka: "*Slava!*" After they had sat down, Vesna offered a tray with a glass of water, a glass filled with spoons, and a plate of *žito*. As described by Seka, *žito* is a dish prepared from wheat, walnuts, and sugar, shaped in the form of a spherical cake, and decorated with oak leaves blessed by the priest—also from Christmas Eve—and caster sugar. She flavors it with orange, vanilla, or lemon as otherwise it is "too sweet." Each new arrival took a spoon from the glass and ate a spoonful of *žito*, afterwards placing the used spoon in the glass of water. The visitor then crossed himself or herself. I remarked that the custom resembled *slatko*, the ritual Yugoslav offering to an arriving guest of a small piece of sweet food, water, and a spoon on a tray, and was told, "Yes, but this is different."

Since, as we have already noted, *žito* is not served for the *Slava* of the Archangel Michael because he is living (saints are reckoned to be dead and the festivals of the other Archangels are not celebrated), there seems to be little doubt that it is a ritual food associated with the dead. It bears some resemblance to the dish eaten in neighboring Greece in memory of the departed. G. F. Abbot, in his *Macedonian Folklore* published at the beginning of the century, refers to "the anniversary of the death [when] a 'feast of remembrance' is celebrated." He continues:

> The grave is decorated with flowers, a Mass is sung, and offerings are made in the church. These offerings consist of a tray of parboiled wheat mixed with powdered walnuts, raisins and parsley, and covered over with a coating of sugar, with the sign of the cross, and sometimes the initials of the deceased, worked on it in raisins. The wheat is interpreted as a symbol of the resurrection: as the grain is buried in the earth, rots, and rises again in the shape of a blooming plant, so will the soul rise from its tomb. An occult meaning is also attached to the sugar and the raisins: the sweetness of the one representing the sweets of the heavenly paradise, and the shrivelled appearance of the other suggesting the state of the soul before it is admitted to the bliss of the Christian Elysium. [Abbot 1969:207–8]

Following the ritual consumption of the *žito* on arrival, guests were offered an aperitif and red caviar bought by Seka on a recent visit to Moscow. Then there was an invitation to help oneself to the liberal buffet in the dining room: salami, cold chicken, cold veal, hot stuffed cabbage, tomato-cucumber ("Serbian") salad, cheese pie, potato salad, and Russian beet salad. It is a cuisine influenced by Austria-Hungary, Turkey, and the presence of a Russian son-in-law. All were pressed to eat their fill. Later in the evening two different cakes and little sweetmeats, crescent-shaped or round and flavored with almonds, were handed round with coffee, brandy, and liquéurs. Wine was served with the buffet supper.

Later in the evening, after the coffee and cakes, the émigré leader from London, his son, the son's girl friend, and Vesna danced a circular dance and various songs were sung. Vesna then took photographs. It was a long, drawn-out event. We arrived soon after 7:00 P.M., among the last of the visitors, and left at 2:15 A.M. Nor were we the last to leave. The old ladies, including Granny, aged eighty-three, stayed till 5:00 A.M., when it ended.

Đorđe and Seka are a pious couple whom I met at the Orthodox Midnight Resurrection Service at the Russian Church in London. They and their children are intellectuals with a keen desire to keep alive the culture and religious customs of their native land, hence the old Slavonic names that they have given to the children. They are self-conscious about their family unity, a feeling enshrined in the observance of *Slava,* which is essentially a family event. The local Serbian community joins with them in their celebration; the presence of an émigré leader from London and the singing and dancing of national songs and dances indicate the significance of the occasion, which Đorđe says is "more important than Christmas or Easter."

The family's celebration of the event shows the interplay of creativity and tradition in an ethnic setting. The family members come from a variety of occupations and intellectual pursuits suggesting the range of behavioral registers available to them. Appropriate to their pursuits, they have effected changes in the custom as it was remembered from the "old country." Yet the family expresses its unity through a distinctive celebration in a folk-culture register. The family strategically uses the tradition to fashion roles and customs for the reinforcement of family and ethnic identity.

The social functions of the feast for this family in particular, and for the Serbian community of Britain in general, are of utmost importance. This ethnic group is not large compared with the population of Britain as a whole, and inevitably its members to a greater or lesser extent feel marginalized. The celebration of the *Slava* functions as an occasion when members of the family and the wider community can gather together to create, express, and hence reinforce their ethnic identity and further experience the spiritual importance of their religious tradition.

REFERENCES
Abbott, G. F.
    1969   Macedonian Folklore. 1903 repr. Chicago: Argonaut.
Halpern, Joel M.
    1972   A Serbian Village in Historical Perspective. New York: Holt, Rinehart, and Winston.
Lodge, Olive
    1941   Peasant Life in Jugoslavia. London: Seely, Service, & Co.

16

TRADITION, CHANGE, AND HMONG REFUGEES

ROGER E. MITCHELL

Among the many issues related to the connection of creativity and tradition are the effects of national "character" on the adaptation of folk narrative. Bill Nicolaisen took up this issue in an essay on "Folk and Habitat" (1976) and concluded with several proposals for future studies, one of which was "an investigation of the behavior of folk-narrative items and genres in bi-cultural situations, whether these are also bi-lingual or not" (Nicolaisen 1976:325, 329). Some of these questions and suggestions I propose to investigate, at least in part, with reference to the hastening acculturation of recent immigrant refugees from Southeast Asia to the United States.

The abrupt departure of American forces from Vietnam in 1975 set in motion an exodus of Southeast Asians that by July 1, 1989, numbered over 1,500,000 people. Of these, nearly a million have come to the United States. While they are to be found in every state in the union, nearly half of them have settled in California (Southeast Asian... 1989:9). The relative ease with which this mixed group of Vietnamese, Cambodian, and Laotian refugees has entered the American mainstream has depended in large part on the education and usable skills that each group brought to America. The least successful thus far has been that Laotian subdivision called in the older literature "Meo" or "Miao" (Barney 1967). These terms, however, have the connotations of "savage" or "barbarian," and today one finds these Laotian hill tribes referred to by their own preferred classifier, "Hmong," meaning "free."

This penchant for freedom, often alluded to by Hmong of my acquaintance, has brought them a long history of wandering and trouble. According to their legends, they came "from the north" (Quincy 1988:14), and were first recorded as dwellers in China (Geddes 1976:19–21), where large numbers of Hmong (Miao) still reside. Hmong scholar Yang Dao and others pick up the trail in China and trace the route taken by rebellious Hmong clans in their wanderings to the contemporary Hmong settlements in North Vietnam, Laos, and Thailand (Yang 1975; Savina 1924).

The events that made the Hmong a part of America's Southeast Asian refugee population are much more recent. At the same time the North Vietnamese Communists were aiding the Viet Cong in South Vietnam, they were also involved in a military action in Laos aimed at upsetting the Royal Laotian government. Many factors combined to put the Laotian Hmong in the thick of things. The battles were waged in those eastern provinces heavily inhabited by the Hmong, who reacted aggressively to this new threat to their freedom. More importantly, the Royal Laotian Army included in its ranks a Hmong lieutenant, Vang Pao, who quickly rose to the level of general because of his leadership qualities, military prowess, and ability to attract substantial aid in food, weapons, and transportation from the Central Intelligence Agency (CIA). General Vang Pao was able to raise a large number of Hmong troops, who, in the beginning at least, saw themselves as fighting against their traditional enemy (Wekkin 1982:181–82).

For this the Hmong paid dearly. Out of an estimated prewar population of 300,000 Laotian Hmong, 12,000 soldiers died in the thirteen years of war (1962–75) with the Communists. Well over 100,000 were forced to flee their homes and live in refugee camps in Laos, where they were fed by a USAID relief program. Another twenty percent (60,000) of the Hmong civilian population is estimated to have died of starvation, disease, and enemy attacks as they fled to refugee camps (Lee 1982:203).

The sudden American withdrawal of support in 1975 left General Vang Pao, his troops, and the many Hmong refugees in a hopeless position clustered about or near his several military camps. There was little choice but to withdraw, and the logical route was south to Thailand. A favored few, such as General Vang Pao and others close to the seats of power, came to America quickly. Many preferred to stay in the Thai refugee camps, waiting for a political miracle that would allow them to return to their homeland. Some hoped against hope that a reluctant Thai government would change its policies and allow them to settle in Thailand permanently (Governor's State Advisory Council 1986). Others delayed until close relatives were able to escape from Laos and join them in Thailand, but eventually a large number accepted the inevitable and headed for America, the most unwilling group of immigrants our shores have seen for many a year. Nearly 100,000 Hmong now reside within our borders, with California playing host to over half of them. The second largest group is in the Minneapolis-St. Paul area (approximately 14,000). Wisconsin has concentrations of about 2,000 in each of her larger cities (approximately 16,000), and smaller settlements are to be found in Illinois, Michigan, and Indiana (Yang and North 1988:19). Other states where refugees were originally placed, especially in the East, have not proved attractive, and many of these Hmong are moving westward to join relatives (Mitchell et al. 1989).

As a group the Hmong are having great difficulty adjusting. Some ex-soldiers, widows, and war orphans I have interviewed are bitter. They firmly believe that they were deserted by the Americans after being told by CIA agents that they would be cared for. Moreover, they are of the opinion, especially after coming to America, that the United States could have won the war if its politicians had wished. Another cause for uncertainty is the belief on the part of many Hmong, especially in the older generation, that someday they will return victorious to their homeland. This hope is fed by a curious combination of religious belief and past military exploits under General Vang Pao. A millenarian movement in Laos called Chao Fa, like many other such religious groups, promises its believers that someday their god will come and rescue his devotees from their oppressors. A great many older Hmong in America and Southeast Asia still anticipate the great day. In addition, General Vang Pao still schemes to reclaim Hmong lands, and his representatives travel from one Hmong community to another, exhorting the faithful and collecting money to finance the soon-to-be expected victorious return (Hammond 1989:14).

In the meantime, many younger Hmong have become more Americanized and less receptive to their elders' demands to follow the old ways, which themselves have been greatly transformed during the years of conflict and forced moves (Smalley 1986:8). Especially disconcerting to the elders are the signs that some younger Hmong are getting into trouble through gang membership and related activities such as car theft (Hopfensperger 1989:4B). Of great concern, too, is the widespread belief that Americans are trying to disrupt the traditional Hmong family.

In prewar Laos, age at marriage was young; for women fourteen or fifteen was not uncommon, and demographic data indicate that this tendency has changed little since the Hmong removal to America. In addition frequently the tradition of elopement, or "marriage by capture" has been misinterpreted by the press as kidnapping (Knight 1987:8; Klein 1989:1A; Goldstein 1986:138). Other areas of strain and misunderstanding are related to shamanism, folk medicine, and various rumors relating to food practices, welfare utilization, and drugs (Conquergood 1989; Osborne 1988; Mitchell 1987).

How do folklorists respond to this latest wave of refugees? Certainly there is much of a traditional nature to warrant interest. Folk music is still much in demand at such important rituals as shamanistic performances and funerals. Traditional games, songs, food, and clothing are very much in evidence at New Year celebrations. Herbal medicine is as yet widely practiced. There exists a vigorous folktale tradition (Johnson 1985; Vang and Lewis 1984).

As could be expected of a recently nonliterate society, the Hmong place high value on competency in verbal expression; they arrived in their new home with much of their expressive culture intact and functional. In the more than a decade that the Hmong have been resident in Eau Claire, Wisconsin, I have worked closely with them, and again and again attention to the polished turn of phrase has been evident. For example, in a recent talk given at a conference concerning minority enrollment, a Hmong college student emphasized the need for more dialogue between university leaders and Hmong community leaders. His precise phrase was: "This is a bridge that should be crossed from the Hmong side" (Vue 1989). This he worked into a major point: Don't select your Hmong liaison personnel on the basis of how well they are liked by Americans. Rather, choose a qualified individual who is highly respected in the Hmong community. In his recommendation that the university strive for closer relations with the Hmong elders, the speaker also made use of proverbs, one of which was:

> Reverence the heavens
> And they will give you good fortune;
> Reverence your parents
> And you will be well off. [Vue 1989:3]

This use of the well-turned phrase and the proverbial saying is an adaptation of traditional Hmong usage. All important Hmong ceremonies and rituals require that older Hmong who are experts in the use of "proper" language be present to represent the family through expressive speech, the least elaborate of which is "Paired Words." Thus, "Hot hand—hot foot" suggests that one is trying to do too many things at once. Or one could say, "Yellow wind—black wind," meaning a storm is brewing (Vang and Lewis 1984:69). This type of figurative language is open to all, and my Hmong informants and aides had no trouble coming up with many examples of the Hmong fondness for verbal elaboration.

Far distant from "Paired Words" is what are called "Flower Words" (Vang and Lewis 1984:67), which are intentionally obscure. While definitely of a traditional and proverbial nature, flower language is the mark of the Hmong orator. When I asked English-speaking Hmong for the meaning of "flower words," I was several times given a proverb: "The tree gives the flower; but no fruit yet" which is interpreted to mean that unless one is well versed in flower language, one must search for the hidden meaning.

The head interviewer in the demographic survey, Touly Xiong, presented several examples of this metaphorical language from the verbal exchanges that take place when two negotiators are arranging a forthcoming marriage. One might say, "I am here to splice our wing to your wing and our tail to your tail." By this he meant that the ceremonies would bind bride to groom and family to family. Then they could "fly together." When the bride left with the groom, her father's negotiator might say, "But remember, I have given you the halter, but I hold the rope." Thus the daughter is let go like an animal on a tether. If she is not treated properly, the father will pull the rope and bring her home.

Although I was able to obtain examples of flower words if I asked for them, they were rarely forthcoming spontaneously. Indeed, I was told several times that elders who used obscure references were often told: "Give us the fruit. Keep the flower." Allied to the fact that many young American Hmong have never experienced much traditional Hmong culture, this does not bode well for metaphorical communication relating to a horticultural way of life that was left behind. In discussing this matter with me, a Hmong college student used a flower expression to illustrate the problem. In his opinion, using such esoteric language to the young was like "playing a flute to a wild buffalo." They don't know what is going on.

When one moves the focus from the oblique proverbial saying to the proverb itself, the signs of a vigorous life are evident. Often books dealing with elements of Hmong culture will contain a segment on proverbs (e.g., Vang and Lewis 1984:71–79; Heimbach 1969:461–66), and my Hmong contacts often use proverbs to comment on whatever matters are under discussion at the time. Some refer to commonplace things as I probe their memories about life on their mountain farms in Laos. It was on one such an occasion that the informant commented: "In the morning we went up to the thunder. In the afternoon we came down to the dragon" (Xiong 1988). By this he meant that they had gone to their opium fields on the hilltops and had returned to their rice fields in the lower land (the traditional abode of the dragon) that afternoon. Others might be uttered to fit a present situation. For example, if an effort to correct something has made it worse, the proverb "Avoid the frog; Meet the snake" (Xiong 1988) might be used.

Although these examples might appear as obscure as the Flower Words, to most Hmong they are immediately recognizable as proverbs. They are in paired lines, they rhyme (in Hmong), and the second line explains the first. Moreover, they are common sayings and understandable to the average Hmong. Many of the proverbs that I have encountered appear also in other published works as examples of the genre or as illustrations of a cultural attitude, but little effort has been made in these sources to indicate which proverbs were collected by the authors and which were borrowed from other collections such as Jean Mottin's *Eléments de Grammaire Hmong Blanc* (1978). Either the authors were not aware of certain well-known, earthy Hmong proverbs, or they chose not to print them. For example, when some Hmong students were discussing the supposed change in Chinese communism with me, Touly Xiong commented: "We have a Hmong proverb about this: 'The music is different, But it smells like the same old shit.' I don't trust them" (Xiong 1988). Nearly all the proverbs cited below are to be found in Heimbach (1969) or Vang and Lewis (1984). If my informant agreed with the published translation, I have cited the published form. Where disagreement exists, I cite my informant (Xiong 1988).

My interest in the Hmong proverb has been guided in large part by necessity. Once I had completed my demographic survey of the Eau Claire Hmong community, I often found myself serving as a source of information for the several agencies, school officials, and service groups that were involved in various services to the Hmong. However, once I got beyond the basic data—age at marriage, size of family, place of birth, I was faced with attitudinal questions: When will the Hmong adopt our marriage patterns? How do they feel about education? Are we creating yet another group of welfare dependents? In reply I was forced to retreat from my statistics and offer answers based on my interview responses. Often I would preface my response with Hmong proverbs that had been recited to me by informants making similar points. Proverbs as indicators of worldview have aided me greatly in giving meaning to my demographic data and conveying that meaning to other Americans.

Antirefugee rumors to the contrary, the Hmong possess a positive world view, which needs little remodeling to earn them success in America, if they can avoid becoming acculturated into what Oscar Lewis (1965:xii) once called the "culture of poverty." First and foremost are the importance of family and the need for cooperation. We cannot expect, at least for a time, that the average Hmong will delay marriage until after college, or indeed until after high school. Over and over, the proverbial point is made: "Grain planted late is mostly chaff. Late marriage leaves orphans" (Heimbach 1969). Common, too, is the advice to choose carefully, for: "If the crops aren't good, you lose only one year; If your wife isn't good, you lose a whole lifetime" (Xiong 1988). That the parents are the ones who ideally aid their child in making the right choice is seen in many proverbs advising filial behavior:

> Young, obey your parents.
> Become a man, be village chief. [Xiong 1988]
>
> Reverence the heavens and they will give you good fortune.

> Reverence your parents and you will be well off.
> [Heimbach 1969]

Nor is this all one-sided, for traditional wisdom emphasizes the duality of family responsibility: "Feed and care for the old and they will remember your kindness. Feed and care for the young and they will stay close by you" (Heimbach 1969). And this concept of family envisions the binding together of two extended families. To quote: "Your chicken rests in my coop; My duck is in your barn" (Xiong 1988). Furthermore, the importance of kinship extends even beyond close blood relations: "If you are not their chief, they do not respect you. If you are not their clan mate they do not support you" (Vang and Lewis 1984:73). Moreover, as blood kinship extends to those of the same clan, so ties to people one knows are emphasized:

> Bitter vegetables are not suitable to eat with rice.
> Strangers are not good companions. [Xiong 1988]

> To eat flavorless vegetables [with friends] is as tasty as meat.
> And to drink water [with them] is as good as alcohol.
> [Heimbach 1969]

Another strong point of emphasis in Hmong proverbs is the importance of hard work and self-sufficiency. For the lazy there is this traditional warning:

> When the others work,
> You don't have to work with them;
> When the others eat,
> You're a dog begging for scraps. [Vang and Lewis 1984:80]

Another castigates the malingerer who, as we would say in Maine, is slow to the plow but fast to the table:

> Grinding corn hurts my hand!
> Pounding rice hurts my foot!
> Carrying water hurts my back!
> But for eating rice you get a big spoon. [Xiong 1988]

Or

> Plant beans late, they are marked with spots.
> Man who works slowly begs at the other's door.
> Plant beans late, they are marked with blight.
> Man who works little begs at the other's fence.
> [Vang and Lewis 1984:73]

Nor is this practical wisdom aimed at merely filling the pot. One should strive for success for as the proverb has it: "Mushrooms come up whether you put them in water or not. If one is rich, it doesn't matter where he lives" (Heimbach 1969).

The path to this desired wealth is marked with practicality, work, and patience:

> Handsome, then get Chinese girl.
> Patient, then become chief. [Vang and Lewis 1984:72]

> Put your heart into something.
> You will win. [Xiong 1988]

> When young, learn to be practical;
> When grown, able to be a wealthy person. [Vang and Lewis 1984:85].

The desired end of this quest for self-sufficiency and wealth is to become an esteemed person, leader of your clan and perhaps even of your village. This brings us back to reverence for age and adds the desired qualities of a leader:

> Tangled hair, use a comb to unsnarl it.
> Complicated dispute, use an elder to solve it.
> [Vang and Lewis 1984:81]

> Look at the river carefully;
> Treat people fairly. [Xiong 1988]

It is also apparent that they feel right living has its own rewards: "Clean water wins over dirty. Good people win over bad" (Xiong

1988). In addition, one must make the effort to get along, to cooperate: "Whether you eat or not, at least hold a spoon. Whether you laugh or not, at least force a smile" (Heimbach 1969). Once you step outside this close circle of kin and friends, you are advised to proceed with caution: "When doing business, don't be father and son. When doing business, be like the Black Chinese" (Vang and Lewis 1984:78). You keep your word: "When you cut off a bit of metal to make a bullet, You don't add to it or take from it" (Heimbach 1969). You make good your debts: "Did you borrow my money like taking a person's rice cake to devour?" (Heimbach 1969). You beware of government officials: "See a tiger, you will die; See an official, you will be poor" (Vang and Lewis 1984:73). There is also the belief that wealth of itself does not buy happiness: "Poor people are happy, Rich people weep" (Xiong 1988). And as a final bit of wisdom: "Rich, don't boast. Poor, don't cry" (Vang and Lewis 1984:71).

The majority of these proverbs celebrate the importance of kin, status, and hard work, and the statistical data emerging from my demographic survey reinforce these same themes. It was kin that sustained these refugees in the difficult journey from Laos to Thailand to America, and the secondary migration from other American cities to Eau Claire was in large part influenced by the desire to repair their fractured families.

The desire for economic independence also comes through strongly in their concern for education and vocational training. A large majority indicated they would move again if they could find a good job. The responses also indicated a great reluctance to state that they were unemployed or on welfare, although over 75 percent fall in this category (see Reder 1985:67 for similarly high rates of dependence in other Hmong settlements). Moreover, a leadership survey that I am now carrying out strongly indicates that positions of respect and leadership in the Hmong community must be worked for.

This is most assuredly a world view Americans can work with, both to benefit the Hmong and the United States as the host society. And most certainly this is not the time for ill-advised attempts to restructure the institution of the Hmong extended family. Change will come with time. To quote a leader among Hmong college students:

> Continued threats of felony charges and jail will only make the Hmong withdraw more and become more suspicious. While

claiming to want to help us, our American friends are doing the opposite. Already some Hmong families are isolated. The elders are distrusting the young and their education. They repeat the proverb: "We escaped from the frog (Communists) but face the snake (Americans)." We are afraid that our families will break up and be lost before we get our feet on new ground. How can we be expected to change so fast? We haven't got by the first step: acceptance in the Eau Claire community. We are the minority and we have been trying to adapt to the majority way. However, the majority is not ready for us. [Xiong 1989]

REFERENCES
Barney, G. Linwood
    1967   The Meo of Xieng Khouang Province, Laos. *In* Peter Kunstadter, ed., Southeast Asian Tribes, Minorities, and Nations. Princeton: Princeton University Press, pp. 271–94.
Conquergood, Dwight
    1989   Establishing the World: Hmong Shamans. Cura Reporter [University of Minnesota] 19, 2:5–10.
Geddes, William R.
    1976   Migrants of the Mountains: The Cultural Ecology of the Blue Miao (Hmong Njua) of Thailand. Oxford: Clarendon Press.
Goldstein, Beth L.
    1986   Resolving Sexual Assault: Hmong and the American Legal System. *In* Glenn L. Hendricks, Bruce T. Downing, and Amos S. Deinard, eds., The Hmong in Transition. New York: Center for Migration Studies, pp. 135–43.
Governor's State Advisory Council for Refugees
    1986   Thailand Trip Report. Minneapolis: State of Minnesota.
Hammond, Ruth
    1989   Rumors of War: Vang Pao. Twin Cities Reader [Minneapolis], October 25–31, pp. 8–14.
Heimbach, Ernest E.
    1969   White Hmong-English Dictionary. Ithaca: Cornell University.
Hopfensperger, Jean
    1989   Anguish, Confusion Remain Behind for Dead Boys' Families. Star Tribune [Minneapolis], November 17, pp. 1b, 4b.
Johnson, Charles
    1985   Dab Neeg Hmoob: Myths, Legends, and Folktales from the Hmong of Laos. St. Paul: Macalester College.

Klein, Michael
    1989   Girl Kidnapped for Marriage. Leader-Telegram [Eau Claire, Wisconsin], October 1, pp. 1a–2a.
Knight, Joe
    1987   Hmong Officials Discuss Conflicting Customs, Laws. Leader-Telegram [Eau Claire, Wisconsin], February 17, pp. 3a.
Lee, Gary
    1982   Minority Policies and the Hmong. In Martin Stuart-Fox, ed., Contemporary Laos: Studies in the Politics and Society of the Lao People's Democratic Republic. St. Lucia: University of Queensland Press, pp. 199–219.
Lewis, Oscar
    1965   La Vida: A Puerto Rican Family in the Culture of Poverty—San Juan and New York. Random House: New York.
Mitchell, Roger
    1987   The Will to Believe and Anti-Refugee Rumors. Midwestern Folklore 13:5–15.
Mitchell, Roger; Xiong, Touly; Vue, Charles; Xiong, Moua; Martin, Leanne
    1989   The Eau Claire Hmong Community: A Cooperative Study. Wisconsin Sociologist 26:33–37.
Mottin, Jean
    1978   Eléments de Grammaire Hmong Blanc. Bangkok: Don Bosco Press.
Nicolaisen, W. F. H.
    1976   Folk and Habitat. Studia Fennica 20:324–30.
Osborne, Garth
    1988   Health Risks from Mineral-Based Traditional Medicine. The Refugee Health Issues Center Update 2, 2:1–2.
Quincy, Keith
    1988   Hmong: History of a People. Cheney, Washington: Eastern Washington University Press.
Reder, Stephen (Project Director)
    1985   The Hmong Resettlement Study. Final Report, Vol I. Washington, D.C.: Office of Refugee Resettlement.
Savina, F. M.
    1924   Histoire des Miao. Paris: Société des Missions-Estrangères.
Smalley, William A.
    1986   Stages of Hmong Cultural Adaption. In Glenn L. Hendricks, Bruce T. Downing, and Amos S. Deinard, eds., The Hmong in Transition. New York: Center for Migration Studies, pp. 7–22.
Southeast Asian Refugee Population Nears One Million
    1989   Asian Business and Community News [Minneapolis] 7:9.
Vang, Lue; and Lewis, Judy
    1984   Grandmother's Path, Grandfather's Way. Folsom, California: Folsom-Cordova School District.

Vue, Charles Chu
- 1989 In Search for Diversity: Hmong Students at the University of Wisconsin-Eau Claire. Paper given at University of Wisconsin-Eau Claire Minority Student Leadership Conference.

Wekkin, Gary D.
- 1982 The Rewards of Revolution: Pathet Lao Policy towards the Hill Tribes since 1975. *In* Martin Stuart-Fox, ed., Contemporary Laos: Studies in the Politics and Society of the Lao People's Democratic Republic. St. Lucia: University of Queensland Press, pp. 181–98.

Xiong, Touly
- 1988 Unpublished family history interviews. Interviewer: Roger Mitchell.
- 1989 Paper written for composition class.

Yang, Dao
- 1975 Les Hmongs du Laos Face au Développement. Vientiane: Siaosavath Publishers.

Yang, Duoa; North, David
- 1988 Profiles of the Highland Lao Communities in the United States. Washington: Office of Refugee Resettlement.

ELABORATING TRADITION:
A Pennsylvania-German Folk Artist Ministers to His Community*

SIMON J. BRONNER

Walking out of a Mahantongo Valley church supper and its loads of Pennsylvania-German delicacies, Charles Rebuck paused by a row of proud, aging stones in the churchyard. Compared to others in the yard, they were highly decorated with rosettes, hearts, and floral designs. Charles remarked, "Now there was a Dutchman, all right." "You mean the fellow who's buried there?" I asked. "No, the fellow who carved them. Stiehly's his name. His descendants are here yet," he offered. Others joined us as we gazed at the stones. The carver had left no signature on the stones, and yet these people easily recognized his creations. I thought it significant that almost 150 years after Stiehly finished his work, residents recalled him even more than those for whom he carved. *"Do iss der Mann, as mer so viel schwetze devun"* (Here is the man that we talk so much about), Rebuck explained later in his native Pennsylvania Dutch. He pointed out the Stiehly farmstead and mill across the road, and tried to explain his role

---

*I am grateful to Charles and Beulah Rebuck, Mahantongo Valley residents, for first pointing me to Salem Church, and for their invaluable assistance afterward. Bill Richardson, also living in the valley, kindly shared his research and accompanied me on several trips to cemeteries. I am indebted to Marilyn Herb and her mother Katie Malick for showing me Stiehly family account books, artifacts, and photographs. Don Yoder, William Aspinall, and Henry Reed also contributed greatly to my understanding of the valley and its folk arts.

by telling me a riddle: *"Was geht un geht, Un steht un steht?"* (What goes and goes, And yet stands and stands?).[1] The answer, he emphasized, was "a mill," but it just as easily could be the Pennsylvania Germans of this valley, still around despite reports to the contrary.

Charles knows about descendants in the valley; his forebears were among its first settlers back in the eighteenth century, and the town name of Rebuck, not far from where we stood, honors his pioneering family. Talking about family is a common way to converse in the valley. People know each other from the family trees that all seem to interconnect, and they easily recount as narrative whose "pap"—maybe a Rothermel, Drumheller, or Klinger—was related to whose cousin going back more than two hundred years.[2] I wasn't surprised, then, when Charles told me, "Well, let's see now—Isaac was the minister, and he had a son Jared, who's the grandfather of Katie Malick, who's over in Valley View now, and she had a daughter Marilyn—yeah, I think that's right."

From where we stood, you couldn't see Valley View in the Hegins Valley, just a few miles south over imposing Mahantongo Mountain, but could see Line Mountain to the north, another giant barrier, running straight across the landscape. I could understand why residents call the place where the Mahantongo and Line mountains meet *der Kessel* or "the kettle." The valley creates a feeling of self-containment (Fig. 1), and residents, marked culturally by their distinctive Pennsylvania-German dialect and traditions, identify strongly with the area they simply call the "Mahantongo."

Some scholars have highlighted the valley's cultural stability in comparison to other areas of central Pennsylvania, but residents tell of waves of change that have come to the region (see Boyer, Buffington, and Yoder 1964; Troutman 9 October 1948). The valley has had several cultural transitions to make from the time the first settlers arrived during the 1770s through a gap in the Blue Mountain in Berks County to the discovery of coal, the introduction of state-controlled common or "free" schools, the advent of the railroad and new immigrants during the 1840s, the second wave of immigration and industrialization during the late-nineteenth century, and the communication and transportation changes and agricultural depressions of the twentieth century (see Wood 1942; Klein and Hoogenboom 1980; Yoder 25 January 1947a; Yoder 1985; Parsons 1985).[3]

Isaac Stiehly (Fig. 2), whose gravestones beckoned Charles Rebuck

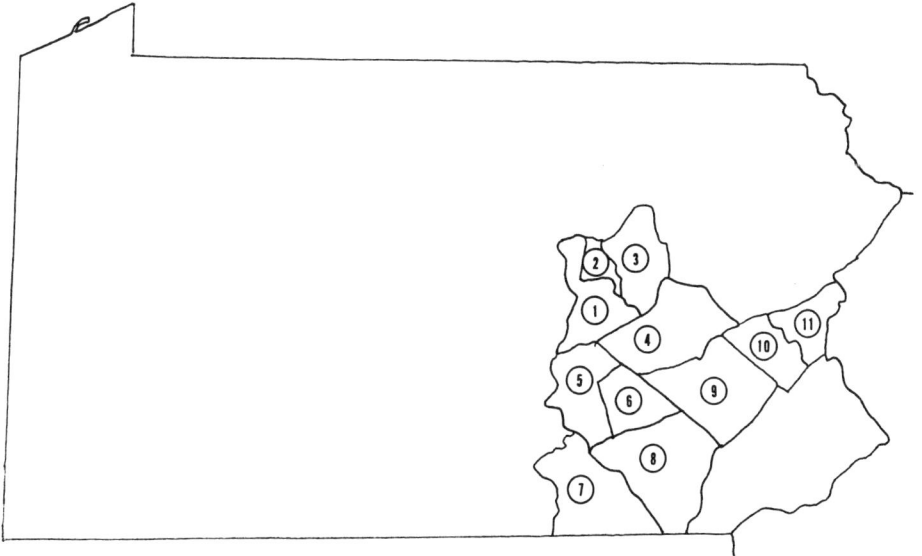

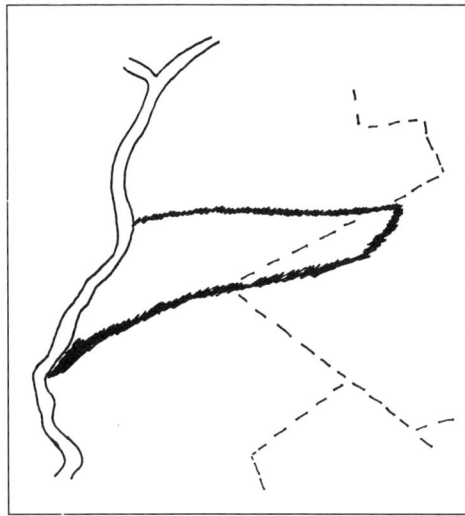

1. Reference Maps: A. Counties of central Pennsylvania discussed in essay
No. 1: Northumberland
No. 2: Montour
No. 3: Columbia
No. 4: Schuylkill
No. 5: Dauphin
No. 6: Lebanon
No. 7: York
No. 8: Lancaster
No. 9: Berks
No. 10: Lehigh
No. 11: Northampton

B. The Mahantongo Valley in central Pennsylvania (Salem Church is situated near Klingerstown where three counties—Dauphin, Schuylkill, and Northumberland—meet)

2. Isaac F. Stiehly (1800–69) late in his life. (Courtesy Marilyn Herb)

and others this day, had experienced transition in the valley more than most. Besides ministering at Salem Church, Stiehly also served at least ten other church congregations, mostly in the Mahantongo and Hegins valleys, between 1827 and 1869 (see Richardson 1990:14). He could vividly see communities form and develop as he ministered to them. Churches—either German Reformed or Lutheran, and often both together in a "Union" church—brought families together even more than markets did and defined communities. They also influenced political attitudes. Stiehly was known to voice his opposition to the National Bank and the prevailing nationalistic politics of Lancaster County.[4] The churches administered holiday celebrations, maintained social services, conducted rituals of life passage (baptisms, confirmations, weddings, funerals), kept family records, and saw to the education of children (see Yoder 1984; Weiser 1987; Frantz 1987). Stiehly lived near Salem Church in Rough and Ready (near Klingerstown), and considered it his base.

Ministering to his congregation in the Mahantongo Valley away from the governing Herman Synod in Lancaster, two counties over to the southeast, Stiehly recognized that his community was developing an ethnic subculture. Although many Pennsylvania-German settlers shared roots in the Rhineland Palatinate region of Europe, their inherited dialect experienced further fragmentation in the various centers of settlement—in the Shenandoah Valley of Virginia, in Lancaster and York counties, and in Berks and Lehigh counties south of the Blue Mountain where the Mahantongo Valley lies, to name a few (see Seifert 1946; Buffington 1948; Yoder 1 February 1947a). Congregations in Stiehly's region used the Pennsylvania-German dialect as their workaday as well as home language, and by the 1840s felt increasingly alienated from the English and High German dictated by the Herman Synod for use in sermons, Bible readings, and church instructions. In his church, Stiehly emphasized oral recitation in the local dialect.[5]

One sign of community identity in the Mahantongo Valley was Stiehly's formation of the Free or Stiehly Synod in 1841, which broke away from the Herman Synod (Reed 1987:51; Richardson 1990:15). Stiehly organized seven churches in the Mahantongo and adjacent valleys to form the new synod, and insisted on adjusting church services to the folk language and culture of the region. In so doing, Stiehly resisted the main synod's demands for contributions to a central education fund and for the use of English (Reed 1987:51; Kuhns 1901: 166–67).

The need to understand what was Pennsylvania German and what was Reformed arose during the 1840s as non-German immigration to coal regions in German-speaking Pennsylvania increased, and Methodist revivalism spread (see Yoder 1959, 1985; Maser 1987:199–211; Frantz 1987:138–39). Near Shamokin and Pottsville, coal mines attracted Irish, Welsh, Scottish, and—later—Italian, Ukrainian, Polish, and Lithuanian workers. With additional coal towns springing up in the Lykens Valley to the southwest, coal country ringed the farms of the Mahantongo and Hegins valleys in on three sides. To the Pennsylvania-German farmers, the coal miners, besides raising ethnic and religious tensions, appeared to be feeding social unrest and defacing the land (see Klein and Hoogenboom 1980:316–19; Wallace 1962:211–13; Korson 1960:72–81; Korson 1964; Bodnar 1985:92–116; Gibbons 1882:423; Yoder 25 October 1947b:8).

The Methodist revivalists, representing Americanizing tendencies, meanwhile "invaded" German-speaking Pennsylvania, accusing the Pennsylvania German Reformed and Lutheran communities of not living according to the Gospel. The Methodists insisted on conversion experiences; calling the Reformed and Lutheran churches *Schlof-Kaerriche* ("asleep churches"), they insisted on reformation and awakening (Yoder 18 January 1947a, 1959; see also Milspaw 1987:286–88). To be sure, the Reformed and Lutheran churches in central Pennsylvania had secularized to an extent, and served social as much as spiritual purposes in the valleys of the region, but they resented the attack on their very way of life as well as their faith (Yoder 18 January 1947a, 25 October 1947b, 1959, 1985:47–50; Wood 1942:85–102; Maser 1987; Milspaw 1987:286–88).

Stiehly represents a bridge between the old and new elements of German-speaking Pennsylvania. He was born south of Blue Mountain near Wernersville, Heidelberg Township, Berks County, on May 13, 1800.[6] Two of his father's sisters had already made the trek into the Mahantongo near Salem Church; Elizabeth married John Knorr and Anna married Peter, John's brother. The Herman Synod licensed Isaac to preach in 1824. In 1827, he married his first cousin, Anna Knorr, daughter of Peter and Anna Knorr at Salem Church; that same year, Isaac was ordained as a minister of the German Reformed Church and began service at Salem Church. In addition to pursuing his ministry, Stiehly ran a gristmill and farm, and, according to account books still in the family, he carved gravestones for payment and kept receipts for making paint. He had other artistic skills on paper with *Fraktur* work (elaborate writing) and *Scherenschnitte* (scissors cutting).[7] As the man who spoke up for the valley's culture against the wealthier and more established regional center in Lancaster, and because he etched his mark on paper and in stone for generations to admire, Stiehly established a name and a place in legendry for himself. A cycle of Stiehly stories appears in print in the first volume of the *Pennsylvania Dutchman* in 1950. William F. Yoder recounts the man who "achieved great renown over the whole Mahantongo and Lykens (Hegins) Valley area. All I know about him is what tradition handed down to our day" (1950:5). "From all reports," Yoder reflects, "he was a diamond in the rough. He was a versatile man. A farmer and a millwright, as well as a preacher, he fitted well into pioneer life." Attesting to Stiehly's central role in the life passage of the valley's people, Yoder remembers, "When I was a boy, we heard people say of the older folks, "Der Parra Schtiely hot sie keiert" (Rev. Stiely married them); "Der Parra Schtiely hot sie gedawft" (Rev. Stiely baptized them); or, "Der Parra Schtiely hot sei Leicht kalta" (Rev. Stiely officiated at his funeral). These things were heard continually in my youth. I never heard any other minister's name of that period mentioned" (Yoder, W. 1950:5).

Stories living on in tradition emphasize his role as one of the people despite his lofty spiritual calling, his exceptional strength and stature, and his protectiveness of the Dutch communities. Possibly indicating secularizing influences on the Reformed Church, William Yoder offers the story from tradition that one Sabbath morning, Stiehly met a fisherman shooting pickerel. "The fisherman did not hit the pickerel, whereupon the minister said, 'Gebe mir das Gewehr' (Give me the gun). He took the gun, shot the fish, and went on to church!" (Yoder, W. 1950:5; see also Yoder, D. 4 October 1947b:8). In a story further underscoring Stiehly's status as local folk hero by bringing out his humble display of extraordinary strength (especially considering the stereotype of the minister as a literary type not engaging in taxing manual labor), as well as his community-mindedness, Yoder tells of the time Stiehly helped a man hew heavy timbers for a building. Without other help available, there arose the problem of raising the timber for hewing. Stiehly self-assuredly "lifted the log so his helper could put a block under the end" (Yoder, W. 1950:5). Yoder's final story has a message of equalizing tendencies in the tight-knit valley communities with everyone taking roles. The story again describes Stiehly as not conforming to the normal ministerial roles.

> Rev. Stiely was an unusual kind of preacher. He could see good in all people. It was the practice of most ministers of his time, when officiating at a funeral, to either raise the dead to heaven or send him to hell. It was almost always one or the other. Stiely never raised the smell of brimstone on account of any person whose funeral sermon he preached. It was his custom always to say something good about the departed regardless of his character and reputation.
>
> It so happened that there was a derelict in that vicinity who had great success making a living without working. He avoided work at all times. He went about day and night with a bag. In it he put things that were movable—vegetables, chickens, and meat from

farmers' smokehouses. He was known as a thief and did not care when people called him "Der Sackmann" (The man with the bag)....

The thief died and Stiely officiated at his funeral. "Now," said the people, "Stiely cannot say anything good about the dead." But they were disappointed. The minister never said a derogative word. He closed his sermon by saying, "Er hat seine Familie gut besorgt. Er hat sie besorgt bei Tag und bei Nacht" (He provided well for his family—he provided for them by day and by night!).

The moral of the story? Yoder concludes, "A good community now is a fitting monument to the pioneer labors of this good man, the *Rev. Isaac Stiely*" (Yoder, W. 1950:5). So although Stiehly promoted community as "one of the people," he was also exceptional because of remarkable skills, including his arts, and stories about him as a kind of culture hero act to justify his distinction.[8]

Stiehly came into the Mahantongo when Pennsylvania-German artistry flowered in the valley's painted furniture. From 1798 to 1828, painted and decorated blanket or "dower" chests (*Kischde*) were in use, probably made by no more than a few makers (Reed 1987; Weiser and Sullivan 1980; see also Fabian 1978; Lasansky 1990; Forman 1983: 140–47; Lichten 1963:85–109; Schlee 1980:69–100)[9] In anticipation of marriage, young men and women received the chests to store treasured household goods used in their adult lives. The young person often placed, or pasted, *Fraktur* manuscripts marking the wedding or birth in a safe place within the chest (Shelley 1961:29; Yoder 1989: 105–6; Weiser 1987:233–34). Some makers of the chests also doubled as *Fraktur* writers (Robacker 1965:143). Decorations on furniture typically appeared between the names of the recipient and the date lettered in *Fraktur* style; a cartouche framed the names and decorations. While the Mahantongo chest may have been painted or grained, the overall appearance is plain, especially compared to the architecturally styled dower chests with whole panels of designs in wealthier Lancaster and Lebanon counties (see Fabian 1978; Kauffman 1949; Kauffman 1964:117–21; Hopf 1970–71; Garvan 1982:18–25; Forman 1983).

During the 1830s there emerged from several makers in the Mahantongo Valley a highly decorated set of painted furniture (see Figs. 3, 4). Apparently the makers engaged in other carpentry and craft pursuits and produced the furniture on an occasional basis (see

Reed 1987:75–85). Against green and reddish-brown backgrounds, birds, horses, angels, stars, trees, flowers, praying children, cartouches, rays, and rosettes boldly graced chests of drawers, slant-top desks, cupboards, and hanging cupboards. This outpouring of folk art came at a time when the creation of decorated furniture had supposedly faded elsewhere (Fabian 1978:70). The furniture may still have been used for the dowry, with the desk and chest of drawers (*Draar*) probably replacing the blanket chest (Weiser 1987:233; Lasansky 1990: 76). This furniture stands out in retrospect as "the most novel, the most distinctive, the most colorful in the Pennsylvania Dutch field" (Robacker 1965:144; see also Earnest 1984:14).

Despite the claim for novelty, the painted-furniture designs show similarities to traditional *Fraktur* baptismal certificates known earlier in the valley (see Reed 1987:55–63; Shelley 1961:nos. 291–92; Weiser and Sullivan 1980; Garvan 1982:302). In a reminiscence, Carrie Haas Troutman writes, "The bureaus were stained with a home-made stain green, red, black or yellow, with designs copied from the old home-made birth certificates with angels, birds and flowers. The flowers were put on with a cork that was cut to resemble a flower, then dipped in the stain and put on alternately, red, then yellow" (Troutman 16 October 1948). Those furniture makers who have been identified worked near one another, suggesting a connection among the artists. Further, indications are that joining, turning, painting, and decorating may have been done by different craftsworkers in the community (Reed 1987:30–40; Forman 1983:134). But by the early 1840s, the colorful furniture passed from favor. "In their place," Robacker comments, "came several other kinds of furniture, still heavy by present-day standards, but almost flimsy by comparison with what they replaced" (1965:145); To Monroe Fabian, the painted furniture was "replaced with sober tonality that reflected much of the manners and morals of nineteenth-century America" (Fabian 1978:70). Yoder points to the intrusion of professional furniture makers and later factories that rendered the pieces obsolete (Reed 1987:86–87).

The Mahantongo furniture makers didn't record their motivations for taking creative license in their distinctive furniture during the 1830s, but what can be said is that in a period of social and political transition the valley's painted softwood furniture stood as Pennsylvania-Dutch products in sharp contrast to the unpainted hardwood chests of English tradition; the furniture appeared as regional products apart from the work of craftsworkers in Lancaster and Lebanon counties (Forman 1983:135). Although the makers used old symbols from the Pennsylvania-German *Fraktur* repertoire, they—especially prominent makers such as Jacob Masser (1812–95) and Johannes Mayer (1794-1883)—demonstrated innovation in their use of colors and designs on furniture, such as desks and chests of drawers, which previously were not usually decorated (see Figs. 3,4). Even the furniture itself was transitional, marking, as Robacker recognizes, "the passing of the heavy early furniture and the advent of pieces which were lighter in weight and therefore easier to handle" (1965:145).

Stiehly must have seen his share of painted furniture in his ministerial travels to homes and in his family connection to furniture-maker Johannes (or John) Mayer (1794–1883), as his son Jared's father-in-law.[10] The couple was married in 1857, but the father of the bride was already well known to Stiehly. John Mayer lived near Salem Church up the Little Mahantongo Creek, and Isaac's son Jared worked for him in addition to helping his father on the farm and at the gristmill. In 1844, Isaac did a *Scherenschnitt* and colored it for Mayer (Fig. 5). The cutting includes red and yellow birds found on Mahantongo furniture (see Reed 1987:41, 53), and, in keeping with Stiehly's political nature, an eagle, which also appeared on *Fraktur* and furniture (Reed 1987:59; Forman 1983:147; Shelley 1961:90; Fabian 1978:166–67; Weiser and Heaney 1976:nos. 501–12; Yoder and Graves 1989:4).

Pennsylvania Germans made such artwork as "well-wishes," or friendship tokens, and as valentines; *Fraktur* inscriptions and motifs commonly accompanied the cutwork (see Hopf 1977; Shelley 1961: 52–54, 67–68; Weiser and Heaney 1976:no. 436; Weiser 1983:262; Schlee 1980:221). The cut well-wishes did not call for a text of passage, and while artists used motifs from the *Geburts- und Tauf-schein* ("birth and baptismal certificate"), they generally didn't use its structure suggesting passage. Stiehly's *Scherenschnitte* consistently have a large cut eagle in the middle with flanking leaf or floral designs. Birds, stars, or vines with leaves run horizontally across the top and bottom; Stiehly also cut out the name of the recipient, or a political phrase, across the top beneath the vine and the artist's name across the bottom (Fig. 5). The emphasis is on the image instead of a text. As with other traditional *Scherenschnitte,* Stiehly's use of the bilaterally symmetrical form *aba* from top to bottom as well as from side to side emphasizes the attractive image in the center to impress the viewer with the

3. Painted and decorated chest of drawers, Mahantongo Valley, 1835–40, made by Jacob Maser. (Courtesy Philadelphia Museum of Art)

4. Painted and decorated desk, Mahantongo Valley, 1834. (Courtesy the Henry Francis du Pont Winterthur Museum)

5. Paper cutting for John Mayer, April 4, 1844, by Isaac Stiehly. Bodies on birds are colored red with wings and heads in yellow except for red eyes. (Photo courtesy Henry Reed)

6. Wedding certificate of Isaac F. Stiehly and Anna Knorr, drawn and lettered by Isaac Stiehly, 1827. (Courtesy Marilyn Herb)

thought and labor that went into the work (see Reed 1987:51–53; Shelley 1961:52–54, 67–68; Hopf 1977). Beyond the sheer discipline, Stiehly's papercutting skills probably also came in handy for the making of stencils used in furniture decorating and gravestone carving (Reed 1987:80; Richardson 1990:36–37).

Isaac Stiehly's earliest known work in *Fraktur* is his own wedding certificate (*Trauschein*) from 1827.[11] Announcing its purpose is *Verheirathet* (for marriage) centered at the top beneath a decorative crown (Fig. 6). The decorative lines done in "roundhand flourishing" continue around the edge and shape the work into a vertical rectangle. Seven lines of text use most of the width between the decorative borders of the paper. At the bottom, *Pennsylvanien* balances the heading at the top. This design is similar to a wedding certificate Stiehly prepared for William Yoder and Brigitta DeLong, also of Upper Mahantongo Township, in 1840, which perhaps shows the influence of furniture design in Stiehly's economical use of border and floral and leaf motifs in red and green around the outside (Reed 1987:77). Three rosette-shaped flowers lie symmetrically across the top. The design resembles the emphasis on verticality and textuality found in some family registers and *Taufscheine* (Mercer 1897:430–33; Weiser 1973; Weiser and Heaney 1976:nos. 436, 439–40, 535–38; Earnest and Hoch 1990:11–12; Hopf 1972).

For birth and baptismal certificates, Stiehly relied on sheets published in Reading, Berks County (Reed 1987:50).[12] In longhand, he filled in sections calling for names and dates with *Fraktur* writing (Fig. 7). The structure of the printed baptismal certificates kept the vertical orientation favored by Stiehly in his wedding certificates (see Fig. 8). At the top, the printed certificate had a central figure flanked by two rectangles of lesser size forming a bilaterally symmetrical head. The top signals the division of the remainder into three parts, with a central text and smaller columns of figures on either side. Throughout the certificate, then, figures accompany texts: the central figure at the top has text below it, and the text in the middle has figures flanking it. The figures suggest an order with an earthly side at the bottom with birds and flowers and a heavenly side with angels at the top. A decorative line frames the text in the middle and outlines seven sections from bottom to top. Stiehly underlined the announcement of the birth and baptism and used small floral figures to divide the central text essentially into three units. The signature of the publisher surrounded by a

290 / COMMUNITY AND IDENTITY

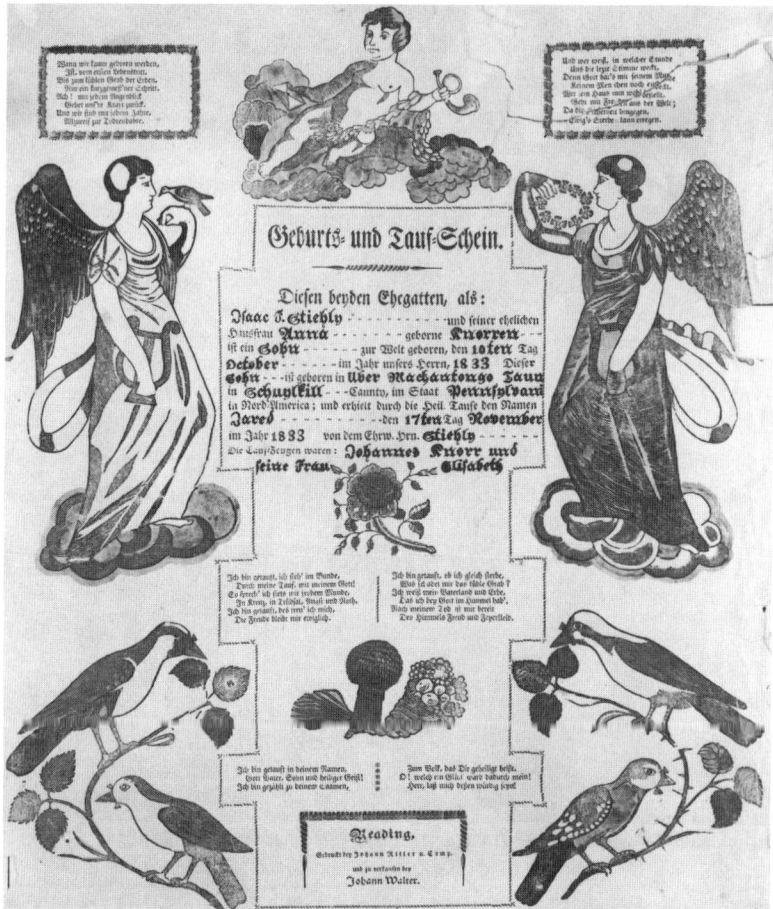

7. Baptismal certificate of Jared Stiehly, son of Isaac F. Stiehly and his wife Anna Knorr, born November 17, 1833, in Upper Mahantongo Township in Schuylkill County. Printed certificate inscribed by Isaac Stiehly. (Courtesy Marilyn Herb)

decorative border appears at the bottom. The figures at the sides and top are large animal or human representations. This alignment of text and figures, using appositions of two and arrangements of three and seven, is the basic structure of Stiehly's gravestones. Thus the printed certificates use motifs from the handmade certificates and standardize their form.

The certificates, then, were religious inspirations, aesthetic expressions, family records, and signs of important life passage, especially in

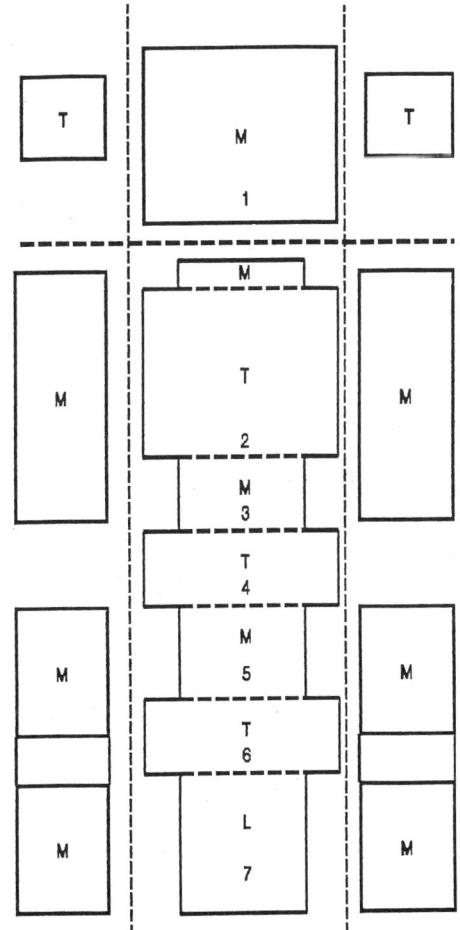

8. Structure of Jared Stiehly's baptismal certificate. M = motif, T = text. (Graphic by William N. Richardson)

rural areas of the Pennsylvania-German region. As celebrations of the arrival of a new member in a community tied by language, family background, occupation, and religion, the certificate is central to the value system of Pennsylvania-German cultural life in the Reformed and Lutheran valleys such as the Mahantongo (see Yoder 1989). "The texts," Frederick Weiser points out, "functioned didactically and hortatorically to see that the child grew into a society-pleasing and God-pleasing adult" (Weiser 1980:141; see also Weiser 1970). The illustrations accompanying the text derive from a variety of sources including religious scripture, central European and Christian folk motifs, and popular prints (Weiser 1980:145; see also Stoudt 1966). The printed forms carry religious texts usually toward the middle and bottom, in keeping with Protestant tradition emphasizing the Word of God, and carry family information toward the top (Mickey 1987:14–19). Usually inscribed by the minister conducting the baptism, the certificate includes the facts of a person's birth: his or her full name, parents' names (including the mother's maiden name), and the date and place of birth followed by the baptism date, the baptizing pastor, the confession, and the sponsors (see Weiser 1980:138; Mickey 1987:14–16).

By using designs based on appositions of two and arrangements of three and seven, the *Taufschein* form uses numerical representations of spiritual and artistic order in Western tradition (Crump 1990:129–32; Dundes 1980; Glassie 1972:273–76; Bronner 1986:16–17). The division of the passage vertically into seven parts suggests the life passage that the certificate honors (see Fig. 8). Seven divisions offers religious symbolism separate from the secular accounting of ten stages of life (see Chew 1962; Kammen 1987:183–85; Joerissen and Will 1983). Psychologically, the division into seven is usually the limit of the cultural grammar guiding construction of the vertical text.[13] Culturally, seven divisions connote the Biblical idea of creation and passage, the world made in seven days, as well as folkloric connections to a magical number (Menninger 1969:182–83; Flegg 1983:273–74; Miller 1956). Pennsylvania-German religious broadsides also used seven stages, particularly in "Roads to Heaven and Hell," also known as "The New Jerusalem" and "The Three Paths of Eternity," and in "The Seven Rules of Wisdom" (Pieske 1989; Shelley 1961:470).

As *Taufschein* recorded the beginning of life, so *Grabstein*, as Stiehly called his gravestones, marked the end of life. Unlike the *Taufschein*, the gravestone was a public statement recognizing the individual as a family member and a member of the Pennsylvania-German community. Many of the designs around the baptismal text surround the gravestone text: hearts, angels, stars, rosettes, tulips. Several stonecutters who advertised during the nineteenth century were also schoolteachers and preachers who produced *Fraktur* (Weiser 1980:158–60). "Thus," Frederick Weiser asserts,

> the tombstone, like the *Taufschein*, was both a personal and a social document. One marked the entrance of the individual into the

community and told him what the community expected of him. The other marked the exit of the individual from the community and told the community what he expected of it. The community preexisted the individual and postexisted the individual. Tombstone and *Taufschein* recorded the individual's pilgrimage through the community; at the same time, they helped the community transcend the individual and preserve its existence apart from the individuals who made it up. [Weiser 1980:151–52]

The structure and content of *Taufscheine* and gravestones were essential links of tradition to the individual; they outlined the "individual's relations to the institutions within the folk-culture—the church, the school, and the family—the three institutions which were the individual's triple focus in life" (Yoder, Gunnion, and Hopf 1969:8). They emphasized the importance of maintaining tradition particularly at moments of greatest social change, and therefore disruption, within the family and community—birth and death.

When observing Pennsylvania-German gravestone design, however, the connection to *Taufschein* structure is not immediately clear. Eighteenth-century stones tend to be small and thick and have a rounded head (suggesting a simple bilaterally symmetrical frame); often made of sandstone, they have a restricted text and single illustrative motif, perhaps a heart or rosette (see Barba 1953; Wust 1970; Graves 1988). Weiser speculates:

> The early Pennsylvania German pioneer came from social levels in Europe which probably did not erect tombstones for the deceased. As more than one European learned and commented, the German peasant in the New World aspired to grandeur. The first stonecutters were obviously well trained, probably in Europe. Their work was three-dimensional and baroque in style. The work of their apprentices was quite different. While neat and carefully done, the products of second generation stonecutters are two-dimensional, relying heavily on the incised line, and provincial in style. Using the standard motifs found on other Pennsylvania German objects, they are more patently folk in every sense. [Weiser 1980:152–53]

The elaboration of gravestones to resemble baptismal certificates became more apparent during the early nineteenth century. Stonecutters switched to marble and used taller, thinner dimensions, thus achieving the look of a certificate—white, vertical, and literary. In keeping with the development of Pennsylvania-German artistry during the 1830s in a number of folk-art genres in response to cultural intrusions, Pennsylvania-German gravestones became more articulated with text and decoration, and at the same time more standardized.[14] One clue to the structure that Isaac Stiehly inherited is in the work of the Sausser brothers, Perry (1800–1879) and Jonathan (1812–1900), the principal carvers of gravestones in the Mahantongo Valley before Stiehly (Richardson 1990:35). Their stonecutting father Jacob (1778–1848) was born in Tulpehocken Township in Berks County near the birthplace of Isaac Stiehly; the sons came along the Tulpehocken Path into the Mahantongo Valley and then established a stonecutting business in the Hegins Valley. Their stones in Mahantongo Valley cemeteries date from 1819 to 1856 and have a tripartite structure. At the top, two quarter-circle sets of rays flank a half-circle set. Other decorations are absent, but the cutters carved cartouches to highlight names of the deceased. The structure has seven components beginning with the announcement *Hier Ruhet* ("Here Rests"); then in German come family information, birth and death dates, years of life, a reference to a Biblical text, and a signature logo (a printer's line) at the bottom (see Figs. 9, 11).

Isaac Stiehly began carving stones in significant numbers around 1846. Each extant stone is slightly different, although he used two consistent structures, one in his early work and a revised one in his later design, and maintained a sequential grammar for handling gravestone text (Richardson 1990:27–28). His early stones use relief techniques found on the Sausser stones, but correspond in design more closely to decorative motifs on *Taufscheine* and Mahantongo furniture (Type I, see Figs. 12, 14). He used rosettes, stars in a variety of geometric patterns, tulips, hearts, rays, vines (sometimes in the form of a "tree-of-life" motif), and flowers. He often headed his stones *Hier Ruhet,* sometimes adding the more religious *Hier Ruhet in Gott.* He carved names of the deceased in relief surrounded by a cartouche followed by family information and birth and death dates in relief, also surrounded by a cartouche and flanked by decorative motifs on either side. At the bottom, he carved in a reference to Biblical text and left his logo in the shape of rays or hearts.[15]

In Berks County during the late 1840s and 1850s, carvers created stones similar in design to Stiehly's, notably Sutter Womelsdorf, who worked near the Tulpehocken Path (see Fig. 10). Yet Stiehly's stones stand apart because of his extra elaboration of decorative motifs within the body of the stone. Other carvers restricted the placement of these decorative motifs to the top; Stiehly's motifs flanked the birth date and other information, and later were even carved between the numbers of the year. Perhaps as a part-time carver and a man of some means, Stiehly was less interested in producing a standard product than he was in making a religious and artistic statement for members of his community at a time when Pennsylvania-German rural identity appeared threatened.

In his work, Stiehly memorializes the pioneers of the valley, most of them born in the eighteenth century. In the first few years of production, Stiehly made fewer than 15 stones annually, mostly for Salem Church. Suddenly in the early 1850s, his production jumped to over 20 stones a year, and he placed stones in nineteen other churchyards (Richardson 1990:19–20). Most of his stones stand in Salem (81), Sacramento (51), Klinger's (45), and Howerter's (27), spanning an area twelve miles wide in the Mahantongo and Hegins valleys. Before he was through in 1869, he would carve over 400 stones (309 still stand today). Although a few of his stones were carved for residents who died during the 1820s and 1830s, Stiehly's account books suggest that he probably produced them much later as replacements for old markers. Stiehly's production jumped around the time when the number of stones produced by the Saussers in the Mahantongo Valley dropped, but his output was never consistent. After a burst in the early 1850s, his production again dropped, then picked up toward the end of the 1850s. He carved just a few stones a year in the twilight of his life, the 1860s.

Stiehly's stones show variety, especially comparing his early and later works. Before the mid-1850s, they mostly have hearts, rosettes, and compass-drawn stars; after that they carry more tulips, rays, floral motifs, and trees of life. Stiehly's signature logo also changed; he gradually shifted from the carved heart at the bottom to the rays. He began his career using square cartouches, but toward the end carved the more elaborate double quarter-round cartouche in relief (see Fig. 15). After the 1850s, the decorations that once were attached to the text become separate from the seven textual statements in the stone and are enclosed in discrete cartouche fields (Type II, see Figs. 13, 15).

9. Example of stone carved by Sausser Brothers: Elizabeth Wolf, 1845, Halifax. (Photo by Simon J. Bronner)

10. Example of stone carved by Sutter Womelsdorf: Martin Derf, 1847, Rehrersburg (Altalaha Lutheran). (Photo by Simon J. Bronner)

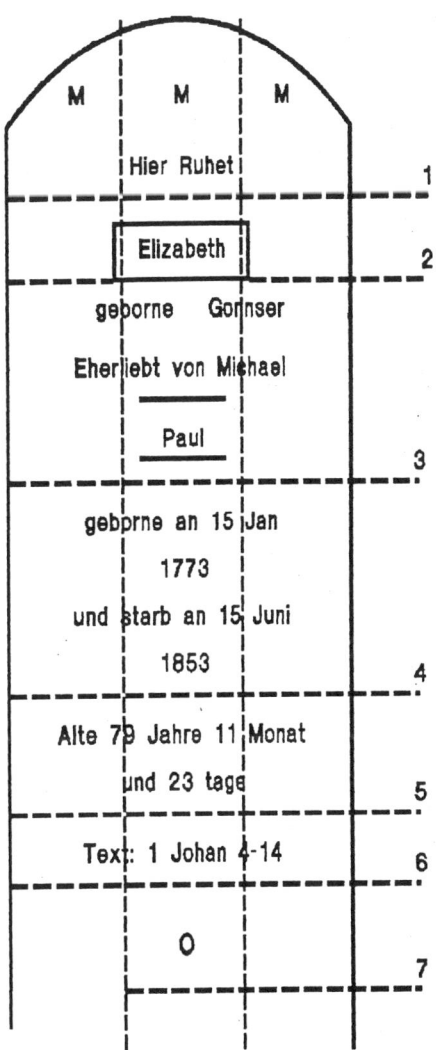

11. Structure of Elizabeth Paul's tombstone carved by Sausser Brothers. (Graphic by William N. Richardson)

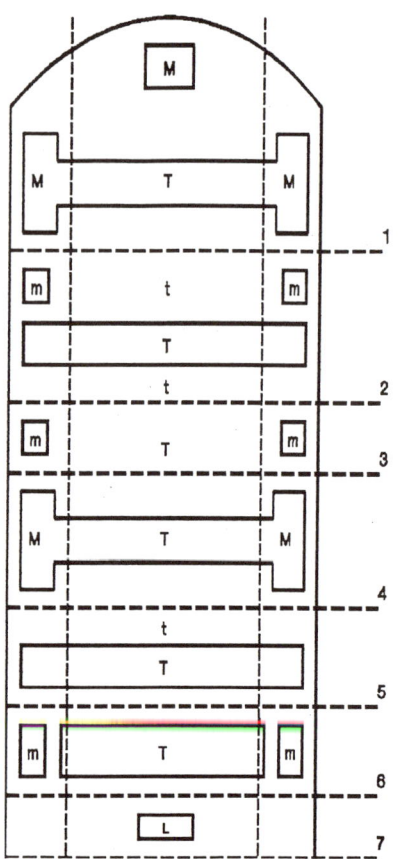

12. Structure of Stiehly tombstone Type I (1840s to mid-1850s). M = motif, T = text. (Graphic by William N. Richardson)

14. Example of Stiehly tombstone Type I: Johannes Stang, 1855, Klingerstown (Klinger's Zion Lutheran). (Photo by Simon J. Bronner)

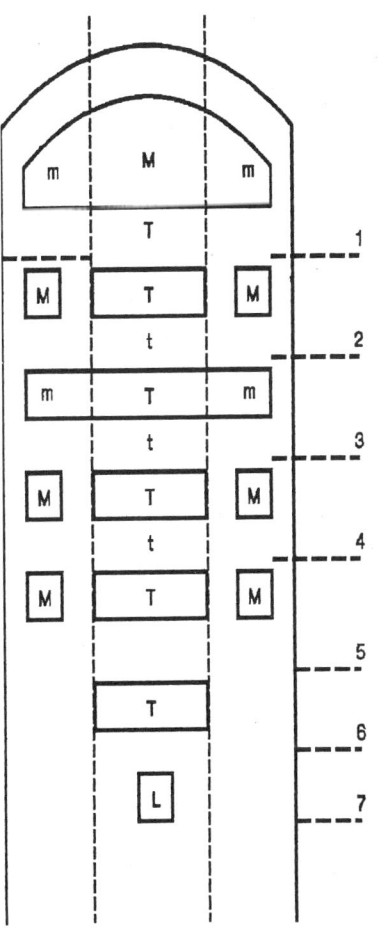

15. Example of Stiehly tombstone Type II: Susanna Maurer, 1861, Rough and Ready (Salem Church). (Photo by Simon J. Bronner)

13. Structure of Stiehly tombstone Type II (mid-1850s to 1869). M = motif, T = text. (Graphic by William N. Richardson)

Stiehly increased his use of relief in the later stones and elaborated the motifs at the top and within the birth and death dates. He liked to mix decorative motifs within a single stone, but after 1855, he sometimes offered a decorative unity in floral motifs, particularly the tree of life. He included the popular Victorian weeping-willow motif on a few stones during the early 1850s (see Fig. 14), but quickly dropped it in favor of Pennsylvania-German tulips (see Fig. 21). During this brief concession to popular taste, Stiehly occasionally replaced the traditional designation of "Here Rests" or "Here Lie the Remains Of" (*Hier ruhen die Gebeine von*) for the heading of "Memorial" (*Denkmal*). He also carved at least two stones that deviated from the usual header design during the disruptive Civil War. The stones commemorate fallen Civil War soldiers from the region (see Fig. 16). Stiehly carved flags and guns at the top and followed with his regular treatment of the text, except to add that they died at their camp.

In their dimensions, Stiehly's stones are an egalitarian effort, making a distinction only between adults and children. Children's stones include relief carving, but are smaller than the adult stones and lack cartouche framing or decoration. One might note that stones carved for relatives such as Heinrich and Peter Knorr received special attention. Heinrich Knorr's stone has flowers between each numeral of his birth and death dates (Fig. 17). At the top, the center of the bilaterally symmetrical design has an intricately carved tree of life with seven star-shaped flowers. Hearts, at the sides of the death date and at the bottom, complete the work. For Peter Knorr's stone, Stiehly altered the design, using hearts between the numerals of the birth and death dates, a single rounded unit with a vine and five rosettes at the top, and a compass-drawn star within a circle flanking the birth date (Fig. 18).

Other community members, not related to Stiehly, also received distinctive treatments. Johannes Birler's stone, completed after 1855, has full-circle rays between each numeral of the birth and death dates, although only the birth date is in relief and framed by a single-line cartouche (Fig. 19). His name, however, receives a double-line cartouche. In the stone for Elizabeth Kohlman completed after 1866, Stiehly framed her first name in a double-line cartouche and informed the viewer of her maiden name (Fig. 20). Showing special attention to altering the rhythm of his usual design, he placed three tulips coming from a single stem at the top center. Flanking this central unit are two tulips bending toward the central tulips. On the body of the stone, Stiehly carved three more sets of tulips, the bottom set pointing downward. The wilting tulips therefore support the text, because they flank the death date at the earthly side of the stone. At the "heavenly side," floral motifs and skyward rays announce vitality (see Fig. 21). Meanwhile Anna Catharina Erdman, whose stone was probably carved years after her death in 1842, has tulips between each numeral of her birth and death dates (Fig. 22). With his alteration of motifs around consistent structures, Stiehly apparently made an effort to give each person a distinctive stone, yet tied each by overall design to the Pennsylvania-German cultural tradition.

Stiehly's stones catch the eye because they are tall and elaborate versions of traditional designs that capture the spirit of the old settlement. Additionally, Stiehly used relief and raised cartouches to give three-dimensional emphasis to family names and dates. In this way, the stones stand as vivid records and profound testimonies to the family traditions of the community. Taken together, they offer a strong visual reinforcement of joined religious and cultural place, and the span of years covered conveys a sense of continuous cultural time. In several churchyards a few miles apart, Stiehly's stones stand one after another, making a case for the use of art to create community. His highly elaborated stones, like the decorated furniture that preceded them, were embellished expressions of regional identity that residents sought out. They presented an image of cultural strength through the emphatic re-use of old symbols, even as their intention suggested an imminent cultural weakening.

There was much of Stiehly, the individual, involved in the stones as well. While he meant to bring out connecting cultural symbols for the community in his designs, in his elaboration of the tradition, he offered a unique statement. The style of his stones is easily recognizable in contrast to others around them, yet it speaks loudly of the cultural traditions he sought to promote. He acknowledged his role as minister in making persuasive public statements of religion, indeed of artistic representations of text. To this day, residents of the valley look at these stones and recognize someone special, firm in his faith, forceful in his cultural pride and feeling for family and community, strong in his expression of skill and individualism. Indeed, it can be said that in combining elements of old and new, tradition and innovation, he created a representational tension within the stone that cried for resolu-

16. "Civil War" stone of Johannes Updegrof, 1863, Sacramento (St. Paul's), carved by Isaac Stiehly. (Photo by Simon J. Bronner)

17. Stone of Heinrich Knorr, 1855, Rough and Ready (Salem Church), carved by Isaac Stiehly. (Photo by Simon J. Bronner)

18. Stone of Peter Knorr, 1855, Rough and Ready (Salem Church), carved by Isaac Stiehly. (Photo by Simon J. Bronner)

19. Stone of Johannes Birler, 1855, Rough and Ready (Salem Church), carved by Isaac Stiehly. (Photo by Simon J. Bronner)

20. Stone of Elizabeth Kohlman, 1866, Sacramento (St. Paul's), carved by Isaac Stiehly. (Photo by Simon J. Bronner)

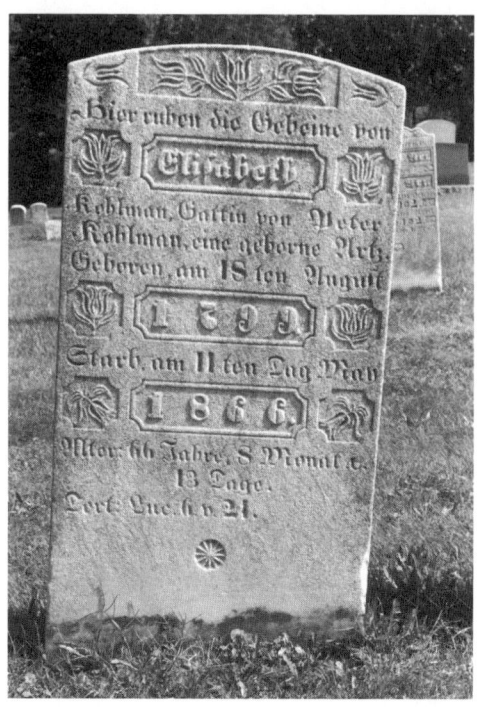

21. Stone of Michael Paul, 1865, Rough and Ready (Salem Church), carved by Isaac Stiehly. (Photo by Simon J. Bronner)

22. Stone of Anna Catharina Erdman, 1842, Rough and Ready (Salem Church), carved by Isaac Stiehly. (Photo by Simon J. Bronner)

tion, thus drawing the viewer to contemplate the forces of continuity and change in life and death, in community and country.[16]

Stiehly the folk artist was versatile, showing talents in carving, cutwork, and calligraphy, not to mention his verbal prowess in the pulpit, for which he received monetary and social rewards.[17] He chose to make the stones his lasting artistic expression. They were larger and more ornate than anything else he presented. They reached out to and flourished within the culture in a way that his other artistic efforts didn't. There's a connection here to an Appalachian chairmaker's artistic elaboration described by Michael Owen Jones (1989). Working within another regional tradition, chairmaker Chester Cornett created an unusually ornate version of the Appalachian rocking chair: "Although nearly every element of the chair has a precedent in Chester's forty-year career as a craftsman, each feature has been elaborated or even carried to an extreme. The chair culminates Chester's chairmaking endeavors; each major element extends a concept previously developed." The elaboration thus transmuted "the commonplace into something uncommon indeed" (Jones 1989:77).

The background of the Mahantongo's Pennsylvania Germans, and their response to cultural transition, gives Stiehly's work a special context in which one can see that his creative elaboration of tradition, a kind of carved narration, emphasized the creation of a past, "both as time and space, through narrating it" in familial, ethnic, and religious terms (Nicolaisen 1990:10). The stone holds a place in space connecting the individual to the church and to the region. Precise dates connect him or her to a time within cultural history (thus the dates given are historical, the age at death are personal). The narrative begins with the family name carved in relief, enduring to remember and reside in the valley. The religious text, a Biblical reference, coming after the other texts culminates the narrative with a spiritual meaning to the individual, and written as reference rather than text, reminds the community of the Bible's force. The ethnic message meanwhile is conveyed differently and probably most timelessly. Carved as image (in hearts, tulips, rosettes) and *Fraktur* style, it transcends words and envelops the narrative to provide a guide to the reading of social identity and cultural meaning. Narration as much as design, Stiehly's stones provide an artistic expression that offers, in Bill Nicolaisen's words, "the illusion of identity and of a continuous self by inventing ourselves in true stories of a past that never was" (Nicolaisen 1990:10). Stiehly the preacher—creatively working a traditional text to relate to a modern context, offering communal stability and individual inspiration—comes through the stones. He is also the masterful folk artist, elaborating a story of cultural transition, conveying through his folk design a cultural past and a manageable future, and thereby ministering to his community.

After Isaac Stiehly died in 1869, his children declined to carry on his stonecarving. Jared, who had learned some stonecutting skills, devoted himself to the mill and farm, unsure of how his father managed to preach, teach, carve, craft, farm, and do all the other things he did (Richardson 1990:17, 44). Additionally, Isaac Stiehly's artistic skills, his intricate, laborious work by hand for each person who died, seemed economically impractical. After Stiehly ceased making stones, few stones in the Mahantongo churchyards appeared in German or with the old symbols. Commercial memorials inscribed in English replaced his hand-cut stones and carried popular Victorian motifs. Fewer *Taufscheine* circulated within the region.

If public expressions of language and symbols left the tombstones by the late nineteenth century, they found their way into regional newspapers in special "dialect columns" (see Reichard 1918, 1942). From the Mahantongo came "The Flying Dutchman" whose dialect prose in the form of humorous letters appeared in the *Valley Echo* (see Yoder 8 February 1947a). In another instance of elaborating tradition, he and other Dutch columnists often used folklore as a basis for their stories and poems, or wrote of bygone days when Pennsylvania-German lifeways had no alternative (Haag 1988). The "tradition" continues today in the Mahantongo and Hegins valleys with the columns, "*En Kats Deitsch Schtick,*" by Bill Klouser in the *Citizen-Standard,* published in Valley View. The heading of his column includes rosettes, birds, hearts, and tulips reminiscent of Stiehly's work. The Dutch literature promotes identity through a popular medium, rather than the folk medium that Stiehly used as a conduit.

As communal institutions, the churches still sponsor activities that promote aspects of folk culture. Salem Church suppers have become a regional attraction twice a year. The church dishes out folk foods with a distinctive regional taste, and the suppers are occasions for socializing and talking in the *Mudderschprooch,* or "mother-tongue." During the fall, the church features stuffed pig's stomachs along with pot pie, hot salad, chow-chow, and shoo-fly pie; the spring special is ham and dandelion salad served with side dishes in plentiful amounts (see Salem U.C.C. Youth Group 1990). As the diners stride toward the entrance, they pass Stiehly's stones, white marble glistening if there's sunshine, arranged neatly in rows along the walk.

Several churches in the region sponsor dialect church services called "folk" or "heritage" worships (see Yoder 1978). Klinger's Lutheran offers an annual Pennsylvania-German picnic featuring theater in the dialect. Men might attend something of a "new tradition," now 50 years old, an annual *Fersommling* ("gathering") at Lykens where they participate in an intensive evening of "Dutchiness." Over 400 participants eat Pennsylvania Dutch food, sing Dutch songs, listen to Dutch humorists from the region, and watch a Dutch play written by schoolmaster Irwin Klinger (see Kemp 1944; Gilbert 1956; Haag 1988:316–22). A design of tulips on either side of two Dutch-styled birds decorates the program cover. In 1991, the guest humorist was the Rev. Phaeres Reitz, a minister from Allentown and a native of the Mahantongo. For many years after World War II, the Rev. Walter Boyer worked within the Mahantongo promoting folklore collecting as well as folk art production to connect the Dutch community (see Boyer, Buffington, and Yoder 1964). According to Don Yoder, "Rev. Walter Boyer is doing what he can to encourage preservation of the folk art of our people, by redecorating chests and bureaus, and painting wooden wall-platters with Dutch designs and humorous Dutch inscriptions." As he relates Boyer's efforts, he brings up the long shadow of the Rev. Isaac Stiehly, for he follows by reflecting: "On a recent visit to Hegins, I noted particularly the distinctively Dutch designs used on the older tombstones... lovely six and eight pointed stars, and the favorite tulip" (Yoder 1 February 1947a). The designs come from the hand of the Rev. Isaac Stiehly; they now help define the distinctiveness of this region.

Charles Rebuck has something to show me when I see him next. I wait for him to bring it out and notice a framed piece of needlework his daughter made for him and his wife. It has the family tree worked into a *Taufschein* design with hearts and tulips. In retirement Charles has made baskets for several years, remembering the technique from when he learned it as a young man in the valley. He gives them to friends who recall the shape of the old "Rebuck" baskets or the *Orschbackekareb* (an egg basket taking its name from the shape of the bottom, or "ass-cheeks"). He shows me an egg basket that he made with the sides extended; the shape is odd yet compelling. By deviating from tradition, it draws more attention to it. It forces recognition of the original shape of the basket when it was part of the Pennsylvania-Dutch workaday world here, even as it conveys the maker's creativity as times and the culture have changed. He smiles and tells me, "It's something *Parre Schtiely* would have liked, don't you think?"

NOTES

1. Charles Rebuck's riddle is documented in Stoudt 1915:71 and Barrick 1987:50. His use of the term "Dutchman" is meant to show admiration, referring to Stiehly as a one of the people. For connotations of "Dutchman," see Yoder 1980a. Don Yoder points out that

    In the eighteenth century, when our peasant forefathers huddled in the emigrant ships sailing from the Rhine ports, there was no proud, united Germany. They had no German "Fatherland" to boast to their descendants of, as did the Nineteenth-century German emigrants. They were not called primarily "Germans," that is, citizens of a united

"Germany."...When they stepped off the boat at Philadelphia, they were called by English-speaking people "Dutch" and "Dutchmen." The term was *not,* as you often erroneously hear, *invented* in America as a mispronunciation of the German word "*Deutsch*" which means "German." No, "Dutch" was in 1750 already an ancient and well-established term. [Yoder 1950]

"Dutch" eventually came to stand specifically for Holland "Low Dutch" but in the eighteenth century, the term described the "High Dutch" (from areas of what is now south Germany). Rather than a mispronunciation, as some scholars assume, "Dutch" approximates "Deitsch" in the dialect. Observing the Pennsylvania Germans during the 1860s, Phebe Gibbons wrote, "Although our 'Pennsylvania Dutch' are of undoubted German origin, yet in common speech they almost always speak of themselves as Dutch, which sounds much more like *Deutsch* than German does; and it is not a great length of time since Germans were so called" (Gibbons 1882:417). During the late nineteenth century, after the unification of Germany, scholars pushed for what Yoder calls the more "bookish" term "Pennsylvania German." Yet many in Pennsylvania of Rhineland Palatinate ancestry resisted the change to "German" because they considered themselves a distinct American group, with sharp contrasts to nineteenth-century German immigrants, and during the twentieth century—to what most Americans considered a bellicose Germany (see Korson 1960:226–28; Parsons 1985:227–59; Yoder 1980b, 1985:51–54). "Pennsylvania German" has received more widespread acceptance today, but "Dutch," a folk term with the connotation of endearment, is still widely used by people in Pennsylvania of Rhineland Palatinate ancestry to refer to themselves and each other.

2. I can point to several indications of the orientation toward family narrative. Don Yoder, the preeminent Pennsylvania-German folklorist, explains his introduction to folklore through family narrative: "Family traditions and identity became important to me as I talked with older members of my family, some of whom told me Indian stories and tales of the first settlers; this happened long before I had ever heard of oral history or folklore. I like to tell my students that when I was a boy I filled a notebook with the stories my grandfather told me. He was born in 1861, and his grandfather was born in 1776" (Yoder 1990:190). During the nineteenth century, Gibbons observed among the Pennsylvania Germans that "the farmer has generally a great 'freundschaft,' or family connection, both his and his wife's; and the paying visits within a range of twenty or thirty miles, and receiving visits in return, help to pass away the time" (1882:34–35). Further, the index to *Pennsylvania Folklife* (1949–86), originally the *Pennsylvania Dutchman,* lists a whopping 137 entries for genealogy. It's also the only index to a folklore journal I've seen that includes a surname index for genealogy and immigration articles. The connection between family name and local tradition is also evident in the high pro-

portion of place names representing family settlement in the Pennsylvania-German region of central Pennsylvania; see Spieler 1953; Espenshade 1925. In the Mahantongo Valley, Klingerstown, Erdman, and Rebuck refer to families in the region. Further, annual family reunions in the valleys—among the most frequent social activities during the summer—foster family storytelling. Among the largest are the Rebuck and Hepler reunions, and having attended the Rebuck reunions for several years, I have noted a strong pattern of narrative repetition from event to event. If there is a historical writing tradition in the valley, it focuses on family history; see, for example, the books by Avis Morgan published by Gateway Press, Baltimore: *The Hepler Family* (1985), *The Morgan Family* (1989), and *The Mattern Family* (1990).

3. The celebration of this valley's stability has been by scholars rather than the public; see Yoder 1990:185–98. The public's attention has been primarily drawn to the Amish in Lancaster County and the "hex-sign" area of Berks County (see Hoffman 1989; Yoder and Graves 1989; Buck 1979). The irony is that while these areas were formerly in the "core" of the Pennsylvania Culture Region, they have commercially developed and have lost much of their active Pennsylvania-German folk culture. Although the Mahantongo Valley is at the northern edge of the Pennsylvania Culture Region, it has retained more of the community cohesion and lifeways associated with Pennsylvania-German folkways; see Glass 1986; Cuff et al. 1989:154; Glassie 1968:36–64; Buffington, Boyer, and Yoder 1964. Nonetheless, residents sense the tension between old and new in their valley. Henry Reed wrote, "Old timers from the area would tell us that the valley is now built-up and greatly changed. True enough, there are now high tension poles and wires scarring the ridges and traversing some farmfields of the valley, telephone lines and a few modern homes are now apparent; yet the serenity and solitude pervading the area seem firmly in place" (Reed 1987:69).

The matter of control over the schools has had a pivotal role in cultural transition throughout the Pennsylvania-German region. Pennsylvania Germans, mostly using parochial schools for their youth, opposed state control of schools and the establishment of common or "free" schools for all children, regardless of denomination and means. The Pennsylvania Germans argued that state control took education out of the hands of family and church, where it properly belonged. They also feared the loss of schools using their native Pennsylvania-German dialect and worried about a campaign to eradicate the dialect in favor of English—fears that turned to realities. In the tolerant spirit of William Penn's holy experiment in cultural freedom, they argued for the right to maintain their language and culture and still live as Pennsylvanians and Americans. State intrusion came as early as 1804, and in 1831, the legislature passed an act to establish through taxation a general system of common schools. The Pennsylvania Germans resisted and managed to preserve Pennsylvania-

German schools into the twentieth century. In 1911, however, the legislature required English as the only language of instruction in the public schools, and eventually forced compliance. See Wood 1942:105–27; Kuhns 1901:143–52; Sharpless 1900:301–6; Weiser 1983:230–34; Klein and Hoogenboom 1980:227–48; Yoder 1985:47.

4. Stiehly (who also went by the spelling Stiely) completed a *Scherenschnitt* or "scissors cutting" with the message "Jackson, Sutherland & Ash Down with the Bank," probably around 1835 (see Reed 1987:51). The bank drew the opposition of locally minded Pennsylvania-German Democrats because it represented the interests of the national government and of growing urban power (the bank was in Philadelphia). Andrew Jackson, with his vernacular rhetoric, held their loyalty because of his stand that "politics and religion should be kept flexible, personal, and close to the people" (see Nye 1960:221); he fought institutional rigidity, much as Stiehly's region fought rigid state control of the schools (see note 3).

Phebe Gibbons also observed the political and ethnic differences between Lancaster County and the counties to the northwest during the nineteenth century. "The most astonishing difference," Gibbons wrote, is "that of politics" (1882:414). "We have returned about five or six thousand majority for the Whig, Anti-Masonic, and Republican ticket, and the adjoining very 'Dutch' county of Berks invariably as great a majority for the Democratic." As an example, she offers the case of the Constitutional Convention of 1874. "The vote of Berks was 5,269 for a convention, and 10,905 against a convention; the vote of Lancaster was, for a convention 16,862, against the same 116" (1882:21). In the northwest counties, as the joke in oral tradition went, German farmers did not see any need of so many parties, "the Democrats and Lutherans were enough," in other words, one party (Gibbons 1882:21; see also Yoder 25 October 1947b:8).

5. Ralph Wood observes that the Lutheran and Reformed churches, while influenced by the pietism of the plain sects and the fervor of American Methodism during the nineteenth century, stood in contrast to them because of their tradition of decentralized administration. Conflict emerged, however, in eastern Pennsylvania, "where the population remained German-speaking and for a long time German-reading, when other German sections of the original colonies had become Anglicized. Anglicized Lutherans and Reformed, chiefly from the cities, of which Philadelphia and Lancaster in the state of Pennsylvania may be mentioned, led the fight against the German language in the Pennsylvania German churches" (1942:88–90). In the German-speaking areas, a further tension existed between those calling for the use of High German and the dialect. Stiehly, in keeping with his reputation for being "one of the people," called for the latter.

In anecdotal style, Gibbons describes the tension within the German-speaking churches:

... in the Reformed and Lutheran Churches, there are many ministers who preach in pure German. Yet, when the minister goes to dine with a parishioner, they generally speak the dialect. The minister who speaks this to his flock is more popular. They could understand the higher German; but they say of him when he speaks the dialect, "Er iss en gemehner Mann" (He is a common, plain man, or one who doesn't put on airs.) A gentleman in Lebanon, born in Berks, told me that he should be pleased to speak German as it is in the Bible. "But," he added, "as soon as a person begins to use pure German here among his acquaintances the Pennsylvania Dutch will say, "Dess iss ane Fratz-Hans," or a high-flown fellow; or, as it may be rendered, "He's full of conceit." [1882:389]

Today, most church services are in English, but several in the Hegins and Mahantongo valleys occasionally still hold "folk" or "heritage" services in Pennsylvania Dutch (for more information on the dialect service, see Yoder 1978). In his survey of folklore from the Mahantongo and Hegins valleys, Yoder notes that the religious differences also had political overtones:

In these valleys the strong pietistic strain expressed itself also in the newer German revivalistic churches such as the Evangelical Association and the Church of the United Brethren in Christ. Occasionally there was tension between the Lutheran and Reformed Churches on the one hand, and the revivalistic churches on the other. In addition to the difference in worship and attitude toward revivalism, an important factor was the fact that most Lutherans were Democrats, most Evangelicals Republicans. The feeling was most bitter during the Civil War. [Yoder 25 October 1947b:8]

6. Stiehly was baptized and confirmed at St. John's Reformed Church in Wernersville. The settlement and church was along the Tulpehocken Path, historically the major route from Reading to Sunbury on the Susquehanna and used by settlers to the Mahantongo.

7. *Fraktur* was typically used on illuminated baptismal certificates and other decorated documents, and was often taught by schoolmasters and ministers. *Fraktur* thus commonly refers to the decorated documents as well as to the style of writing. Curtis Bentzel explains: "In handwritten *Fraktur,* the writing instrument is lifted from the paper after each letter is completed, which leaves a break or "fracture" between the letters, making it look more like a printed text than a handwritten text" (Bentzel 1987:10; see also Shelley 1961; Hopf 1972; Weiser 1983). The decoration of the *Fraktur* documents was characteristic of the Pennsylvania Germans. According to Bentzel, "Pennsylvania German *Fraktur* are decorated with colorful birds, flowers, and angels. Such colorful secular decoration of handwritten texts was virtually unknown in Europe and first practiced widely by Germans who came to America, as was the introduction of the individual *Taufschein*" (Bentzel 1987:13). For other historical and cultural

surveys of *Fraktur,* see Mercer 1897; Shelley 1961; Yoder 1989; Weiser 1973; Weiser and Heaney 1976; Faill 1987; Yoder, Gunnion, and Hopf 1969.

8. Stiehly was exceptional in the community not only because of his arts, but also because of his later wealth. While Stiehly defined himself according to the 1850 census as a "reformed preacher," not a lucrative position in those days (see Weiser 1983), he is known to have run a gristmill and farm and carved gravestones in addition to his preaching. He received $25 a year from Salem Church for his preaching and supplemented the income with service at baptisms, weddings, and funerals. He is also probably exceptional because of his literary and calligraphic abilities. As Weiser points out, ministers, often doubling as schoolmasters and scriveners (completing family registers and other documents), were often the only literary people in early nineteenth-century Pennsylvania-German communities (Weiser 1983). Although portrayed in narrative as "one of the people" because of his humble roots, interests, dialect language abilities, versatility, and farmwork, in the 1860 census Stiehly is listed as the wealthiest man in his township (Richardson 1990:52).

Folklorists will recognize in William Yoder's account common characteristics of folk hero narratives. As Jan Harold Brunvand summarizes, "These figures might... be pictured mainly as powerful men or great hunters, or they might possess a special repertoire..." (Brunvand 1986: 171; see also Dorson 1977:199–243; Abrahams 1966; Jones 1971). The Aarne-Thompson Motif Index includes several entries that apply under the section "Marvels": F661 Skillful marksman, F610 Remarkable strength (cf. A526.7 Culture hero performs remarkable feats of strength and skill). These narrative motifs help support admiration for Stiehly's artwork (cf. F660 Remarkable skill) and his many talents. Thus the narratives structurally emphasize Stiehly as one of the people, even as they allow him to distinguish himself. Thus, as Robert Georges offers, "legends appear to be metaphorizations of basic kinds of relationship sets" (Georges 1971:18; see also Nicolaisen 1990). The story about Stiehly's dealing kindly with the thief falls under motif H500 Test of cleverness or ability, and is related more specifically to the motif for clever retorts, J1269.8 Robber's defense for stealing from rich, God will not permit them to enter heaven unless we take their ill-gotten goods from them. Related to the stories about Stiehly's hunting prowess, Don Yoder collected a story in 1947:

> The Reformed pastor Isaac F. Stiely (1800–1869) is another whose memory is green in these valleys. He must have felt "at one" with his congregations, if the following story is true! An outlying appointment of his was at the old log schoolhouse in wild and romantic Williams Valley, across the Broad Mountain from Hegins. One time when he was holding church there, a deer was sighted near the church. The men of the congregation, including *der Parre,* grabbed their guns,

which were stacked in the back of the church, and went after the deer. They shot it and carried it back to the church, and the service was resumed! [Yoder 4 October 1947b:8]

William Yoder offers a fragment of a story about Stiehly that makes little sense, unless the reader is familiar with a common anecdote (X411 Parson put to flight during sermon). During a sermon, a member of the congregation sees a fox out the window. Stiehly interrupts his sermon by saying, "I smell a fox!" He rushes out of the church with his gun along with the rest of the congregation (for a variant, see Yoder 4 October 1947b:8). For surveys of anecdotes and humorous narratives about preachers in central Pennsylvania, see Yoder 4 October 1947b:8; Barrick 1969; Troutman 2 October 1948.

9. There may be technical reasons for painting the furniture. Pennsylvania Germans typically used soft woods in their furniture, and these woods take paint for protection very well. Carroll Hopf suggests that in America wood was abundant and used in a number of household items, many of them painted in eastern Pennsylvania. "In terms of furnishings, two or three and sometimes more varieties of wood were used in a single piece of furniture. It must have been a challenge to try to disguise so much raw wood surface which normally appeared in the home." Therefore, "coloring was applied, as part explanation to conceal the raw wood" (Hopf 1970–71:7; see also Fabian 1978:50–58). From available materials the Pennsylvania-Germans fashioned, and apparently favored, red and green pigments (Hopf 1970–71:4–6; Fabian 1978:52–58). In addition to using paint as a cultural symbol, Pennsylvania Germans may have decorated "unpretentious woods to resemble something made of finer wood such as mahogany, rosewood, cedar, and maple" (Hopf 1970–71:8; see also Glassie 1968:43–44). Mahantongo furniture makers used mostly tulip poplar and pine, sometimes in the same piece (Forman 1983:133). Yet Fabian argues for cultural preference in the choice of painted furniture: "Given its availability and its beauty when properly finished, it is surprising that [walnut] is not found more often than it is in Pennsylvania-German chests. Among the rural customers natural walnut was definitely a second choice to painted wood. This fact in itself is an indication of the prevalence of Southern-German taste and tradition in Pennsylvania" (Fabian 1978:37). Practical or not, "decorated furniture, along with building crafts the most visible of Old-World traditions, was among the first to suffer from the inroads of urban taste and fashion" (Fabian 1978:70).

10. Henry Reed makes a case for some direct involvement by Stiehly in Mahantongo furniture making and/or decorating; see Reed 1987:45–53. Stiehly used designs similar to the ones used on the furniture and had in his family decorated wooden spice cups. "Conclusive?" Reed writes. "No, hardly, just a tantalizing problem. As we know Stiehly was a very talented artist in every sense of the word. His journals mention ingredients in paint for grain painting, and, most importantly, his son married

the daughter of Mahantongo's principal furniture maker, John Mayer, to whom Stiehly dedicated the Scherenschnitt" (Correspondence 21 May 1991).

11. The text announces the "marriage by Rev. Adam Scheffer on March 9, 1827, of Rev. Isaac Stiely to Anna Knorr of Upper Mahontongo [sic] Township, Schuylkill County in the State of Pennsylvania." My thanks to Henry Reed for making this copy available and to Marilyn Herb for permission to reproduce the work.

12. Use of published birth and baptismal certificates, usually lettered and sometimes colored in by hand, became more common practice during the nineteenth century (Yoder 1989:108–11; Weiser and Heaney 1976:nos. 453–523; Shelley 1961:63–68). Besides printed certificates of Johann Walter of Reading, which Stiehly used, others were available from G. S. Peters in Carlisle and Harrisburg; Jacob Baab and John S. Wiestling of Harrisburg; Johann Ritter, Heinrich B. Sage, and Carl A. Bruckman of Reading; H. Ebner and Blumer and Busch of Allentown, to name a few (see Shelley 1961:63–68, 135–40; Weiser and Heaney 1976:nos. 453–523; Sommer 1983:290–95).

13. The culturally accepted structure using these numbers provides a grammar governing the selection and sequence of designs into a coherent visual expression (see Glassie 1975:13–40). The design used by Stiehly is also found in architecture, furniture, needlework, and *Fraktur* (see Barba 1953:24–27). The German timber house, for example, "was sustained by two rows of posts dividing the interior into a nave and two aisles"; the timbers "divided the space of the house lengthwise into a modular sequence of timber-framed bays" (Crump 1990:132). I have argued that the reliance on oppositions and bilateral symmetry in our cultural grammar is an extension of reliance on human form as a model (Bronner 1986:16–17). This makes Stiehly's design of the erect stone (with its references to head, shoulders, and body) particularly powerful as a cultural expression for the individual lying in the ground. Stiehly's stones extend the grammar used by others by emphasizing the seven segments of text into a tall, certificate-looking marker (see Richardson 1990:27–28). Stiehly's compass-stars, a fundamental symbol on his stones and on other Pennsylvania-German folk art, reinforce the structure by showing seven points. Seven as a structuring principle governs the basic unit of time, the week, and Judeo-Christian writing (Flegg 1983:273–74). The number seven takes some significance from its exceptionalism; Flegg points out that it may have acquired its special folkloric and religious status because it is neither "produced" (i.e., has factors) nor "produces" (i.e., is a factor of another number) (Flegg 1983:274). Psychologically, seven has been shown to be the limit of instantaneous cognitive recognition; ten used in official counting is a reference to an external source. Seven, according to these psychological tests, represents a limit to our visual processing of information (Miller 1956; see also Crump 1990:18–19).

14. Milspaw describes the use of "Classical" white marble stones in Pennsylvania-German areas with new symbols: "crosses, Bibles, roses, hands pointing heavenward or clasped in fellowship, doves, lambs, and other symbols of popular American Christianity" (Milspaw 1987:287). Stiehly rejected these symbols while using the certificate form; he additionally rejected the "European winged cherub" from New England adapted in German areas of Dauphin and Lancaster counties (see Milspaw 1980, 1987:288). The revival of the old Pennsylvania-German motifs within the certificate form on stone is more evident, then, in the areas resistant to the anglicization of the Reformed and Lutheran churches, especially in Berks, Schuylkill, and Northumberland counties around the Mahantongo and Hegins valleys. Despite the growing ostentation in American gravestone carving during the mid-nineteenth century, the work of Stiehly and others in the valleys stands out because of their extended use of the old symbols on the new face, their handling of text in *Fraktur*, and their elaboration of birth and death dates, for example, that Victorian design avoided (cf. Jack 1968; Gillespie 1969–70; Graves 1988; Lucas 1990).

    There is some dispute whether the old motifs retained religious (and some ancient mystical) symbolism or were intended as cultural signs of ethnic identity and aesthetic preference. The use of the designs on furniture and later stones suggest that they were intended as cultural signs. Still, they might have held appeal to Stiehly as an implicit religious reminder. Milspaw describes the Pennsylvania-German gravestone symbolism as affirming the tripartite Christian life, resurrection, and salvation:

    > The tulip or lily, an immensely popular design, was a thinly veiled symbol of life arising out of death; the tulip growing from a heart or an urn was called the Rod of Jesse, and was popularly interpreted as an analogy for Christ and the resurrection. The Sechsstern or compass star, an ancient symbol of the sun, and the image of the sun itself, were both clear symbols of eternal life. The heart was regularly used and was interpreted as a symbol of both romantic and heavenly love. [Milspaw 1987:288; see also Stoudt 1966; Barba 1953]

15. Stiehly carved at least two stones in English after 1860, in the twilight of his stonecarving career. Although the designs on the stones are plainer than the Pennsylvania-German ones, the stones nonetheless exhibit the *Taufschein* structure used on his other stones.

    One stone located at Salem Church reads "IN MEMORY of GEORG SIMMY. Was born the 4 of July 1796. Died; the 8 of January 1860. Aged 63 years, 6 month, 4 days." Stiehly completed the stone according to the structural pattern he used on other stones during his later period. Stiehly avoided using the old Pennsylvania-German symbols in the cartouches, and instead placed floral motifs at the center of the top and the three side sections. At the shoulders, Stiehly carved in two half-circle sets of rays.

According to Henry Reed, "George Simmy was a black freeman who owned a farm near the Salem Church. He enjoyed the respect and friendship of the entire community.... He is the only black person ever buried in Salem Cemetery. Isaac Stiehly conducted his funeral and carved his gravestone" (Reed 1987:53).

The other English stone is in Leck Kill, within the Mahantongo Valley. It has a floral motif at the head flanked by two sets of half-circle rays, but lacks decoration in the body of the stone. It reads: "In Memory of Lewis Kehler, Son of Elias and Ester Kehler, was born the 9th of October 1859, Died the 30th of May 1864, Aged 4 years, 7 M, 21 days."

16. I have discussed this artistic technique of drawing attention to social dilemmas in *Chain Carvers* (1985). There old men of rural backgrounds, feeling that urban-industrial society had ignored their heritage and failed to acknowledge their skills, carved chains out of wood. The tension of something intended to be strong yet made out of a weak material created a visual riddle that attracted viewers to ask the old carvers about their mastery of the object. Other examples are included in my *Grasping Things* (1986:63–86); see also Jones 1989; Hufford, Hunt, and Zeitlin 1987:37–67.

17. According to Stiehly's account books, he received compensation (approximately $.75 per day) for his stones in line with other skilled craftsworkers in the community (Richardson 1990:16–17). According to Bill Richardson's calculations based on Stiehly's account books, the average adult stone cost $12 (minus about $3.25 in costs, the profit would be around $8.75) and children's stones cost an average of $5.64 (or about $4.39 in profit). He received a nominal wage for his ministry at Salem ($25 per year) and supplemented this amount with earnings from service at weddings, baptisms, funerals, and donations from other congregations. Still, the total from ministering and artwork would not have netted him great gains. Calculating the earnings recorded in the account book and his worth reported in the census, it appears that the bulk of his wealth came from his gristmill and farm. My case for Stiehly's cultural intentions is based on the fact that motivations other than economic must have been at work. The Sausser Brothers, in contrast, covered a wider area in the three counties around the Mahantongo Valley, established a shop specifically for stonecutting and memorials, produced more stones, and used a plainer, standardized design to facilitate production.

REFERENCES

Abrahams, Roger D.
1966   Some Varieties of Heroes in America. Journal of the Folklore Institute 3:343–62.

Barba, Preston
 1953 Pennsylvania German Tombstones: A Study in Folk Art. Pennsylvania German Folklore Society, vol. 18. Allentown: Schlechter's.

Barrick, Mac
 1969 Pulpit Humor in Central Pennsylvania. Pennsylvania Folklife 19, 1:28–36.
 1987 German-American Folklore. Little Rock: August House.

Bentzel, Curtis C.
 1987 Calligraphy and Linguistics: A Different Look at the F&M *Fraktur*. In Fraktur: A Selective Guide to the Franklin and Marshall *Fraktur* Collection. Lancaster: Franklin and Marshall College, pp. 9–13.

Bodnar, John
 1985 The Transplanted: A History of Immigrants in Urban America. Bloomington: Indiana University Press.

Boyer, Walter; Buffington, Albert F.; Yoder, Don
 1964 Songs Along the Mahantongo: Pennsylvania Dutch Folksongs. 1951 repr. Hatboro, Pennsylvania: Folklore Associates.

Bronner, Simon J.
 1985 Chain Carvers: Old Men Crafting Meaning. Lexington: University Press of Kentucky.
 1986 Grasping Things: Folk Material Culture and Mass Society in America. Lexington: University Press of Kentucky.

Brunvand, Jan Harold
 1986 The Study of American Folklore: An Introduction. 3d ed. New York: W. W. Norton.

Buck, Roy
 1979 Bloodless Theatre: Images of the Old Order Amish in Tourism Literature. Pennsylvania Mennonite Heritage 2:2–11.

Buffington, Albert F.
 1948 Linguistic Variants in the Pennsylvania German Dialect. Publications of the Pennsylvania German Folklore Society 13:216–52.

Chew, Samuel C.
 1962 The Pilgrimage of Life. New Haven: Yale University Press.

Crump, Thomas
 1990 The Anthropology of Numbers. Cambridge: Cambridge University Press.

Cuff, David J.; Young, William J.; Muller, Edward K.; Zelinsky, Wilbur; Abler, Ronald F.
 1989 (eds.) The Atlas of Pennsylvania. Philadelphia: Temple University Press.

Dorson, Richard M.
 1977 American Folklore. 1959 repr. Chicago: University of Chicago Press.

Dundes, Alan
    1980   The Number Three in American Culture. *In* Interpreting Folklore. Bloomington: Indiana University Press, pp. 134–59.

Earnest, Adele
    1984   Folk Art in America: A Personal View. Exton, Pennsylvania: Schiffer.

Earnest, Corinne Pattie; Hoch, Beverly Repass
    1990   The Genealogist's Guide to *Fraktur* for Genealogists Researching German-American Families. Albuquerque, New Mexico: Russell D. Earnest Associates and Beverly Repass Hoch.

Espenshade, A. Howry
    1925   Pennsylvania Place Names. State College, Pennsylvania: Pennsylvania State College.

Fabian, Monroe
    1978   The Pennsylvania-German Decorated Chest. Publications of the Pennsylvania German Society, vol. 12. New York: Universe Books.

Faill, Carol E.
    1987   *Fraktur*. *In* Fraktur: A Selective Guide to the Franklin and Marshall *Fraktur* Collection. Lancaster, Pennsylvania: Franklin and Marshall College, pp. 5–8.

Fisher, Sydney George
    1908   The Making of Pennsylvania. 2d ed. (1st ed., 1896). Philadelphia: J. B. Lippincott.

Flegg, Graham
    1983   Numbers: Their History and Meaning. New York: Schocken.

Forman, Benno M.
    1983   German Influences in Pennsylvania Furniture. *In* Scott T. Swank, Arts of the Pennsylvania Germans. New York: W. W. Norton, pp. 102–70.

Frantz, John B.
    1987   United Church of Christ. *In* Robert Grant Crist, ed., Penn's Example to the Nations: 300 Years of the Holy Experiment. Harrisburg: Pennsylvania Council of Churches for the Pennsylvania Religious Tercentenary Committee, pp. 129–46.

Garvan, Beatrice B.
    1982   The Pennsylvania German Collection. Philadelphia: Philadelphia Museum of Art.

Georges, Robert A.
    1971   The General Concept of Legends: Some Assumptions to be Reexamined and Reassessed. *In* Wayland D. Hand, ed. American Folk Legend. Berkeley: University of California Press, pp. 1–19.

Gibbons, Phebe Earle
    1882   "Pennsylvania Dutch," and Other Essays. Philadelphia: J. B. Lippincott.

Gilbert, Russell
    1956   Pennsylvania German Versammling Speeches. Pennsylvania Speech Annual 13 (1956):3–20.

Gillespie, Angus K.
    1969–70 Gravestones and Ostentation: A Study of Five Delaware County Cemeteries. Pennsylvania Folklife 19, 2:34–43.

Glass, Joseph
    1986   The Pennsylvania Culture Region: A View from the Barn. Ann Arbor, Michigan: UMI Research Press.

Glassie, Henry
    1968   Pattern in the Material Folk Culture of the Eastern United States. Philadelphia: University of Pennsylvania.
    1972   Folk Art. In Richard M. Dorson, ed., Folklore and Folklife: An Introduction. Chicago: University of Chicago Press, pp. 253–80.
    1975   Folk Housing in Middle Virginia. Knoxville: University of Tennessee Press.

Graves, Thomas E.
    1988   Pennsylvania German Gravestones: An Introduction. Markers 5:61–95.

Haag, Earl C.
    1988   (ed.) A Pennsylvania German Anthology. Selinsgrove: Susquehanna University Press.

Hoffman, William N.
    1989   Going Dutch: A Visitor's Guide to the Pennsylvania Dutch Country. New Rochelle, New York: Spring Garden Publications.

Hopf, Carroll
    1970–71 Decorated Folk Furniture. Pennsylvania Folklife 20, 2:2–8.
    1972   Calligraphic Drawings and Pennsylvania German Fraktur. Pennsylvania Folklife 22, 1:2–9.

Hopf, Claudia
    1977   *Scherenschnitte:* Traditional Paper Cutting. Lebanon, Pennsylvania: Applied Arts.

Hufford, Mary; Hunt, Marjorie; Zeitlin, Steven
    1987   The Grand Generation: Memory, Mastery, Legacy. Seattle: University of Washington Press for the Smithsonian Institution.

Jack, Phil R.
    1968   A Western Pennsylvania Graveyard, 1787–1967. Pennsylvania Folklife 17, 3:41–48.

Joerissen, Peter; Will, Cornelia
    1983   (eds.) Die Lebenstreppe: Bilder der menschlichen Lebensalter. Köln: Schriften des Rhenisches Museumsamtes.

Jones, Michael Owen
    1971   (PC + CB) X SD (R + I + E) = Hero. New York Folklore Quarterly 27:243–60.

1989 Craftsman of the Cumberlands: Tradition and Creativity. Lexington: University Press of Kentucky.

Kammen, Michael
1987 Changing Perceptions of the Life Cycle in American Thought and Culture. *In* Selvages & Biases: The Fabric of History in American Culture. Ithaca: Cornell University Press, pp. 180–221.

Kauffman, Henry J.
1949 Decorated Chests in the Pennsylvania Dutch Country. Pennsylvania Dutchman 1, 8:1.
1964 Pennsylvania Dutch American Folk Art. 1946 repr. New York: Dover.

Kemp, A. F.
1944 The Pennsylvania German Versammlinge. Publications of the Pennsylvania German Folklore Society, Vol. 9, pp. 185–218.

Klein, Philip S.; Hoogenboom, Ari
1980 A History of Pennsylvania. University Park: Pennsylvania State University Press.

Korson, George
1960 Black Rock: Mining Folklore of the Pennsylvania Dutch. Baltimore: Johns Hopkins Press.
1964 Minstrels of the Mine Patch: Songs and Stories of the Anthracite Industry. Hatboro, Pennsylvania: Folklore Associates.

Kuhns, Oscar
1901 The German and Swiss Settlements of Colonial Pennsylvania: A Study of the So-Called Pennsylvania Dutch. New York: Henry Holt.

Lasansky, Jeanette
1990 A Good Start: The Aussteier or Dowry. Lewisburg, Pennsylvania: Oral Traditions Project of the Union County Historical Society.

Lichten, Francis
1963 Folk Art of Rural Pennsylvania. New York: Scribners.

Lucas, Jennifer
1990 Stonecarvers of Monroe County, Indiana, 1828–1890. Markers 7:195–212.

Maser, Frederick E.
1987 Methodists. *In* Robert Grant Crist, ed., Penn's Example to the Nations: 300 Years of the Holy Experiment. Harrisburg: Pennsylvania Council of Churches for the Pennsylvania Religious Tercentenary Committee, pp. 196–218.

Menninger, Karl
1969 Number Words and Number Symbols: A Cultural History of Numbers. Cambridge: M.I.T. Press.

Mercer, Henry C.
  1897 The Survival of the Mediaeval Art of Illuminative Writing Among Pennsylvania Germans. Proceedings of the American Philosophical Society, vol. 26 (December), pp. 424–33.

Mickey, Robert G.
  1987 Religious Dimensions. In Fraktur: A Selective Guide to the Franklin and Marshall *Fraktur* Collection. Lancaster, Pennsylvania: Franklin and Marshall College, pp. 14–19.

Miller, G. A.
  1956 The Magical Number Seven, Plus or Minus Two: Some Limits to Our Capacity for Processing Information. Psychological Review 63:81–97.

Milspaw, Yvonne
  1980 Plain Walls and Little Angels: Pioneer Churches in Central Pennsylvania. Pioneer America 12:77–96.
  1987 The Churches of Central Pennsylvania: Doctrine in Wood and Stone. In Daniel W. Ingersoll, Jr., and Gordon Bronitsky, eds., Mirror and Metaphor: Material and Social Constructions of Reality. Lanham, Maryland: University Press of America, pp. 277–96.

Nicolaisen, W. F. H.
  1990 Why Tell Stories? Fabula 31:5–10.

Nye, Russel Blaine
  1960 The Cultural Life of the New Nation, 1776–1830. New York: Harper Torchbooks/Harper & Row.

Parsons, William T.
  1985 Pennsylvania Germans: A Persistent Minority. Collegeville, Pennsylvania: Chestnut Books.

Pieske, Christa
  1989 The European Origins of Four Pennsylvania German Broadsheet Themes: Adam and Eve; The New Jerusalem—The Broad and Narrow Way; The Unjust Judgment; The Stages of Life. Der Reggeboge (The Rainbow): Journal of the Pennsylvania German Society 23:7–32.

Reed, Henry M.
  1987 Decorated Furniture of the Mahantongo Valley. A Center Gallery Publication, Bucknell University. Distributed by University of Pennsylvania Press, Philadelphia.

Reichard, Harry
  1918 Pennsylvania German Dialect Writing and Writers. Pennsylvania German Society: Proceedings and Addresses, Vol. 26. Lancaster, Pennsylvania.
  1942 Pennsylvania German Literature. In Ralph Wood, ed., The Pennsylvania Germans. Princeton: Princeton University Press, pp. 165–224.

Richardson, William N.
 1990 The Pennsylvania German Tombstones of Isaac F. Stiehly (1800-1869). Northumberland Historical Society Proceedings 30:1–67.
Robacker, Earl F.
 1965 Touch of the Dutchland. New York: A. S. Barnes.
Salem U.C.C. Youth Group
 1990 Mahantongo Valley Cookbook. Olathe, Kansas: Cookbook Publishers.
Schlee, Ernst
 1980 German Folk Art. Tokyo: Kodansha International.
Seifert, Lester W. J.
 1946 Lexical Differences Between Four Pennsylvania German Regions. Pennsylvania German Folklore Society 11:154–69.
Sharpless, Isaac
 1900 Two Centuries of Pennsylvania History. Philadelphia: J. B. Lippincott.
Shelley, Donald A.
 1961 The Fraktur-Writings or Illuminated Manuscripts of the Pennsylvania Germans. Allentown: Pennsylvania German Society.
Shoemaker, Alfred L.
 1952a (ed.) Early Program for Wiping Out Pennsylvania Dutch, by Swatara. Pennsylvania Dutchman 3, 15:2–3.
 1952b (ed.) Early Attitude to Pennsylvania Dutch, by Swatara. Pennsylvania Dutchman 3, 15:2.
Sommer, Frank H.
 1983 German Language Books, Periodicals, & Manuscripts. In Scott T. Swank, Arts of the Pennsylvania Germans. New York: W. W. Norton, pp. 265–304.
Spieler, Gerhard G.
 1953 Pennsylvania Dutch Place Names. Pennsylvania Dutchman 5, 7:5–6.
Stoudt, John Baer
 1915 The Folklore of the Pennsylvania-German. Lancaster: Pennsylvania German Society.
Stoudt, John Joseph
 1966 Pennsylvania German Folk Art: An Interpretation. Allentown, Pennsylvania: Schlechter's.
Troutman, Carrie Haas
 1948 Pioneer Days in Mahantongo Valley. 'S Pennsylfawnisch Deitsch Eck, Morning Call (Allentown, Pennsylvania), October 2 (p. 6), 9 (p. 6), 16 (p. 6).
Wallace, Paul A. W.
 1962 Pennsylvania: Seed of a Nation. New York: Harper and Row.
Weiser, Frederick S.
 1970 The Concept of Baptism among Colonial Pennsylvania German

Church People. Lutheran Historical Conference Essays and Reports 4:1–45.
1973 Piety and Protocol in Folk Art: Pennsylvania German Fraktur Birth and Baptismal Certificates. Winterthur Portfolio 8:19–43.
1980 Baptismal Certificate and Gravemarker: Pennsylvania German Folk Art at the Beginning and the End of Life. In Ian M.G. Quimby and Scott T. Swank, eds., Perspectives on American Folk Art. New York: W. W. Norton, pp. 134–61.
1983 Fraktur. In Scott T. Swank, Arts of the Pennsylvania Germans. New York: W. W. Norton, pp. 230–64.
1987 The Lutherans. In Robert Grant Crist, ed., Penn's Example to the Nations: 300 Years of the Holy Experiment. Harrisburg: Pennsylvania Council of Churches for the Pennsylvania Religious Tercentenary Committee, pp. 74–84.

Weiser, Frederick S.; Heaney, Howell J.
1976 The Pennsylvania German Fraktur of the Free Library of Pennsylvania. 2 vols. Publications of the Pennsylvania German Society, Vol. 10. Breinigsville: Pennsylvania German Society.

Weiser, Frederick S.; Sullivan, Mary Hammond
1980 Decorated Furniture of the Schwaben Creek Valley. Publications of the Pennsylvania German Society 14:333–94.

Wood, Ralph
1942 (ed.) The Pennsylvania Germans. Princeton: Princeton University Press.

Wust, Klaus
1970 Folk Art in Stone: Southwest Virginia. Edinburg, Virginia: Shenandoah History.

Yoder, Don
1947a Hegins Valley in Song and Story. 'S Pennsylfawnisch Deitsch Eck, Morning Call (Allentown, Pennsylvania), January 11 (p. 6), 18 (p. 6), 25 (p. 8); February 1 (p. 8), 8 (p. 8).
1947b Folklore from the Hegins and Mahantongo Valleys. 'S Pennsylfawnisch Deitsch Eck, Morning Call (Allentown, Pennsylvania), October 4 (p. 8), 11 (p. 8), 18 (p. 8), 25 (p. 8); November 2 (p. 6), 8 (p. 8), 15 (p. 8), 22 (p. 8).
1950 "Pennsylvania Dutch"... Or "Pennsylvania German"? Pennsylvania Dutchman 2, 2:1.
1959 The Bench Versus the Catechism: Revivalism and Pennsylvania's Lutheran and Reformed Churches. Pennsylvania Folklife 10, 2:14–23.
1978 The Dialect Church Service in the Pennsylvania German Culture. Pennsylvania Folklife 27, 4:2–13.
1980a "Palatine, Hessian, Dutchman: Three Images of the German in America." Publications of the Pennsylvania German Society, vol. 14. Breinigsville: Pennsylvania German Society, pp. 105–30.

1980b Pennsylvania-Germans. *In* Stephan Thernstrom, ed., Harvard Encyclopedia of American Ethnic Groups. Cambridge: Belknap Press of Harvard University Press, pp. 770–72.

1983 The Reformed Church and Pennsylvania German Identity. Yearbook of German-American Studies 18:63–82.

1984 The Baptismal Records of St. Jacob's (Howerter's) Lutheran and Reformed Union Church, Upper Mahanoy Township, Northumberland County, Pennsylvania, 1803–1869. Northumberland County Historical Society Proceedings and Addresses 29:127–250.

1985 The Pennsylvania Germans: Three Centuries of Identity Crisis. *In* Frank Trommler and Joseph McVeigh, eds., America and the Germans: An Assessment of a Three-Hundred-Year History. Volume One: Immigration, Language, Ethnicity. Philadelphia: University of Pennsylvania Press, pp. 41–65.

1989 A Fraktur Primer. *In* James Hardin and Alan Jabbour, eds., Folklife Annual 1988–89. Washington, D.C.: Library of Congress, pp. 100–111.

1990 Discovering American Folklife: Studies in Ethnic, Religious, and Regional Culture. Ann Arbor, Michigan: UMI Research Press.

Yoder, Don; Graves, Thomas E.

1989 Hex Signs: Pennsylvania Dutch Barn Symbols and Their Meaning. New York: E. P. Dutton.

Yoder, Don; Gunnion, Vernon S.; Hopf, Carroll

1969 Pennsylvania German Fraktur and Color Drawings. Lancaster, Pennsylvania: Landis Valley Associates.

Yoder, William F.

1950 A Pioneer Minister. Pennsylvania Dutchman 1, 25:5.

W. F. H. NICOLAISEN:
A Selected Bibliography

1957
Die alteuropäischen Gewässernamen der britischen Hauptinsel. Beiträge zur Namenforschung 8:211–68.

The Semantic Structure of Scottish Hydronymy. Scottish Studies 1:211–40.

1958
Notes on Scottish Place-Names: 1. Armaidh; 2. Caddon Water; 3. Livet; 4. Forth. Scottish Studies 2:109–12.

Notes on Scottish Place-Names: 5. Shin; 6. Tain; 7. Gaelic *lon* in Stream-Names. Scottish Studies 2:189–205.

1959
Notes on Scottish Place-Names: 9. Dryfesdale. 10. The Type "Burn of—" in Scottish Hydronymy. Scottish Studies 3:88–102.

Notes on Scottish Place-Names: 12 Nevis. Scottish Studies 3:214–18.

W. M. Alexander (1881–1959). Onoma 8 (1958–59):475–76.

1960
Norse Place-Names in South-West Scotland. Scottish Studies 4:49–70.

The Fascination of Scottish Place Names. The Scots Magazine 73:261–67.

Notes on Scottish Place-Names: 13. Some Early Name-Forms of the Stirlingshire *Carron*. Scottish Studies 4:96–104.

Notes on Scottish Place-Names: 14. Avon; 15. Names Containing the Preposition of. Scottish Studies 4:187–205.

1961
Field-Work in Place-Name Research. Studia Hibernica 1:74–88.

The Historical Stratification of Scottish Hydronymy. Sixth International Congress of Onomastic Sciences, Munich 1958, Reports, Vol. 3. Munich, pp. 561–71.

Notes on Scottish Place-Names: 16. The Interpretation of Name-Changes. Scottish Studies 5:85–96.
Notes on Scottish Place-Names: 17. *Sike* and *Strand*. Scottish Studies 5: 99–201.
Some Minor Manuscript Sources of Scottish Place-Names. Scottish Studies 5:209–11.

1962
Notes on Scottish Place-Names: 18. *Lane* in Galloway. Scottish Studies 6:85–87.
Notes on Scottish Place-Names: 19. Further Minor Elements in Scottish River-Names. Scottish Studies 6:210–17.
Council for Name Studies: Great Britain and Ireland. Scottish Studies 6:93–94.
Calum Maclean (1915–1960). Fabula 5:162–64.

1963
The Collection and Transcription of Scottish Place-Names. Atti e Memorie del VII Congresso Internazionale di Sciense Onomastiche, Vol. 4. Florence, pp. 105–14.
A Short Comparative List of Celtic Bird Names of the British Isles. *In* Birds of the British Isles, Vol. 12. Edinburgh, pp. 405–23.
Notes on Scottish Place-Names: 20. Path. Scottish Studies 7:83–85.
Notes on Scottish Place-Names: 21. Kilwinning. Scottish Studies 7:199–200.
Some Gaelic Place-Rhymes. Scottish Studies 7:100–102.

1964
Anglo-Saxons and Celts in the Scottish Border Counties. Scottish Studies 8:141–71.
Notes on Scottish Place-Names: 23. Old Norse *øveit*, etc. Scottish Studies 8:96–103.
Notes on Scottish Place-Names: 23. The Distribution of Old Norse *byr* and *fjall*. Scottish Studies 8:208–13.
A Gaelic Map of Scotland. Cartographic Journal 1, 1:44.

1965
Regional Ethnology in European Universities (Summary). Volkskunde 66: 103–5.
Scottish Studies in 1964: An Annual Bibliography. Scottish Studies 9:225–35.
Scottish Place-Names: 24. *Slew-* and *sliabh*. Scottish Studies 9:91–106.
Scottish Place-Names: "Hill of—" and "Loch of—." Scottish Studies 9:175–82.

1966
Scottish Water-Courses as Boundaries. Proceedings of the Eighth International Congress of Onomastic Sciences, Amsterdam. The Hague, pp. 327–33.

Scottish Studies in 1965: An Annual Bibliography. Scottish Studies 10:214–24.
Index to *Scottish Studies* Vols. 1 (1957)–10 (1966). Scottish Studies 10:225–68.
Scottish Place-Names: 26. Blackadder and Whiteadder. Scottish Studies 10: 78–87.
Scottish Place-Names: 27. Thurso. Scottish Studies 10:171–76.

1967
Scottish Studies in 1966: An Annual Bibliography. Scottish Studies 11:252–64.
Scottish Place-Names: 28. Old English *wic* in Scottish Place-Names. Scottish Studies 11:75–84.
Scottish Place-Names: 29. Scandinavian Personal Names in the Place-Names of South-East Scotland. Scottish Studies 11:223–36.
IX Internationaler Kongress für Namenforschung. Beiträge zur Namenforschung (Neue Folge) 2:121–23.

1968
Editor. Transactions of the Third International Congress of Celtic Studies, Edinburgh, 1967. Edinburgh.
The Prodigious Jump: A Contribution to the Study of the Relationship Between Folklore and Place-Names. Volksüberlieferung: Festschrift für Kurt Ranke. Göttingen, pp. 431–42.
Place-Names of the Dundee Region. *In* S. J. Jones, ed., Dundee and District. British Association for the Advancement of Science. Dundee, pp. 144–52.
Scottish Studies in 1967: An Annual Bibliography. Scottish Studies 12:207–18.
Scottish Place-Names: 30. Fintry. Scottish Studies 12:179–82.

1969
Norse Settlement in the Northern and Western Isles. Scottish Historical Review 48:6–17 + 4 maps.
Some Problems of Chronology in Southern Scotland. Proceedings of the Ninth International Congress of Onomastic Sciences, London, 1966. Louvain, pp. 340–47.
The Distribution of Certain Gaelic Mountain-Names. Transactions of the Gaelic Society of Inverness 45:113–28 + 7 maps.
Aspects of Scottish Mountain-Names. Disputationes ad Montium Vocabula alierumque nominum significationes pertinentes. Tenth International Congress of Onomastic Sciences, Vienna, 1969, Vol. 1. Vienna, pp. 109–15.
Scottish Studies in 1968: An Annual Bibliography. Scottish Studies 13:189–202.
Place-Names on Maps of Scotland and Wales. Scottish Section, Ordnance Survey, Southampton.
Scottish Place-Names: 31. Falkirk. Scottish Studies 13:47–59.
Scottish Place-Names: 32. Gaelic *tulach* and *barr*. Scottish Studies 13:159–66.

1970
Editor. The Place-Names of Birsay by Hugh Marwick. Aberdeen: Aberdeen University Press.
With M. Gelling and M. Richards. The Names of Towns and Cities in Britain. London: B. T. Batsford.
Gaelic Place-Names in Southern Scotland. Studia Celtica 5:15–35.
Council for Name Studies in Great Britain and Ireland. Onoma 15:151–53.
O.K. Schram (1900–1968). Onoma 15:179–80.

1971
National and International Folklore. The Bulletin of the Pennsylvania State Modern Language Association 49 (Fall 1970–Spring 1971):17–24.
Early Spellings and Scottish Place-Names. Edinburgh Studies in English and Scots. London, pp. 210–33.

1972
The Mapping of Folk Culture as Applied Folklore. *In* Dick Sweterlitsch, ed., Papers on Applied Folklore. Folklore Forum, Bibliographic and Special Studies, No. 8, pp. 26–30.
Great Britain and Old Europe. Namn och Bygd 59:85–105.
Onomastics—An Independent Discipline? Indiana Names 3:33–47.
P-Celtic Place-Names in Scotland: A Reappraisal. Studia Celtica 7:1–11.

1973
Folklore and Geography: Towards an Atlas of American Folk Culture. New York Folklore Quarterly 29:3–20.
Place-Names in Traditional Ballads. Folklore 84:299–312.

1974
Assistant Editor. Educational Opportunity Programs: Another Look. Proceedings of the Institute on Innovative Teaching and Counseling IV. Binghamton, New York.
Place-Names in Traditional Ballads. Literary Onomastics Studies 1:84–102 (revised version of paper published in Folklore 1973).
Names as Verbal Icons. Names 22:104–10.

1975
The Place-Names of Wessex. Literary Onomastics Studies 2:58–82.
Place-Name Evidence (16 maps and accompanying text). *In* An Historical Atlas of Scotland c. 400–c. 1600. St. Andrews, pp. 2–7 and 106–13.
Surveying and Mapping North American Culture. Mid-South Folklore 3:35–40.
Place-Names in Bilingual Communities. Names 23:167–74.
Onomastic Activities in the United States: A Personal Postscript. Onoma 19:555–73.

1976
Scottish Place-Names. London. B. T. Batsford.
Folk and Habitat. Studia Fennica 20:324–30.
Celtic Toponymics in Scotland. Word 28:117–39.
The Place-Names of Barsetshire. Literary Onomastics Studies 3:1–21.
Scandinavian Place Names in Scotland as a Source of Knowledge. Northern Studies 7–8:14–24.
Place-Name Legends: An Onomastic Mythology. Folklore 87:146–59.
Words as Names. Onoma 20:142–63.
Name Aesthetics. Midwestern Journal of Language and Folklore 2:56–63.

1977
Some Humorous Folk-Etymological Narratives. New York Folklore 3:1–14.
Line and Sentence in Dunbar's Poetry. *In* A. J. Aitken et al., eds., Bards and Makars. Glasgow, pp. 61–71.
Place-Names and their Stories. Ortnamnssallskapets i Uppsala Årsskrift:23–29.
Between Berne and Cracow—Some Reflections. Onoma 21:549–56.
Folk Literature. *In* The Year's Work in Scottish Literary Studies. Scottish Literary Journal, Supplement No. 4 (Autumn):9–14.

1978
The Folk and the Region. New York Folklore 2:143–49.
Are There Connotative Names? Names 26:40–47.
Desert Island Onomastics. Literary Onomastics Studies 5:110–51.
English Jack and American Jack. Midwestern Journal of Language and Folklore 4:27–36.
Recognition and Identity: Place Names as Keys and Disguises in the Regional Novel. Onomastica 53:1–9.
Ordering the Chaos: Name Strategies in Robert Kroetsch's Novels. Essays on Canadian Writing 11:55–65.
How Incremental is Incremental Repetition? *In* Patricia Conroy, ed., Ballads and Ballad Research. Seattle: University of Washington, pp. 122–33.

1979
Celtic Place Names in America B.C. Vermont History 47:148–60.
The Toponymy of Literary Landscapes. Literary Onomastics Studies 6:75–104.
Field Collecting in Onomastics. Names 27:162–78.
"Distorted Function" in Material Aspects of Culture. *In* Simon J. Bronner and Stephen P. Poyser, eds., Approaches to the Study of Material Aspects of American Folk Culture. Folklore Forum 12:223–35.
Literary Names as Text: Personal Names in Sir Walter Scott's *Waverley*. Nomina 3:29–39.
"When I First Remember Talcottville...": Place Names in a Recollected Landscape. Names Northeast 1:17–27.

1980

Early Scandinavian Naming in the Northern and Western Isles. Northern Scotland 3 (1979–80): 105–21.

Variant, Dialect and Region: An Exploration in the Geography of Tradition. New York Folklore 6:137–49.

Onomastic Dialects. American Speech 55:36–45.

Place Names as Evidence for Linguistic Stratification in Scotland. *In* Vibeke Dalberg et al., eds., Sprogvidenskabelig Udnyttelse af Stednavnematerialet. NORNA-rapporter 18:211–31.

Tension and Extension: Thoughts on Scottish Surnames and Medieval Popular Culture. Journal of Popular Culture 14:119–30.

Masks and Illusions: The Function of Names of Robertson Davies' "Deptford Trilogy." Onomastica 58:1–12.

AT 1535 in Beech Mountain, North Carolina. ARV: Scandinavian Yearbook of Folklore 36:99–106.

Space in Folk Narrative. *In* Nikolai Burlakoff and Carl Lindahl, eds., Folklore on Two Continents: Essays in Honor of Linda Dégh. Bloomington, Indiana: Trickster Press, pp. 14–18.

Scottish Folk Literature 1977 and 1978. Scottish Literary Journal, Supplement 13:21–29.

Time in Folk-Narrative. *In* Venetia J. Newall, ed., Folklore Studies in the Twentieth Century. Woodbridge, Suffolk: D. S. Brewer, pp. 314–19.

Über Namen in der Literatur. Namenkundliche Informationen 38:13–25.

What Is Your Name? The Question of Identity in Some of the Waverley Novels. Names 28, 4:255–66.

"A Colony for New England": New York Places and Their Names in Timothy Dwight's *Travels in New England and New York*. Names Northeast 2:100–111.

1981

Personal Names in Traditional Ballads: A Proposal for a Ballad Onomasticon. Journal of American Folklore 94:229–32.

Bagimond's Roll as a Toponymic Text. *In* Michael Benskin and M. L. Samuels, eds., So Many People Longages and Tonges, Philological Essays in Scots and Mediaeval English Presented to Angus McIntosh. Edinburgh, pp. 173–85.

Inverlochy: Place Names as Ruins. Literary Onomastics Studies 8:27–38.

Zur Namenforschung in den USA. Namenkundliche Mitteilungen 39:37–45.

Robinsons as Namers. *In* Fred Tarplay, ed., The Scope of Names, South Central Names Institute Publication 7. Commerce, Texas, pp. 1–9.

1982

Why Study Names in Literature? Literary Onomastics Studies 9:1–20.

Lexical and Onomastic Fields. Proceedings of the Thirteenth International Congress of Onomastic Sciences, Cracow 1978, Vol. II. Cracow, pp. 209–16.

P. W. Joyce and Scotland. Topothesia: Essays in Honour of T. S. O Maille Galway, Ireland, pp. 72–89.
Scandinavians and Celts in Caithness: The Place-Name Evidence. *In* John R. Baldwin, ed., Caithness: A Cultural Crossroads. Edinburgh, pp. 75–85.
Salterton and Deptford: A Comparison of Onomastic Structures. Onomastica Canadiana 62:14–22.
Thirty Years Later: Thoughts on a Viable Concept of Old European Hydronymy. *In* Otto Winkelmann and Maria Braisch, eds., Festschrift für Johannes Hubschmid zum 65, Geburtstag. Bern, Switzerland, pp. 139–48.
The Viking Settlement of Scotland: Evidence of Place Names. In: R. T. Farrell, ed., The Vikings. Chichester: Phillimore, pp. 95–115.
"The Lord is Not at Home": A Brief Diversion. Proceedings of the 12th International Folk Ballad Conference. CVV-Studies 1:206–13.
Opening Address to the XIVth International Congress of Onomastic Sciences at Ann Arbor, 1981. Onoma 26:28–31.
The Folk in Literature: Some Comments on Sir Walter Scott's Scottish Novels. Kentucky Folklore Record 28:48–60.
"Old European" Names in Britain. Nomina 6:37–42.
Leopold Schmidt (1912–1981). Folklore 93:224.

1983
Scott and the Folk Tradition. *In* Alan Bold, ed., Sir Walter Scott: The Long-Forgotten Melody. London: Vision Press, pp. 127–42.
"What a Name. Stephen Halifax." Onomastic Modes in Three Novels by Margaret Drabble. Literary Onomastics Studies 10:269–83.
Concepts of Time and Space in Irish Folktales. *In* Patrick K. Ford, ed., Celtic Folklore and Christianity: Studies in Memory of William W. Heist. Santa Barbara: McNally and Lofton, pp. 150–58.
The Post-Norse Place-Names of Shetland. *In* Donald J. Withrington, ed., Shetland and the Outside World 1469–1969. Aberdeen University Studies 157. Oxford: Oxford University Press, pp. 69–85.
An Onomastic Vernacular in Scottish Literature. *In* J. Derrick McClure, ed., Scotland and the Lowland Tongue. Aberdeen: Aberdeen University Press, pp. 209–18.
Theodor Fontane's "Sir Patrick Spens." *In* James Porter, ed., The Ballad Image: Essays Presented to Bertrand Harris Bronson. Los Angeles: Center for the Study of Comparative Folklore and Mythology, University of California, pp. 3–19.
Articles on Ecclesiastical Place Names (pp. 228–29), Gaelic Place Names in Scotland (pp. 231–33), Pre-Celtic Place Names (pp. 235–36), and Pre-Gaelic Place Names (p. 236). *In* Derick S. Thomson, ed., The Companion to Gaelic Scotland. Oxford: Basil Blackwell.
Scandinavian Shore Names in Shetland: The Onomastic Subdialect of a Coastscape. Språk och tradition. Festskrif till Sven Benson. Uppsala: Almqvist & Wiksell, pp. 144–52 [= Svenska Landsmål och Svenskt Folkliv 106 (1983)].

Folklore and... What? New York Folklore 9:89–98.
Sir Walter Scott: The Folklorist as Novelist, *In* J. H. Alexander and David Hewitt, eds., Scott and His Influence. Aberdeen: Association for Scottish Literary Studies, pp. 169–79.

1984
What Crisis in Onomastics? Names 32:14–25.
Folklore and Names. Names Northeast 3:14–21.
Place Names in Early New England Literature. Names Northeast 4:67–76.
The Structure of Narrated Time in the Folktale. Le conte pourquoi? comment? Paris: Editions du Centre National de la Recherche Scientifique, pp. 417–36.
Names and Narratives. Journal of American Folklore 97:259–72.
Legends as Narrative Response. *In* Paul Smith, ed., Perspectives on Contemporary Legend. CECTAL Conference Paper Series No. 4. Sheffield: University of Sheffield, pp. 167–78.
Maps of Space—Maps of Time. Names 32:358–66.
Henri Draye (1911–1983). Names 32:74–76.

1985
Socio-onomastics. *In* Ernst Eichler et al., eds., Der Eigenname in Sprache und Gesellschaft. Verhandlungen im Plenum, XV. Internationaler Kongress für Namenforschung, August 1984. Leipzig: Karl-Marx-Universität, pp. 118–32.
The Semantics of Place Names and Their Elements. NORNA-rapporter 28: 60–71.
Nomen, Noun and Name: The Lexical Horns of an Onomastic Dilemma, *In* Mary Jo Arn and Hanneke Wirtjes, eds., Historical & Editorial Studies in Medieval & Early Modern English. Groningen: Wolters-Noordhoff, pp. 63–72.
Tartan and Kilt, Whisky and Bagpipe: Living Scottish Traditions in America. New Jersey Folklore 10:17–21.
Burnside of Duntrune: An Essay in Praise of Ordinariness. Names 33:29–38.
"There was a Lord in Ambertown": Fictitious Place Names in the Ballad Landscape, *In* Carol L. Edwards and Kathleen E. B. Manley, eds., Narrative Folksong—New Directions: Essays in Appreciation of W. Edson Richmond. Boulder, Colorado: Westview Press, pp. 73–81.
Recent Publications in German Onomastics. Names 33:158–68.
Introduction, Special Issue on Theory About Names. Names 33:109–10.
Rehearsing the Future in the Folktale. New York Folklore 11:231–38.
Reminiscences. New York Folklore 11:18–20.
Perspectives on Contemporary Legend. Fabula 26:213–18.

1986
Paperback edition of Scottish Place Names (1976). London: B. T. Batsford.
Paperback edition of The Names of Towns and Cities in Britain (1970). With Margaret Gelling and Melville Richards. London: B. T. Batsford.

Response to James Porter's "Ballad Explanations, Ballad Reality, and the Singer's Epistemics." Western Folklore 45:125–27.
Anthologization of Names as Verbal Icons (1974). *In* Kelsie B. Harder, ed., Names and their Varieties: A Collection of Essays in Onomastics. Lanham, Maryland: University Press of America, pp. 246–52.
Names Reduced to Words?: Purpose and Scope of a Dictionary of Scottish Place Names. *In* Dietrich Strauss and Horst W. Drescher, eds., Scottish Language and Literature, Medieval and Renaissance. Frankfurt am Main: Peter Lang, pp. 47–54.
Gaelic Place Names in Scots. Scottish Language 5:140–46.
Names of Strangers in Traditional Ballads: A Response to Sheila Douglas. *In* Hugh Shields, ed., Ballad Research: The Stranger in Ballad Narrative and Other Topics. Dublin: Folk Music Society of Ireland, pp. 111–13.
Fun and Names. Grazer Linguistische Studien 25:215–20.
Personal Names as Place Names. *In* Ola Stemshaug, ed., Personnamn i Stadnamn. NORNA-rapporter 33:207–16.
The Structure and Function of Names in English Literature. Studia Anglica Posnaniensia 18:139–52.
Naming and Abstraction, *In* Edward Callary, ed., From Oz to Onion Patch. Publications of the North Central Name Society 1:11–26.
Names as Intertextual Devices. Onomastica Canadiana 68:58–66.
The Official Treatment of Non-English Placenames in the United States. *In* Amtlicher Gebrauch des Geographischen Namengutes. Bozen, pp. 253–65.
Kurt Ranke (1908–1985). Folklore 97:110–11.

1987

Is There Room for Name Studies in Geolinguistics? *In* Jesse Levitt et al., eds., Geolinguistic Perspectives. Lanham: University Press of America, pp. 129–37.
Names in Derivative Literature and Parodies. Literary Onomastics Studies 14:49–67.
Imitation and Innovation in the Scandinavian Place-Names of the Northern Isles of Scotland. Nomina 11:75–85.
The Linguistic Structure of Legends. *In* Gillian Bennett et al., eds., Perspectives on Contemporary Legend, Vol. II. CECTAL Conference Paper Series No. 5. Sheffield: Sheffield Academic Press, pp. 61–67.
Semantic Causes of Structural Changes in Place Names. NORNA-rapporter 34:9–19.
Entries Nechtan (p. 91) and Picts (pp. G41–G43) *In* Joseph R. Strayer, ed., Dictionary of the Middle Ages. New York: Charles Scribner's Sons.

1988

Anthologization of The Place Names of Wessex (1975). *In* Grace Alvarez-Altman and Frederick M. Burelbach, eds., Names in Literature: Essays from Literary Onomastics Studies. Lanham, Maryland: University Press of America, pp. 35–45.

Introduction: Folk-Narrative Research in the U.S.A. Fabula 29:286–89.
Once Upon a Place, or Where Is the World of the Folktale? *In* Albrecht Lehmann and Andreas Kuntz, eds., Sichtweisen der Volkskunde: Zur Geschichte und Forschungspraxis einer Disziplin. Lebensformen 3. Berlin-Hamburg: Dietrich Reimer, pp. 359–66.
German *Sage* and English *Legend:* Terminology and Conceptual Problems. *In* Gillian Bennett and Paul Smith, eds., Monsters with Iron Teeth, Perspectives on Contemporary Legend III. Sheffield: Sheffield Academic Press, pp. 79–87.
The Toponymy of Remembered Childhood. Names 36:133–142.

1989
Name Spelling and Identity. Journal of the North Central Name Society (Winter 1988–89):13–21.
Place-Name Maps: How Reliable Are They? Studia Onomastica: Festskrift till Thorsten Anderson 26 Februari 1989. Lund: Bloms, pp. 261–68.
Kurt Ranke and Einfache Formen. Folklore 100:113–19.
The Spelling of Scottish Place Names as a Linguistic Resource: Stirling vs. Dunfermline. *In* J. Lachlan Mackenzie and Richard Todd, eds., In Other Words. Dordrecht, Holland: Foris, pp. 301–14.
What Have Our Histories Taught Us? Folklore Historian 6:13–15.
Hartland, Edwin-Sidney. Enzykloypädie des Märchens 6, 2–3:528–30.
Henderson, Hamish. Enzykloypädie des Märchens 6, 2–3:812–13.
Definitional Problems in Oral Narrative. *In* Gillian Bennett and Paul Smith, eds., The Questing Beast, Perspectives on Contemporary Legend IV. Sheffield: Sheffield Academic Press, pp. 77–89.
Editor's Foreword. Special Issue: Type 425, "The Search for the Lost Husband." Midwestern Folklore 15:69–70.

1990
Variability and Creativity in Folk Narrative. *In* Veronika Görög-Karady, ed., D'un conte...a l'áutre: la variabilité dans la littérature orale. Paris: Editions du Centre National de La Recherche Scientifique, pp. 39–46.
Linguistic Aspects of the Vanishing Hitchhiker. *In* Leander Petzoldt and Stefaan Top, eds., Dona Folcloristica: Festgabe für Lutz Röhrich zu seiner Emeritierung. Frankfurt: Peter Lang, pp. 187–99.
Preface. *In* Gillian Bennett and Paul Smith, comps. Contemporary Legend: The First Five Years, Abstracts and Bibliographies from the Sheffield Conferences on Contemporary Legend 1982–1986. Sheffield, England: Sheffield Academic Press, pp. 7–15.
The Past as Place. Dolphin Newsletter 9 (May):25–26.
Why Tell Stories? Fabula 13:5–10.
Gaelic and Scots 1300–1600: Some Place-Name Evidence. *In* Derick S. Thomson, ed., Gaelic and Scots in Harmony. Glasgow: Department of Celtic, University of Glasgow, pp. 20–35.
Placenames and Politics. Names 38:193–207.

Onomastic Onomastics. *In* Jean-Claude Boulanger, ed., Proceedings of the XVIth International Congress of Onomastic Sciences, Quebec 1987. Quebec: Les Presses de l' Universite Laval, pp. 3–14.
Maps of Fiction: The Cartography of the Landscape of the Mind. Onomastic Canadiana 72:57–68.
The Growth of Name Systems. *In* Eeva Maria Nähri, ed., Proceedings of the XVIIth International Congress of Onomastic Sciences. Helsinki, pp. 203–10.
Aberdeen: A Toponymic Key to the Region. Northern Studies 27:50–63.
A Folklorist Looks at (S)NACS. North American Culture 6:3–11.

1991
The Past as Place: Names, Stories, and the Remembered Self. Folklore 102:3–15.
Name That Past: Place Names in Autobiographical Writings. Names 39: 239–48.
Scottish Analogues of Scandinavian Place Names. *In* Gordon Albøge et al., eds. Analogi i Navngivning. NORNA-rapporter 45:147–55.
Die ältesten Namenschichten auf den britischen Inseln. *In* Ernst Eichler, ed., Probleme der alteren Namenschichten. Heidelberg: Carl Winter, Universitätsverlag, pp. 67–74.
Celtic and Pre-Celtic Place-Name Elements in Scotland. *In* Benjamin T. Hudson and Vickie Ziegler, eds., Crossed Paths: Methodological Approaches to the Celtic Aspect of the European Middle Ages. Lanham, Maryland: University Press of America, pp. 1–10.
Anthologization of Onomastics—An Independent Discipline? (1972). *In* Ronald L. Baker, ed., The Study of Place Names. Terre Haute: Indiana Council of Teachers of English and Hoosier Folklore Society, pp. 9–22.
Reprint of Place-Name Maps: How Reliable Are They? (1989). *In* Namn och Bygd 79: 43–50.

Forthcoming
Wortloses Erzählen [Stories Without Words]. *In* Proceedings of the Conference on "Bild und Text," Innsbruck, October 1990.
Gaelic *-ach* > Scots *-o* in Scottish Place Names. Scottish Gaelic Studies. Special Issue in Honor of Professor D. S. Thomson.
Contemporary Legends: Narrative Texts vs. Summaries. Contemporary Legend 2.
Humour in Traditional Ballads (Mainly Scottish). Folklore 103, pp. 27–39.
On Arran Place Names. Northern Studies 29.
Pictish Place Names as Scottish Surnames. Nomina 14.
Why Tell Stories about Innocent, Persecuted Heroines? *In* Cristina Bacchilega and Steven Swann Jones, eds., Mirror, Mirror, on the Wall: Models of Female Initiation in Folklore.
The Teller and the Tale. *In* William B. McCarthy, ed., Jack in Two Worlds: Contemporary North American Taletellers.

Onomastic Aspects of Clerk Colvill. Arv (1992).
The *Dee* at Chester and Aberdeen: Thoughts on Rivers and Divinities. *In* Alex. Rumble, ed., Memorial Volume for John McN. Dodgson.

CONTRIBUTORS

Ronald L. Baker is professor of English and chair of the English Department at Indiana State University. Past president of the Hoosier Folklore Society, he is editor of *Midwestern Folklore* and *Folklore Historian,* and author of *Folklore in the Writings of Rowland E. Robinson, Indiana Place Names, Hoosier Folk Legends, Jokelore: Humorous Folktales from Indiana,* and *French Folklife in Old Vincennes.* He has received Indiana State University's award for outstanding research and the Centennial Commendation Award of the American Folklore Society's History and Folklore Section.

Cristina Bacchilega is associate professor of English at the University of Hawaii at Manoa. Her degrees are from the Università degli Studi di Roma, "La Sapienza," Italy, and State University of New York (SUNY) at Binghamton, where Bill Nicolaisen was her folklore adviser. She is the editor and translator of *La narativa postmoderna in America: testi e contesti* and coeditor of the 1986 and 1988 Proceedings of the Conference on Literature and Hawaii's Children. She has published in *Textual Practice, Journal of Folklore Research, Fabula, La ricerca folklorica, New York Folklore,* and other journals in folk narrative, contemporary fiction, and feminist theory. Her current research is on gender and narrativity in contemporary revisions of classic fairy tales.

Simon J. Bronner is distinguished professor of folklore and American Studies and coordinator of the American Studies Program at Penn

State Harrisburg. He is the author of *American Folklore Studies: An Intellectual History, Piled Higher and Deeper: Folklore of Campus Life, American Children's Folklore* (awarded the Opie Prize), *Old-Time Music Makers of New York State* (awarded the John Ben Snow Foundation Prize), *Grasping Things: Folk Material Culture and Mass Society in America,* and *Chain Carvers: Old Men Crafting Meaning.* He is the editor of five books, including volumes on folk art, material culture, and cultural history. He has served as president of the Pennsylvania Folklore Society and the Middle Atlantic Folklife Association, and as editor of the journals *Material Culture, Folklore Forum,* and *Folklore Historian.*

Mary Ellen Brown is director of the Women's Studies Program, professor of folklore and women's studies, and adjunct professor of English at Indiana University, Bloomington. Author of *Burns and Tradition;* editor of "Folklore and Literature," a special issue of the *Journal of the Folklore Institute;* and contributor to *History of Scottish Literature* (vol. 3) and *The Eighteenth-Century Poets: The Dictionary of Literary Biography,* she has published a number of other folklore-related articles. She has served on the Executive Board of the American Folklore Society and received fellowships from the Institute for Advanced Studies in the Humanities, the University of Edinburgh, and the American Council of Learned Societies.

Linda Dégh is Distinguished Professor of Folklore at Indiana University, Bloomington. Recipient of the Giuseppe Pitrè Prize, she is the author of twenty-two books in Hungarian, German, and English, including *Folktales and Society, Folktales of Hungary,* and *People in the Tobacco Belt.* She is the editor of *Indiana Folklore* and *Studies in East European Folk Narrative,* among other volumes. She has received fellowships from the Guggenheim Foundation, the National Humanities Center, the National Endowment for the Humanities, and the American Council of Learned Societies. Formerly president of the American Folklore Society and currently vice-president of the International Society for Folk Narrative Research, she has taught at several universities in Europe and the United States.

Alexander Fenton is professor of Scottish ethnology and director of the School of Scottish Studies at the University of Edinburgh and of the European Ethnological Research Centre in the National Museums of Scotland. His publications include *Scottish Country Life, The Northern Isles: Orkney and Shetland, The Shape of the Past* (2 vols.), *Country Life in Scotland, The Rural Architecture of Scotland, The Turra Coo,* and

Wirds an' Wark 'e Seasons Roon on an Aberdeenshire Farm. He is the editor of the *Review of Scottish Culture.*

Eleanor R. Long-Wilgus is cataloguer of D. K. Wilgus' papers for deposit in the John Edwards Memorial Foundation Archives at the University of North Carolina. Formerly research associate at the Center for the Study of Comparative Folklore and Mythology at the University of California, Los Angeles, she has taught English and folklore at Santa Clara University, the University of Saskatchewan, the University of Idaho, California State University, Long Beach, and the University of California, Los Angeles. She is the author of *The Maid and the Hangman: Myth and Tradition in a Popular Ballad* (awarded the Chicago Folklore Prize) and a contributor to *Ballad Research, Narrative Folksong: New Directions, Journal of American Folklore, Western Folklore, Fabula,* and *Jahrbuch fur Volksliedforschung.*

J. Derrick McClure is senior lecturer in the Department of English, Aberdeen University, Scotland, and has previously taught in Germany and Canada. His publications include *Why Scots Matters, Scotland and the Lowland Tongue, Bryght Lanternis: Essays on the Language and Literature of Medieval and Renaissance Scotland,* and *Minority Languages Today.* He is the editor of *Scottish Language* and chair of the Language Committee of the Association for Scottish Literary Studies.

W. K. McNeil is folklorist at the Ozark Folk Center, Mountain View, Arkansas. Past president of the Ozark States Folklore Society, he has published eleven books, including *Ghost Stories from the American South, Southern Folk Ballads, Ozark Mountain Humor,* and *Appalachian Images in Folk and Popular Culture.* He is the editor of *Rejoice* and *Old Time Country,* and is on the editorial boards of *Folklore Historian, Mid-America Folklore,* and *Appalachian Journal.*

Wolfgang Mieder is professor of German and folklore and chair of the Department of German and Russian at the University of Vermont, Burlington. His publications have appeared in German and English in Europe, the United States, and Canada. Among his books in English are *The Wisdom of Many: Essays on the Proverb, International Proverb Scholarship: An Annotated Bibliography* (2 vols.), *Disenchantments: An Anthology of Modern Fairy Tale Poetry, Encyclopedia of World Proverbs, Talk Less and Say More: Vermont Proverbs, Tradition and Innovation in Folk Literature, Yankee Wisdom: New England Proverbs, American Proverbs: A Study of Texts and Contexts, Salty Wisdom: Proverbs and the Sea, Not by Bread Alone: Proverbs of the Bible,* and *Dictionary of American*

Proverbs. He is a Folklore Fellow of the Finnish Academy of Science and Letters, Fellow of the American Folklore Society, and editor of *Proverbium: Yearbook of International Proverb Scholarship*.

Roger E. Mitchell is professor of anthropology and chair of the Sociology and Anthropology Department at the University of Wisconsin, Eau Claire. His publications include *The Folktales of Micronesia, A Micronesian Hornbook: Folklore and Sexuality, George Knox: From Man to Legend, I'm a Man That Works: The Biography of Don Mitchell of Merrill, Maine, The Press, Rumor, and Legend Formation,* and *From Fathers to Sons: A Wisconsin Family Farm*. He has received fellowships from the Ford and Guggenheim foundations and received an Excellence in Scholarship Award from the University of Wisconsin.

Venetia Newall is honorary research fellow in folklore in the Department of English at University College, London (University of London). She is also honorary visiting fellow in folklore in the School of Slavonic and East European Studies at the University of London. She was visiting professor of folklore at the University of California, Berkeley, and has lectured at many universities in the United States and Europe. She received the Chicago Folklore Prize for *An Egg at Easter: A Folklore Study*. Other publications include *Encyclopedia of Witchcraft and Magic, The Folklore of Birds and Beasts, The Witch Figure: Festschrift for K. M. Briggs,* and *Folklore Studies in the 20th Century*. She is a fellow of the Royal Anthropological Institute, the Finnish Academy of Sciences, and the American Folklore Society. She is editor of *International Folklore Review*.

Ian A. Olson is an Aberdeen physician whose principal literary research is into Scottish traditional culture and its history, especially of the North East of Scotland. He has a special interest in Scottish song and has written extensively on the *Greig-Duncan Folk Song Collection*. He has published in *Folk Music Journal, Folklore, Folk Song Journal, Review of Scottish Culture, Scottish Literary Journal, Cencrastus, Northern Scotland,* and *Anglistik und englischunterricht*. He has written chapters for *The History of Scottish Literature* and *Scotland: Literature, Culture and Politics*. He is editor of the *Aberdeen University Review*.

Klaus Roth is professor of folklore and European ethnology at the Institut für deutsche und vergleichende Volkskunde, University of Munich, Germany. He was visiting professor of anthropology at the University of California at Berkeley. He has written widely on folk song and narrative research, historical material culture, and various aspects of contemporary southeast European folk culture. He has published *Ehebruchschwänke in Liedform: Eine Untersuchung zur deutsch- und englischsprachigen Schwankballade, Handwerk in Mittel- und Sudosteuropa: Mobilität, Vermittlung und Wandel im Handwerk des 18. bis 20. Jahrhunderts,* and *Probate Inventories: International Bibliography.*

Elizabeth Tucker is associate professor of English and undergraduate director of the English Department at the State University of New York (SUNY) at Binghamton, where she is a colleague of W. F. H. Nicolaisen. Her dissertation was on "Tradition and Creativity in the Storytelling of Pre-Adolescent Girls." She has contributed essays on children's folklore, folk narrative, African folklore, and witchcraft to *Folklore on Two Continents, Western Folklore,* and *Arv: Yearbook of Scandinavian Folklore,* among other books and journals.

D. K. Wilgus was professor emeritus of English, music, and folklore at the University of California, Los Angeles. He died in 1989. He served as president of the American Folklore Society, the California Folklore Society, and the Kentucky Folklore Society. He edited *Western Folklore* and *Kentucky Folklore Record.* He is the author of more than 250 scholarly articles and reviews, *Anglo-American Folksong Scholarship Since 1898* (awarded the Chicago Folklore Prize), and editor of *Folklore International* and *Folk-Songs of the Southern United States.*

Wilbur Zelinsky is professor emeritus of geography at Penn State University Park, where he served as head of the department from 1970 to 1976. Formerly president of the Association of American Geographers and the Society for the North American Cultural Survey, his major research interests have been population geography and all aspects of the cultural and social geography of North America. His major publications are *The Cultural Geography of the United States, Nation into State: The Shifting Symbolic Foundations of American Nationalism,* and *The Atlas of Pennsylvania.*

INDEX*

Abbott, G. F.: *Macedonian Folklore*, 261
Adler, Margot, 147: *Drawing Down the Moon*, 143, 146
Ágoston, Ambrus (storyteller), 122
Aitken, Adam J., 209
Albig, William (sociologist), 187
America, 57-104, 141-52, 169-203, 263-325. *See also* Hmong, Pennsylvania Germans, proverbs
American Folklore and the Historian. See Dorson, Richard M.
American Murder Ballads and Their Stories. See Burt, Olive Woolley
American Tragedy, An. See Dreiser, Theodore
Anderson, Walter (folklorist), 8-9, 27n.5
Andrásfalvi, György (storyteller), 122
Arora, Shirley L., 186
art, folk, 277-325

Azadovskij, Mark A.: *Eine sibirische Märchenerzählerin*, 3

Bain, Read (sociologist), 187
ballads: *aisling* tradition, 57-58, 61, 62, 64, 68; bothy ballads, 48; formulas, 95-96; influence on Scottish local poet tradition, 247-49; about Pearl Bryan, 95-96, 100, 102, 103; and place-names, 41-53; titles: "Annan Water," 25; "The Battle of Harlaw" (Child 163 and Greig-Duncan 112), 51-52; "The Battle of Sheriff Muir," 248; "Bonny House o' Airlie,"248; "The Cherry Tree Carol," (Child 54), 63; "Chevy Chace," 248; "Collier Laddie," 58; "The Country Girl," 58-62; "The Cowboy's Lament" (Laws B1), 57, 61; "Dainty Davie," 248; "The Factory Girl," 58-62;

---

*Index prepared by Alan E. Mays, Pennsylvania State University at Harrisburg, with support from the Office of Research and Graduate Studies

"Geordie" (Child 209), 44-45; "Gightie's Lady" (Greig-Duncan 249), 44-45; "Gilderoy," 248; "The High Blantyre Explosion," 62; "Jealous Lover" (Laws F1), 95, 102; "Jock o' Hazeldean," 248; "Johnie Cock" (Child 114), 45-47; "Johnnie o' Braidisleys" (Greig-Duncan 250), 45-47; "Lord Randall," 61, 63; "The Lost Jimmy Whalen," 62; "The Old Man Rocking the Cradle," 62-63; "Sleepy Toon" (Greig-Duncan 356), 48-49; "Wreck on the Southern Old '97," 75. *See also* folksongs
Bausinger, Hermann, 142
Beattie, James: *Scoticisms Arranged in Alphabetical Order*, 206-20
Beckwith, Marc, 162
belief and custom, 105-26, 141-52, 255-62, 277-325. *See also* witchcraft
Ben-Amos, Dan, 2
Boas, Franz, 3
Boyer, Rev. Walter, 307-8
Breadalbane Account Books, 229-30
Bronson, Bertrand, 45, 46
Brothers Grimm. *See* Grimm, Jacob and Wilhelm
Brown, Grace, 96
Bryan, Pearl: ballads, 95-96, 100, 102, 103; legends, 95, 96-103; murder, 93-95
Buchan, Peter, 45
Buckland, Raymond: *Witchcraft from the Inside*, 143
Bulgaria, 127-39; Eleanor Smollett's study in, 132
Burns, Robert, 208, 215, 216, 246, 249
Burns Club, 246
Burt, Olive Woolley: *American Murder Ballads and Their Stories*, 95
Cadenhead, William (poet), 247

Calvino, Italo: *Italian Folktales*, 154-63
Campbell, Sir Duncan, 225-26
Carolina Tar Heels, The, 75
Carpenter, James, 45
Child, Francis James, 44, 45
Clark, William (Boyd), 48
Companion to Gaelic Scotland, 233
Cornett, Chester (chairmaker), 305-6
Crabtree, Lillian, 71, 82, 84
crafts. *See* art, folk
creativity: concept of, 1-7, 122-23, 143, 306
Crowley, Daniel: *I Could Talk Old-Story Good*, 4
Cultural Literacy. *See* Hirsch, E. D.
cultural register: concept of, 9-10, 16, 127, 142, 255

Dante: *Inferno*, 146
Darby, Walter C., 78
de Beauvoir, Simone, 155, 158
Defoe, Daniel: *Memoirs of the Church of Scotland*, 206
Dégh, Linda, 144; *People in the Tobacco Belt*, 142
DePauw University, 93, 96, 97, 98, 99, 100
Description of the Western Islands. *See* Martin, Martin
Dialect of Banffshire, The. *See* Gregor, Walter
Dictionary of Cultural Literacy. *See* Hirsch, E. D.
Dictionary of the Older Scottish Tongue, 226
Dorson, Richard M. (folklorist): *American Folklore and the Historian*, 94-95
Douglas, Sylvester, 209
Drawing Down the Moon. *See* Adler, Margot
Dreini, Raffaella (storyteller), 162-63
Dreiser, Theodore: *An American Tragedy*, 96

Duff, James, 250
Duncan, Rev. James Bruce, 44, 45
Dundes, Alan, 4, 127-28, 186
Dwelly, Edward, 230

Eléments de Grammaire Hmong Blanc. See Mottin, Jean
Eliade, Mircea, 154
England: nobility in, 227, 228; Serbs in, 255-62
English Proverbs. See Mieder, Wolfgang

Fabian, Monroe, 285
Fazakas, Mrs. Lajos, 122
feminism, 160-61, 164n.3. See also women
folk: definition, 4
folklore: concept of, 2
folksongs: influence on Scottish local poet tradition, 247-49; titles: "Cradle Hushaby," 64; "The Dollar and the Devil," 71, 74-87; "Get Along Little Dogies," 63-64; "*Hushabu Cliabhán*," 64; "Lonesome Road Blues," 75; "Rock All Our Babies to Sleep," 66-68; "Rocking the Baby to Sleep," 65-66; "The Two Rulers," 71, 73, 82-86. See also ballads
folktales: heroes in, 141, 144-50; innocent persecuted heroine subgenre, 154-63; titles: "The Black and White Bride" (AT 403), 156; "Bluebeard" (AT 312), 146; "Catherine, Sly Country Lass" (AT 875), 162; "Catherine the Wise" (AT 891), 162; "The Fine Greenbird" (AT 707), 157-58; "The Handless Maiden," 157, 158; "The Handmade King" (AT 425), 162; "Hansel and Gretel" (AT 327A), 146; "The Healing Fruits" (AT 610), 149-50; "The Heifer Hide," 17; "John the Bear" (AT 301), 148; "King Krin" (AT 425B), 155; "The King of Spain and the English Milord" (AT 881), 156; "The King of the Peacocks" (AT 403), 157; "The Myrtle Child" (AT 407A), 155-56, 161, 162-63; "Rapunzel" (AT 310), 159; "The Rich and the Poor Peasant," 17; "The Six Swans" (AT 451), 149; "The Turkey Hen," 157; "The Twelve Dancing Princesses" (AT 306), 146; "Uliva" (AT 706), 156-57; "The Youth Who Wanted to Know What Fear Is" (AT 326), 146
foodways: church suppers, 277, 307; at *Krsna Slava* celebration, 255-62
From Proverb to Folk-Tale. See Permiakov, Grigorii L'vovich

Gardner, Gerald B.: *Witchcraft Today*, 143
Gardner, Robert. See Mac and Bob
Garry, Flora (poet), 46-47, 53
Geddes, Alexander, 218
Germany: proverbs, 193-94. See also Pennsylvania Germans
Gillette, Chester, 96
Gordon, Sir Robert, 227
Gordon, Susan (storyteller), 158-59
Graham, William: *The Scots Word Book*, 220
Green, Archie, 71
Gregor, Walter: *The Dialect of Banffshire*, 220
Greig, Gavin, 44, 45
Grimm, Jakob and Wilhelm (Brothers Grimm), 161
Grzybek, Peter (linguist), 190; *Semiotische Studien zum Sprichwort*, 186

Halloween, 144
Harris, Carlyle, 95

Henderson, Hamish, 43, 45
Hickerson, Joe, 96
Hicks, Ray, 17
Higgins, Lizzie, 46, 47
Hirsch, E. D.: *Cultural Literacy*, 195; *Dictionary of Cultural Literacy*, 195-96, 198
History of Scottish Literature, 239
Hmong: adaptation in America, 265-66, 269, 272-73; history, 263-65; use of proverbs, 266-73
How Proverbs Mean. See Norrick, Neal
Hume, David: *Political Discourses*, 206, 209-10, 212, 213, 218, 220
Hungary, 105-26

I Could Talk Old-Story Good. See Crowley, Daniel
Inferno. See Dante
Ireland, 57-69
Italian Folktales. See Calvino, Italo
Italy, 153-66

Jackson, George, 94
Jackson, Scott, 93, 94, 97, 99
jokes: political, 127-28, 130-31
Jones, Michael Owen (folklorist), 6, 305
Jones, Steven Swann, 160-61

Kanyo, Zoltan: *Sprichwörter-Analyse einer Einfachen Form*, 186
Kent Club, 245
Kerekes, Anna, 105
Kett, Joseph, 195
Kirshenblatt-Gimblett, Barbara, 5
Klauser, Bill, 307
Kóka, Rozália (folklore performer), 106
Kristeller, Paul Oskar (philosopher), 5
Krsna Slava (Slavic feast of the patron saint of the family), 255-62
Kuusi, Matti, 189, 190; *Towards an International Type-System of Proverbs*, 186

Laos. See Hmong
legend conduits, 107, 120-23
legends, 17, 63, 107, 142, 154; Pearl Bryan, 95, 96-103; urban, 128, 131-32, 134; titles: "Another Candle," 114; "The Bouncing Frog," 115; "The Candle," 113-14; "Fasting on Rózsi Diszke," 115-17; "Fishing Adventure," 112-13; "Frog That Turns into a Dog," 115; "The Lüdércburján," 109-11; "Mara-Tukhlata" ("Mara-the-Brickstone"), 134; "Playing Ghost," 108-9; "Pledge on Mrs. Fazakas," 117-19; "Son Cursed by Father for Stealing," 119; "Towel Mistaken for Ghost," 109; "White Woman Ghost," 114-15; "The Woman Who Can Talk to the Dead," 111-12; "Zhoro-Paveto" ("George-the-Paving-Stone"), 134
Leslie, Charles (poet), 241, 244, 248, 249
Levin, Isidor (folklorist), 188
Lewis, Oscar, 269
Linnell, Avis, 96
Lomax, Alan, 45, 64
Lomax, John, 63
Lopašić, Aleksandar, 255n, 257
Lowth, Bishop, 209
Luhrmann, T. M.: *Persuasions of the Witch's Craft*, 143-44
Lüthi, Max, 154, 157

Mac and Bob (country singers), 80-81, 86
McClintock, Henry F.: *Old Irish and Highland Dress*, 226
McCravy Brothers (country singers), 81, 86
Macdonald, Donald, 50-52

Macedonian Folklore. See Abbott, G. F.
McFarland, Lester. *See* Mac and Bob
McKenna, Kevin J., 189
McNeill, Robert H. (lawyer), 77-78
Mahantongo Valley, 277-78, 281, 284-85, 306-7
Major, John, 226
Makem, Sarah (folksinger), 58-61, 68
Malleus Maleficarum, 148
Martin, Martin: *Description of the Western Islands,* 225
Marzolf, Stanley S. (psychologist), 190
Mason, John Hope (philosopher), 6
Masser, Jacob (furniture maker), 286
Matras, Christian, 231
Mayer, Johannes (furniture maker), 286
Memoirs of the Church of Scotland. See Defoe, Daniel
Messia, Agatuzza (storyteller), 163
Mieder, Wolfgang: *American Proverbs,* 198; *English Proverbs,* 196, 198
Mitchell, Adam (farmer), 48-49
Mitchell, Hugh, *Scotticisms, Vulgar Anglicisms and Grammatical Improprieties Corrected,* 207, 209, 213, 215-18
Modern Proverbs and Proverbial Sayings. See Whiting, Bartlett Jere
Moryson, Fynes, 227
Mottin, Jean: *Eléments de Grammaire Hmong Blanc,* 268
Murray, Margaret: *The Witch-Cult in Western Europe,* 143
Murison, David, 224

names: definition, 170-71; and dress, 225-28; folk naming, 176; geography of, 176-77; and land use, 228-30; naming codes, 172-77; neologisms, 217; nicknames, 176; personal, 175-76, 182-83. *See also* onomastics, place-names, Scotticisms
narratives: everyday, 8, 127-37, 142; family, 278, 309n.2; gravestones as narration, 306; about Isaac F. Stiehly, 280-84; Nicolaisen's study of, 16-18; types, 128-29. *See also* folktales, legends, personal experience narratives, storytelling
New (Second) Statistical Account (Scotland), 228
Nicolaisen, W. F. H., 1-2, 6-21, 25, 41, 42, 47, 52, 57, 71, 86, 103, 122, 127, 142, 150n.1, 168-69, 205-6, 223, 234, 239, 255, 263, 306; academic career, 7-8, 18-19; bibliography, 327-38; and concept of cultural register, 9-10, 16, 142; and concept of individual inviolability, 142; and concept of onomasticon, 185; presidential address to American Folklore Society, 1, 11-12; publications of, 15, 18, 19; *Scottish Place-Names,* 15, 42; and study of narratives, 16-18; as teacher, 19-21
Norrick, Neal: *How Proverbs Mean,* 186
Novaković, Đorđe: celebration of the *Krsna Slava,* 258-62

Observations on the Scottish Dialect. See Sinclair, John
oicotype: concept of, 9, 28n.7
Old Irish and Highland Dress. See McClintock, Henry F.
Ong, Walter, 242
onomastics, 15-16; and idiolect, 16, 29n.9; and onomasticon, 185. *See also* names, place-names
Ot pogovorki do skazki. See Permiakov, Grigorii L'vovich

Paisley Literary and Convivial Association, 246
Palkó, Zsuzsanna (storyteller), 105, 106, 122

paremiological minimum. *See* proverbs
Peacock, James, 5-6
Pearson, James Larkin (poet), 71-87; *Pearson's Poems*, 73, 74, 76; *Plowed Ground*, 73, 86
Pearson's Poems. See Pearson, James Larkin
Peer, Ralph, 76-77, 81
Pennsylvania Germans: churches, 307, 311n.5; connotations of name "Dutchman," 308n.1; *Fersommling*, 307; *Fraktur*, 282, 284, 285, 286, 289-94, 306, 312n.7, 315n.13; furniture, painted, 284-86, 314nn.9, 10; gravestones, 277, 292-95, 300-1, 305, 306-7, 316nn.14, 15, 317n.17; newspaper columnists, 307; religious broadsides, 292; *Scherenschnitte*, 282, 286, 289, 311n.4; use of Pennsylvania "Dutch," 308n.1
People in the Tobacco Belt. See Dégh, Linda
Permiakov, Grigorii L'vovich (linguist and folklorist), 188-90, 194, 196; *From Proverb to Folk-Tale*, 186; *Ot pogovorki do skazki*, 185
personal experience narratives: definition, 142, 150n.1; of witches, 141-50. *See also* narratives, storytelling
Persuasions of the Witch's Craft. See Luhrmann, T. M.
Philologus, 209, 210-11, 212
Pitrè, Giuseppe, 161-62
place-names, 205-6; and ballads, 41-53; definition, 169-71; generic vs. specific, 171-72; and naming codes, 173-75, 177-84. *See also* names, onomastics
Plowed Ground. See Pearson, James Larkin
Political Discourses. See Hume, David

poetry, 137n.6; *aisling*, 57-58, 61, 62, 64, 68; relationship to ballads and folksongs, 247-249; Scottish local poet tradition, 239-51; Standard Habbie verse form, 249-50; titles: "Epistle to Andrew Scot," 250; "Fifty Acres," 72-73; "The Life and Death of Habbie Simson," 249; "Macleod's Defeat at Inverury," 249; "On Raising the Dead," 243; "On the Times, 1799," 249-50; "The Two Rulers" 71, 82-86; "When the Dollar Rules the Pulpit," 73-87; "When the War Is Going to End," 73, 87n.2
Potts, Helen, 95
Proverbium, 188, 189
proverbs, 161, 219; American, 186-88, 190-93, 194-99; German, 193-94; Hmong, 266-73; and paremiological minimum, 189-99; Russian, 188-90
Puckett, Riley (country singer), 66

Ranke, Kurt (folklorist), 8-9, 27n.5, 142
Rebuck, Charles, 277-78, 308
Reitz, Rev. Phaeres, 307
Richson, Rev. Clarence, 96
riddles, 233-34, 278
Robacker, Earl F., 285, 286
Robertson, Jeannie (singer), 43-44, 45, 46
Rodgers, Jimmie, 67
Röhrich, Lutz, 128, 130
Ross, James, 228
Russell, Miss: "Gaelic Element in the Spoken Language of the South of Scotland," 224-25
Russia: proverbs, 188-90

Sausser, Jonathan and Perry (stone carvers), 294, 295
Scoticisms Arranged in Alphabetical Order. See Beattie, James
Scotland, 41-55, 205-54. *See also*

Scotticisms
Scots Word Book, The. See Graham, William
Scott, Sir Walter, 45, 50, 51, 216, 217, 228
Scotticisms, 206-20
Scotticisms, Vulgar Anglicisms and Grammatical Improprieties Corrected. See Mitchell, Hugh
Scottish National Dictionary, 224, 226
Scottish Place-Names. See Nicolaisen, W. F. H.
Sebestyén, Ádám (native folklorist), 105-6, 108, 120, 122
Sebestyén, Emma (storyteller), 105-6, 122
semiotics, 159
Semiotische Studien zum Sprichwort. See Grzybek, Peter
Semphill, Robert (poet), 249
Serbians, 255-62
Shakespeare, 213, 214
sibirische Märchenerzählerin, Eine. See Azadovskij, Mark A.
Sinclair, John: *Observations on the Scottish Dialect*, 206, 208, 212-15, 217
Slavic. *See* Serbians
Smith, R. A. *See* Tannahill, Robert
Smollett, Eleanor. *See* Bulgaria
Smollett, Tobias (novelist), 215
Smout, T. C., 251
Sprichwörter-Analyse einer Einfachen Form. See Kanyo, Zoltan
Stewart, David, 228
Stiehly, Isaac F.: as folk hero, 283, 313n.8; *Fraktur*, 282, 289-90, 306, 315n.13; furniture, painted, 314n.10; gravestones, 277, 292, 294, 316n.15, 317n.17; as minister, 278, 280-82, 306; narratives about, 280-84, 313n.8; *Scherenschnitte*, 282, 286, 289, 311n.4; Stiehly, Jared (son of Isaac), 286, 306
storytelling, 10-11, 12, 105-25; and everyday narrating, 8, 127-37. *See also* folktales, legends, narratives, personal experience stories
Szentes, Mári (storyteller), 105, 108, 120-22
Szentes, Mátyás (storyteller), 105, 107 8, 121 22

Tannahill, Robert, 241, 243, 245-47, 248; and R. A. Smith (musical friend), 248
Tannahill Club, 246
Tannahill-Macdonald Club, 247
Thom, William (poet), 243
Thomson, Derick S., 232-33
Thomson, James (poet), 240-41, 243, 244-45, 247, 249
Tillhagen, Carl-Herman (folklorist), 188
Towards an International Type-System of Proverbs. See Kuusi, Matti
tradition: concept of, 1-7, 122-23, 143, 306
Treaty of Union (Scotland), 211
Trefil, James, 195
Troutman, Carrie Haas, 285

Utley, Francis Lee (folklorist), 8, 26n.4

Vang Pao, 264-65
vernacular literature, 249, 252n.3
Vlach, John, 95
Voigt, Vilmos, 103
von Sydow, Carl Wilhelm (folklorist), 13, 28n.7

Xiong, Touly, 267, 268

Walling, Alonzo, 93, 94
Walsh, Dock (country recording artist), 74-76
Weiser, Frederick, 291, 292-93
Whiting, Bartlett Jere, 186; *Modern Proverbs and Proverbial Sayings*, 196-98

Whitter, Henry, 71, 74, 75-76, 77, 80-81
witchcraft: contemporary, 143-44; as Satanism, 144. *See also* witches
Witchcraft from the Inside. *See* Buckland, Raymond
Witchcraft Today. *See* Gardner, Gerald B.
The Witch-Cult in Western Europe. *See* Murray, Margaret
witches: as heroes, 141, 144-50; personal experience narratives of, 141-50. *See also* witchcraft
Womelsdorf, Sutter (stone carver), 295
women: and discourse of pregnancy, 153-54; as innocent persecuted heroines in folktales, 154-63; and nature metaphor, 154-63. *See also* feminism
Wood, David (poet), 247
Wood, William, 93
Wörter und Sachen ("Words and Things"): concept of, 13, 223-24, 228, 231-34

Yang Dao, 264
Yoder, Don, 285, 308, 308n.1, 309n.2
Yoder, William F., 282-84

Zaicz, János (storyteller), 122
Zhivkova, Ludmila, 133-34